The Chatto Book of
NONSENSE
POETRY

The Chatto Book of
NONSENSE
POETRY

Edited, with an Introduction, by
HUGH HAUGHTON

Chatto & Windus
LONDON

Published in 1988 by
Chatto & Windus Ltd
30 Bedford Square
London WC1B 3SG

A CIP Catalogue record for this book is available
from the British Library

ISBN 0 7011 3105 5

Typography by Humphrey Stone
Photoset by Rowland Phototypesetting Ltd
Bury St Edmunds, Suffolk
Printed in Great Britain by
Redwood Burn Ltd
Trowbridge, Wiltshire

Contents

EDGAR. Pillicock sat on Pillicock Hill. Alow, alow, loo, loo!
FOOL. This cold night will turn us all to fools and madmen.

WILLIAM SHAKESPEARE
King Lear, Act III.iv.

> For Nonsense I will tax all Christendom;
> Great Emperours and Kings shall pay me some;
> Strong Hull, with fatal Hell and Halifax
> Shall naturally bring me toll and tax;
> The mighty stock of Nonsense I will win
> Shall be the universal Magazine,
> For Universities to work upon
> The Rich Philosophers' admired Stone;
> Then I make Poets rich, and Usurers poor,
> And thus resolved at this time write no more.

JOHN TAYLOR (1580–1653)
The Essence, Quintessence,
Incense, Innocence, Lye-sence and Magnificence of
Nonsense upon Sense: or Sense upon Nonsense.

CHARON. (to the Goddess of Nonsense). An't please Your Majesty, there's an odd sort of a man o't' other side the water, says he's recommended to you by some people of quality. Egad, I don't care to take him aboard, not I. He says his name is Hurloborumbo-rumbo – Hurloborumbo, I think he calls himself. He looks like one of Apollo's people in my opinion; he seems mad enough to be a real poet.
NONSENSE. Take him aboard.

HENRY FIELDING
The Author's Farce. III. 542 ff.

De joie, je prenais une expression bouffonne et égarée au possible . . . Je devins un opéra fabuleux: je vis que tous les êtres ont une fatalité de bonheur.

ARTHUR RIMBAUD
'Une Saison en Enfer'. *Délires*, II

I can explain all the poems that ever were invented – and a good many that haven't been invented just yet.

Humpty Dumpty in LEWIS CARROLL's
Through the Looking-Glass

JACK. 'If you don't take care, your friend Bunbury will get you into a serious scrape some day.'
ALGERNON. 'I love scrapes. They are the only things that are never serious.'
JACK. 'Oh, that's nonsense, Algy. You never talk anything but nonsense.'
ALGERNON. 'Nobody ever does.'

OSCAR WILDE
The Importance of Being Earnest, Act I

If . . . nonsense is really to be the literature of the future, it must have its own version of the Cosmos to offer; the world must not only be the tragic, romantic, and religious, it must be nonsensical also.

G. K. CHESTERTON
'A Defence of Nonsense', *The Defendant*, 1901

Hang coersion everyhow! And smotthermock Gramm's laws! But we're a drippindrhue gayleague all at ones. In the buginning is the woid, in the muddle is the sound-dance and thereinofter you're unbewised again, vund vulsyvolsy. You talker dunsker's brogue men we our souls speech obstruct hostery. Silence in thought! Spreach! Wear anartful of outer nocense!

JAMES JOYCE *Finnegans Wake*

The writing of nonsense poetry which appeals to the Unconscious, and of poetry for children who live in a world before self-consciousness, was an attempt to find a world where the divisions of class, sex, occupation did not operate, and the great Victorian masters of this kind of poetry, Lewis Carroll and Edward Lear, were as successful in their day as Mr. Walt Disney has been in ours.

W. H. AUDEN
Introduction to *The Oxford Book of Light Verse*, 1938

We say: At night an Arabian in my room,
With his damned hoobla-hoobla-hoobla-how,
Inscribes a primitive astronomy

Across the unscrawled fores the future casts
And throws his stars around the floor. By day
The wood-dove used to chant his hoobla-hoo

And still the grossest iridescence of ocean
Howls hoo and rises and howls hoo and falls.
Life's nonsense pierces us with strange relation.

WALLACE STEVENS
from 'Notes Towards the Supreme Fiction'

'It is now known that there may be several codes for one amino acid and that there are nonsense codes that do not code anything.'

Encyclopaedia Britannica Micropaedia, vol. IV (1974)

Powerless green ideas sleep furiously.

NOAM CHOMSKY

Introduction

I

Hey diddle diddle
The Cat and the Fiddle,
The Cow jumped over the Moon;
The little Dog laughed
To see such Craft,
And the Dish ran away with the Spoon.

The familiar song of 'Hey Diddle Diddle' is described by the editors of the *Oxford Dictionary of Nursery Rhymes* as 'probably the best known nonsense verse in the language'.[1] Such rhymes are as easy as ABC, yet their combination of airy deadpan plain sailing with riddling oddity has a perennial charm that is a bit of a puzzle. What is the appeal of such nonsense?

'Hey Diddle Diddle' was first published in the earliest anthology of English nursery-rhymes, *Mother Goose's Melody*, produced by the enterprising John Newbery in the 1760s.[2] That epoch-making little book was introduced by a mock-scholarly preface by 'a very Great Writer of Little Books' which, no doubt parodying the fashion for antiquarian literature launched by Bishop Percy's *Reliques*, related the 'custom of making Nonsense Verses in our schools' to the traditional practices of nurses in the Middle Ages. Each rhyme was headed by a jokey title, such as 'Aristotle's Song', and followed by a mock-serious moral or maxim, as if making fun of the idea of making sense out of nonsense, though at the same time displaying a certain embarrassment about the significance to be attached to the conspicuously insignificant traditional children's rhymes. After 'Jack and Jill', for example, we find the moral 'The more you think of dying the better you shall live'; and after 'There were two birds sat on a stone, / One flew away and then there was none', the maxim 'This may serve as a Chapter of Consequences in the next new book of Logick'. In the same vein 'Hey Diddle Diddle' is framed by the grave editorial observation that 'It must be a little Dog that laughed, for a great Dog would be ashamed to laugh at such Nonsense'.

There was a tradition of mock-scholarship in eighteenth-century English literature, and such editorial gravity seems to mock its own adult moral authority (as a 'great Dog'), when faced by the spontaneous laughter of the 'little Dog' (or little child) who naturally enjoys the 'Craft' of the cow's impossible athleticism and the poem's defiant levity. It's a song which celebrates a literal defiance of gravity, of course, as it records the animal's unlikely lunar (or lunatic) levitation, and the topsy-turvy coupling of such familiar household items as the cat and fiddle, the dish and spoon. The absurdly exuberant story is launched by a spirited nonsensical formula or tune ('Hey diddle diddle'), reminiscent of such song-writers' phrases as 'hey nonny no' and 'be-bop-a-lula' but marked by the nursery-rhyme's characteristic taste for phonetic pairings (like 'Humpty Dumpty' and 'Hickory Dickory'), freed of obvious semantic reference. The poem itself is written in a highly sprung, bouncy alternating metre that runs away with the nouns and savours the clatter of the patently arbitrary rhymes. Only a very self-consciously serious 'great Dog' could resist the appeal of such lyric nonsense – and such genially nonsensical lyricism.

Yet for all that, nonsense is a bit of a problem – as *Mother Goose*'s first editor – probably that notorious displaced Irishman Oliver Goldsmith – seemed to realise.[3] There is something paradoxical after all in editing an anthology of nonsense, just as there is something inherently paradoxical about nonsense poetry itself. It involves taking pleasure in kinds of language and thinking which are normally treated as being beneath serious consideration, and intrinsically beyond the pale of what 'great Dogs' consider important. Unlike other kinds of verse, nonsense alone emphasises its essentially absurd status as an anomaly, a linguistic and logical misfit. It is based upon the curiously self-cancelling premiss that it is 'only nonsense'. In normal circumstances after all, it is a basic precondition of all language and behaviour that it should at least make sense. A writer who signally and deliberately fails to make sense, in order to 'make nonsense', is therefore apparently doing something exceptionally perverse in verse. Nonsense is a term of dismissal: for a poet – or editor – to specialise in a kind of language which flaunts its own conspicuous incompetence or oddity is odd indeed.

The 'sense' of nonsense has something to do with its opposition to what is normally considered 'sense'. It defies sense, and yet works in implicit dialogue with it, as if setting a diction against its contradictions. Such classic works of nonsense as *Through The Looking-Glass* thrive on puzzling out the relationships between sense and nonsense and the boundary disputes between them, as in Alice's knotty debate with the magisterial Red Queen:

'When you say "hill",' the Queen interrupted, 'I could show you hills, in comparison with which you'd call that a valley.'

'No, I shouldn't,' said Alice, surprised into contradicting her at last: 'a hill can't be a valley, you know. That would be nonsense –'

The Red Queen shook her head. 'You may call it "nonsense" if you like', she said, 'but *I've* heard nonsense, compared to which that would be as sensible as a dictionary!'[4]

As in the inverted world of *Through the Looking-Glass*, with its domineering argumentative Queens, so in normal usage the term 'nonsense' is mainly used to police the frontiers of acceptable meaning and establish the limits of significant argument. The senses of 'nonsense' recorded in the sensible dictionary produced in the reign of Alice's Queen, Victoria, make this abundantly clear.

Nonsense (nǫ·nsĕns), *sb.* Also 7–8 **-sence,** 8 **-scense.** [f. NON- 2 + SENSE *sb.* Cf. F. *non-sens* (from 12–13th c.).]

1. That which is not sense; spoken or written words which make no sense or convey absurd ideas; also, absurd or senseless action.

Often used exclamatorily to express disbelief of, or surprise at, a statement.

1614 B. JONSON *Bart. Fair* IV. iv, Here they continue their game of vapours, which is Nonsense. *a* **1643** VISC. FALKLAND, etc. *Infallibility* (1646) 121 You leave out those words .. and so make non-sence of that period. *a* **1680** BUTLER *Rem.* (1759) I. 222 For learned Nonsense has a deeper Sound, Than easy Sense, and goes for more profound. **1707** LADY M. W. MONTAGUE *Lett.* II. xlvi. 33, I understand architecture so little, that I am afraid of talking nonsense in endeavouring to speak of it particularly. **1711** ADDISON *Spect.* No. 35 P 1 If they speak Nonsense, they believe they are talking Humour. **1790** BURKE *Fr. Rev.* 17 This doctrine .. either is nonsense, and therefore neither true nor false, or it affirms a most .. dangerous .. position. **1816** SCOTT *Antiq.* xiii, Come, let us have no more of this nonsense. **1859** HAWTHORNE *Fr. & It. Note-bks.* (1871) II. 345, I am writing nonsense, but it is because no sense within my mind will answer the purpose. **1894** FENN *In Alpine Valley* I. 28 'You are not [dying], John dear. It's all stuff and nonsense,' said the little lady.

†b. In particularized use: A piece of nonsense.

a **1643** VISCT. FALKLAND, etc. *Infallibility* (1646) 98 Every new nonsense will be more acceptable .. then any old sense. **1655** tr. *Sorel's Com. Hist. Francion* II. 36 He understood not French very well, nor I his Fustian Language, so our discourse was a perpetuall Nonsense.

c. *No nonsense*: no foolish or extravagant conduct; no foolery or humbug. Chiefly in phr. *stand no nonsense* (also used as adj.).

1821 *Sporting Mag.* VIII. 233 Smith would stand *no nonsense.* **1836** SIR G. STEPHEN *Search of a Horse* i. (1841) 4 There was 'no nonsense about him' [*sc.* a horse], .. but he unluckily moved like a castle! **1849** MISS MULOCK *Ogilvies* ii, Mr. Ogilvie would allow 'no nonsense' of late rising. **1904** SLADEN *Lovers Japan* xiii, Rich was the only stand-no-nonsense Englishman of the lot.

2. Absurdity, nonsensicalness.

1630 W. BEDELL in *Ussher's Lett.* (1686) 421, I shewed the false Latin, Non-sence, injustice of it. **1660** T. PIERCE *Inq. Nat. Sin* To Rdr. *marg.*, Compare the non-sense with the impiety of the expression. **1841** L. HUNT *Seer* II. 2/1 The nonsense of ill-will.

3. Unsubstantial or worthless stuff or things.

1638 COWLEY *Love's Riddle* IV. Wks. 1711 III. 113 Our

Desires .. are Love's Nonsence, wrapt up in thick Clouds. **1648** J. BEAUMONT *Psyche* V. i, What royal Nonsence is a Diadem Abroad, for One who's not at home supreme? **1687** NORRIS *Coll. Misc.* 24, I find This busie World is Non-sense all. **1900** *Westm. Gaz.* 2 Feb. 12/1 Six dollars a week for slippers, and three more for 'ribbons and bits of chiffon nonsense'.

4. A meaning that makes no sense.

1650 WEEKES *Truth's Conflict* i. 11 This is to put a non-sense upon the place, and to destroy the savor that is in it. **1711** POPE *Lett.* (1735) I. 166 How easy it is to a Caviller to give a new Sense, or a new Nonsence to any thing.

†5. Want of feeling or physical sensation. *Obs.*

1621 in T. Bedford *The Sinne*, etc. A i b, Disquietnesse of Conscience [growes] into a numbdnesse or non-sense.

6. *attrib.* and *Comb.*, as *nonsense-proof* adj., *-talker*, *-writer*; **nonsense-book,** a book of non-sense or nonsense verses; **nonsense-name** (see quot.); **nonsense verses,** verses consisting of words and phrases arranged solely with reference to the metre and without regard to the sense; also *non-sense song*, etc.

1887 *Spectator* 17 Sept. 1251 Lear's *Nonsense Books. **1842** *Rep. Brit. Assoc.* 118 *Nonsense names.—Some authors .. have adopted the plan of coining words at random without any derivation or meaning whatever. **1778** *Love Feast* 12 Led by the Spirit to John's pantil'd Roof, Which many a vagrant Paul makes *Nonsense-Proof. **1871** E. LEAR (*title*), *Nonsense Songs, Stories, Botany and Alphabets. *a* **1832** BENTHAM *Deontol.* ii. (1834) I. 26 The moralist .. would call his enemy .. hypocrite, and *nonsense-talker. **1830** COLERIDGE *Table-t.* 5 Oct., I did not seem much interested with a piece of Rossini's, which had just been performed. I said, it sounded to me like *nonsense verses. **1870** *Spectator* 26 Dec. 30 Mere musical sounds are no other than nonsense verses are in poetry. **1887** *Ibid.* 17 Sept. 1251 The parent of modern *nonsense-writers.

b. That is nonsense; full of nonsense; † in the 17th c. often used as *adj.* = Nonsensical.

1621 BURTON *Anat. Mel.* II. iv. I. v. (1651) 375 A few simples well .. understood are better than such an heap of nonsense confused compounds. **1638** CHILLINGW. *Relig. Prot.* I. iv. § 47. 217 Some empty unintelligible non-sense distinction. **1642** ROGERS *Naaman* 191 Put case the way of washing in Jordan bee irrationall and non-sense to thy wit and reason. **1757** FOOTE *Author* I. (1782) 23 You are a Non-sense man, and I won't agree to any such Thing. **1858** MRS. OLIPHANT *Laird of Norlaw* II. 127 This is not a nonsense letter—will you read it, mother? **1862** PALGRAVE in *Times* 15 May, A learned mockery, a nonsense sculpture.

It is only under meaning number 6 here that the *OED* refers to nonsense as a literary genre, with its allusion to the 'parent of modern nonsense-writers', presumably Edward Lear. Yet the genre depends on the dismissive nature of the other meanings, the first of which ('spoken or written words which make no sense or convey absurd ideas') seems to underpin them all. By its

[3]

means the authors quoted by the dictionary dismiss phenomena as varied as a 'game of vapours', a written sentence or period, a style of learning, an attempt at humour, a political doctrine, a private journal entry, 'Fustian' language, and an attitude towards one's health. As the other examples show, it can be used to outlaw things as different as linguistic usage and intellectual belief, 'false Latin' and 'impiety'. In failing to make sense a speaker or writer is seen as failing in the most drastic way imaginable, at either the level of linguistic competence or ideological coherence. The appeal and authority of the term 'nonsense' largely consists in its important function as an instrument for declaring other utterances to be unimportant and functionless. This confirms the uniquely anomalous status of a deliberately nonsensical literature. With its brazen incompetence at the level of logic or language, nonsense poetry itself would seem little more than a 'game of vapours'. Yet, as the examples concerned with 'impiety', moral disagreement and 'dangerous' political subversion suggest, it is a game which might engage in the questionable domain of transgression, however innocently.

Nursery-rhymes apart, the traditional literary view of 'nonsense' – developed most effectively by the neo-classical satirists and critics of the age of Dryden and Pope – is as dismissive as the dictionary's other usages suggest. Since the late seventeenth century, 'nonsense' has been the ultimate critical put-down, the most lethal term in the hostile critic's armoury of abuse. In his brilliant mock-epic, *Mac Flecknoe,* John Dryden damns his true-blue poetical hero by declaring that he 'In prose or verse, was owned, without dispute / Through all the realms of Nonsense absolute'.[5] In Dryden's view, to hold sovereignty over the realms of nonsense would be a travesty of literary authority: the realms of nonsense are the dumping-ground for literary failures, the limbo of the unachieved and meaningless. Ever since, the term 'nonsense' has remained the basic formula for rubbishing literature that is incompetent, difficult or even experimental. You still hear it and see it as the ultimate put-down. To be accused of writing nonsense is to be written off.

Yet, as 'Hey Diddle Diddle' with its little laughing dog reminds us, poetry and nonsense was originally intertwined – in nursery rhymes, children's games, and our earliest wordplay as babies. Children's oral rhymes and rhyming are indeed our usual introduction to the formal pleasures of poetry and stand as the most conspicuous surviving monument of the earliest play with – and play of – language in our lives. The realms of poetry and the realms of nonsense were originally closely allied. The twentieth-century Russian apologist for children's literature, Kornei Chuvovsky, has linked the primitive pleasure in rhyme-making to language-learning itself, and given particular emphasis to the affinity between a child's taste for nonsense and poetry as such.[6] He recalls watching a two-year-old girl chanting:

> Kunda, munda, karamunda,
> Dunda, bunda, Paramun

just as the poet Pushkin had greeted a seven-year-old boy as a born 'Romantic' when he heard him improvise the strange chant:

> Indijanda, Indijanda, Indija!
> Indijadi, Indijad, Indija![7]

The 'speech-play' of children is full of such pleasurable but non-referential sound-patterns, such as are ritualised in the counting-rhymes and counting out formulae which play such a large part in the culture of the playground in English-speaking countries, as in Russia, France, Germany and elsewhere. In America children chant:

> Inty, ninty, tibbety fig
> Deema, dima doma nig
> Howchy powchy domi nowday
> Hom tom tout
> Olligo bolligo boo
> Out goes you.[8]

In France they sing:

> Am stram gram
> Pic et pic et colégram
> Bour et bour et ratatam
> Am stram gram.[9]

While in Germany they say:

> Annchen Dannchen
> Diddchen Daddchen
> Ewerde Bewerde
> Bittchende Battchen
> Ewerde Bewerde Bu
> Ab bist du![10]

The taste for formulaic babble is international, and the need to play about with sounds and meanings seems to be a universal feature of childhood. You learn codes by breaking them. You learn how language and logic are built by breaking them down. You also enjoy the pleasures of going beyond the bounds. The truth is that word formation and word deformation are closely allied. Language is built up between babble and Babel.

In both the *Beano*-like subculture of the playground documented in Iona and Peter Opie's *Lore and Language of Schoolchildren*, and the traditional culture of nursery song, Mother Goose's Melodies play a part in introducing us to the oral pleasures of the mother tongue, while at the same time initiating us into the thrills of goosing father's logic.[11] In fact, though they may seem inconsequential in adult eyes, children's rhymes may serve as chapters of consequences (as the first editor of *Mother Goose* parodically suggested), and miniature ABC's of linguistic order. They deal regularly with the basic constituents of language and number as well as the regular ins and outs and ups and downs of childhood. Alphabetical poems are an obvious example, from the traditional:

> Great A, little a,
> > Bouncing B;
> The cat's in the cupboard,
> > And she can't see.

(where the child may not see, but will certainly hear the pun on C), to the nonsense alphabets of Edward Lear and Edward Gorey. Counting rhymes are a comparable case, like the following:

> 1,2,3,4,5,
> Once I caught a fish alive;
> 6,7,8,9,10,
> Then I let him go again.

Here the rhyme makes counting come alive, numerically and metrically. It first helps catch the fish alive and then lets it go again, to swim free of the wholly arbitrary grid of the counting-rhyme and our arithmetic. Nonsensical and nursery rhymes are particularly drawn to serial order of one kind or another: number as in 'Green grow the rushes-o'; names such as London churches in 'Oranges and Lemons'; days of the week, as in 'Solomon Grundy'; fingers and toes, like 'This little pig went to market'; chains of consequences like 'This is the House that Jack Built'; absurd rhyme-schemes as in Lear's 'Mousy, Bousey, Sousy, Mousy', and loopy refrains like 'With a rolypoly, gammon and spinach'. Inconsequence is of huge consequence in the world of children's rhymes, with their double fascination with sequentiality and *non sequiturs*.

One of the first patterns that emerges when we look at nonsense poems of this sort is that patterns emerge. To make nonsense, you have to do more than gabble or scrabble. If anything, nonsense is more shapely, more brazenly formalised and patterned than other kinds of language – not the reverse, as is often assumed.[12] Indeed it might be argued that, far from being a very special case of poetry, nonsense represents what makes poetry itself a special case. I suspect there is a pleasure in nonsense at the core of all poetry, a pleasure ultimately rooted in the child's free play with sounds, words, rhythms and patterns of repetition – experiments with meaning which are made in defiance of the obligation to make sense.

At any rate the *Chatto Book of Nonsense Poetry* is intended to invite readers to take a fresh look at both poetry and nonsense, and to explore their playful interaction across the centuries. Some of this material is familiar. There is a fair sprinkling of children's rhymes of various kinds, and a generous selection from the Victorian godfathers of nonsense, Edward Lear and Lewis Carroll, writers whose names are almost synonymous with nonsense, and whose work stands at the centre of the eccentric 'nonsense canon'. Without 'Jabberwocky' and 'The Dong with the Luminous Nose', neither nonsense nor poetry would look as it does. There is also a varied sample of comic and off-beat 'light verse', such as Thomas Hood's punning ballads and Ogden Nash's bagatelles. Yet I have cast my net further afield, in space and time, to include less familiar material from the remoter past and some more unpredictable material from the present, with the idea of extending our sense of the 'realm of nonsense', and enlarging the bounds of the canon of poetry that goes beyond the bounds of sense.

I have therefore taken samples from some of the obscurer reaches of medieval and renaissance poetry as well as from recognised past masters like Rabelais and Shakespeare; from seventeenth-century song-books and drolleries as well as from the bizarre farragos of John Taylor the Water Poet, the unacknowledged pioneer of English nonsense poetry; from eighteenth-century spoofs and satires, by Pope, Swift, Fielding, and others; from lesser known areas of the great Romantic writers like Blake, Keats, and Coleridge, giving particular space to the neglected satirical ballads of Thomas Love Peacock; and from Victorian songs, like Hood's and Gilbert's. Yet if I have trawled my net across the literature of the past, searching for linguistic oddities and absurd narratives, it is in large measure because the poetry of our century has proved especially open to nonsense. Perhaps partly as result of the liberating examples of Freud and the Surrealists, twentieth-century poets have been fascinated by nonsense tricks and plots, by linguistic absurdity and logical puzzles and elaborately arbitrary poetic forms. As a result I have collected a rich assortment of modern poetry of all sorts and shapes and sizes – Dadaist and Surrealist performances, experimental and modernist poems by Joyce, Khlebnikov and others, miscellaneous idiosyncratic lyrics by traditionalists like W. B. Yeats and Robert Graves, and free inventions by post-moderns like John Ashbery. I hope this demonstrates the enduring vitality of the English nonsense tradition – one of the greatest of all English inventions – as well as the wider currency of nonsense poetry in America and modern Europe on both sides of the Iron Curtain. As the haunting work of Eastern European writers like the Czech Miroslav Holub and the Romanian Marin Sorescu remind us, nonsense may be a liberating way of dealing with the intolerable, or at least handling the impermissible.

Nonsense is a permissive form, but unfortunately the cost of permissions is high. I would have liked to include more poetry by twentieth-century writers, but have had to limit the number of poems in copyright. If nonsense highlights the arbitrariness of order, an anthology like this one is a conspicuous case of such arbitrariness. In the past the Nonsense Canon has tended to be thought of as surprisingly fixed and restricted, and I hope that this anthology will draw new as well as familiar material into play, while also including questionable, marginal, and controversial items. Nonsense poetry is less a genre than a possibility, a dimension, a boundary which poetry touches more frequently than we usually imagine. It may take the form of nursery-rhyme, utopian protest, riddle, parody, fable, automatic writing, madsong, limerick, futurist experiment, learned joke, satire, or *jeu d'esprit*, but at its heart lies a playful formal inventiveness and delight in transgression, a protest against the arbitrariness of order and an affirmation of the pleasure-principle applied to language.

The obsessively moralistic Duchess in *Alice in Wonderland* tells the young Alice to 'Take care of the sense and the sounds will take care of themselves.'[13] That is certainly sensible advice in most situations, but in nonsense the reverse is true. If you take care of the sounds, the sense will take care of itself. In making nonsense of something, a writer brings to light ideas or feelings camouflaged by the serious mask of Sense. As a misfit itself, it rejoices in the misfit of language and the world, allowing words – especially the sound of words – a freer rein than usual, favouring puns, tight rhymes, assonance, neologism, inversions, twinnings, formal elaboration, *double entendres*, secret codes and private languages. When Alice questions Humpty Dumpty's assumption that he can make a word mean whatever he wants it to mean, however wayward, he replies: 'the question is . . . which is to be master – that's all'.[14] In nonsense, words are master, and this mastery is a cause for celebration, though at the same time a sign of absurdity. We, our language and our world, appear in all our arbitrariness to be absurder than we know in nonsense poems, and the best of them give a salutary and savoury sense of the saving incongruity between our language mastery and all it does not and can never master. Alice first discovered nonsense when she went underground, and it may well be that nonsense is a kind of underground language – something to do with the unconscious, the rich world of sleep, slips of the tongue, and literary rejection slips. The literature of nonsense certainly has its roots in childhood, pleasure, and the revaluation of what has been dismissed or rejected. Alice rejects her garbled versions of poetry as mere nonsense, and yet Lewis Carroll has made a kind of triumph out of garbling, out of *faux pas* and false logic, as all the best nonsense poetry does.

2

At the opening of Thomas Lovell Beddoes's neglected Gothic tragedy *Death's Jest-Book*, one of the characters named Homunculus Mandrake holds forth to a brother fool on the decline of folly, in a style that is a pastiche of the patter of Shakespearean fools like Feste:

In truth I mark our noble faculty is in decay. The world shall see its ears in a glass no longer; so we are laid aside and shall soon be forgotten; for why should the feast of asses come but once a year, when all the days are foaled of one mother? O world, world! The gods and fairies left thee, for thou wert too wise; and now, thou Socratic star, thy demon, the great Pan, Folly, is parting from thee. The oracles still talked in their sleep, shall our grandchildren say, till Master Merriman's kingdom was broken up: now is every man his own fool, and the world's grown cheerless.[15]

Beddoes's elegiac Romantic Fool speaks with understandable professional bias but he is extremely well-informed about the history of folly, and his views may throw light on the elusive history of folly's close relation, Nonsense. It may be that nonsense is the modern descendant of his long-eared 'noble faculty', 'oracles' talking in their sleep, feasts of asses, and the culture of fools and folly.

   This anthology is organised chronologically, to display something of the history of nonsense and the curious interaction between nonsense and history. The early traces, if we exclude the special code-nonsense of riddles and riddle-books, are scattered and elusive, glimpsed in the corners of obscure texts and in reports of feasts and fools that have been indeed 'laid aside' and 'forgotten'. Nonsense thrives in oral performance – and most of it inevitably fails to outlive the occasions which give it birth. It must have played a significant part in the popular culture of the Middle Ages and the Renaissance, as part of the ritual clowning associated with carnival and religious feasts, such as the feasts of assess mentioned by Homunculus Mandrake, as well as in the courtly culture where the licensed fool in his motley brandished his bauble. We can see glimpses of these worlds in the wordplay of Shakespeare's fools, Elizabethan jest-books, nonsense carols, French *fatrasies* and *sotties*, Skelton's learned linguistic fantasias like *Phyllyp Sparowe*, and, above all, in the encyclopaedic grotesquery of the Renaissance Humanist François Rabelais whose *Gargantua and Pantagruel* is a playful, learned monument to the popular culture of carnival in the Middle Ages. These glimpses are tantalising signs of the lost nonsense of the medieval period. The Russian critic Mikhail Bakhtin, in his influential book *Rabelais and His World*, has created a renewed interest in this whole culture

[9]

of carnival which he argues lies at the heart of Rabelais's exuberantly licentious literary masterpiece, with its systematic transgressions, inversions, and travesties of social and religious authority.[16] Carnival, in fact, permitted a kind of officially licensed protest against the social hierarchy, strict moral code, and authority of the church, working by parodying, burlesquing and inverting sacred texts and rites, while affirming bodily excess and carnality against the transcendental claims of the Christian Church. An example of this kind of festive burlesque is the thirteenth-century 'Prose of the Ass' from Beauvais, which was sung in church to celebrate the authority of a donkey. It begins:

> Orientis partibus
> Adventavit Asinus,
> Pulcher et fortissimus,
> Sarcinis aptissimus.
> Hez, Sire Asnes, car chantez[17]

Such travesties of church services and priestly functions were particularly associated with the Feast of Fools which formed part of the church calendar in many places throughout the Middle Ages. E. K. Chambers quotes a late but representative account of the Feast of Fools in Antibes, where the choir and office were left to cooks and gardeners rather than priests or friars, vestments were put on inside out, books held upside down, spectacles replaced by orange peel, and in place of the correct liturgy, the participants chanted 'confused and inarticulate gibberish'.[18] It may be that such antics, which were the bane of reforming bishops in the period, would have made Alfred Jarry's outrageous surrealist play *Ubu Roi* or the notorious Dadaist café performances at the Cabaret Voltaire, look like a vicarage tea-party.

Much of what remains from that carnivalesque culture is inaccessible or untranslatable. I have begun with an enigmatic lyric by William of Aquitaine, a Provençal writer who is credited as the first important European vernacular poet, and included a modernised version of the Middle-English *Land of Cockaygne*, a gentle utopian satire shot through with absurd gusto as well as radical social criticism, which probably emanated from Ireland; parts of John Skelton's exuberant mock-elegy for a pet bird, 'Phyllyp Sparowe', which like his play *Magnificence* makes magnificent play with extravagant speech; and a nonsense burlesque and ludicrous inventory of games from Rabelais's *Gargantua and Pantagruel*, in seventeenth-century English translation. These form the main set-pieces from this earliest period. Around them I have set a nonsense carol and song, as well as makeshift versions of the utterly untranslatable nonsense genre of French *fatrasies*, a formally strict but semantically anarchic genre which flourished in France in the thirteenth to fifteenth centuries, owing something to popular entertainments but more perhaps to sophisticated literary *jeux de société*, based on elaborately absurd improvisation in a tight formal corset – rather like a longer, more intricate limerick of eleven lines.[19] In fact the *fatrasie* is the first fully-fledged nonsense genre that I know of, and, like the limerick, only used for nonsensical effects. It seems to have been a lightweight, letting-the-hair-down affair, which mischievously travestied the elaborately codified official poetics of the medieval period, and revelled in batty, downbeat free association often with possible political overtones. Like the limericks of Lear, food and place-names were crucial to the fun. Here is an example:

> Uns saiges sans sense,
> Sans bouche, sans dens,
> Le siècle mengea
> Et uns sors harens
> Manda les Flamens
> Qui les vengera;
> Mais tout ce ne lor vaura
> La plume de deus mellens
> Qui quatre nés affondra.
> Mais je ne sai que pens;
> De murdre les apela.[20]

Sadly, this is a kind of nonsense which is hard for even modern French readers to tune into and is almost wholly untranslatable. Like the gibberish and horseplay of carnival, such festive poetic deviance lives on only in scholarship.

Shakespeare's quicksilver wordplay, quibbling, and comic inventiveness survive out in the open (with the help of footnotes). For the anthology I have taken an absurd pastiche from *Love's Labour's Lost*, Bottom's Dream as a genial translation of the carnivalesque feast of asses, Feste's lilting Fool's song from *Twelfth Night*, and the scene on the heath in *King Lear* where the mad king, bewildered Fool and Edgar disguised as a Tom O'Bedlam beggar, confront each other's folly in the howling storm. Familiar as it is, the scene from *Lear* has as vivid a place in the history of nonsense as in that of madness. The dialogue is shot through with queer, garbled oracular language, and shifts back and forth between reason and madness, pathos and absurdity. It's not only the most vivid representation of the fool in literature, but in its vision of violent social disorder and broken authority suggests that through the language of madness and adopted madness the characters make touch with truths and feelings outside the pale of their normal language. What they say in their terrible crisis makes sense all right, but it takes a route that zigzags giddily across the border with nonsense.

The border with nonsense never seems that far away in the best poetry of the seventeenth century. What we now call the 'metaphysical' poetry of the school of Donne, is full of absurd conceits and extravagant hyperbole which, for all the passionate wit and high-wire argumentativeness of the poetry, have affinities with nonsense. Though I have included a couple of instances of this highly sophisticated verse, the popular entertaining books of drolleries that appeared in the mid-century, especially at the end of the Commonwealth period, have proved a more fertile source of deliberate nonsense. The drolleries, such as *Wit and Drollery* and *The Westminster Drollery*, tended to specialise in jolly drinking-songs, bawdy anti-Puritan satire, and fun, in protest against the seriousness of the Puritan ethos. Much of this cheerful flim-flam has ceased to be funny, but there are a few bawdy trifles, ingenious absurdities like Dr Corbett's, and memorable Bedlamite songs such as 'Tom O'Bedlam', which speak with inspired licence. The series of Bedlamite songs look back to *Lear* and sometimes tap a vein of tough, zany lyricism in their mask of simulated madness. Beside them, I have set one poem by the authentic Bedlamite, James Carkesse, whose poems, *Lucida Intervalla*, were written late in the century while their author was incarcerated in Finsbury Hospital.[21]

A poem with the title 'Nonsense' appeared in one of the drolleries without attribution, and has since done the rounds of all the nonsense anthologies as the work of Anon. It is in fact the work of the now obscure hack John Taylor – known as the Water-Poet because he was a Thames bargeman – the author of an immense literary output of travelogues, joke-books, second-rate poems, pro-royalist tracts and anti-Puritan satires. Though he was the writer of a heap of ephemeral trash, Taylor also deserves to be recognised as the first pioneer of English nonsense verse on the strength of a series of distinctively bizarre poetic travesties: *Odcomb's Lament*, which includes poems in a spoof Utopian language, *Jack O'Lent*, a work with carnival overtones, *Sir Gregory Nonsense his News from No-Place*, and the magnificently titled *The Essence, Quintessence, Incense, Innocence, Lye-sence, and Magnificence of Nonsense upon Sense; or Sense upon Nonsense.*[22] Though almost forgotten now, Taylor's nonsense narrative poems are certainly worth reading for all their hit-or-miss quirkiness and jumbled-up style and stories. They contain phrases of surrealist charm and inspired bathos, which look forward to Lewis Carroll and even James Joyce: 'As I upon a gnat was riding late / In quest to parley with the Pleiades', 'then on the banks of Shoreditch shall be seen / What 'tis to serve the great Utopian Queen' and 'Give me a medlar in a field of blue, / Wrapt stigmatically in a dream'. His nonsense grotesques depend on oscillating bewilderingly between high and low, exotic and local, classical and Cockney, sublime and ridiculous, with giddy volubility. The effect is of a Bedlamite parody of literary order itself. In the 1640s Taylor wrote an anti-puritan propaganda allegory called *Mad Fashions, Odd Fashions, All out of Fashions*, which used the same techniques of nonsensical inversion and topsyturvydom to deplore the 'World turned upside down' advocated by the Puritans ('The world's turned upside down, from bad to worse / Quite out of frame, the cart before the horse').[23] 'England's face and language is estranged', he wrote there, and such an assertion suggests the connection between the defiant linguistic utopianism of his nonsense works and his recoil from what he saw as political anarchy, between his attraction to and fear of *estrangement*.

A comparable ambivalence informs the neo-classical satire of the Restoration and eighteenth century. For writers like Dryden, Pope, Fielding and Swift, 'nonsense' was a term of abuse, to be applied to cultural phenomena that were felt to be abuses. The representative critic Addison, for example, writing in the influential periodical *The Spectator* in 1711, opposed true and false humour by drawing up two neatly allegorical charts.[24] In the first 'Truth was the Founder of the Family, and the Father of Good Sense. Good Sense was the Father of Wit, who married a lady of Collateral Line called Mirth, by whom he had Issue Humour'. In the second the 'impostor' false Humour 'descends originally from Falsehood who was the Mother of Nonsense, who was brought to bed of a Son called Frenzy, who married one of the Daughters of Folly, commonly known by the name of Laughter, on whom he begot that Monstrous Infant'. People who think they are being humorous 'if they speak Nonsense' are in Addison's view almost qualified for Bedlam, being prone to indulge in 'boundless freedoms'. As a consciously 'great Dog' himself, Addison sees Nonsense as the affair of very little dogs indeed – and closely associated with Falsehood, Madness and Folly, those bugbears of the Man of Sense.

Within the literary satire of the time, it became the standard strategy of conservative satirists, in defence of their own neo-classicising standards, to knock their opponents over the head with the idea of nonsense – along with folly, anarchy and such like anathemas. In *Mac Flecknoe*, John Dryden made his lampooned poet hero absolute monarch of the 'realms of nonsense', and subjected him to nonsensical indignities in mock-heroic verse. In *The Dunciad*, Alexander Pope's darker cultural burlesque in the same vein, 'new-born Nonsense' is portrayed as the first stage in the evolution of the unclassical trash culture of excretion, exhibitionism and hallucination which holds sway in his nightmare vision of Grub Street *Götterdämmerung*.[25] In *The Author's Farce*, a play within the same tradition, Henry Fielding presents his audience with a theatrical burlesque in which a 'great number of passengers arrived from England' are shown en route to the Court of Nonsense; they include Don Tragedio, Sir Farcical Comic, Dr Orator, Signior Opera, Monsieur Pantomime and Mrs Novel, along with a Bookseller described as 'the Prime Minister of Nonsense' and a Presbyterian Parson called Murder-text who cries out 'Shall you abuse Nonsense, when all the town supports it?'[26]

In such spoofs and critiques 'Nonsense' is a way of abusing the taste of the town. It's not a recognisable genre itself, but the name for the degeneration of the other genres ('Don Tragedio', 'Signior Opera'). It seems to be intimately bound up with the idea of travestied authority and spurious dignity; the conservative satirists conjure up great anarchs, laureates of dullness, goddesses and even a prime minister of nonsense. Obviously neither Dryden, Pope or Fielding would have taken kindly to the idea of a poetry of nonsense. Nevertheless, when fired by the idea of nonsense, the very nonsense they are attacking, their satire tends to take on an anarchic kind of inventiveness and pleasurable absurdity, akin to nonsense. They travesty what they see as travesties of order with a grotesque gusto of their own, and seem to explore – even as they deplore – the dangerous vitality of linguistic folly. The effect is of a kind of bilious negative carnival, paradoxically licensed by the writers' exacerbated commitment to the classical ethos of literary decorum. As a result the history of nonsense has been enriched, not impoverished, by the satire of the Augustan period and the work of writers such as Pope, Dryden, Swift and Fielding. Fielding's spoof songs, Swift's parody cantata, Samuel Johnson's improvised burlesques, show a light-footed relish for absurdity typical of the time – a happy confirmation of the motto of Sterne's Yorick 'Vive la bagatelle'.[27] Swift, though the author of an important polemical pamphlet advocating rationalisation and stabilisation of the English language, had a lifelong fascination with language games and deformations. *Gulliver's Travels* represents samples of imaginary languages, his private *Journal to Stella* is full of secret codewords and absurd pet-names, and his poetry includes elaborate riddling verses for his friend Dr Delaney, English poems in the guise of warped Latin, as well as quirky burlesques, and a curious couplet written in his sleep. Even as they pilloried unconscious nonsense as a kind of literary madness, writers like Swift and Pope showed a taste for the consciously nonsensical bagatelle.

Later in the century, the certifiably Bedlamite poet Christopher Smart, who under the pseudonym of 'Mother Midnight' had turned out his fair share of comic bagatelles for money, found himself hospitalised in Bethlem after suffering a serious breakdown, and produced one of the most arrestingly *sui generis* poems in the English language, the idiosyncratic and encyclopaedic song of praise, *Jubilate Agno*. For all its copious learning and Augustan elegance of diction, it is a work of sublimely incongruous and incongruously sublime style, and has something of the fascination with amazingly arbitrary schemes of order and absurdly heterogeneous language, which characterises the best nonsense poetry. Its eccentrically felicitous linguistic panache certainly aligns it, albeit in a visionary mode, with the nonsense tradition. William Blake, another visionary poet sometimes accused of madness, tried his hand at knockabout literary burlesque in an early chaotic satire on his contemporaries called *The Island in the Moon*. In its improvised songs the voice of the romantic bard is heard in surprisingly playful vein, as he lets off steam in inspired unbardic buffoonery.

The Romantic poets are not generally associated with lighter or satirical poetry, Byron excepted. All the same, not only Blake, but Lamb, Coleridge, Keats and Beddoes, in more relaxed moods (and modes) threw off a number of nonsensical poems, and Thomas Love Peacock, in his pastiche-medieval ballad *Sir Proteus*, deployed the idea of Nonsense as a term and technique of abuse, to parody the affectations of the Lake Poets and current literary fashions. Unexpectedly the funniest of the Romantic writers, Lord Byron, author of that swinging comic epic *Don Juan*, rarely taps the vein of nonsense at all while the most earnest of them, William Wordsworth, accused by Hazlitt of writing 'mere *nonsense verses*' in some of the *Lyrical Ballads*, surprisingly uses a couplet which is just that, when the idiot boy tells the story of his midnight journey in his own peculiar upsidedown way:[28]

> 'The cocks did crow to-whoo, to-whoo,
> And the sun did shine so cold',
> – Thus answered Johnny in his glory
> And that was all his travel's story.[29]

'The Idiot Boy' is something of an exception in the output of the poet Shelley called 'solemn and unsexual', and the same might be said of Keats's improvised idiotic ballad, 'There was a naughty boy', in relation to his output. On the other hand, it does not seem surprising that Thomas Lovell Beddoes, writer of Homunculus Mandrake's praise of folly quoted earlier, should have had a taste for the nonsensical, and he concocted a small number of very queer romantic legends indeed – one about an egg-laying tailor, another about a new kind of Dodo, and another celebrating a grosser St Cecilia. From the mythological to the ridiculous is only a step. And Samuel Taylor Coleridge, a poet accused of writing nonsense in his enigmatically mythopoeic dream-poem 'Kubla Khan', once commented on a particular passage: 'Well! that . . . is what I call the sublime dashed to pieces by cutting too close with the fiery four-in-hand round the corner of nonsense.'[30] It remained an open question whether the fiery four-in-hand of nonsense mightn't retrace the famous step from the sublime to the ridiculous, and become a new sublime.

3

It was not until the middle of the nineteenth century, however, and in the heart of the Victorian era, that nonsense poetry as such came into its own, thanks to the genius of Edward Lear and Lewis Carroll. Ironically perhaps, this Victorian Nonsense Renaissance was indirectly a legacy of Wordsworthian romanticism – as well as a reaction to the cult of moral sublimity of the age. It forms part at any rate of the inspiring critique of seriousness generated by a culture with a huge investment in ideas of social and intellectual authority and a dedication to the ideal of moral earnestness – a critique played out in the children's books of Lear and Carroll, the punning lyrical ballads of Thomas Hood, the squibs and satires of Thackeray, the grotesque novels of Charles Dickens, and the elegantly subversive dialogues and plays of Oscar Wilde. Such writers implicitly brought into question the earnestness of being important, and the importance of being earnest.

But it was the romantic invention of childhood and the Wordsworthian cult of the child which licensed the Victorian literature of nonsense. Lear and Carroll are successors of Wordsworth's idiot boy Johnny 'in his glory' and their art depends upon the 'glory' celebrated in Wordsworth's 'Ode on Intimations of Immortality', the wakeful creativity associated with childhood. Edward Lear first published what he called his 'nonsenses' – the word limerick came later – as a children's book, *The Book of Nonsense*, in 1846, and had improvised them to amuse the children at Knowsley Hall a couple of years earlier, taking 'There was an old man of Tobago' from the anonymous *Anecdotes and Adventures of Fifteen Gentlemen* as his model. Lear's spontaneously improvised brief lives of memorable eccentrics caused 'uproarious delight and welcome at the appearance of every new absurdity' in the Knowsley children (as he wrote in *More Nonsense*), and afterwards the world at large responded with similar comic relief.[31] Lear was a world-travelled landscape artist and natural history illustrator by profession, but it was in his limericks, songs, and haywire doodles for children that he found his true voice – and vocation – in the expression of his own ruefully funny sense of displacement and eccentricity. A taste for children and a gift for nonsense happily coincided for Charles Lutwidge Dodgson of Christ Church College, Oxford, a conservative logician and amateur photographer. Under the pseudonym of Lewis Carroll he too found a kind of vocation not in the Church or indeed as a don in Christ Church, but as an inventor of ingenious nonsense for the young. *Alice in Wonderland* began as an 'extemporaneous romance'[32] spun for the amusement of the daughters of Dean Liddell on a rowing picnic outside Oxford in July 1862, and was finally published as a fully-fledged children's book in 1865, to great acclaim.

For both Lear and Carroll nonsense sponsored by the presence of children and the idea of the child yielded a strangely expressive art with an enigmatic appeal not only to children but adults. Looking back on their work now, we can see they not only transformed children's literature, and gave it an escape-route from the domain of moral responsibilities, but opened up possibilities through the looking-glass and underground, which would in the twentieth century attract the avant-garde. They extended the poetic licence.

For Lear and Carroll, nonsense was a kind of dialect of innocence, a language associated with childhood but somehow divested of the burden of meaning. '"Nonsense" pure and absolute' was the declared 'aim' of Lear's limericks, free of any 'symbolical meaning' other than 'administering innocent mirth to thousands', as he wrote in the introduction to *More Nonsense*.[33] Asked about his intentions in writing *The Hunting of the Snark*, Carroll wrote 'I'm afraid I didn't mean anything but nonsense!' – though he conceded that 'words mean more than we mean to express when we use them', and said he would be prepared to accept 'whatever good meanings are in the book'.[34] Of the *Alice* books too, he wrote that every idea and word 'came of itself', without calculation or intentional significance.[35] Faced with his own work he turns out to be in much the same position as his imperturbable, but perpetually puzzled heroine Alice when, on slipping through the mirror, she encounters the poem 'Jabberwocky': 'It fills my head with ideas – only I don't know what they are!'[36] For a man otherwise so scrupulously preoccupied by correct logic, propriety, and good meanings (he wanted to bowdlerise Bowdler's Shakespeare to fit it for children), nonsense clearly offered a most effective escape-hatch, letting quite other kinds of meaning 'innocently' into the air. 'Who or why or which or what is the Akond of Swat?' Lear asked in a famous poem. The poem never answers its own questions and remains a questionnaire about an incognito from some *terra incognita*. Similarly, in *The Hunting of the Snark*, Carroll's dark mock-epic readers never find out the identity of the enigmatic object of the poem's anxious quest, its nonsensical equivalent of Moby Dick. We face the poem rather as the ship's crew face the absurd figure of their captain the Bellman – a solemnly idiotic figure with the manners of a Victorian Sage but not the slightest idea of navigation or topography:

> 'Other maps are such shapes, with their islands and capes!
>   But we've our brave captain to thank'
> (So the crew would protest) 'that he's bought *us* the best –
>   A perfect and absolute blank!'

In a world which put so high a premium on moral duty, sexual purity, commercial expansion, and the importance of Mr Gradgrind's 'Fact', the chartered 'innocence' of nonsense must have held an unspoken promise of provisional freedom, the freedom of play.

Yet the innocent maps of Victorian nonsense are not blank. They chart familiar territory in absurd disguise. Lear's limericks and lyrics rehearse the facts and fantasies of his saddened life in a misfittingly funny form. Lear was what he described as 'a dirty landscape painter',[37] recorder of natural history, travel-writer and picturesque tourist. He was also a sociable and melancholic man, plagued by recurrent epilepsy and financial anxiety, whose letters and diaries reflect chronic depression and loneliness, the price in part of unhappily repressed (because 'unspeakable') homosexual longings and unreciprocated friendship. Like his life, his nonsense combines the search for the exotic and the persistence of the melancholic, like Byron's *Childe Harold* in a more childlike, clowning key. All his writing is geographical, and almost every poem is about leaving or being left. It is a record of travel to strange lands and by strange means – the Jumblies go to sea in a sieve to the Torrible Zone and the hills of Chankly Bore, the Owl and the Pussycat sail for a year and a day to the land where the Bong Tree grows, the Dong wanders the great Gromboolian Plain. Like Lear's official art, it records unknown flora like the Bottelphorkia Spoonifolia and Manypeeplia Upsidedownia of his *Nonsense Botany*, and outlandish fauna like the Pobble and Scroobious Pip. It is peopled by misfits and travellers, melancholics and eccentrics, who suffer from unhappy love like the Dong or Yonghy-Bonghy-Bo, impossible aspirations like Mr Daddy Long-Legs, inappropriate appetites like the person from Florence with a fatal taste for eating Bustards in mustard, physical peculiarities such as huge noses or voluminous beards, and with a propensity for behaviour that is 'scroobious and strange', such as sitting in tubs, reading Homer on one leg, or dancing with a raven – all of which tends to outrage the respectable citizenry, 'the legions of cruel and inquisitive They' as Auden called the intolerant moral majority represented in Lear's nonsensical *Baedeker*.[38] The limerick form which Lear made his own is beautifully suited to his purposes; with its tightly-bound rhyme-scheme and energetically bouncing rhythms, it catches both the forces which constrict figures within a geographical space defined by a place-name, and the deviant energies which defy such definition and break out of the shell of social conventions. As the spikily energetic drawings that accompany the poems show, these miniature confrontations tap whirlwinds of social passion, and the outcome is often the defeat of individual initiative – as in the case of the dancing ornithologist of Whitehaven:

> There was an Old Man of Whitehaven,
> Who danced a quadrille with a Raven;
> But they said – 'It's absurd to encourage this bird!'
> So they smashed that Old Man of Whitehaven.

However, among a host of disappointed eccentrics and would-be travellers, there is at least one triumphant success-story:

> There was an Old Person from Basing,
> Whose presence of mind was amazing;
> He purchased a steed, which he rode at full speed,
> And escaped from the people of Basing.

Though we don't know where he escapes to – anywhere outside Basing will do – we relish the hero's defiance of the forces of conventional inertia, and the suggestion that anyone with any presence of mind at all would want to get out of Basing, though it will require initiative and great speed to make the great escape.

Lear's longer lyrics are like warped Tennyson.[39] They take the form of poignant *reductiones ad absurdum* of the high romantic themes of wandering, lost love, madness, and quests for the paradisal place. Some, like 'Incidents in the Life of my Uncle Arly' and 'How Pleasant to Meet Mr. Lear', are transparently autobiographical, but all of them deal with the materials of romantic tragedy in light-footed, comic guise, with a delicately tuned musical bathos, such as marks the 'impossible' epithalamium for the Owl and the Pussycat, that odd coupling of nocturnal mouse-eaters, or the Poe-like portrait of the distraught Dong on the great Gromboolian Plain.[40] Lear's use of nonsense lyricism seems to serve the same functions as the Dong's strangely constructed Luminous Nose – as a defence against the absurdity of his intense feelings, and a parodic expression of them which will send out light in 'gleaming rays on the dismal night'.

Lewis Carroll's poetry lacks the poignantly loopy grace of Lear's, but it too transposes romantic and everyday material into a disconcertingly absurd key. 'Jabberwocky' parodies the heroic ballad and Anglo-Saxon epic, as the White Knight's Song parodies Wordsworth's high seriousness; 'Twinkle twinkle little bat' and 'How doth the little crocodile' mock the piously sentimental children's hymns of Ann Taylor and Isaac Watts; and *The Hunting of the Snark* travesties such romantic ballads as Coleridge's *Ancient Mariner* and quest-poems such as Tennyson's *Ulysses* and Browning's *Childe Roland*. The *Alice* books themselves convert the romantic dream-book into a joke-book, the Kings and Queens of Romance into cards and chess-pieces, fairy tales into puzzles, and the whole paraphernalia of Victorian childhood into bizarre, curiously sinister intellectual pantomime. Underlying them is the Wordsworthian myth of childhood innocence and 'glory', but Humpty Dumpty's definition of 'glory' as a 'knock-me-down argument' catches the queer nature of the book's idiom of nonsense argumentativeness as Alice sails courageously through a world of childish adults, bossy pedants and governesses, bullying her with crazily arbitrary rules and morals, while she undergoes a series of abrupt transformations on her way to assuming her own authority as a Queen.[41] Carroll's nonsense is full of Kings and Queens, rules and conventions, yet presents a beautifully pedantic burlesque upon adult authority and codes of manners, as its jokes harp on the nature of identity, the fascination of eating, and the fact of death. The alibi of 'innocence' enabled Carroll to write a kind of children's book which paradoxically slipped through the cordon sanitaire of moral innocence, and gave rein to the perverse, subversive, anxious areas of the child's – and the adult's – mind, as well as that delight in nonsense, a nonsense as clever as Lear's is idiotic, which relieves us from the burden of taking the world seriously. In doing so, he anticipated a much later literature. Poems like the *Hunting of the Snark* and 'Jabberwocky' point forwards to poetic experiments still to come – the Surrealist Aragon translated the first, and the absurdist Artaud the latter, into modern surrealised French. When Humpty Dumpty tells little Alice that he can 'explain all the poems that ever were invented – and a good many that haven't been invented just yet', his words were more prophetic than he or his author probably knew.[42]

Lear and Carroll never refer to each other's work and may well have invented their poetries of nonsense quite independently of each other. It is as if the Victorian *Zeitgeist* needed nonsense as a blessed relief from the authority of seriousness and the seriousness of authority. They may have been influenced by J. O. Halliwell's *Nursery Rhymes of England* published in the early 1840s, but Hood, Thackeray, Gilbert and others were also being drawn to verbal and narrative absurdity, and Hood in particular fabricated a series of memorable nonsense ballads, revelling in virtuoso wordplay, and cutting social pretensions down to size. In the lunatic sci-fi ballad, 'A Flying Visit', describing the descent of the man in the moon by balloon into nineteenth-century England, the lunar luminary speaks an unrecognisable tongue which is recognisably nonsense: 'Thus he said or he sung, Mi criky bo biggamy kickery bung'. This enigmatic tongue is compared by bystanders to slang, high Dutch, Greek, 'hotch-potch', glossolalia, Dickens, mad speech, and all 'the babble of Babel'; as the language of a quasi-'angel' descended from above it is also a travesty of the idiom of romantic transcendentalism. In fact, Hood's flying visitor, though only a figure in a light-hearted Victorian spoof, is like a compendium of the alibis for the strangeness of nonsense language in the nineteenth century. Things have changed in the twentieth century. Now we tend, with the Russian futurists, to insist art makes it strange, and have made of the language of estrangement a fine art.

On the threshold of the twentieth century, looking back at the progressive achievements of the Victorian era, G. K. Chesterton wrote that:

The matters which most thoroughly evoke this abiding childhood of the world are those which are really fresh, abrupt and inventive in any age: and if we were asked what was the best proof of this adventurous growth in the nineteenth century we should say, with all respect for its portentous science and philosophy, that it was to be found in the rhymes of Mr Edward Lear and the literature of nonsense. The Dong with the Luminous Nose, at least, is original, as the first ship and the first plough were original.

Having made this mischievously portentous claim for Lear's nonsense as some equivalent of the neolithic revolution, playing down Lear and Carroll's debt to the past traditions of children's rhymes and satirical parody, Chesterton went on to proclaim this new literary technology as 'the literature of the future'.[43]

Chesterton's claim for the absolute novelty of Victorian nonsense is exaggerated, as I hope this anthology shows, but his metaphors of plough and ship are happy ones, since nonsense can well be seen as a device for turning over exhausted soil and a means of transport to new territories, beyond the range of authorised official maps. At any rate, his joke has become prophetic, and in the present century the once marginal border-games of nonsense have become strangely central to artists, novelists and poets. The legacy of Lear and Carroll's fine art of nonsense was not so much to the often drearily predictable Victorian and Edwardian light verse brigade, as to literature at large, which was enlarged by their licence.[44] For poets in particular, at all levels of seriousness, high and low, mandarin and popular, in English and nearly every European language, the queer formations and deformations associated with nonsense poetry have played a curiously influential part in their work. T. S. Eliot is a representative case. He once told Stravinsky that he considered Edward Lear a great poet in company with George Herbert and the French Symbolist Mallarmé, and in *The Waste Land*, his shattered *collagiste* epic of post-war Europe, he made vivid use of nonsense effects among the 'fragments' shored against his 'ruins':

> O the moon shone bright on Mrs Porter
> And on her daughter
> They wash their feet in soda water
> – *Et O ces voix d'enfants, chantant dans la coupole!*[45]

From 'Prufrock' to *Old Possum's Book of Practical Cats*, Eliot had an acute ear for the resonantly nonsensical phrase, and in the *Waste Land* such riddling, nervous stammerings, sometimes childlike, sometimes hysterical, serve an almost choric function in the anxious echo-chamber of his requiem for European culture.

Such receptivity to the nonsensical has been a hallmark of much modern culture, with our premium on making it new, and our attraction towards making it stranger and stranger. Rimbaud claimed to have a key to the 'parade sauvage', and the late nineteenth-century Symbolisme of Mallarmé and Rimbaud created a new mystique around French poetic language in its search for the unknown by 'le dérèglement de tous les sens' – a mystique which had a powerful influence on twentieth-century poets across Europe, opening the way to the restless poetic experimentalism of Russian and Italian futurism, Anglo-American modernism, German and French Dada-ism and Surrealism and the other avant-garde Isms with which literary history is crowded.[46] For those unlikely pioneers of the avant-garde, Edward Lear and Lewis Carroll, nonsense was a dialect of innocence, but after Alice had returned from behind the looking-glass, nonsense lost its innocence. This may be in large measure to do with the terrifying dominion of centralised social authority over all areas of our lives, but can also be traceable to the influence of Freudian psychoanalysis and the example and theory of Surrealism. After Freud had created a way of reading which conferred intelligibility on phenomena hitherto treated as essentially meaningless – slips of the tongue, hysterical symptoms, jokes and dreams – and after the Surrealists had made a thriving cult of chance and the Unconscious, the status of nonsense changed. Nonsense has gone up in the world, it can now give itself airs – as well as air. The twentieth century has proved especially hospitable to nonsense in art – for traditionalists like A. E. Housman and Robert Graves, as well as innovators like e. e. cummings and Robert Desnos. The danger may be that nonsense becomes less hospitable as it becomes more programmatic. The poetic refuge from seriousness has often become a very serious place indeed. The vein of oracular nonsense encouraged by the French Surrealists, like the ʒaum or 'trans-rational' language pursued by the Russian futurists, means that the Old Man of Thermopylae of Lear's limerick might nowadays easily turn out to be the oracle at Delphi. Though nonsense is still an important defence against high seriousness, it has got beyond a joke.

But then so have jokes. Freud's revolutionary interpretation of the function and nature of jokes and dreams has placed nonsense in a new light. In Jokes and the Unconscious Freud put what he called 'the pleasure in nonsense' at the root of all joking and humour.[47] Just as in his view dreams are disguised expressions of repressed desires with roots in early childhood experience, so jokes are partially disguised devices for expressing not only our normally concealed protests against the norms we live by, but our suppressed infantile pleasure in nonsense, in playing with words and ideas. He even suggests that the pleasure in jokes as such derives from either 'play with words or from the liberation of nonsense'; their 'meaning' is 'merely intended to protect that pleasure from being done away with by criticism'.[48] Commentators on psychoanalysis universally recognise that the suppression of desire is central to Freud's account of individual development; they rarely consider the implications of the closely related repression of nonsense.

The Interpretation of Dreams analyses the apparent absurdity of dreams in terms of a transfigured and defigured sense. From his own and his patients' dreams, Freud notices not only weird narrative and figurative distortions, but the frequency of Jabberwocky-style nonsense coinages such as 'Autodidasker' and 'Norekdal', verbal freaks that he identifies as improvised compound words based on free association, so that 'Autodidasker' joins 'autodidact' and 'Lasker' while 'Norekdal' parodies such German superlatives as 'kolossal' by referring to two characters from Ibsen, Nora and Ekdal – just as Humpty Dumpty analysing 'Jabberwocky' broke 'slithy' down into 'lithe' and 'slimy'.[49] Freud suggests that the dreamer produces absurd dreams or elements of dreams when disguising any 'criticism, ridicule or derision' present in the disguised underlying 'dream-thoughts'. His general comments on this aspect of the dream-work cast a striking light on the nonsense art-work:

Dreams, then, are often most profound when they seem most crazy. In every epoch of history those who have had something to say but could not say it without peril have eagerly assumed a fool's cap. The audience at whom their forbidden speech was aimed tolerated it more easily if they could at the same time laugh and flatter themselves with the reflection that the unwelcome words were clearly nonsensical. The Prince in the play, who had to disguise himself as a madman, was behaving just as dreams do in reality; so that we can say of dreams what Hamlet said of himself, concealing the true circumstances under a cloak of wit and unintelligibility: 'I am but mad north-north-west; when the wind is southerly, I know a hawk from a handsaw!'[50]

There was something rotten in Hamlet's Denmark, and the appeal of nonsense to twentieth-century writers, perhaps especially in Eastern Europe, must have something to do with a comparable sense of threat and rot. The 'antic disposition' of nonsense may be a compromise formation like Freud's idea of the dream. It may enable the poet to tune into forbidden and 'absurd' sources of pleasure, while giving vent to scepticism in the face of the absurdity of authority. There is a vein of protest in all nonsense, as well as of self-doubt. The 'liberation of nonsense' invoked by Freud has a way of suggesting the bad faith of good sense, especially in societies perceived as dully repressive, or repressively dull.

In twentieth-century art, the liberation of nonsense is generally associated with Dadaism and Surrealism. The legendary history of the anti-traditionalist Dadaist movement traditionally begins with a cabaret, the Cabaret Voltaire set up by the German poet Hugo Ball in Zurich in 1916.[51] In a room decorated with the latest paintings by the latest experimental artists, Ball organised a series of provocatively bizarre performances, including both simultaneous readings of newly devised babble-poems by himself and Huelsenbeck, and recitations of work by the unlikely father-figures of Dada: Rimbaud, Jarry and Apollinaire. The word 'Dada' was meant to have been chosen at random from the dictionary, being a baby-word for a horse, and the Dadaist poetry performed at the notorious café was in danger of riding baby-talk and glossolalic babble to death. A typical performance from the year 1919 has been described by Georges Hugnet:

On the stage keys and boxes were pounded to provide the music, until the infuriated public protested. Serner instead of reciting poems, set a bunch of flowers at the foot of a dressmaker's dummy. A voice, under a huge hat in the shape of a sugar-loaf, recited poems by Arp. Huelsenbeck screamed his poems louder and louder, while Tzara beat out the same rhythm crescendo on a big drum. Huelsenbeck and Tzara danced around grunting like bear cubs, or in sacks with top hats waddled around in an exercise called 'noir cacadou'.[52]

Simultaneous poems such as 'L'Amiral cherche une maison à louer' by Huelsenbeck, Janco and Tzara, sound poems like Ball's 'Karawane', and random *collage* poems by Kurt Schwitters and others, survive as paradoxical monuments of this art against art, the Dadaist rage for chaos. Then soon after the war, the surrealists came to the cabaret, and the art of shocking the bourgeois entered a new phase.

In the declaration of 27 January 1925, signed by 26 newly-baptised Surrealists, and in the year of the first Surrealist art exhibition, Surrealism was defined as 'a means of total liberation of the mind and of all that resembles it'.[53] The Surrealists under their 'Pope', André Breton, were never renowned for modesty, and their strategies of total liberation may now look naively incomplete to their successors, yet in the plastic arts and poetry their invention of new styles of inventiveness certainly changed the cultural climate, and helped emancipate the absurd. That first exhibition included work by the Cubist Picasso, the Dadaist Hans Arp, that free spirit Paul Klee, as well as such full-blown surrealist painters as Joan Miró, Giorgio de Chirico and Max Ernst; and from the first, Surrealism like Dadaism was a question of literature and aesthetics as well as the visual arts. Its poets dreamed up new devices which, like the *frottage* and *collage* practised by the artists, would trigger a new kind of provocative free association on the page. So Robert Desnos became an expert at trance-like 'automatic writing', individuals tried to recreate the bizarre logic of dreams, and groups engaged in solemn grown-up versions of such children's games as Consequences, renamed *Le Cadavre exquis* after the first sentence, improvised in this arbitrary way: 'The exquisite corpse will drink new wine'.[54] Describing themselves as 'specialists in Revolt',[55] the Surrealists devised new kinds of bottle for their linguistic Bacchanalias, and their new line in wine.[56] Many of these involve nonsense, like Desnos's ingenious game of variations 'Rrose Sélavy', or his punning 'P'Oasis' which is a jokey apologia for a new poiesis; or the zany poetic narratives of Benjamin Péret, with their dreamily precise inconsequentiality.

Impressed by Freud's account of dreams, the Surrealists attempted to create a public equivalent of the dream-work, based on free association or pure chance. As it developed, however, especially under the influence of its polemical entrepreneur André Breton, it tended to become increasingly programmatic. Most of its dreams take the form of disguised allegories of the fight of Surrealism versus the tyranny of the Reality Principle and Bourgeois Normality. What is disguised in such 'dream' poems is not unconscious wishes such as Freud detected, but conscious programmatic calculation. Too much French Surrealist poetry was hoist by its own petard, its categorical imperative being the classic paradoxical injunction 'Be spontaneous' or, in its case, 'Be surrealist'. Nevertheless, in the early work of Aragon and Desnos, and throughout the exuberantly free-floating career of Benjamin Péret, we experience something of that 'liberation of nonsense' described by Freud. As Breton's notion of a pseudo-transcendental higher reality of the dream took hold, its initial jokes, japes and dream songs lost their innocence in the incense of a new cult of the imagination, with its own brand of orthodoxy, and its own kind of higher code.

Though the prime movers of literary surrealism were French, their iconoclastic poetics and their new brand of poetic tricks sent shock-waves of influence across Europe and beyond. What seemed at the time anti-art and even anti-language became something like an absurd lingua franca in modern art. It's obviously not possible to represent this wider currency in an anthology like this one, but I have included one of Rafael Alberti's early surrealistic poems – one of a set of deadpan tributes to comic silent movie-stars – and a few of the young Lorca's spontaneously quirky, childlike songs, such as 'Corridor' and 'Tío-Vivo', which have a touch of aeriel nonsensicality about them: small tokens of the impact of Surrealism on Spanish poetry.

In Russia before the First World War it was the iconoclastic poetics and inventions of the Futurists which opened up the frontiers between non-sense and poetry. In 1913 Kruchenykh published a pamphlet called 'Declaration of the Word as such', in which he announced:

Thought and speech cannot catch up with the emotional experience of someone inspired; therefore, the artist is free to express himself not only in common language (concepts), but also in a private one (a creator is individual), as well as in a language that does not have a definite meaning (is not frozen), that is *transrational*. A common language is binding; a free one allows more complete expression.[57]

Kruchenykh was the first practitioner as well as theorist of what was called *zaum* verse, transrational or trans-sense poetry (*um* meaning 'reason' or 'intelligence' and *za* the prefix 'trans'); in the same year he published a book called *Pomade* which included the following:

> dyr bul schchyl
> uleshshchur
> skum
> vy so bu
> r l èz[58]

Poems like this aren't decipherable in terms of normal 'sense'; some of the groups of letters at the start resemble Russian or Ukranian words, others look like fragments of words, while the last two lines simply consist of syllables and letters, ending with a distinctively non-Russian sounding-suffix, 'èz'. 'In *zaum*,' said Igor Terentyev, 'one can howl, squeak, ask for the unaskable, and touch the unapproachable subjects'.[59] For non-Russian readers such trans-sensical experiments must inevitably remain a some-what inapproachable subject in themselves, but they played a provocative part in the lively debates about meaning, language and poetry that took place in the decade of the Futurists and in the criticism of the Formalists. Kruchenykh's 'Declaration of Transrational Language' (1921) asserted that *zaum* was the historically and individually 'primary form of poetry', while Igor Terentyev, in his 'Seventeen Nonsensical Implements' of 1919, affirmed that 'any poet is a *zaumnik*', whether he knows it or not.[60]

Velimir Khlebnikov's *Incantation by Laughter* is perhaps the most cele-brated poem in the *zaumnik* tradition, an attempt to sound out the inherent resonances of the word 'laughter' by etymological, semantic and phono-logical variation. The Russian (transliterated) begins:

> O, rassmeites', smekhachi!
> O, zasmeites', smekhachi!
> Chto smeyutsa smekhami, chto smeyanstvuyut smeyal'no.
> O zasmeites' usmeyal'no.

Trans-sense is hard to translate, and Gary Kern translates this as:

> O laugh it out, you laughsters!
> O laugh it up, you laughsters!
> So they laugh with laughters, so they laugherize delaughly.
> O laugh it up belaughably![61]

whereas Paul Schmidt gives it a more archaic Anglo-Saxon ring (after all 'Jabberwocky' started out as a 'Fragment of Anglo-Saxon Poetry'):

> Hlahla! Uthlofan, lauflings!
> Hlaha! Ufhlofan, lauflings!
> Who lawghen with lafe, who hlachen lewchly,
> Hlahla! Ufhlofan hlouly![62]

For such *zaum* experiments the Italian equation of *traduttore* and *traditore*, translator and traitor, is laughably apt, yet these versions enable us to guess the kind of poetry Futurists like Khlebnikov invented during the creative ferment of Russia before and after the Revolution. As Paul Schmidt, in his introduction to his magnificent selection of Khlebnikov's work, *The King of Time*, says, they opened up 'an entire poetics in that area of language the Anglo-Saxon tends to belittle as play – neologisms, palindromes, riddles, puns'.[63] Poems like 'Laughter' or Kruchenykh's 'Heights' (Universal language) illustrate the Futurist's genial work (or play) at the margins of language, a play that came to its strange apotheosis in Khlebnikov's nonsensical 'Supersaga' *Zangesi*, staged by Tatlin in Petrograd in 1923 – an extravaganza which invents *zaum* language for birds, Eros, the Gods, and stars, and is a kind of modern mystery play, in bizarre guise, about the mystery of language itself. There the hero Zangesi sings a song in star-language and says:

These are star-songs, where the algebra of words is muddled with yardsticks and clocks. And this is only the first draft! Someday this language will unite us all, and that day may some soon.[64]

Sadly that day did not come as quickly as Zangesi dreamed, and Khlebnikov with his blend of the playfully folkloric and the utopian died in 1922, already marginalised, as was Futurism itself with the inauguration of the Stalin era. The writers of the slightly later 'Oberiu' group, such as Daniil Kharms, went on to produce their own brand of nonsensical poems, stories and plays, at first in live performances, rather like those at the Café Voltaire, then, under the pressure of official disapproval, through children's litera-ture. George Gibian's *Russia's Lost Literature of the Absurd* gives a vivid sample of their writing, which, like the nonsensical machine Kharms made out of boxes and bicycle wheels and twine, are literary machines, made out of jetsam and bric-à-brac, designed to do nothing.[65] Stalin's Russia was not a hospitable place for Kharms's enigmatic miniatures, with their patent illogicality, and his work, like that of many of the Futurists, was refused official recognition in the epoch of Socialist Realism, and discarded as jetsam in its turn. In 1937 Daniil Kharms walked out of his house and disappeared.

[27]

The Russian children's writer Kornei Chukovsky, who had himself been involved in the Futurist movement, worked hard, like Kharms and Vvedensky, to rehabilitate nonsense and fairy tales within the utilitarian, and authoritarian Soviet culture of the time, and Eastern European poetry this century has shown a particular fascination with logical nonsense and the absurd fairy tale as a means of refreshing the world and the word. The romantic imagination often survives incognito in the guise of nonsense, and the folktale has adapted itself to our dark times by dipping itself in the waters of the absurd. Certainly the warped parable or twisted fairy tale has proved a haunting, questioning genre in the hands of such poets as Miroslav Holub from Czechoslovakia, Vasko Popa from Yugoslavia, and Marin Sorescu from Romania, and Polish and Russian poets have drawn freely on the resources of nonsense logic and the surreal encyclopedia, in the face of the pseudo-logic of the 'rational' state. The old confrontation between nonsense and authority, between earnest orthodoxy and liberating eccentricity, has been writ large within Eastern Europe in the struggle between socialist realism and the sceptical unrealism of mobile invention. Vladimir Nabokov translated the Alice books into Russian, and translations of Eastern European poetry in *Through the Looking-Glass* style have had a correspondingly inspirational impact this side of the Iron Curtain, and on our own poetic looking-glasses. Holub, Popa, Sorescu, seem peculiarly well-equipped to tell us about the secret tyrannies and disguised absurdity of our ordinary world.

We tend perhaps to associate German culture with high seriousness and the deadly earnest, the cult of leaders and *lieder*, yet there is a rich and various tradition of nonsense-writing in German, as the recent anthology, *Deutsche Unsinnspoesie*, edited by Klaus Peter Dencker makes abundantly clear.[66] In the nineteenth-century Eduard Mörike's quirky *Wispeliaden*, the *Sommersprossen* (or 'freckles') produced by one of his imaginary characters called Wispel, and comic performances by Wilhelm Busch and Paul Scheerbart, prepared the way for the *Galgenlieder* or 'Gallows Songs' of Christian Morgenstern, first published in 1905 – poems which brought together the popular and intellectual possibilities of nonsense in the form of quirky metaphysical arabesques, built around gallows humour, and the oddities of two invented inventors named Korf and Palmstroem. Morgenstern's own inventions show something like Lear's interest in unlikely creatures such as the Nosobame, as well as Carroll's interest in philosophical puzzles, while making fun of the German romantic traditions of fairy tales and 'Gothic' ballads. Morgenstern preferred to think of his lyrics in terms of 'folly' rather than 'nonsense', arguing that they were attempts to 'lure our cornered and restricted imagination into an area where it can roam at liberty'.[67] As he saw it, the German language was incorrigibly middle-class and middle-of-the-road: 'to drive it to one side or the other, or even off the road' was, he wrote, 'the noblest task of the future'.[68] Many subsequent German poets, including Dadaists such as Hans Arp, have shared Morgenstern's distrust of language, and experimented with driving it to extremes – or even off the road. In their struggle to avoid the prestigious language of the literary tradition and the assumptions of the ruling 'middle class', many German poets have resorted to nonsense as a language of conscious subversion and evasion, such as Peter Handke in his world-turned-upside-down poem 'The Wrong Way Round'. A fierce distrust of ordinary language and poetic convention also marks the refractory lyric poetry of Paul Celan, perhaps the most important German-language poet since the war, and it might be said of it, however paradoxically, that it too draws on the technology of nonsense poetry. This is apparent in the quite untypical joke poem 'Grosses Geburtstagsblaublau' ('Great Birthdayblueblue'), but can be detected at the heart of his great poem 'Todesfuge' ('Deathfugue'), a solemn requiem in grotesquely *fugato* style for the Jewish victims of the Nazi camps. More recently, Hans Magnus Enzensberger, one of Germany's most interesting political poets, has translated the *Complete Nonsense of Edward Lear*.[69] This might seem an unlikely project for a serious German intellectual in English eyes, yet in a cultural tradition with a terrible investment in the idea of intellectual and political authority, and enmeshed in the rites of bureaucratic order, perhaps nonsense, while solving nothing, can act as a kind of solvent.

Twentieth-century poetry in English, though superficially outside the reach of the continental currents of Surrealism and Futurism, is rich in versions of nonsense too. The oral tradition is still a fertile breeding-ground of nonsense songs and ballads and jokes – as can be heard in playground rhymes, blues, folksongs, radio comedy, and pop music, though much of this lyric nonsense has to be heard to be believed, and looks lifeless on the page. The jazz singer's 'scat' or the pop singer's 'be-bop-a-lula' depend on live performance and can't properly be represented in an anthology of this kind. Nevertheless, we should remember that where song lyrics are concerned zaniness has been a vital instrument in renovating the drab conventions of modern pop music: when David Byrne of Talking Heads called an album *Stop Making Sense*, it certainly made sense. Music is happy with nonsense.

Nonsense still survives as one strand of children's poetry in the wake of Lear and Carroll, and as one style of light verse, in the wake of W. S. Gilbert and Thomas Hood. It's there in A. E. Housman's wicked travesties of poetic innocence and E. C. Bentley's minimalist lives of the great, his neatly bathetic Clerihews, in Hilaire Belloc's mock-didactic *Cautionary Tales* and Harry Graham's *Ruthless Rhymes*, in Ogden Nash's tricksy trifles and T. S.

Eliot's *Old Possum's Book of Practical Cats*, as well as later in the children's poems of Theodore Roethke and Kenneth Patchen, and in James Fenton's calculatedly Absurd poetry-exhibits such as 'This Octopus Exploits Women'. Yet more surprisingly nonsensicality breaks surface in some of the most ambitious, haunting poetry of Europe and America this century, written by writers we think of as traditionalists as well as the heroes and *agents provocateurs* of the modernist avant-garde.

'Life's nonsense pierces us with strange relation', wrote Wallace Stevens in his musical meditation upon twentieth-century poetics, 'Notes Towards a Supreme Fiction'.[70] In Stevens's poetry there is a recurring note of dainty clowning, a self-mocking vein of fastidious linguistic absurdity – 'Such tink and tank and tunk-a-tunk' or 'hoobla-hoo'. Conscious both of 'the poem's gibberish' and 'the gibberish of the vulgate', Stevens regularly brings a dandyishly nonsensical register into his high-toned reflections, sending waves of sceptical playfulness – like signs of the modern climate – to ripple across the immaculate surface of his notes towards a serene fiction.[71] Stevens affirmed the 'gaiety of language', and the combination of linguistic gaiety with philosophical scepticism may underlie many of the versions of nonsense current in twentieth-century poetry. It seems to have a particular appeal for poets with a taste for intricate formality but who are intellectually suspicious of the claims of poetic form to mirror the order of things: linguistic scepticism and celebration seem to go hand in hand. In 'The Idea of Order at Key West' Stevens speaks of man's 'blessed rage for order' in the face of the sea, and in the best modern nonsense the idea of order and the threatening appeal of randomness seem to converge.[72] As an inherently mischievous or suspect border dialect, nonsense may face both ways: towards the modernist's anxious rage for order, and towards the Dadaist's iconoclastic rage for chaos.[73]

James Joyce's *Finnegans Wake* is our great nonsense epic, an epic mock-epic, a cryptographic travesty of sacred scriptures and high literary forms, which draws on the Freudian dreamworld of slips of the tongue, riddles, inversions, condensations, and every imaginable form of verbal deformation. Though a forbiddingly obscure text, it is also a kind of encyclopaedic resumé of popular nonsense – like a modern Rabelais. Interestingly, Joyce makes both Lewis Carroll and Humpty Dumpty avatars of his Irish hero, H. C. Earwicker or Here Comes Everybody, and his book of the night is riddled not only with 'ibsenest nanscence' but with 'nonsery reams', children's games, popular songs, carnival clowning, and festive parody of all things sacred.[74] Only in the twentieth century could such a gigantically ambitious literary venture take such a bizarre linguistic form and 'wear anartful of outer nocense'.[75] Yet in such burlesques as 'The Ballad of Persse O'Reilly' there still hums the ghost of popular song, and the child's 'sound-dance'.[76] The book is both a wake for Western Literature, and an awakening.

Joyce, as usual, is an extreme case, but nonsense threads its way through many poems of much more mainstream writers. W. B. Yeats resurrected the bedlamite mad-song in 'Crazy Jane' and other late poems, while Robert Graves, John Crowe Ransom and W. H. Auden among others resurrected popular ballad forms in strange riddling guises, as in Auden's 'As I walked out one evening' where the traditional lyric forms gleam through a warped twentieth-century mirror. In Auden's poetry, as in Marvell's, nonsense is never far away, though there are few fully-fledged nonsense poems, save the long surrealised contemporary ballad, 'The Month was April'. Stevie Smith on the other hand proves to be one of the exceptions to Auden's rule that women don't favour nonsense, and her poetry makes great play with absurdity as part of its cunningly adopted mask of chatty naiveté: she distrusts high seriousness, and gives her often polemical revampings of traditional materials a disconcertingly eccentric twist, as well as relishing the opportunity to concoct nonsensical scenarios like 'Who killed lawless Lean?' or the punning 'Private Means is dead'. Nonsense is one of her private means.

Stevie Smith's songs of innocence and experience seem quintessentially middle-class and English, but in America e. e. cummings invented his own brand, typographically and grammatically askew, to give a novel, jazzy air to *his* reworking of the traditional lyric themes.[77] John Berryman in the *Dream Songs* adopted a vaudeville version of the Jacobean madsong as a way of exploring his own manic disarray through the fool's mask of a distraught *alter ego*, Henry. Nonsense-style dislocations play their part in such different contexts as Jack Spicer's last-ditch West Coast Beat Rimbaud act, Elizabeth Bishop's haunting poetry of voyeuristic estrangement, Frank O'Hara's free-wheeling New York School improvisations, and John Ashbery's dreamily sophisticated meditations on the miscellaneousness of America and its fictions. But of all modern American poets, it is perhaps Bob Dylan who makes most memorable use of nonsense in his vernacular-oracular songs, especially such junkyard do-it-yourself mythological poems as 'Ballad of a Thin Man' and 'Desolation Row'.

Nonsense poetry faces the same difficulties as other kinds of poetry. It is hard to make it new. After nearly a century of making it strange, strangeness has become depressingly familiar. The repertoire of nonsense must pall too. But I hope this anthology shows something of the possibilities of nonsense and something of its obscure and chequered history.

To call something nonsensical is normally a way of putting it down. Yet despite this, or maybe because of it, reading a piece of inspired nonsense is curiously rather tonic. It sets us up. It makes desolation row more bearable.

It recalls our early pleasure in playing about with words and logic, and happily tells us something about our unhappiness in the face of ordinary order. Over and over again, in its comic guise, it deals with the serious things of our lives – desire and death, identity and authority, language and meaning, fun and games. Yet it is inherently a protest against the tyranny of orthodox seriousness, and serious orthodoxy. It comes in many shapes and sizes, but whether it take the form of nursery-rhyme, utopian exercise, joke, riddle, parody, limerick, carnival, madsong, absurdist fable, surrealist automatic writing, private language, literary satire or *jeu d'esprit*, it tends to be a poetry of playful formal inventiveness and genially defiant transgression. It is generally suspicious of higher kinds of meaning and Romanticism, yet is grounded in a carnivalesque affirmation of language and the pleasure of language. With its worlds turned upside down and logics turned inside out, nonsense poetry has its roots in the most familiar world. Just as failing to make sense is an absurdly primary matter, it tends to raise primary matters in all their blank absurdity and make us question the order of the ordinary. Good nonsense poetry is so resonantly lyrical because, like the marginalised madtalk of the exiled King Lear and Edgar in Shakespeare's play, it can tap central intuitions about the binding institutions of language and logic – and all that language and logic bind and contain. As a result I hope that this anthology will display what John Taylor back in the seventeenth century called the Essence, Quintessence, Incense, Innocence, Lye-sence and Magnificence of Nonsense upon Sense – or Sense upon Nonsense.

A Note on Translations

Poetry is notoriously untranslatable, and nonsense, being notoriously verbal, is even more so. Much translation makes a nonsense of the original, nonsense translations have the difficult task of making comparable nonsense. Since I have been keen to include a wide sample of nonsense poetry from outside English, I have made heavy use of translations, where possible drawing on existing versions, though in many cases having to make do with my own. Sometimes I have included original poems in a foreign language, French in particular, though where feasible I have included English versions as well to suggest something of the gusto of the original. Some French poems stay untranslated because they seem easy, others because they are too difficult, and I have preferred to be inconsistent rather than needlessly exclusive. I hope the untranslated poems will be intelligible to most readers, enjoyable to more, and only minimally irritating to the rest. There is a fine line between gibberish and nonsense, Utopian languages and our own, and I hope the mix of translated and untranslated poems will suggest the pleasures of nonsense as well as the pains of Babel.

Prologue

A dialogue between Fools

MANDRAKE. . . . O world, world, the gods and fairies left you, for thou wert too grave, and now, Socratic star, thy Demon, thy great Pan, Folly, is waning from thy side. The oracles still talked in their sleep, shall our grand-children say, till Master Merryman's Kingdom was broken up; now is every man his own Fool, and Fate for us all. So much for my dying speech and confession as the last Fool, or indeed, the last Man, for he who hath no leaven of the original father Donkey in any corner of him, may be an angel, black, white or piebald: he has lost his title to humanity. And now a ballad to the speech, a rhyme to the reason:

> Folly hath now turned out of door
> Mankind and Fate, who were before
>   Jove's Harlequin and Clown.
> The world's no stage, no tavern more,
>   Its sign, the Fool's ta'en down.
> With poppy rain and cypress dew
> Weep all, for all, who laughed for you:
> For goose-grass is no medicine more,
> But the owl's brown eye's the sky's new blue.
>   Heigho! Foolscap!

ISABRAND. Well said and truly. 'Twas no idle joke of Heaven's that Tarquin's fool and Manlius' geese saved Earth's only Rome, and in her freedom, civilized manners, art and science, for all future times, but a hint and token which man has overlooked. Why not an owl or a philosopher? If the good lord of the creation, being a beggar in foolery, will in spite of Destiny ride a cock-horse on Wisdom, why! he must needs gallop to Bedlam. I wash my hands of him. Well, now the Fates are no more humorous, they have been converted by the Knowledge Society tracts, and to make something useful of their cotton, do now with the threads of noble men's destinies knit matrimonial night-caps for old Goody Nature and Gaffer Mankind to play Punch and Judy in. But I grow delirious, and utter grave Truths.

THOMAS LOVELL BEDDOES (1803–49)
from Act I, Scene i, *Death's Jest-Book*

Before Play

One shuts one eye
Peers into oneself into every corner
Looks at oneself to see there are no spikes no thieves
No cuckoos' eggs

One shuts the other eye too
Crouches then jumps
Jumps high high high
To the top of oneself

Thence one drops by one's own weight
For days one drops deep deep deep
To the bottom of one's abyss

He who is not smashed to smithereens
He who remains whole and gets up whole
He plays

VASKO POPA
trans. Anne Pennington,
in *Collected Poems 1943–76*.

Old-Saxon Fragment

Syng a song of Saxons
In the Wapentake of Rye
Four and twenty eaoldormen
Two eaold to die . . .

Beoleopard

OR

The Witan's Whail

Whan Cnut Cyng the Witan wold enfeoff
Of infanthief and outfangthief
Wonderlich were they enwraged
And wordwar waged
Sware Cnut great scot and lot
Swingë wold ich this illbegotten lot.

Wroth was Cnut and wrothword spake.
Well wold he win at wopantake.
Fain wold he brakë frith and crackë heads
And than they shold worshippe his redes.

Swingéd Cnut Cyng with swung sword
Howléd Witanë hellë but hearkened his word
Murië sang Cnut Cyng
Outfangthief is Damgudthyng.

Recorded by W. C. Sellar and R. J. Yeatman

WILLIAM OF AQUITAINE

1071–1127

'I will write a poem about nothing'

Farai un vers de dreyt nïen:
Non er de mi ni d'autra gen,
Non er d'amor ni de joven,
   Ni de ren au;
Qu'enans fo trobatz en durmen
   Sobre chevau.

No sai en qual guiza.m fuy natz:
No suy alegres ni iratz,
No suy estrayns ni sui privatz,
   Ni no.n puesc au;
Qu'enaissi fuy de nueitz fadatz
   Sobr'un pueg au.

No sai quora.m suy endormitz,
Ni quora.m velh, s'om no m'o ditz.
Per pauc no m'es lo cor partitz
   D'un dol corau.
E no m'o pretz una soritz,
   Per sanh Marsau!

Malautz suy e tremi murir,
E ren no sai mas quan n'aug dir;
Metge querrai, al mieu albir,
   E no.m sai tau;
Bos metges er si.m pot guerir,
   Mas ja non, si amau.

Amigu'ai ieu, no sai qui s'es,
Qu'anc non la vi, si m'ajut fes!
Ni.m fes que.m plassa ni que.m pes,
   Ni no m'en cau,
Qu'anc non ac Norman ni Frances
   Dins mon ostau.

Anc non la vi et am la fort,
Anc no n'aic dreyt ni no.m fes tort;
Quan non la vey, be m'en deport,
   No.m pretz un jau,
Qu'ie.n sai gensor et bellazor,
   E que mais vau.

Fag ai lo vers, no say de cuy;
E trametrai lo a selhuy
Que lo.m trametra per autruy
   Lay vers Anjau,
Que.m tramezes del sieu estuy
   La contraclau.

Translation

I will write a poem about nothing
not about myself or other people,
nor about love or youth,
   nor about anything else;
composed, in fact, as I slept
   on horseback.

I don't know how I was born,
I'm neither happy nor sad,
neither stranger nor intimate,
   nor can act otherwise,
entranced thus, by night,
   on a high hill.

I don't know if I'm awake
or asleep unless told.
My heart is near broken
   with real grief,
yet I don't give a hoot
   by Saint Martial.

Sick and afraid to die,
I know only what I hear.
I'll find my kind of doctor
    though I know none such:
a good doctor, should he cure me
    – but if not, a quack.

I have a mistress, I don't know who,
whom I've never seen, I swear.
She's neither a pleasure nor a pain
    nor of interest to me.
And I've never had Normans or French
    at my house.

I've never seen her and adore her.
She's never done me right nor even wrong.
When I don't see her, that's fine
    I couldn't care less:
I know someone nobler, lovelier,
    who means much more.

So I've made a poem about I don't know what,
and I'll send it on to him
who will send it on to another
    and on to Anjou,
so that he, from his own pocket,
    may send the key to me.

ANONYMOUS

The Land of Cockaygne

Out to sea, far west of Spain,
Lies the land men call Cockaygne.
No land that under heaven is,
For wealth and goodness comes near this;
Though Paradise is merry and bright
Cockaygne is a fairer sight.
For what is there in Paradise
But grass and flowers and greeneries?
Though there is joy and great delight,
There's nothing good but fruit to bite,
There's neither hall, bower, nor bench,
And only water thirst to quench.
And of men there are but two,
Elijah and Enoch also;
Sadly thither would I come
Where but two men have their home.

   In Cockaygne we drink and eat
Freely without care and sweat,
The food is choice and clear the wine,
At fourses and at supper time,
I say again, and I dare swear,
No land is like it anywhere,
Under heaven no land like this
Of such joy and endless bliss.

   There is many a sweet sight,
All is day, there is no night,
There no quarreling nor strife,
There no death, but endless life;
There no lack of food or cloth,
There no man or woman wroth,
There no serpent, wolf or fox,
Horse or nag or cow or ox,
Neither sheep nor swine nor goat,
Nor creeping groom, I'd have you note,

Neither stallion there nor stud.
Other things you'll find are good.
In bed or garment or in house,
There's neither flea nor fly nor louse,
Neither thunder, sleet nor hail,
No vile worm nor any snail,
Never a storm, nor rain nor wind,
There's no man or woman blind.
All is sporting, joy and glee,
Lucky the man that there may be.

There are rivers broad and fine
Of oil, milk, honey and of wine;
Water serveth there no thing
But for sight and for washing.
Many fruits grow in that place
For all delight and sweet solace.

There is a mighty fine Abbey,
Thronged with monks both white and grey,
Ah, those chambers and those halls!
All of pasties stand the walls,
Of fish and flesh and all rich meat,
The tastiest that men can eat.
Wheaten cakes the shingles all,
Of church, of cloister, bower and hall.
The pinnacles are fat puddings,
Good food for princes or for kings.
Every man takes what he will,
As of right, to eat his fill.
All is common to young and old,
To stout and strong, to meek and bold.

There is a cloister, fair and light,
Broad and long, a goodly sight.
The pillars of that place are all
Fashioned out of clear crystal,
And every base and capital
Of jasper green and red coral.
In the garth there stands a tree
Pleasant truly for to see.

Ginger and cyperus the roots,
And valerian all the shoots,
Choicest nutmegs flower thereon,
The bark it is of cinnamon.
The fruit is scented gillyflower,
Of every spice is ample store.
There the roses, red of hue,
And the lovely lily, too,
Never fade through day and night,
But endure to please men's sight.
In that Abbey are four springs,
Healing and health their water brings,
Balm they are, and wine indeed,
Running freely for men's need,
And the bank about those streams
With gold and with rich jewels gleams.
There is sapphire and uniune,
Garnet red and astiune,
Emerald, ligure and prassiune,
Beryl, onyx, topasiune,
Amethyst and chrystolite,
Chalcedony and epetite

　　There are birds in every bush,
Throstle, nightingale and thrush,
Woodpecker and the soaring lark,
More there are than man may mark,
Singing with all their merry might,
Never ceasing day or night.
Yet this wonder add to it –
That geese fly roasted on the spit,
As God's my witness, to that spot,
Crying out, 'Geese, all hot, all hot!'
Every goose in garlic drest,
Of all food the seemliest.
And the larks that are so couth
Fly right down into man's mouth,
Smothered in stew, and thereupon
Piles of powdered cinnamon.
Every man may drink his fill
And needn't sweat to pay the bill.

When the monks go in to mass,
All the windows that were glass,
Turn them into crystal bright
To give the monks a clearer light;
And when the mass has all been said,
And the mass-books up are laid,
The crystal pane turns back to glass,
The very way it always was.

Now the young monks every day
After dinner go to play,
No hawk not any bird can fly
Half so fast across the sky
As the monk in joyous mood
In his wide sleeves and his hood.
The Abbot counts it goodly sport
To see his monks in haste depart,
But presently he comes along
To summon them to evensong.
The monks refrain not from their play,
But fast and far they flee away,
And when the Abbot plain can see
How all his monks inconstant flee,
A wench upon the road he'll find,
And turning up her white behind,
He beats upon it as a drum
To call his monks to vespers home.
When the monks behold that sport
Unto the maiden all resort,
And going all the wench about,
Every one stroketh her white toute.
So they end their busy day
With drinking half the night away,
And so to the long tables spread
In sumptuous procession tread.

Another Abbey is near by,
In sooth, a splendid nunnery,
Upon a river of sweet milk,
Where is plenteous store of silk.
When the summer day is hot
The younger nuns take out a boat,

And forth upon the river clear,
Some do row and some do steer.
When they are far from their Abbey,
They strip them naked for their play,
And, plunging in the river's brim,
Slyly address themselves to swim.
When the young monks see that sport,
Straightway thither they resort,
And coming to the nuns anon,
Each monk taketh to him one,
And, swiftly bearing forth his prey,
Carries her to the Abbey grey,
And teaches her an orison,
Jigging up and jigging down.
The monk that is a stallion good,
And can manage well his hood,
He shall have, without a doubt,
Twelve wives before the year is out,
All of right and nought through grace,
So he may himself solace.
And the monk that sleepeth best,
And gives his body ample rest,
He, God knows, may presently
Hope an Abbot for to be.

    Whoso will come that land unto
Full great penance he must do,
He must wade for seven years
In the dirt a swine-pen bears,
Seven years right to the chin,
Ere he may hope that land to win.
Listen Lords, both good and kind,
Never will you that country find
Till through the ordeal you've gone
And that penance has been done.
So you may that land attain
And never more return again,
Pray to God that so it be,
Amen, by holy charity.

Modernised version by A. L. Morton

[45]

CERVERI De GIRONA*

14 c

Iflimit iflimis haflamard foflomor meflemen toflomo
    eflemerr aflamamioflomong goofloomood
    peofleomeople
aflamand eafleameasyflymy aflamamoflomong thoflomose
    whoflomo haflamaye noflomo
    loflomoyaflamaltyflymy,
  oflomor soflomo thefleme woflomorld
  coflomonsiflimideflemers.

Ifirri difirrislifirrike afarra houfourrouse wheferrere
    boforroth lafarradyfyrry afarrand
    seferrervafarrant
laufaurraugh wheferren theferre loforrord
    referretufurrurns toforro seefeerree whafarrat
    bafarrad woforrork
  theyfeyrrey've doforrone (Iflirri dafarrare sayfayrray
  noforro moforrore).

Howpowpow fipipine woupoupould bepepe apapa
     wopoporld ipipin whipipich sipipilvepeper
wepepere lepepess pripipized thapapan apapa
     wopoporthypypy waypaypay opopof lipipife,
   apapas ipipin lepepent apapand capaparnipipivapapal.

Imimi woumoumould bememe gaymaymay amamand
    hamamappymymy imimin amama
    romomoyamamal coumoumourt
imimif amamall thememe vamamaliamamant
    peomeomeople thememere gomomot
    pleameameasumumure
  fromomom thememe womomorks Imimi wrimimite.

*For an explanation of this poem please see the Notes on page 502.

Forrovor jurruvust orrovone Chrirrivistmarravas Irrivi
    wourrouvould lirrivike torrovo rurruvule
therreve grearreaveat barravarorrovons, arravand
    errevextrarravact arrava toorroovooth frorrovom
        earreaveach
marravan whorrovo worrovon't gorrovo
    orrovoverreversearreaveas.

Soforrobreferrepreferretz, wifirrith goofoorrood
    jufurrudgmeferrent afarrand noforro
    flafarratteferreryfyrry,
Ifirri praifairraise boforroth youfourrou afarrand
    heferrer oforrof Cafarrartz.[7]

Iflimi woufloumould thaflamat fiflimive kiflimings
    weflement wheflemere Goflomod
    peflemeriflimished,
leflemed byflymy oufloumours, whoflomo
    oufloumoutshiflimines theflemem aflamall.

translated by Anthony Bonner

[47]

A QUARTET OF FATRASIES

Fatrasie de Beaumanoir

Uns grans herens sors
Eut assis Gisors
D'une part et d'autre,
Et dui homes mors
Vinrent a esfors
Portant une porte;
Ne fust une vielle torte
Qui ala criant; 'Ahors!'
Li cris d'une quaille morte
Les eust pris a esfors
Desous un capel de fautre.

Translation

Just as Gisors had placed
A great herring
In a clearing
Two men freshly deceased
Came by in great haste
With a door they were carrying.
Were it not for a starling
That 'Out, out' was swearing
A dead quail in her nest
Would have called up a tempest
Under the hat they were wearing.

ANONYMOUS

Three Fatrasies from Arras

Uns biaus hom sans teste
Menoit mout grant feste
Por on com velut,
Et une fenestre
A mis hors sa teste,
Si vit le fendu;
Ja fust grant max avenu,
Quant li songes d'une beste
S'escria: 'Hareu! le fu!'
Trestout voloit ardoir l'aitre
Pour ce c'om i ot foutu.

Translation

A headless young Beau
Was having it cushy
Admiring some pussy
When a local high window
Put its head out in dumbshow
And spied the crack down below.
It'd have been a disaster
Had a beast's dream not passed there
And yelled 'Tallyho!'.
He'd have fired the whole cloister
For the pussy he'd kissed there below.

ANONYMOUS

Uns saiges sans sens
Sans bouche et sans dens
Le siecle mangea
Et uns sors harens
Manda les Flamens
Qui les vengera;
Mais tout ce no lor vaura
La plume de deus mellens
Qui quatre nés affondra.
Mais je ne sai que je pens:
De murder les apela.

Translation

A senseless prof
Without teeth or mouth
Ate the era
And a red herring
Summoned the Fleming
To act as avenger.
But all this is no better
Than two whiting's feather
Causing four ships to sink.
I don't know what I think:
The charge was murder.

ANONYMOUS

Anglois de Hollande
Embloient Illande
Por mengier as aus;
Uns lymecons mande
Gent de huppelande
Sor deus syminiaus . . .
Uns paniers ce fist chevaus
Quant une mouche truande
Qui fist parler deus muiaus
Avoit ja tolu l'offrande
A deus abbés de Cytiaus.

Translation

An Englishman from Holland
Carried off Ireland
To eat it with mayonnaise.
A snail does command
Those with a waistband
On two monkelays.
A basket makes the drays
When a gnat from the highland
That'd made two mutes praise
Had stolen the *offrande*
From two abbots of Cytaise.

JOHN SKELTON
?1460–1529

Phyllyp Sparowe

compyled by Mayster Skelton, poete laureate

Pla ce bo,
Who is there, who?
Di le xi,
Dame Margery,
Fa, re, my, my.

Wherefore and why, why?
For the sowle of Phyllyp Sparowe,
That was late slayn at Carowe
Among the Nones Blake.
For that swete soules sake,
And for all sparowes soules
Set in our bede rolles,
Pater noster qui,
With an *Ave Mari,*
And with the corner of a Crede,
The more shal be your mede.

Whan I remember agayn
How mi Phyllyp was slayn,
Never halfe the payne
Was betwene you twayne,
Pyramus and Thesbe,
As than befell to me.
I wept and I wayled,
The tearys downe hayled;
But nothing it avayled
To call Phyllyp agayne
Whom Gyb our cat has slayne.
. . . .

Of fortune this the chaunce
Standeth on varyaunce:
Oft tyme after pleasaunce,

Trouble and grevaunce.
No man can be sure
All way to have pleasure.
As well perceyve ye maye
How my dysport and play
From me was taken away
By Gyb, our cat savage,
That in a furyous rage
Caught Phyllyp by the head,
And slew him there starke dead.
  Kyry, eleyson
  Christe, eleyson
  Kyry, eleson!

For Phyllyp Sparowes soule
Set in our bede rolle,
Let us now whysper
A *Pater noster*.

Lauda, anima mea, Dominum!
To wepe with me loke that ye come,
All maner of byrdes in your kynd;
So none be left behynde.
To mornynge loke that ye fall
With dolorous songes funerall,
Some to synge, and some to say,
Some to wepe, and some to pray,
Every byrde in his laye:
The goldfynche, the wagtayle;
The janglynge jay to rayle,
The fleckyd pye to chatter
Of this dolorous mater.
And Robyn Redbrest
He shall be the preest,
The requiem masse to synge,
Softly warbelynge,
With helpe of the red sparow
And the chattrynge swallow,
This herse for to halow.
The larke with his longe to;
The spynke and the martynet also;
The shovelar with his brode bek;

[53]

The doterell, that folyshe pek;
And also the mad coote,
With a balde face to toote;
The feldefare and the snyte;
The crowe and the kyte;
The ravyn called Rolfe,
His playne songe to solfe;
The partryche, the quayle;
The plover with us to wayle;
The woodhacke, that syngeth 'chur',
Horsly, as he had the mur;
The lusty chauntyng nyghtyngale;
The popyngay to tell her tale,
That toteth oft in a glasse,
Shall rede the gospell at masse;
The mavys with her whystell
Shall rede there the pystell.
   But with a large and a longe
To kepe just playne songe
Our chaunters shalbe the cuckoue,
The culver, the stockedowve,
With Puwyt the lapwyng,
The versycles shall syng.
   The bitter with his bumpe,
The crane with his trumpe,
The swan of Menander,
The gose and the gander,
The ducke and the drake,
Shall watche at this wake;
The pecocke so prowde,
Bycause his voyce is lowde,
And hath a glorious tayle,
He shall syng the grayle;
The owle, that is so foule,
Must helpe us to houle;
The heron so gaunce,
And the cormoraunce,
With the fesaunte,
And the gaglynge gaunte,
And the churlysshe chowgh;
The knoute and the rowgh;
The barnacle, the bussarde,

With the wylde mallarde;
The dyvendop to slepe;
The wather-hen to wepe;
The puffyn and the tele,
Money they shall dele
To poore folke at large,
That shall be theyr charge;
The semewe and the tytmose;
The wodcocke with the longe nose;
The threstyl with her warblyng;
The starlyng with her brablyng;
The roke, with the ospraye
That putteth fysshes to a fraye;
And the denty curlewe,
With the turtyll most trew.

    At this *Placebo*
We may not well forgo
The countrynge of the coe;
The storke also,
That maketh his nest
In chymneyes to rest;
Within those walles
No broken galles
May there abyde
Of cokoldry syde,
Or els phylosophy
Maketh a great lye.
    The estryge, that wyll eate
An horshowe so great,
In the stede of meate
Such fervent heat
His stomake doth freat;
He can not well fly,
Nor synge tunably;
Yet at a brayde
He hath well assayde
To solfe above E-la –
Fa, lorell, *fa, fa* –
Ne quando
Male cantando,
The best that we can,

To make hym our belman,
And let hym ryng the bellys;
He can do nothyng ellys.

    Chaunteclere, our coke,
Must tell what is of the clocke
By the astrology
That he hath naturally
Conceyved and cought,
And was never tought
By Albumazer
The astronomer,
Nor by Ptholomy,
Prince of astronomy,
Nor yet by Haly;
And yet he croweth dayly
And nyghtly the tydes
That no man abydes,
With Partlot his hen,
Whom now and then
He plucketh by the hede
Whan he doth her trede.
    The byrde of Araby,
That potencyally
May never dye
And yet there is none
But one alone;
A phenex it is
This herse that must blys
With armatycke gummes
That cost great sumes,
The way of thurifycation
To make a fumigation
Swete of reflayre,
And redolent of eyre,
This corse for to sence
With greate reverence,
As patryarke or pope
In a blacke cope.
Whyles he senseth the herse,
He shall synge the verse
Libe ra me,

In *de, la, soll, re,*
Softly bemole
For my sparowes soule.
Plinni sheweth all
In his *Story Naturall,*
What he doth fynde
Of this phenyx kynde;
Of whose incyneracyon
There ryseth a new creacyon
Of the same facyon
Without alteracyon,
Savyng that olde age
Is turned into corage
Of fresshe youth agayne;
This matter trew and playne,
Playne matter indede,
Whoso lyst to rede
    But for the egle doth flye
Hyest in the skye,
He shall be the sedeane,
The quere to demeane,
As provost pryncypall,
To teach them theyr ordynall;
Also the noble fawcon,
With the gerfawcon,
The tarsell gentyll,
They shall morne soft and styll
In theyr amysse of gray;
The sacre with them shall say
Dirige for Phyllyppes soule;
The goshauke shall have a role
The queresters to controll;
The lanners and the marlyons
Shall stand in their morning gounes;
The hobby and the muskette
The sensers and the crosse shall fet;
The kestrell in all this warke
Shall be holy wather clarke.
    And now the darke cloudy nyght
Chaseth away Phebus bryght,
Taking his course toward the west;
God sende my sparoes sole good rest!

[57]

Requiem eternam dona eis, Domine.
Fa, fa, fa, my, re,
A por ta in fe ri,
Fa, fa, fa, my, my.
Credo vydere bona Domini,
I pray God, Phillip to heven may fly.
Domine, exaudi oracionem meam,
To heven he shall, from heven he cam.
Do mi nus vo bis cum,
Of al good praiers God send him sum!
   Oremus.
Deus, cui proprium est miserere et parcere,
On Phillips soule have pyte!

For he was a prety cocke,
And came of a gentyll stocke,
And wrapt in a maidenes smocke,
And cherysshed full dayntely,
Tyll cruell fate made him to dy:
Alas, for dolefull desteny!
But whereto shuld I
Lenger morne or crye?
To Jupyter I call,
Of heven emperyall,
That Phyllyp may fly
Above the starry sky,
To treade the prety wren
That is our Ladyes hen.
Amen, amen, amen!

ANONYMOUS

'Hay, hey, hey, hey! I will have
the whetstone and I may'

I saw a dog sethying sows
And an ape thatching an house
And a pudding eating a mouse;
I will have the whetstone and I may.

I saw an urchin shape and sew
And another bake and brew
Scour the pots as they were new;
I will have the whetstone and I may.

I saw a codfish corn sow,
And a worm a whistle blow
And a pye treading a crow;
I will have the whetstone and I may.

I saw a stockfish drawing a harrow
And another driving a barrow
And a saltfish shooting an arrow;
I will have the whetstone and I may.

I saw a boar burdens bind
And a frog clewens wind
And a toad mustard grind;
I will have the whetstone and I may.

I saw a sow bear kerchers to wash,
The second sow had an hedge to plash
The third sow went to the barn to thresh
I will have the whetstone and I may.

I saw an egg eating a pie;
Give me a drink, my mouth is dry;
It is not long since I made a lie;
I will have the whetstone and I may.

ANONYMOUS
(French traditional)

Les Mensonges

Oh j'ai vu, j'ai vu
Compèr' qu'as-tu vu?
J'ai vu une vache
Qui dansait sur la glace
A la Saint Jean d'été
Compèr' vous mentez.

Ah j'ai vu, j'ai vu
Compèr' qu'as-tu vu?
J'ai vu une grenouille
Qui faisait la patrouille
Le sabre au côté
Compèr' vous mentez.

Ah, j'ai vu, j'ai vu
Compèr' qu'as-tu vu?
Ah j'ai vu un loup
Qui vendait des choux
Sur la place Labourée,
Compèr' vous mentez.

Ah j'ai vu, j'ai vu,
Compèr' qu'as-tu vu?
J'ai vu une anguille
Qui coiffait une fille
Pour s'aller marier,
Compèr' vous mentez.

ANONYMOUS

My heart of gold as true as steel,
  As I me leaned to a bough,
In faith, but if you love me well,
  Lord, so Robin lough!

My lady went to Canterbury,
  The saint to be her boot;
She met with Kate of Malmesbury;
  Why weepest thou in an apple root?

Nine mile to Michaelmas,
  Our dame began to brew;
Michael set his mare to grass;
  Lord, so fast it snew!

For you, love, I brake my glass;
Your gown is furred with blue;
The devil is dead, for there I was;
  Iwis, it is full true.

And if ye sleep, the cock will crow;
  True heart, think what I say;
Jacknapes will make a mow,
  Look who dare him say nay.

I pray you, have me now in mind;
  I tell you of the matter:
He blew his horn against the wind;
  The crow goeth to the water.

Yet I tell you mickle more:
  The cat lieth in the cradle;
I pray you, keep true heart in store,
  A penny for a ladle.

I swear by Saint Katherine of Kent,
  The goose goeth to the green;
All our dogges tail is brent,
  It is not as I ween.

'Tyrlery lorpyn', the laverock sang;
  So merrily pipes the sparrow;
The cow brake loose; the rope ran home;
  Sir, God give you good morrow.

ANONYMOUS

(A carol)

Gebit, gebit, gebit, gebit,
Lux fulgebit hodie.

Ipse mocat me;
An apple is no pear tree
  In civitate David.

Notum fecit Dominus;
By the bill one knoweth a goose
  In civitate David.

Aparuit Esau;
A red gown is not blue
  In civitate David.

Verbum caro factum est;
A sheep is a perilous beast
  In civitate David.

ANONYMOUS

(*French traditional*)

Il Était un Petit Homme

Il était un p'tit homme
Qui s'appelait Guilleri,
    Carabi;
Il s'en fut à la chasse,
A la chasse aux perdrix,
    Carabi,
      Toto carabo.
Marchand d' carabas,
Compère Guilleri,
Te lairas-tu mouri?

Il s'en fut à la chasse,
A la chasse aux perdrix,
    Carabi;
Il monta sur un arbre
Pour voir ses chiens couri,
    Carabi;
      Toto carabo.
Marchand d' carabas,
Compère Guilleri,
Te lairas-tu mouri?

Il monta sur un arbre
Pour voir ses chiens couri,
    Carabi;
La branche vint à rompre,
Et Guilleri tombi,
    Carabi,
      Toto carabo.
Marchand d' carabas,
Compère Guilleri,
Te lairas-tu mouri?

La branche vint à rompre,
Et Guilleri tombi,
        Carabi;
Il se cassa la jambe,
Et le bras se démit,
        Carabi,
        Toto carabo.
Marchand d' carabas,
Compère Guilleri,
Te lairas-tu mouri?

Il se cassa la jambe
Et le bras se démit,
        Carabi;
Les dam's de l'Hôpital
Sont arrivé's au bruit,
        Carabi,
        Toto carabo.
Marchand d' carabas,
Compère Guilleri,
Te lairas-tu mouri?

Les dam's de l'Hôpital
Sont arrivé's au bruit,
        Carabi;
L'une apporte un emplâtre,
L'autre, de la charpi,
        Carabi,
        Toto carabo.
Marchand d' carabas,
Compère Guilleri,
Te lairas-tu mouri?

L'une apporte un emplâtre,
L'autre, de la charpi,
        Carabi;
On lui banda la jambe
Et le bras lui remit,
        Carabi,
        Toto carabo.

Marchand d' carabas,
Compère Guilleri
Te lairas-tu mouri?

On lui banda la jambe,
Et le bras lui remit,
     Carabi;
Pour remercier ces dames,
Guilleri les embrassi,
     Carabi,
       Toto carabo.
Marchand d' carabas,
Compère Guilleri,
Te lairas-tu mouri?

Pour remercier ces dames,
Guilleri les embrassi,
     Carabi,
Ça prouv' que par les femmes
L'homme est toujours guéri;
     Carabi,
      Toto carabo.
Marchand d' carabas.
Compère Guilleri,
Te lairas-tu mouri?

ANONYMOUS
(French traditional)

Monsieur de la Palisse

Messieurs, vous plaît-il d'ouïr
L'air du fameux La Palisse?
Il pourra vous réjouir,
Pourvu qu'il vous divertisse.
La Palisse eut bien peu de biens,
Pour soutenir sa naissance;
Mais il ne manqua de rien,
Tant qu'il fut dans l'abondance.

Bien instruit dès le berceau,
Jamais, tant il fut honnête,
Il ne mettait son chapeau,
Qu'il ne se couvrit la tête.
Il était affable et doux.
De l'humeur de feu son père
Et n'entrait guère en courroux,
Si ce n'est dans la colère.

Ses valets étaient soigneux
De le servir d'andouillettes,
Et n'oubliaient pas les œufs
Surtout dans les omelettes.
De l'inventeur du raisin
Il révérait la mémoire;
Et pour bien goûter le vin,
Jugait qu'il fallait en boire.

Il disait que le nouveau
Avait pour lui plus d'amorce;
Et moins il y mettait d'eau
Plus il y trouvait de force.
Il consultait rarement
Hippocrate et sa doctrine,
Et se purgeait seulement
Lorsqu'il prenait médecine.

Il aimait à prendre l'air
Quand la saison était bonne,
Et n'attendait pas l'hiver
Pour vendanger en automne.
Il épousa, ce dit-on,
Une vertueuse dame;
S'il était resté garçon,
Il n'aurait pas eu de femme.
Il en fut toujours chéri;
Elle n'était pas jalouse;
Sitôt qu'il fut son mari,
Elle devint son épouse.

[66]

D'un air galant et badin,
Il courtisait sa Caliste,
Sans jamais être chagrin
Qu'au moment qu'il était triste.

Il brillait comme un soleil,
Sa chevelure était blonde;
Il n'eût pas eu son pareil,
S'il eût été seul au monde.
Il eut des talents divers;
Même on assure une chose:
Quand il écrivait des vers
Il n'écrivait pas en prose.

Il voyageait volontiers,
Courant par tout le royaume;
Quand il était à Poitiers,
Il n'était pas à Vendôme.
Il se plaisait en bateau,
Et soit en paix, soit en guerre,
Il allait toujours par eau,
Quand il n'allait pas par terre.

Il choisissait prudemment
De deux choses la meilleure;
Et répétait fréquemment
Ce qu'il disait à toute heure.
Il fut, à la vérité,
Un danseur assez vulgaire;
Mais il n'eût pas mal chanté,
S'il n'avait voulu se taire.

Regretté de ses soldats,
Il mourut digne d'envie;
Et le jour de son trépas
Fut le dernier de sa vie.
Il mourut le vendredi,
Le dernier jour de son âge;
S'il fût mort le samedi,
Il eût vécu davantage.

The Lily and the Rose

The maidens came
When I was in my mother's bower,
I had all that I would.
    The bailey beareth the bell away;
    The lily, the rose, the rose I lay.
The silver is white, red is the gold;
The robes they lay in fold.
    The bailey beareth the bell away;
    The lily, the rose, the rose I lay.
And through the glass windows shines the sun.
How should I love, and I so young?
    The bailey beareth the bell away;
    The lily, the rose, the rose I lay.

ANONYMOUS

mid-16th century

Little John Nobody

In december, when the days draw to be short,
After november, when the nights wax noisome and long;
As I past by a place privily at a port,
I saw one sit by himself making a song:
His last talk of trifles, who told with his tongue
That few were fast i' th' faith. I freyned that freak,
Whether he wanted wit, or some had done him wrong.
    He said, he was little John Nobody, that durst not speak.

John Nobody, quoth I, what news? thou soon note and tell
What manner men thou mean, thou art so mad.
He said, These gay gallants, that will construe the gospel,
As Solomon the sage, with semblance full sad;

To discuss divinity they nought adread;
More meet it were for them to milk kye at a fleyk.
Thou liest, quoth I, thou losel, like a lewd lad.
    He said he was little John Nobody, that durst not speak.

It is meet for every man on this matter to talk,
And the glorious gospel ghostly to have in mind;
It is sooth said, that sect but much unseemly skalk,
As boys babble in books, that in scripture are blind:
Yet to their fancy soon a cause will find;
As to live in lust, in lechery to leyk:
Such caitives count to become of Cain's kind;
    But that I, little John Nobody durst not speak.

For our reverend father hath set forth an order,
Our service to be said in our seignour's tongue;
As Solomon the sage set forth the scripture;
Our suffrages, and services, with many a sweet song,
With homilies, and godly books us among,
That no stiff, stubborn stomachs we should freyk:
But wretches nere worse to do poor men wrong;
    But that I little John Nobody dare not speak.

For bribery was never so great, since born was our Lord,
And whoredom was never less hated, sith Christ harrowed hell,
And poor men are so sore punished commonly through the world,
That it would grieve any one, that good is, to hear tell.
For al the homilies and good books, yet their hearts be so quell,
That if a man do amiss, with mischief they will him wreak;
The fashion of these new fellows is so vile and fell:
    But that I little John Nobody dare not speak.
· · · · · · · · · · · · · · · ·

Thus in no place, this Nobody, in no time I met,
Where no man, ne nought was, nor nothing did appear;
Through the sound of a synagogue for sorrow I swet,
That *Aeolus* through the echo did cause me to hear.
Then I drew me down into a dale, whereas the dumb deer
Did shiver for a shower, but I shunted from a freyk:
For I would not wight in this world wist who I were,
    But little John Nobody, that dare not once speak.

[69]

FRANÇOIS RABELAIS
1494?–c.1563

The Antidoted Fanfreluches: or,
a Galimatia of extravagant
Conceits found
in an ancient Monument

No sooner did the Cymbrians overcommer
Pass through the air to shun the dew of summer
But at his coming streight great tubs were fill'd;
With pure fresh Butter down in showers distill'd
Wherewith when water'd was his Grandam heigh
Aloud he cryed, Fish it, Sir, I pray ye;
Because his beard is almost all beray'd,
Or that he would hold to 'm a scale he pray'd.

To lick his slipper, some told was much better,
Then to gaine pardons and the merit greater,
In th' interim a crafty chuff approaches,
From the depth issued, where they fish for Roches,
Who said, Good sirs, some of them let us save,
The Eele is here, and in this hollow cave
You'll finde, if that our looks on it demurre,
A great wast in the bottome of his furre.

To read this chapter when he did begin,
Nothing but a calves hornes were found therein;
I feel (quoth he) the Miter which doth hold
My head so chill, it makes my braines take cold.
Being with the perfume of a turnup warm'd,
To stay by chimney hearths himself he arm'd,
Provided that a new thill horse they made
Of every person of a hair-braind head.
They talked of the bunghole of Saint Knowles,
Of Gilbathar and thousand other holes;
If they might be reduc'd t' a scarry stuffe,
Such as might not be subject to the cough:
Since ev'ry man unseemly did it finde,

To see them gaping thus at ev'ry winde:
For, if perhaps they handsomely were clos'd,
For pledges they to men might be expos'd.

In this arrest by Hercules the raven
Was flayed at her returne from Lybia haven,
Why am not I said Minos there invited,
Unlesse it be my self, not one's omitted:
And then it is their minde, I do no more
Of Frogs and Oysters send them any store;
In case they spare my life and prove but civil,
I give their sale of distaffs to the Devil.

To quell him comes Q. R. who limping frets
At the safe passe of trixie crackarets,
The boulter, the grand Cyclops cousin, those
Did massacre whil'st each one wip'd his nose:
Few ingles in this fallow ground are bred,
But on a tanners will are winnowed:
Run thither all of you th' alarmes sound clear,
You shall have more then you had the last year.

Short while thereafter was the bird of Jove
Resolv'd to speak, though dismal it should prove;
Yet was afraid, when he saw them in ire,
They should or'throw quite flat down dead th' empire
He rather chus'd the fire from heaven to steale,
To boats where were red Herrings put to sale;
Then to be calm 'gainst those who strive to brave us,
And to the Massorets fond words enslave us.

All this at last concluded galantly,
In spite of Ate and her hern-like thigh,
Who, sitting saw Penthesilea tane,
In her old age, for a cresse-selling quean;
Each one cry'd out, Thou filthy Collier toad,
Doth it become thee to be found abroad?
Thou hast the Roman Standard filtch'd away,
Which they in rags of parchment did display.

[71]

Juno was borne who under the Rainbow,
Was a bird-catching with her Duck below:
When her with such a grievous trick they plyed,
That she had almost been bethwacked by it:
The bargain was that of that throatfull she
Should of Prosperina have two egges free;
And if that she thereafter should be found,
She to a Haw-thorn hill should be fast bound.

Seven moneths thereafter, lacking twenty two,
He, that of old did Carthage town undo:
Did bravely midd'st them all himself advance,
Requiring of them his inheritance;
Although they justly made up the division,
According to the shoe-welt-lawes decision;
By distributing store of brews and beef
To those poor fellows, that did pen the Brief.

But th' year will come signe of a Turkish Bowe,
Five spindles yarnd, and three pot-bottomes too,
Wherein of a discourteous King the dock
Shall pepper'd be under an Hermits frock,
Ah that for one she hypocrite you must
Permit so many acres to be lost:
Cease, cease, this visard may become another,
Withdraw your selves unto the Serpents brother.

'Tis in times past, that he who is shall reigne
With his good friends in peace now and againe;
No rash nor heady Prince shall then rule crave,
Each good will its arbitrement shall have:
And the joy promised of old as doome
To the heavens guests, shall in its beacon come:
Then shall the breeding mares, that benumm'd were,
Like royall palfreys ride triumphant there.

And this continue shall from time to time,
Till Mars be fettred for an unknown crime,
Then shall one come who others will surpasse,
Delightful, pleasing, matchlesse, full of grace;
Chear up your hearts, approach to this repast,
All trusty friends of mine for hee's deceast,

Who would not for a world return againe,
So highly shall time past be cri'd up then.

He who was made of waxe shall lodge each member
Close by the hinges of a block of timber:
We then no more shall Master, master, whoot
The swagger, who th' alarum bell holds out;
Could one seaze on the dagger which he bears,
Heads would be free from tingling in the eares,
To baffle the whole storehouse of abuses,
And thus farewell Apollo and the Muses.

translated from the French by Sir Thomas Urquhart

The Games of Gargantua

Then blockishly mumbling with a set on countenance a piece of scurvie grace, he wash't his hands in fresh wine, pick't his teeth with the foot of a hog, and talked jovially with his Attendants: then the Carpet being spred, they brought plenty of cardes, many dice, with great store and abundance of checkers and chesse-boards.

There he played

At Flusse.	At the last couple in hell.
At Primero.	At the hock.
At the beast.	At the surlie.
At the rifle.	At the lanskenet.
At trump.	At the cukoe.
At the prick and spare not.	At puffe, or let him speak that hath it.
At the hundred.	
At the peenie.	At take nothing and throw out.
At the unfortunate woman.	
At the fib.	At the marriage.
At the passe ten.	At the frolick or jack daw.
At one and thirtie.	At the opinion.
At post and paire, or even and sequence.	At who doth the one, doth the other.
At three hundred.	At the sequences.
At the unluckie man.	At the ivory bundles.

[73]

At the tarots.
At losing load him.
At he's gulled and *esto*.
At the torture.
At the handruf.
At the click.
At honours.
At love.
At the chesse.
At Reynold the fox.
At the squares.
At the cowes.
At the lottery.
At the chance or mum-
chance.
At three dice or maniest
bleaks.
At the tables.
At nivinivinack.
At the lurch.
At doublets or queens-
game.
At the failie.
At the French tictac.
At the long tables or fer-
keering.
At feldown.
At Tods body.
At needs must.
At the dames or draughts.
At bob and mow.
At primus secundus.
At Mark-knife.
At the keyes.
At span-counter.
At even or odd.
At crosse or pile.
At bal and huckle-bones.
At ivory balls.
At the billiards.
At bob and hit.
At the owle.

At the charming of the hare.
At pull yet a little.
At trudgepig.
At the magatapies.
At the horne.
At the flower'd or shrove-
tide oxe.
At the madge-owlet.
At pinch without laughing.
At prickle me tickle me.
At the unshoing of the
Asse.
At the cocksesse.
At hari hohi.
At I set me down.
At earle beardie.
At the old mode.
At draw the spit.
At put out.
At gossip lend me your
sack.
At the ramcod ball.
At thrust out the harlot.
At Marseil figs.
At nicknamrie.
At stick and hole.
At boke or him, or flaying
the fox.
At the branching it.
At trill madam, or graple
my Lady.
At the cat selling.
At blow the coale.
At the rewedding.
At the quick and dead
judge.
At unoven the iron.
At the false clown.
At the flints, or at the nine
stones.
At to the crutch hulch
back.

At the Sanct is found.
At hinch, pinch and laugh
    not.
At the leek.
At Bumdockdousse.
At the loose gig.
At the hoop.
At the sow.
At belly to belly.
At the dales or straths
At the twigs.
At the quoits.
At I'm for that.
At tilt at weekie.
At nine pins.
At the cock quintin.
At tip and hurle.
At the flat bowles.
At the veere and tourn.
At rogue and ruffian.
At bumbatch touch.
At the mysterious trough.
At the short bowles.
At the daple gray.
At cock and crank it.
At break-pot.
At my desire.
At twirlie whirlietrill.
At the rush bundles.
At the short staffe.
At the whirling gigge.
At hide and seek, or are
    you all hid.
At the picket.
At the blank.
At the pilfrers.
At the caveson.
At prison barres.
At have at the nuts.
At cherrie-pit.
At rub and rice.
At whip-top.

At the casting top.
At the hobgoblins.
At the O wonderful.
At the soilie smutchie.
At fast and loose.
At scutchbreech.
At the broom-beesome.
At St Cosme, I come to
    adore thee.
At the lustie brown
    boy.
At I take you napping.
At faire and softly passeth
    lent.
At the forked oak.
At trusse.
At the wolfes taile.
At bum to busse, or nose
    in breech.
At Geordie give me my
    lance.
At swaggie, waggie or
    shoggieshou.
At stook and rook, sheare,
    and threave.
At the birch.
At the musse.
At the dillie dilli darling.
At oxe moudie.
At purpose in purpose.
At nine lesse.
At blinde-man-buffe.
At the fallen bridges.
At bridled nick.
At the white at buts.
At thwack swinge him.
At apple, peare, plum.
At mumgi.
At the toad.
At cricket.
At the pounding stick.
At jack and the box.

At the queens.

At the trades.

At heads and points.

At the vine-tree hug.

At black be thy fall.

At ho the distaffe.

At Joane Thomson.

At the boulting cloth.

At the oats seed.

At greedie glutton.

At the morish dance.

At feebie.

At the whole frisk and
gambole.

At battabum, or riding of
the wilde mare.

At Hinde the Plowman.

At the good mawkin.

At the dead beast.

At climbe the ladder Billie.

At the dying hog.

At the salt doup.

At the pretty pigeon.

At barley break.

At the bavine.

At the bush leap.

At crossing.

At bo-peep.

At the hardit arsepursie.

At the harrowers nest.

At forward hey.

At the fig.

At gunshot crack.

At mustard peel.

At the gome.

At the relapse.

At jog breech, or prick him
forward.

At knockpate.

At the Cornish cough.

At the crane-dance.

At slash and cut.

At bobbing, or the flirt on
the nose.

At the larks.

At filipping.

After he had thus well played, reveled, past and spent his time, it was thought fit to drink a little, and that was eleven glassefuls the man, and immediately after making good cheer again, he would stretch himself upon a faire bench, or a good large bed, and there sleep two or three houres together, without thinking or speaking any hurt. After he was awakened he would shake his eares a little. In the mean time they brought him fresh wine, there he drank better than ever. Ponocrates shewed him, that it was an ill diet to drink so after sleeping. It is, (answered Gargantua,) the very life of the Patriarchs and holy Fathers; for naturally I sleepe salt, and my sleep hath been to me in stead of so many gamons of bacon.

translated by Sir Thomas Urquhart

GEORGE PEELE
1556–96

Song

When as the rye reach to the chin,
And chopcherry, chopcherry ripe within,
Strawberries swimming in the cream,
And school-boys playing in the stream;
 Then O, then O, then O my true love said,
  Till that time come again,
She could not live a maid.

A Voice speaks from the Well

Fair maiden, white and red,
Comb me smooth, and stroke my head;
And thou shalt have some cockle bread.
Gently dip, but not too deep,
For fear thou make the golden beard to weep.
Fair maid, white and red,
Comb me smooth, and stroke my head;
And every hair a sheave shall be,
And every sheave a golden tree.

WILLIAM SHAKESPEARE
1564–1616

Holofernes's Letter

The preyful princess pierc'd and prick'd a pretty pleasing pricket;
Some say a sore; but not a sore, till now made sore with shooting.
The dogs did yell; put 'ell to sore, then sorel jumps from thicket;
Or pricket sore, or else sore'll the people fall a-hooting.
If sore be sore, then 'ell to sore makes fifty sores – O – sorel!
Of one sore I an hundred make, by adding but one more l.

Love's Labour Lost

Feste's Song

When that I was and a little tiny boy,
   With hey, ho, the wind and the rain:
A foolish thing was but a toy,
   For the rain it raineth every day.

But when I came to man's estate,
   With hey, ho, the wind and the rain:
'Gainst knaves and thieves men shut their gate,
   For the rain it raineth every day.

But when I came alas to wive,
   With hey, ho, the wind and the rain:
By swaggering could I never thrive,
   For the rain it raineth every day.

But when I came unto my beds,
   With hey, ho, the wind and the rain:
With toss-pots still had drunken heads,
   For the rain it raineth every day.

A great while ago the world begun,
   With hey, ho, the wind and the rain:
But that's all one, our play is done,
   And we'll strive to please you every day.

Twelfth Night, or What You Will

Bottom's Dream

– I have had a most rare vision. I have had a dream past the wit of man to say what dream it was. Man is but an ass if he go about to expound this dream. Methought I was – there is no man can tell what. Methought I was – and methought I had – but man is but a patched fool if he will offer to say what methought I had. The eye of man hath not heard, the ear of man hath not seen, man's hand is not able to taste, his tongue to conceive, nor his heart to report what my dream was! I will get Peter Quince to write a ballad of this dream. It shall be called 'Bottom's Dream', because it hath no bottom; and I will sing it in the latter end of a play before the Duke. Peradventure, to make it the more gracious, I shall sing it at her death.

A Midsummer Night's Dream

The Fool's prophecy

FOOL. This is a brave night to cool a courtesan.
   I'll speak a prophecy ere I go:

> When priests are more in word than matter;
> When brewers mar their malt with water;
> When nobles are their tailors' tutors;
> No heretics burned, but wenches' suitors;
> When every case in law is right;
> No squire in debt nor no poor knight;
> When slanders do not live in tongues;
> Nor cutpurses come not to throngs;
> When usurers tell their gold i' th' field;
> And bawds and whores do churches build;
> Then shall the realm of Albion
> Come to great confusion:
> Then comes the time, who lives to see't,
> That going shall be used with feet.

This prophecy Merlin shall make; for I live before his time.

King Lear

Lear's Madness

Enter FOOL

FOOL. Come not in here, Nuncle, here's a spirit. Help me, help me!

KENT. Give me thy hand. Who's there?

FOOL. A spirit, a spirit. He says his name's Poor Tom.

KENT. What are thou that dost grumble there i' th' straw?
Come forth.

Enter EDGAR [*disguised as a madman*].

EDGAR. Away! the foul fiend follows me. Through the sharp hawthorn
blows the cold wind. Humh! Go to thy cold bed, and warm thee.

LEAR. Didst thou give all to thy daughters? And art thou come to this?

EDGAR. Who gives anything to Poor Tom? Whom the foul fiend hath led
through fire and through flame, through ford and whirlpool, o'er bog and
quagmire; that hath laid knives under his pillow and halters in his pew,
set ratsbane by his porridge, made him proud of heart, to ride on a bay
trotting horse over four-inched bridges, to course his own shadow for a
traitor. Bless thy five wits, Tom's a-cold. O, do, de, do, de, do, de. Bless
thee from whirlwinds, star-blasting, and taking. Do Poor Tom some
charity, whom the foul fiend vexes. There could I have him now – and
there – and there again – and there.

Storm still.

LEAR. What, has his daughters brought him to this pass?
Couldst thou save nothing? Wouldst thou give 'em all?

FOOL. Nay, he reserved a blanket, else we had been all shamed.

LEAR. Now all the plagues that in the pendulous air
Hang fated o'er men's faults light on thy daughters!

KENT. He hath no daughters, sir.

LEAR. Death, traitor; nothing could have subdued nature
To such a lowness but his unkind daughters.
Is it the fashion that discarded fathers
Should have thus little mercy on their flesh?
Judicious punishment – 'twas this flesh begot
Those pelican daughters.

EDGAR. Pillicock sat on Pillicock Hill. Alow, alow, loo, loo!

FOOL. This cold night will turn us all to fools and madmen.

EDGAR. Take heed o' th' foul fiend; obey thy parents; keep thy word's justice; swear not; commit not with man's sworn spouse; set not thy sweet heart on proud array. Tom's a-cold.

LEAR. What hast thou been?

EDGAR. A servingman, proud in heart and mind; that curled my hair, wore gloves in my cap; served the lust of my mistress' heart, and did the act of darkness with her; swore as many oaths as I spake words, and broke them in the sweet face of heaven. One that slept in the contriving of lust, and waked to do it. Wine loved I deeply, dice dearly; and in woman out-paramoured the Turk. False of heart, light of ear, bloody of hand; hog in sloth, fox in stealth, wolf in greediness, dog in madness, lion in prey. Let not the creaking of shoes nor the rustling of silks betray thy poor heart to woman. Keep thy foot out of brothels, thy hand out of plackets, thy pen from lenders' books, and defy the foul fiend. Still through the hawthorn blows the cold wind; says suum, mun, nonny. Dolphin my boy, boy, sessa! let him trot by.

Storm still.

LEAR. Thou wert better in a grave than to answer with thy uncovered body this extremity of the skies. Is man no more than this? Consider him well. Thou ow'st the worm no silk, the beast no hide, the sheep no wool, the cat no perfume. Ha! here's three on's are sophisticated. Thou art the thing itself; unaccommodated man is no more but such a poor, bare, forked animal as thou art. Off, off, you lendings! Come, unbutton here.

[*Tearing off his clothes.*]

FOOL. Prithee, Nuncle, be contented, 'tis a naughty night to swim in. Now a little fire in a wild field were like an old lecher's heart – a small spark, all the rest on's body, cold. Look, here comes a walking fire.

Enter GLOUCESTER, *with a torch.*

EDGAR. This is the foul fiend Flibbertigibbet. He begins at curfew, and walks till the first cock. He gives the web and the pin, squints the eye, and makes the harelip; mildews the white wheat, and hurts the poor creature of earth.

 Swithold footed thrice the old;
 He met the nightmare, and her nine fold;
  Bid her alight
  And her troth plight,
 And aroint thee, witch, aroint thee!

KENT. How fares your Grace?

LEAR. What's he?

KENT. Who's there? What is't you seek?

GLOUCESTER. What are you there? Your names?

[81]

EDGAR. Poor Tom, that eats the swimming frog, the toad, the todpole, the wall-newt and the water; that in the fury of his heart, when the foul fiend rages, eats cow-dung for sallets, swallows the old rat and the ditch-dog, drinks the green mantle of the standing pool; who is whipped from tithing to tithing, and stocked, punished, and imprisoned; who hath had three suits to his back, six shirts to his body,

> Horse to ride, and weapon to wear,
> But mice and rats, and such small deer,
> Have been Tom's food for seven long year.

Beware my follower! Peace, Smulkin, peace, thou fiend!

GLOUCESTER. What, hath your Grace no better company?

EDGAR. The Prince of Darkness is a gentleman. Modo he's called, and Mahu.

GLOUCESTER. Our flesh and blood, my Lord, is grown so vile
That it doth hate what gets it.

EDGAR. Poor Tom's a-cold.

GLOUCESTER. Go in with me. My duty cannot suffer
T' obey in all your daughters' hard commands.
Though their injunction be to bar my doors
And let this tyrannous night take hold upon you,
Yet have I ventured to come seek you out
And bring you where both fire and food is ready.

LEAR. First let me talk with this philosopher. What is the cause of thunder?

KENT. Good my lord, take his offer; go into th' house.

LEAR. I'll talk a word with this same learnèd Theban.
What is your study?

EDGAR. How to prevent the fiend, and to kill vermin.

LEAR. Let me ask you one word in private.

KENT. Importune him once more to go, my lord.
His wits begin t' unsettle.

GLOUCESTER.   Canst thou blame him?

Storm still.

His daughters seek his death. Ah, that good Kent,
He said it would be thus, poor banished man!
Thou say'st the King grows mad – I'll tell thee, friend,
I am almost mad myself. I had a son,
Now outlawed from my blood; he sought my life
But lately, very late. I loved him, friend,
No father his son dearer. True to tell thee,
The grief hath crazed my wits. What a night's this!
I do beseech your Grace –

[82]

LEAR.   O, cry you mercy, sir.
  Noble philosopher, your company.
EDGAR. Tom's a-cold.
GLOUCESTER. In, fellow, there, into th' hovel; keep thee warm.
LEAR. Come, let's in all.
KENT.   This way, my lord.
LEAR.   With him!
  I will keep still with my philosopher.
KENT. Good my lord, soothe him; let him take the fellow.
GLOUCESTER. Take him you on.
KENT. Sirrah, come on; go along with us.
LEAR. Come, good Athenian.
GLOUCESTER. No words, no words! Hush.
EDGAR. Child Rowland to the dark tower came;
        His word was still, 'Fie, foh, and fum,
        I smell the blood of a British man.'   *Exeunt.*

.   .   .   .

Enter LEAR, EDGAR, *and* FOOL.

EDGAR. Fraretto calls me, and tells me Nero is an angler in the lake of
  darkness. Pray, innocent, and beware the foul fiend.
FOOL. Prithee, Nuncle, tell me whether a madman be a gentleman or a
  yeoman.
LEAR. A king, a king.
FOOL. No, he's a yeoman that has a gentleman to his son; for he's a mad
  yeoman that sees his son a gentleman before him.
LEAR. To have a thousand with red burning spits
  Come hizzing in upon 'em –
EDGAR. The foul fiend bites my back.
FOOL. He's mad that trusts in the tameness of a wolf, a horse's health, a
  boy's love, or a whore's oath.
LEAR. It shall be done; I will arraign them straight.
  [*To* EDGAR] Come, sit thou here, most learned justice.
  [*To the* FOOL] Thou sapient sir, sit here. Now, you she-foxes –
EDGAR. Look, where he stands and glares. Want'st thou eyes at trial,
  madam?
  Come o'er the bourn, Bessy, to me.
FOOL. Her boat hath a leak,
        And she must not speak
        Why she dares not come over to thee.
EDGAR. The foul fiend haunts Poor Tom in the voice of a nightingale.

[83]

Hoppedance cries in Tom's belly for two white herring. Croak not, black angel; I have no food for thee.

KENT. How do you, sir? Stand you not so amazed. Will you lie down and rest upon the cushions?

LEAR. I'll see their trial first. Bring in their evidence.

[*To* EDGAR] Thou, robèd man of justice, take thy place.

[*To the* FOOL] And thou, his yokefellow of equity

Bench by his side. [*To* KENT] You are o'th' commission;

Sit you too.

EDGAR. Let us deal justly.

　　Sleepest or wakest thou, jolly shepherd?

　　　Thy sheep be in the corn;

　　And for one blast of thy minikin mouth

　　　Thy sheep shall take no harm.

Purr, the cat is gray.

LEAR. Arraign her first. 'Tis Goneril, I here take my oath before this honorable assembly, she kicked the poor King her father.

FOOL. Come hither, mistress. Is your name Goneril?

LEAR. She cannot deny it.

FOOL. Cry you mercy, I took you for a joint stool.

LEAR. And here's another, whose warped looks proclaim

What store her heart is made on. Stop her there!

Arms, arms, sword, fire! Corruption in the place!

False justicer, why hast thou let her 'scape?

EDGAR. Bless thy five wits!

KENT. O pity! Sir, where is the patience now

That you so oft have boasted to retain?

EDGAR. [*Aside*] My tears begin to take his part so much

They mar my counterfeiting.

LEAR. The little dogs and all,

Tray, Blanch, and Sweetheart – see, they bark at me.

EDGAR. Tom will throw his head at them. Avaunt, you curs.

　　Be thy mouth or black or white,

　　Tooth that poisons if it bite;

　　Mastiff, greyhound, mongrel grim,

　　Hound or spaniel, brach or lym,

　　Or bobtail tike, or trundle-tail –

　　Tom will make him weep and wail;

　　For, with throwing thus my head,

　　Dogs leaped the hatch, and all are fled.

Do, de, de, de. Sessa! Come, march to wakes and fairs and market towns.

Poor Tom, thy horn is dry.

LEAR. Then let them anatomize Regan. See what breeds about her heart. Is there any cause in nature that make these hard hearts? [*To* EDGAR] You, sir, I entertain for one of my hundred; only I do not like the fashion of your garments. You will say they are Persian; but let them be changed.
KENT. Now, good my lord, lie here and rest awhile.
LEAR. Make no noise, make no noise; draw the curtains.
So, so. We'll go to supper i' th' morning.
FOOL. And I'll go to bed at noon.

ANONYMOUS

Will you buy a fine dog

Will you buy a fine dog with a hole in his head?
    With a dildo
    With a dildo dildo
    With a dildo dildo dildo dildo.
Muffs, cuffs, rebatoes and fine sister's thread,
    With a dildo, etc.

I stand not on points, pins, periwigs, combs, glasses,
Gloves, garters, girdles, busks for the brisk lasses,
    But I have other dainty tricks,
    Sleek stones and poking sticks,
    With a dildo dildo dildo dildo dildo dildo.

And for a need, my pretty pretty pretty pods,
Amber, civet and musk cods,
    With a dildo, with a diddle diddle dildo,
    With a dildo diddle dildo diddle dildo.

ANONYMOUS

Of One that Died of the Wind-Colic

Here lies John Dumbelow,
Who died because he was so.
If his tail could have spoke
His heart had not broke.

ANONYMOUS

The first beginning

The first beginning was Sellinger's Round
    Where the cow leapt over the moon,
And the goodwife shit in the pisspot,
    And the cream ran into her shoon,
        With hey, stitch your nose in her breech
           And turn about knaves all three,
           And we'll have another as good as the other
           If you'll be ruled by me.

My sister went to market
    To buy her a taffety hat.
Before she came there her arse lay bare.
    Lay you your lips to that.
        Hey, stitch, etc.

The fiddler played his wife a dance
    And there sprang up a rose.
The butcher bit his wife by the arse
    And she beshit his nose.
        Hey, stitch, etc.

ANONYMOUS
1608

Fara Diddle Dyno

Ha ha! ha ha! This world doth pass
  Most merrily I'll be sworn,
For many an honest Indian ass
  Goes for a unicorn.
            Fara diddle dyno,
            This is idle fyno.

Tie hie! tie hie! O sweet delight!
  He tickles this age that can
Call Tullia's ape a marmasyte
  And Leda's goose a swan.
            Fara diddle dyno,
            This is idle fyno.

So so! so so! Fine English days!
  For false play is no reproach,
For he that doth the coachman praise
  May safely use the coach.
            Fara diddle dyno,
            This is idle fyno.

ANONYMOUS

Martin and his Man

Martin said to his man,
        Fie! man, fie!
Oh, Martin said to his man,
        Who's the fool now?
Martin said to his man,
Fill thou the cup, and I the can;
Thou hast well drunken, man:
        Who's the fool now?

[87]

I see a sheep shearing corn,
      Fie! man, fie!
I see a sheep shearing corn,
      Who's the fool now?
I see a sheep shearing corn,
And a cuckoo blow his horn;
Thou hast well drunken, man:
      Who's the fool now?

I see a man in the moon,
      Fie! man, fie!
I see a man in the moon,
      Who's the fool now?
I see a man in the moon,
Clouting of St Peter's shoon,
Thou hast well drunken, man:
      Who's the fool now?

I see a hare chase a hound,
      Fie! man, fie!
I see a hare chase a hound,
      Who's the fool now?
I see a hare chase a hound,
Twenty mile above the ground;
Thou hast well drunken, man:
      Who's the fool now?

I see a goose ring a hog,
      Fie! man, fie!
I see a goose ring a hog,
      Who's the fool now?
I see a goose ring a hog,
And a snail that bit a dog;
Thou hast well drunken, man:
      Who's the fool now?

I see a mouse catch the cat,
    Fie! man, fie!
I see a mouse catch the cat,
    Who's the fool now?
I see a mouse catch the cat,
And the cheese to eat the rat;
Thou hast well drunken, man:
    Who's the fool now?

ANONYMOUS

The Fly's Wedding

The Fly she sat in Shamble row
And shambled with her heels I trow,
And then came in Sir Cranion
With legs so long and many a one.

And said 'Jove speed Dame Fly, Dame Fly,'
'Marry you be welcome, good sir', quoth she;
'The Master Humble-bee hath sent me to thee,
To wit and you will his true love be.'

But she said 'Nay, that may not be,
For I must have the Butterfly;
For and a greater Lord there may not be';
But at the last consent did she.

And there was bid to this wedding
All Flies in the field and Worms creeping;
The Snail she came crawling all over the plain,
And with all her jolly trinkets at her train.

Ten Bees there came clad all in Gold,
And all the rest did them behold;
But the Thornbud refused this sight to see
And to a cow-pat away flies she.

[89]

'But where now shall this wedding be?'
'For and hey nonny no in an old Ivy tree.'
'And where now shall we bake our bread?'
'For and heynonny no, in an old horse's head.'

'And where now shall we brew our ale?'
'But even with one Walnut Shell.'
'And also where shall we our dinner make?'
'But even upon a galled Horse back.

For there we shall have good company,
With humbling and bumbling and much melody.'
When ended was this wedding day,
The Bee he took his Fly away.

And laid her down upon the Marsh,
Between one Marigold and one long grass;
And there they begot good Master Gnat,
And made him the heir of all, that's flat.

JOHN DAVIES OF HEREFORD
?1565–1618

THE AUTHOR LOVING THESE HOMELY MEATS
SPECIALLY, VIZ.: CREAM, PANCAKES, BUTTERED
PIPPIN-PIES (LAUGH, GOOD PEOPLE) AND
TOBACCO; WRIT TO THAT WORTHY AND
VIRTUOUS GENTLEWOMAN, WHOM HE
CALLETH MISTRESS, AS FOLLOWETH

If there were, oh! an Hellespont of cream
Between us, milk-white mistress, I would swim
To you, to show to both my love's extreme,
Leander-like, – yea! dive from brim to brim.
But met I with a buttered pippin-pie
Floating upon 't, that would I make my boat
To waft me to you without jeopardy,
Though sea-sick I might be while it did float.
Yet if a storm should rise, by night or day,
Of sugar-snows and hail of caraways,

Then, if I found a pancake in my way,
It like a plank should bring me to your kays;
   Which having found, if they tobacco kept,
   The smoke should dry me well before I slept.

JOHN DONNE
1572–1631

Song

Goe, and catche a falling starre,
Get with child a mandrake roote,
Tell me, where all past yeares are,
   Or who cleft the Divels foot,
Teach me to heare Mermaides singing,
   Or to keep off envies stinging,
         And finde
         What winde
Serves to advance an honest minde.

If thou beest borne to strange sights,
   Things invisible to see,
Ride ten thousand daies and nights,
   Till age snow white haires on thee,
Thou, when thou retorn'st, wilt tell mee
All strange wonders that befell thee,
         And sweare
         No where
Lives a woman true, and faire.

If thou findst one, let mee know,
   Such a Pilgrimage were sweet;
Yet doe not, I would not goe,
   Though at next doore wee might meet,
   Though shee were true, when you met her,
   And last, till you write your letter,
         Yet shee
         Will bee
False, ere I come, to two, or three.

The Computation

For the first twenty yeares, since yesterday,
  I scarce beleev'd, thou could'st be gone away,
For forty more, I fed on favours past,
  And forty'on hopes, that thou would'st, they might last.
Teares drown'd one hundred, and sighes blew out two,
  A thousand, I did neither thinke, nor doe,
  Or not divide, all being one thought of you;
  Or in a thousand more, forgot that too.
Yet call not this long life; But thinke that I
Am, by being dead, Immortall; Can ghosts die?

BEN JONSON
1572–1637

A Catch

Buzz! quoth the Blue-Fly,
Hum! quoth the Bee;
Buzz and hum! they cry,
  And so do we.
In his ear! in his nose!
Thus, – do you see?
He eat the Dormouse –
  Else it was he.

Cocklorrel

Cocklorrel woulds needs have the devil his guest,
  And bade him once into the Peak to dinner,
Where never the fiend had such a feast
  Provided him yet at the charge of a sinner.

His stomach was queasy (he came hither coached)
    The jogging had caused some crudities rise;
To help it he called for a puritan poached,
    That used to turn up the eggs of his eyes.

And so recovered unto his wish,
    He sat him down, and he fell to eat;
Promoter in plum broth was the first dish –
    His own privy kitchen had no such meat.

Yet though with this he much were taken,
    Upon a sudden he shifted his trencher,
As soon as he spied the bawd and the bacon,
    By which you may note the devil's a wencher.

Six pickled tailors sliced and cut,
    Sempsters and tirewomen, fit for his palate;
With feathermen and perfumers put
    Some twelve in a charger to make a great sallet.

A rich fat usurer stewed in his marrow,
    And by him a lawyer's head and green sauce:
Both which his belly took up like a barrow,
    As if till then he had never seen sauce.

Then carbonadoed and cooked with pains,
    Was brought up a cloven sergeant's face:
The sauce was made of his yeoman's brains,
    That had been beaten out with his own mace.

Two roasted sherriffs came whole to the board;
    (The feast had been nothing without 'em)
Both living and dead they were foxed and furred,
    Their chains like sausages hung about 'em.

The very next dish was the mayor of a town,
    With a pudding of maintenance thrust in his belly,
Like a goose in the feathers, dressed in his gown,
    And his couple of hinch-boys boiled to a jelly.

A London cuckold hot from the spit,
    And when the carver up had broken him,
The devil chopped up his head at a bit,
    But the horns were very near like to choke him.

The chine of a lecher too there was roasted,
    With a plump harlot's haunch and garlic,
A pandar's pettitoes, that had boasted
    Himself for a captain, yet never was warlike.

A large fat pasty of a midwife hot;
    And for a cold baked meat into the story,
A reverend painted lady was brought,
    And coffined in crust till now she was hoary.

To these, an over-grown justice of peace,
    With a clerk like a gizzard trussed under each arm;
And warrants for sippits, laid in his own grease,
    Set over a chafing dish to be kept warm.

The jowl of a gaoler served for fish,
    A constable soused with vinegar by;
Two aldermen lobsters asleep in a dish.
    A deputy tart, a churchwarden pie.

All which devoured, he then for a close
    Did for a full draught of Derby call;
He heaved the huge vessel up to his nose,
    And left not till he had drunk up all.

Then from the table he gave a start,
    Where banquet and wine were nothing scarce,
All which he flirted away with a fart,
    From whence it was called the Devil's Arse.

JOHN TAYLOR, THE 'WATER-POET'

1580–1653

Odcomb's Complaint

A sad, joyful, lamentable, delightful, merry-go-sorry elegy or funeral poem upon the supposed death of the famous Cosmographical Surveyor and Historiographical Relator, Mr Thomas Coriat of Odcomb.

O for a rope of Onions from Saint Omers
And for the muse of golden tongued Homer's,
That I might write and weep and weep and write
Odcombian Coriat's timeless last good-night!
O were my wit inspir'd with Scoggins vein,
Or that *Will Summers' ghost* had seiz'd my brain!
Or *Tarlton, Lanum, Singer, Kemp* and *Pope*,
Or she that danc'd and tumbled on the rope!
Or Tilting *Archy*, that so bravely ran
Against Don Phoebus's knight, that wordy man!
O all you crew, inside pied-coloured garments,
Assist me to the height of your preferments;
And with your wits and spirits inspire my pate full
That I in Coriat's praise be no ungrateful.
If ever I lamented loss of folly,
If ever man had cause of Melancholy,
Then now's the time to wail his ruthless wrack,
And weep in tears of *Claret* and of *Sack*.

*

And now Dame *Thetis*, in thy vasty womb
Is odd Odcombian *Coriat's* timeless Tomb,
Where *Nereids, Dryads*, and sweet sea-nymphs tend him,
And with their daily service do befriend him.
There all-shaped *Proteus* and shrill-trumping *Triton*
And many more, which I can hardly write on,
In servile troops they wait on *Coriat*,
That though like hell, the sea were far more dark, as
Yet these would guard his unregarded Carcass.
You *Academick, Latin, Greek Magisters*,

[95]

You offspring of the three-times treble Sisters,
Write, teach, until your tongues have blisters!
For now the *Haddocks* and the shifting *Sharks*
That feed on *Coriat*, will become great Clerks.
The wry-mouthed *Plaice* and mumping *Whiting-mops*
Will in their maws keep *Greek* and *Latin* shops;
The Pork-like *Porpoise*, *Thorn-back* and the *Skate*
Like studious *Grecian Latinists* will prate;
And men with eating them, by inspiration,
With these two tongues shall fill each barbarous Nation!
Then though the Sea hath rudely him bereft us,
Yet, midst our woes, this only comfort left us,
That our posterities by eating fishes
Shall pick his wisdom out of divers dishes;
And then, no doubt, but thousands more will be
As learned, or perhaps as wise, men as he!
    But to conclude, affection makes me cry;
    Sorrow provokes me sleep, grief dries mine eye.

*

Epitaph in the Bermuda tongue, which must be pronounced with the accent of the grunting of a hog

Hough gruntough wough Thomough
          Coratough, Odcough robunquogh
Warawogh bogh Comitogh
          sogh wogh termonatogrogh,
Callimogh gogh whobogh Kaqa-
          magh demagorgogh Palemogh,
Lomerogh nogh Tottertogh ille-
          montogh eagh Allaquemquog,
Isracominogh Jagogh Jamerogh
          mogh Carnogh pelepsogh,
Animogh trogh deradzogh maramogh,
          hogh Flonzagh salepsogh.

*

Epitaph *in the Utopian Tongue*

Nortumblum callimuquash omysteliton quashte burashte,
Scribuke woshtay solusbay perambulatushte;
Grekay fons Turkay Paphay zums Ierusalushte.
Neptus esht Ealors Interremoy diz Dolorushte,
Confabuloy Odcumbay Prozeugmolliton tymorumynoy,
Omulus oratushte paralescus tolliton umbroy.

The same *in English, translated by Caleb Quishquash, an Utopian born, and principal Secretary to the great Adelontado of Barmoodoes.*

Here lies the wonder of the English Nation,
Involved in Neptune's brinish vasty maw.
For fruitless travel and for strange relation,
He past and repast all that e'er eye saw.
Odcomb produced him; many Nations fed him;
And worlds of Writers through the world have spread him.

Sonnet *in praise of Mr Thomas the Deceased, fashioned of divers stuffs, as mockado, fustian, stand-further-off and Motley*

Sweet semi-circled Cynthia played at maw
The while *Endymion* ran the wild-goose chase;
Great Bacchus with his Cross-bow kill'd a daw
And sullen Saturn smiled with pleasant face.
The nine-fold Bugbears of the Caspian lake
Sate whistling Ebon horn-pipes to their Ducks;
Madge-owlet straight for joy her Girdle brake,
And rugged Satyrs frisk'd like Stags and Bucks.
The untam'd tumbling fifteen-footed Goat,
With promulgation of the Lesbian shores,
Confronted Hydra in a sculler Boat,
At which the mighty mountain Taurus roars.
Meantime great Sultan Soliman was born
And Atlas blew his rustick rumbling horn.

[97]

Sir Gregory Nonsense his News from No Place
1622

It was in June the eight and thirtieth day,
That I embarkéd was on Highgate Hill,
After discourteous friendly taking leave
Of my young father *Madge* and Mother *John*.
The Wind did ebb, the tide flowed North South-East,
We hoist our Sails of Colloquintida,
And after 13 days and 17 nights,
(With certain Hieroglyphic hours to boot)
We with tempestuous calms and friendly storms,
Split our main top-mast, close below the keel.
But I with a dull quick congruity
Took 19 ounces of the Western wind,
And with the pith of the pole Artichoke,
Sailed by the flaming Coast of Trebizond.
There in a Fort of melting Adamant,
Armed in a Crimson Robe, as black as jet,
I saw *Alcides* with a Spider's thread
Lead *Cerberus* to the Pronontic Sea.
Then cutting further through the marble Main,
'Mongst flying Bulls and four-legged Turkeycocks,
A dumb fair-spoken, well-faced agéd youth
Sent to me from the stout Stimphalides,
With tongueless silence thus began his speech:
'Illustrious flapjack, to thy hungry doom
Low as the ground I elevate my cause.
As I upon a Gnat was riding late,
In quest to parley with the Pleiades,
I saw the Duke of Hounsditch gaping close
In a green Arbour made of yellow starch,
Betwixt two Brokers howling Madrigales.
A Banquet was served in of Lampreys' bones,
Well pickled in the Tarbox of old time,
When *Demogorgon* sailed to *Islington*;
Which I perceiving, with nine chads of steel,
Straight flew unto the coast of Pimlico,
T'inform great *Prester John* and the *Moghul*
What exc'lent Oysters were at *Billingsgate*.

The *Moghul*, all enraged with these news,
Sent a black snail post to *Tartaria*
To tell the Irishmen in *Saxony*
The dismal downfall of old Charing Cross.
With that nine butter Firkins in a flame
Did coldly rise to Arbitrate the cause:
Guessing by the Sinderesis of Wapping
Saint *Thomas Waterings* is most ominous.
For though an Andiron and a pair of Tongs
May both have breeding from one teeming womb,
Yet by the Calculation of Pickt-hatch,
Milk must not be so dear as Muskadell.
First shall Melpomene in Cobweb Lawn
Adorn great *Memphis* in a Mussel boat,
And all the muses clad in Robes of Air
Shall dance Levoltons with a Whirligig.
Fair *Pluto* shall descend from Brazen Dis,
And *Polyphemus* keep a Seamsters' shop,
The Isle of *Wight* shall like a dive-dapper
Devour the Egyptian proud *Piramides*,
Whilst *Cassia Fistula* shall gourmandise
Upon the flesh and blood of Croydon coal dust.
Then on the banks of Shoreditch shall be seen
What 'tis to serve the great Utopian Queen.'
This fearful period with great joyful care
Was heard with acclamations, and in fine,
The whilst a lad of aged Nestor's years,
Stood sitting in a Throne of massy yeast,
(Not speaking any word) gave this reply:
'Most conscript Umpire in this various Orb,
I saw the Caedars of old *Lebanon*,
Read a sad Lecture unto *Clapham heath*,'
At which time a strange vision did appear.
His head was Buckram and his eyes were sedge;
His arms were blue bottles, his teeth were straw;
His legs were nine well squared Tobacco Pipes,
Cloath'd in a garment all of Dolphins' eggs.
Then with a voice erected to the ground,
Lifting aloft his hands unto his feet,
He thus began: 'Cease friendly cutting throats,
Clamour the Promulgation of your tongues,
And yield to Demagorgon's policy.

[99]

Stop the refulgent method of your moods;
For should you live old *Paphlagonia's* years
And with *Sardanapalus* match in virtue,
Yet *Acropos* will with a Marigold
Run through the Mountains of the Caspian Sea.
When you shall see above you and beneath
That nothing kills a man so soon as death,
Aquarius joined with *Pisces* in firm league,
With Reasons and vindictive Arguments
That pulveriz'd the King of Diamonds
And with a diogorical relapse
Squeezed through the Sinders of a Butterfly.'
Great *Oberon* was mounted on a Wasp
To signify this news at Dunstable.
The weathercock at Pancrage in a fume
With Patience much distracted hearing this
Replied thus briefly without fear or wit:
'What madness doth thy Pericranion seize,
Beyond the Dragon's tail Artyphilax?
Think'st thou a Wolf thrust through a sheepskin glove
Can make me take this Gobling for a Lamb?
Or that a Crocodile in Barley broth
Is not a dish to feast Don Beelzebub?
Give me a Medlar in a field of blue,
Wrapt up stigmatically in a dream,
And I will send him to the gates of Dis
To cause him fetch a sword of massy Chalk,
With which he won the fatal Theban field
From Rome's great mitred Metropolitan.'
Much was the quoile this braving answer made,
When presently a German Conjurer
Did ope a learned book of Palmistry
Crammed full of mental reservations.
The which beginning, with a loud low voice,
With affable and kind discourtesy,
He spake what no man heard or understood,
Words tending unto this or no respect:
'Spawn of a Tortoise, hold thy silent noise!
For when the great Leviathan of Trumps
Shall make a breach in *Sinon's* Tennis Court,
Then shall the pigmy mighty *Hercules*
Skip like a wilderness in Woodstreet Counter;

Then *Taurus* shall in league with *Hannibal*
Draw *Bacchus* dry, whilst *Boreas* in a heat,
Envelloped in a Gown of Icicles,
With much discretion and great want of wit,
Leave all as wisely as it was at first.'
I mused much how those things could be done,
When straight a water Tankard answered me,
That it was made with a Parenthesis,
With thirteen yards of Kersey and a half,
Made of fine flax which grew on Goodwin Sands.
Whereby we all perceived the Hernshaw's breed,
Being trusted with a charitable doom,
Was near Bunhill, when straight I might descry
The Quintessence of Grubstreet, well distilled,
Through Cripplegate in a contagious Map.
Bright *Phaeton* all angry at the sight,
Snatch'd a large Wool-pack from a pismire's mouth
And in a Tailor's Thimble boil'd a cabbage.
Then all the standers by, most Reverend Rude,
Judged the case was most obscure and clear,
And that three salt Enigmates well applied,
With fourscore Pipers and *Arion's* Harp,
Might catch Gargantua through an augur-hole;
And 'twas no doubt but mulley *Mahomet*
Would make a quaffing bowl of *Gorgon's* skull.
While gourmandizing *Tantalus* would weep
That *Polypheme* should kiss *Aurora's* lips,
Tri-formed *Cynthia* in a Cinque-foil shape
Met with the Dogstar on Saint *David's* day,
But said *Grimalkin* mumbling up the Alps
Made fifteen fustian fumes of Pastreycrust.
This was no sooner known at *Amsterdam*,
But with an Ethiopian Argosy,
Mann'd with Flap-dragons drinking upsifreeze,
They passed the purple gulf of Basingstoke.
This being finish'd, search to any end,
A full odd number of just sixteen dogs,
Drench'd in a sulphur flame of scalding Ice,
Sung the Besonian Whirlpools of *Argeire*,
Mix'd with pragmatical potato Pies.
With that I turned my eyes to see these things,
And on a Crystal wall of Scarlet dye

I with mine eyes began to hear and note
What these succeeding Verses might portend,
Which furiously an Anabaptist squeak'd,
The audience deafly list'ning all the while.

A most learned-Lye and Illiterate Oration, in lame galloping Rhyme, fustianly pronounced by Nimshag, A Gymnosophical Phoolosopher, in the presence of Achitophel Smell-smock, Annani-Ass Aretine, Iscariot-Nabal, Franciscus Ra-viliaco, Garnetto Jebusito, Guido Salpetro Favexit Pouderio, and many other grave Senators of Limbo. Translated out of the vulgar language of Terra incognita, and is as material as any part of the Book, the meaning whereof a blind man may see without Spectacles as well as midnight as at noon-day.

· · · · · · · · · · · · · · · · · · ·

Quoth he, 'Shall we whose Ancestors were war-like,
Whose rich Perfumes were only Leeks and Garlike,
Whoe noble deeds nocturnal and diurnal
Great Towns and Towers did topsy-turvy turn all,
Shall all their valour be in us extinguished?
Great Jove forbid, there should be such a thing wished!
Though *Cleopatra* was *Octavian's* rival,
It is a thing that we may well connive all,
Amongst the Ancient it is undisputable,
That women and the winds were ever mutable;
And 'tis approved where people are litigious,
That every Epicure is not religious.'
Old *Oceanus* knowing what they meant all,
Brought *Zephyrus* unto the Oriental,
And he by Argument would prove that love is
A thing that makes a wise man oft a Novice.
For 'tis approved, a Greyhound or a Beagle
Were not ordained or made to hunt the Eagle;
Nor can the nimblest Cat that came from *Gotham*
Search the profundity of *Neptune's* bottom.

· · · · · · · · · · · · · · · · · · ·

Thus do I make a hotch-potch messe of Nonsense,
In dark Enigmas and strange sense upon sense:
It is not foolish all, nor is it wise all,
Nor is it true in all, nor is it lies all.
I have not shew'd my wits acute or fluent,
Nor told which way the Wandering Jew went,

For mine own part I never cared greatly
(So I fare well) where those that dress the meat lie.
. . . .

My care is that no captious Reader bear hence
My understanding, wit or reason here-hence.
On purpose to no purpose I did write all,
And so at noon, I bid you here good night all.'

Then with a touchbox of transalpine tar,
Turning thrice round and stirring not a jot,
He threw five ton of red hot burning Snow
Into a Pigmy's mouth, nine inches square,
Which straight with melancholy mov'd
Old *Bembus*, Burgomaster of *Pickt-hatch*
That plunging through the Sea of Turnbull Street,
He safely did arrive at Smithfield Bars.
Then did the Turne-tripes on the Coast of *France*
Catch fifteen hundred thousand Grasshoppers,
With fourteen Spanish Needles bumbasted,
Poach'd with the eggs of fourscore Flanders Mares;
Mounted upon the foot of *Caucasus*
They whorl'd the football of conspiring fate
And brake the shins of smugfaced *Mulciber*.
With that grim *Pluto* all in Scarlet blue
Gave fair *Proserpina* a kiss of brass,
At which all Hell danc'd Trenchmore in a string,
Whilst *Acheron* and *Termagant* did sing.
The Mold-warp all this while in white broth bath'd
Did carrol Dido's happiness in love,
Upon a Gridiron made of whiting-mops,
Unto the tune of '*John* come kiss me now'.
At which Avernus Music 'gan to roar,
Inthroned upon a seat of three-leav'd grass,
Whilst all the Hibernian Kernes in multitudes
Did feast with Shamrocks stew'd in Usquebagh.
At which a banquet made of Monopolies
Took great distaste, because the Pillory
Was hunger-starv'd for want of Villains' ears,
Whom to relieve there was a Mittimus
Sent from *Tartaria* in an Oyster-boat,
At which the King of China was amaz'd,
And with nine grains of Rhubarb stellified,

[103]

As low as to the altitude of shame,
He thrust sour Onions in a Candle-case
And spoil'd the meaning of the world's misdoubt.
Thus with a Dialogue of crimson starch,
I was inflamed with a numb-cold fire
Upon the tenterhooks of *Charlemagne*.
The Dogstar howled, the Cat-a-Mountain smil'd,
And Sysiphus drank Muskadell and Eggs
In the horn'd hoof of huge *Bucephalus*.
Time turn'd about, and shew'd me yesterday,
Clad in a Crown of mourning had I wist.
The motion was almost too late, they said,
Whilst sad despair made all the World stark mad.
They all arose, and I put up my pen;
It makes no matter where, why, how or when.

Some sense at last to the Learned.

You that in *Greek* and *Latin* learned are,
And of the ancient *Hebrew* have a share;
You that most rarely oftentimes have sung
In the *French*, *Spanish* or *Italian* tongue;
Here I in *English* have employed my pen,
To be read by the learned'st Englishmen,
Wherein the meanest Scholar plain may see,
I understand their tongues, as they do me.

ANONYMOUS
(after John Taylor)

Non-sense

Oh that my lungs could bleat like butter'd pease!
But bleating of my lungs hath caught the itch,
And are as mangy as the *Irish* seas,
That doth ingender wind-mills on a bitch.

I grant that Rain-bows being lull'd asleep,
Snort like a woodknife in a Ladies eyes;
Which makes her grieve to see a pudding creep,
For creeping puddings only please the wise.

Not that a hard-roe'd Herring should presume
To swing a tithe-pig in a Cat-skin purse;
For fear the hailstones which did fall at *Rome*,
By lessening of the fault should make it worse.

For 'tis most certain winter wool-sacks grow
From geese to swans, if men could keep them so,
Till that the sheep-shorn Planets gave the hint
To pickle Pancakes in *Geneva* print.

Some men there were that did suppose the skye
Was made of carbonado'd antidotes:
But my opinion is, a whales left eye
Need not be coyned all King-*Harry*-groats;

The reason's plain, for *Charons* western barge
Running a-tilt at the Subjunctive mood,
Beckned to *Bednal-green*, and gave him charge
To fatten Pad-locks with Antartick food.

The end will be the mill-pools must be laded,
To fish for whitepots in a countrey dance;
So they that suffer'd wrong and were upbraded,
Shall be made friends in a left-handed trance.

ANONYMOUS

If All the World were Paper

If all the world were Paper,
And all the seas were Ink;
If all the trees were bread and cheese,
How should we do for drink?

If all the world were sand'o
Oh then what should we lack'o,
If as they say there were no clay;
How should we take Tobacco?

If all our vessels ran'a,
If none but had a crack'a;
If Spanish Apes eate all the Grapes,
How should we do for Sack'a?

If Fryers had no bald pates,
Nor Nuns had no dark Cloysters;
If all the Seas were Beanes and Peas,
How should we do for Oysters?

If all the World were men,
And men lived all in trenches,
And there were none but we alone
How should we do for Wenches?

If there had been no projects,
Nor none that did great wrongs;
If Fiddlers shall turn Players all,
How should we do for songs?

If all things were eternal,
And nothing their end bringing;
If this should be, then how should we
Here make an end of singing?

RICHARD CORBETT
1582–1635

Nonsence

Like to the thund'ring tone of unspoke speeches,
Or like a lobster clad in logick breeches,
Or like the gray freeze of a crimson cat,
Or like a moon-calf in a slipshoo hat,
Or like a shadow when the sunne is gone,
Or like a thought that neere was thought upon,
   Even such is man, who never was begoten
   Untill his children were both dead and rotten.

Like to the fiery touchstone of a cabbage,
Or like a crablouse with his bagge and baggage,
Or like th' abortive issue of a fizle,
Or like the bagge-pudding of a plowmans whistle,
Or like the foure square circle of a ring,
Or like the singing of hey downe a ding,
   Even such is man, who, breathles without doubt,
   Spake to smal purpose when his tongue was out.

Like to the greene fresh fading withered rose,
Or like to rime or verse that runs in prose,
Or like the humbles of a tinder-box,
Or like a man that's sound, yet hath the poxe,
Or like a hobnaile coyn'd in single pence,
Or like the present preterperfect tense,
   Even such is man, who dy'd and then did laffe
   To see such strange lines writ on 's Epitaph.

A Non Sequitur

Marke how the Lanterns clowd mine eyes!
See where a moone drake ginnes to rise!
Saturne craules much like an *Iron Catt*
To see the naked moone in a slippshott hatt.
    Thunder-thumping toadstooles crock the pots
        To see the Meremaids tumble;
    Leather catt-a-mountaines shake their heeles
        To heare the gosh-hawke grumble.
           The rustic threed
           Begins to bleed,
        And cobwebs elbows itches;
           The putrid skyes
           Eat mulsacke pies,
        Backed up in logicke breches.

Munday trenchers make good hay,
    The Lobster weares no dagger;
Meale-mouth'd shee-peacockes powle the starres,
    And make the lowbell stagger.
        Blew Crocodiles foame in the toe,
        Blind meal-bagges do follow the doe;
        A ribb of apple-braine spice
        Will follow the Lancasheire dice.
Harke, how the chime of *Plutoes* pispot cracks,
To see the rainbowes wheele ganne, made of flax.

HENRY LAWES
1596–1662

Tavola – 'In quel gelato core'

In quel gelato core una voce; piagne
Madonna segl'occhi vostri a due voci; O
sempre e quando, tudi salvar mi cirche,
certe e scorno, misera non creda, ohi me
de lumi gia, macche squallido dalli pallida
labra; Cosi mia vita, a tre voci.

Table of Contents

In that icy heart one voice; My Lady weeps
if your eyes for two voices; O always and
when, you save me from some and scorn,
O wretch do not imagine . . . Ah! me, that your
eyes, with what pale lips that wan lover,
And so my life for three voices.

translated from the Italian by Peggy Forsyth

FRIEDRICH VON LOGAU
1604–55

A.E.I.O.U.

A ist derer, die nicht wollen
E ist derer, die nicht sollen.
I ist derer, die da zagen.
O ist derer, die da klagen.
U ist derer, die da plagen.

Translation

A is the one that won't.
E is the one that shan't.
I is the one who explains.
O is the one that complains.
U is the one that pains.

ANDREW MARVELL
1621–78

From *Upon Appleton House*

. . . .

Then, to conclude these pleasant acts,
Denton sets ope its cataracts,
And makes the meadow truly be
(What it but seemed before) a sea.
For, jealous of its Lord's long stay,
It tries t'invite him thus away.
The river in itself is drowned,
And isles the astonished cattle round.

Let others tell the paradox,
How eels now bellow in the ox;
How horses at their tails do kick,
Turned as they hang to leeches quick;
How boats can over bridges sail;
And fishes do the stables scale.
How salmons trespassing are found;
And pikes are taken in the pound.

. . . .

'Tis not, what once it was, the world,
But a rude heap together hurled,
All negligently overthrown,
Gulfs, deserts, precipices, stone.
Your lesser world contains the same,
But in more decent order tame;
You, heaven's centre, Nature's lap,
And paradise's only map.

But now the salmon-fishers moist
Their leathern boats begin to hoist,
And like Antipodes in shoes,
Have shod their heads in their canoes.
How tortoise-like, but not so slow,
These rational amphibii go!
Let's in: for the dark hemisphere
Does now like one of them appear.

ANONYMOUS

Tom Tell-Truth

All you that will not me believe, disprove it if you can;
You by my story may perceive I am an Honest Man.

        To the Tune of, *Tanta ra ra ra, Tantivee.*

I killed a man, and he was dead, *fa la la, la la la*;   (Repeat, *passim.*)
  I killed a man, and he was dead, and run to *St. Alban's* with a
      head: *Passim.*
    With a fa la, fa la la la, fa la la la la la la.

I asked him why he run so wild? He told me he got a maid [beguil'd].
And in his head there was a spring: a thousand great salmons about there
      did swim.

I saddled a mare and rid to *Whitehall*, and under the Gate-house she gave
      me a fall.
I lay in a swound three-and-twenty long year, and when I awak'd I was
      fill'd with fear.

The thing that did fright me I cannot express: I saw a man big as the
      Tower, no less.
This man with the Monument would run away, but at *Algate* Watch they
      did him stay.

I got up again and rid to *Hyde Park*, and made the old mare to sneeze [until
      dark].
Atop of *Paul's* steeple there did I see a delicate, dainty, fine Apple-Tree.

The Apples were ripe, and ready to fall, and kill'd seven hundred men on a
    stall.
The blood did run both to and fro, which caused seven water-mills for to
    go.

I see *Paul's* steeple run upon wheels, *fa la la, la la la*;
I see *Paul's* steeple run upon wheels and in the middle of all *Moor-fields*,
    With a fa la, fa la la la, fa la la la la la la.

ANONYMOUS

Ad Johannuelem Leporem, *Lepidissimum, Carmen Heroicum.*

I sing the furious battails of the Sphæres
Acted in eight and twenty fathom deep,
And from that time, reckon so many yeares
You'l find *Endimion* fell fast asleep.

And now assist me O ye Musiques nine
Tht tell the Orbs in order as they fight,
And thou dread *Atlas* with thine eyes so fine,
Smile on me now that first begin to write.

Pompey that once was Tapster of *New-Inne*,
And fought with *Cæsar* on th' *Æmathian* plaines,
First with his dreadfull *Myrmidons* came in
And let them blood in the Hepatick veines.

But then an *Antelope* in Sable blew,
Clad like the Prince of *Aurange* in his Cloke,
Studded with Satyres, on his Army drew,
And presently *Pheanders* Army broke.

Philip, for hardiness sirnamed *Chub*,
In Beauty equall to fork-bearing *Bacchus*,
Made such a thrust at *Phæbe*, with his Club,
That made the *Parthians* cry, she will becack us.

Which heard, the *Delphick* Oracle drew nigh,
To wipe fair *Phœbe*, if ought were amiss,
But *Heliotrope*, a little crafty spye,
Cry'd clouts were needless, for she did but piss

A subtle Gloworme lying in a hedge
And heard the story of sweet cheek't *Appollo*,
Snatch'd from bright *Styropes* his Antick sledge
And to the butter'd Flownders cry'd out, *Holla*.

Holla you pamper'd Jades, quoth he, look here,
And mounting straight upon a Lobsters thigh
An *English* man inflam'd with double Beere,
Swore nev'r to drink to Man, a Woman by.

By this time grew the conflict to be hot,
Boots against boots 'gainst Sandals, Sandals, fly.
Many poor thirsty men went to the pot,
Feathers lopt off, spurrs every where did lie.

Cætera desiderantur.

ANONYMOUS

A SEQUENCE OF BEDLAMITE SONGS

From the Hag and Hungry Goblin

From the hag and hungry goblin
That into rags would rend ye,
And the spirit that stands by the naked man,
In the Book of Moons defend ye,
That of your five sound senses,
You never be foresaken,
Nor wander from your selves with Tom,
Abroad to beg your bacon
    While I do sing any food, any feeding,
    Feeding, drink or clothing,
    Come Dame or Maid, be not afraid,
    Poor Tom will injure nothing.

Of thirty bare years have I
Twice twenty been enraged,
And of forty been three times fifteen
In durance soundly caged,
And the lordlie loftes of Bedlam
With stubble softe and dainty,
Brave braceletts strong, sweet whips, ding dong,
With wholesome hunger plenty,
 And now I sing, any food, any feeding etc.

With a thought I took for Maudlin
And a cruse of cockle pottage,
With a thing thus tall, sky bless you all,
I fell into this dotage.
I slept not since the Conquest,
Till then I never waked,
Till the roguish boy of love where I lay
Me found and stripped me naked.
 And now I sing, any food, any feeding, etc.

When I short have shorn my sow's face
And swigged my horny barrel,
In an oaken Inn I pound my skin
As a suit of gilt apparel.
The moon's my constant mistress
And the lonely owl my morrow,
The flaming drake and the nightcrow make
Me music to my sorrow.
 While I do sing, any food, any feeding etc.

The palsy plagues my pulses
When I prig your pigs or pullen,
Your culvers take, or matchless make
Your chanticlere or sullen.
When I want provant with Humfrey
I sup, and when benighted,
I repose in Paul's with waking souls,
Yet never am affrighted.
 But I do sing, any food, any feeding etc.

I know more than Apollo,
For ofte when he lies sleeping,
I see the stars at bloody wars
In the wounded welkin weeping;
The moon embrace her shepherd
And the Queen of Love her warrior,
While the first doth horn the Star of Morn
And the next the heavenly Farrier.
    While I do sing, any food, any feeding etc.

The Gipsy Snap and Pedro
Are none of Tom's comradoes,
The punk I scorn and the cutpurse sworn
And the roaring boy's bravados.
The meek, the white, the gentle,
Mee handle, touch and spare not,
But those that cross Tom Rhinoceros
Do what the Panther dare not.
    Although I sing, any food, any feeding etc.

With an host of furious fancies
Whereof I am commander,
With a burning spear, and a horse of air,
To the wilderness I wander.
By a knight of ghosts and shadows,
I summoned am to tourney,
Ten leagues beyond the wide world's end,
Me thinks it is no journey.
    Yet will I sing, any food, any feeding,
    Feeding, drink or clothing,
    Come Dame or Maid, be not afraid,
    Poor Tom will injure nothing.

Loving Mad Tom

I'll bark against the Dog-star,
And crow away the morning;
   I'll chase the moon
   Till it be noon,
And I'll make her leave her horning.
But I will find Bonny Maud, Merry Mad Maud,
   And seek what e'er betides her,
     Yet I will love
     Beneath or above,
   That dirty Earth that hides her.

I'll crack the Poles asunder,
   Strange things I will devise on.
I'll beat my brain against Charles's Wain,
   And I'll grasp the round horizon.
But I will find Bonny Maud, Merry Mad Maud etc.

I'll search the caves of Slumber,
   And please her in a night-dream;
I'll tumble her into Lawrence's fen,
   And hang myself in a sunbeam;
But I will find Bonny Maud, Merry Mad Maud etc.

I'll sail upon a millstone,
   And make the sea-gods wonder,
I'll plunge in the deep, till I wake asleep,
   And I'll tear the rocks in sunder.
But I will find Bonny Maud, Merry Mad Maud,
   And seek what e'er betides her,
     Yet I will love
     Beneath or above
   The dirty Earth that hides her.

Mad Maudlin is Come

From forth th' *Elisian* Fields,
    A place of restlesse souls,
Mad *Maulkin* is come, to seek her naked *Tom*;
    Hells fury she controuls:
    The damned laugh to see me,
    Grim *Pluto* scolds and frets,
Caron is glad to see poor *Maulkin* madd,
    And away his Boat he gets,
Through the Earth, through the Sea, through unknown I'les,
    Through the lofty Skies,
    I have sought with sobbs and cryes
For my hungrie mad *Tom*, and my Naked sad *Tom*,
Yet I know not whether he lives or dyes.

    My plaints make Satyrs civil,
    The Nymphs forget their singing,
The Fairies have left their Gamballs and their theft,
    The Plants and the Trees there Springing.

Mighty *Leviathan* took a Consumption,
    Triton broke his Organ;
    Neptune despis'd the Ocean,
    Floods did leave their flowing,
    Churlish Winds their blowing,
And all to see poor *Maudlins* Action;
    The Torrid Zone left Burning,
    The Deities stood a striving,
Despised *Jove* from *Juno* took a Glove
    And strook down *Pan* from Whistling.

    Mars for fear lay Couching,
    Apollo's cap was fir'd;
Poor *Charles's Wain* was thrown in the Main,
    The Nimble Post lay tir'd,
    Saturn, Silenus, Vulcan, Venus,
    All lay hushd and Drunk;

Hells fire through Heaven was seen,
Fates and Men remorseless
Hated our Grief and hoarsness,
And yet not one could tell of *Tom.*

Whither shall I wander,
Whither shall I fly?
The Heavens do weep, the Earth, the Air, and the deep
Are wearied with my Cry.
Let me up and steal the Trumpet
That Summons all to Doom,
At one poor blast the Elements shall cast,
All Creatures from their Womb.
Plato with his *Proserpine*, Death with Destruction,
Stormy Clouds and Weather,
Shall call all Souls together.
Against I find my *Tomken* I'le provide a Pumken,
And we will both be blithe together.

From the Top of High Caucasus

From the top of high *Caucasus*,
To *Pauls wharf* near the Tower,
In no great haste I easily past
In less than half an hour.
The Gates of old *Bizantium*
I took upon my shoulders,
And them I bore twelve Leagues and more
In spight of *Turks* and Soldiers
Sigh, sing, and sob, sing, sigh, and be merry,
Sighing, singing, and sobbing,
Thus naked *Tom* away doth run,
And fears no cold nor robbing.

From *Monsieur Tillies* Army
I took two hundred Bannors,
And brought them all to *London* Hall
In sight of all the Tannors;
I past *Parnassus* Ferry
By the hill call'd *Aganip,*
From thence on foot without shoo or boot

I past to the Isle of Ship,
    Sigh, sing, &c.

O're the *Piranean* Valley
'Twixt *Europe* and *St Giles*,
I walk't one night by Sun-shine light
Which fifteen thousand miles is.
I Landed at *White Chapel*
Next to Saint *Edmonds Berry*
From thence I stept while *Charon* slept,
And stole away his Ferry.
    Sigh, sing, &c.

One Summers day at *Shrovetide*
I met old *January*,
Being male content, with him I went
To weep o're old Canary.
The Man ith' Moon at *Pancrass*,
Doth yield us excellent Claret,
Having steel'd my nose, I sung old Rose,
Tush, greatness cannot carry it,
    Sigh, sing, &c.

I met the Turkish Sulton
At *Dover* near St *Georges*
His train and him did to *Callis* swim
Without ships, Boats, or barges.
I taught the King of *Egypt*
A trick to save his Cattle,
I'le Plough with dogs, and Harrow with Hogs,
You'd think it I do prattle,
    Sigh, sing, &c.

In a boat I went on dry Land
From *Carthage* to St *Albons*,
I saild to *Spain*, and back again
In a vessel made of Whalebones.
I met *Diana* hunting
With all her Nymphs attending,
In *Turnball* street with voices sweet
That honest place commending,
    Sigh, sing, &c.

[119]

Diogenes the Belman
Walkt with his Lanthorn duely,
Ith' term among the Lawyers throng
To find one that speaks truly,
The Sun and Moon eclipsed,
I very friendly parted,
And made the Sun away to run
For fear he should be Carted,
    Sigh, sing, *&c.*

Long time have I been studying,
My brains with fancies tearing,
How I might get old *Pauls* a hat,
And a Cross-cloth for old *Charing.*
Thus to give men and women
In cloaths full satisfaction,
These fruitless toyes robb'd me of joyes,
And keeps my brains in action,
    Sigh, sing, *&c.*

To Find my Tom of Bedlam

To find my Tom of Bedlam, ten thousand years I'll travel.
Mad Maudlin goes with dirty toes to save her shoes from gravel.
   Yet I will sing, Bonny boys, bonny mad boys, Bedlam Boys are
      bonny,
   They still go bare and live by the air, and want no drink or money.

I now repent that ever poor Tom was so disdained,
My wits are lost since I him crossed, which makes me go thus chained.
   Yet will I sing, Bonny boys etc.

My staff hath murdered giants, my bag a long knife carries,
To cut mince pies from children's thighs, with which I feast the fairies,
   Yet will I sing, Bonny boys etc.

My horn is made of thunder, I stole it out of Heaven,
The rainbow there is this I wear, for which I hence was driven.
   Yet will I sing, Bonny boys etc.

I went to Pluto's kitchen, to beg some food one morning,
And there I got souls piping hot, with which the spits were turning.
    Yet will I sing, Bonny boys etc.

Then I took up a cauldron, where boiled ten thousand harlots,
'Twas full of flame yet I drank the same, to the health of all such
      varlets.
    Yet will I sing, Bonny boys etc.

A Spirit as hot as lightning did in that journey guide me,
The sun did shake and the pale moon quake, as soon as e'er they spied
      me.
    Yet will I sing, Bonny boys etc.

And now that I have gotten a lease, than Doomsday longer,
To live on earth with some in mirth, ten whales shall feed my hunger.
    Yet will I sing, Bonny boys etc.

No gipsy, slut or doxy shall wind my mad Tom from me,
We'll weep all night, and with stars fight, the fray will well become me.
    Yet will I sing, Bonny boys, etc.

And when I have beaten the Man i'the Moon to powder,
His dog I'll take, and him I'll make as could no Daemon louder.
    Yet will I sing, Bonny boys, etc.

A health to Tom of Bedlam, go fill the seas in barrels,
I'll drink it all well brewed with gall, and Maudlin drunk I'll quarrel.
    Yet will I sing, Bonny boys, bonny mad boys, Bedlam Boys are
      bonny,
    They still go bare and live by the air, and want no drink nor money.

ANONYMOUS

A Messe of Nonsense

Upon a dark, light, gloomy, sunshine day,
As I in *August* walkt to gather *May*,
It was at noon neer ten a clock at night,
The Sun being set did shine exceeding bright,
I with mine eyes began to hear a noise,
And turn'd my Ears about to see the voice,
When from a cellar seven stories high,
With loud low voice *Melpomene* did cry,
What sober madness hath possest your brains,
And men of no place? shall your easie pains
Be thus rewarded? passing *Smithfield* bars,
Cast up thy blear-ey'd eyes down to the stars,
And see the Dragons head in Quartile move,
Now *Venus* is with *Mercury* in love:
Mars patient rages in a fustian fume,
And *Jove* will be reveng'd or quit the room:
Mild *Juno*, beauteous *Saturn*, *Martia* free,
At ten leagues distance now assembled be.
   Then shut your eyes and see bright *Iris* mount
Five hundred fathoms deep by just account,
And with a noble ignominious train
Pass flying to the place where *Mars* was slain:
Thus silently she spake, whilst I mine eyes
Fixt on the ground advanced to the skies.
And then not speaking any word reply'd
Our noble family is near ally'd
To that renowned peasant George a Green:
Stout *Wakefield* Pinner, he that stood between
Achilles and the fierce *Eacides*,
And them withstood with most laborious ease,
Yet whilst that *Boreas* and kind *Auster* lie
Together, and at once the same way flie;
And that unmoved wandring fixed star,
That bloody peace foretells, and patient War,
And scares the earth with fiery apparitions,
And plants in men both good and bad conditions;

I ever will with my weak able pen
Subscribe myself your Servant
Francis Ben.

JAMES CARKESSE
fl. 1679

His Petition to Mr Speaker

A man of Sense in Bedlam, I recount
Among our Grievances, a Tant-amount:
To rescue me, then Serjeant send at Arms:
The Circle in the Crown, Mad-Devil charms;
And Man in Moon, so sure his Bush at Back,
Must fall by Mace, as fire by Malaga Sack.

JOHN DRYDEN
1631–1700

From *Mac Flecknoe*

All humane things are subject to decay,
And, when Fate summons, Monarchs must obey:
This *Fleckno* found, who, like *Augustus*, young
Was call'd to Empire, and had govern'd long:
In Prose and Verse, was own'd, without dispute
Through all the Realms of *Non-sense*, absolute.
This aged Prince now flourishing in Peace,
And blest with issue of a large increase,
Worn out with business, did at length debate
To settle the succession of the State:
And pond'ring which of all his Sons was fit
To Reign, and wage immortal War with Wit;
Cry'd, 'tis resolv'd; for Nature pleads that He
Should onely rule, who most resembles me:
Shadwell alone my perfect image bears,
Mature in dullness from his tender years.

[123]

Shadwell alone, of all my Sons, is he
Who stands confirm'd in full stupidity.
The rest to some faint meaning make pretence,
But *Shadwell* never deviates into sense.
Some Beams of Wit on other souls may fall,
Strike through and make a lucid intervall;
But *Shadwell*'s genuine night admits no ray,
His rising Fogs prevail upon the Day:
Besides his goodly Fabrick fills the eye,
And seems design'd for thoughtless Majesty:
Thoughtless as Monarch Oakes, that shade the plain,
And, spread in solemn state, supinely reign.
Heywood and *Shirley* were but Types of thee,
Thou last great Prophet of Tautology:
Even I, a dunce of more renown than they,
Was sent before but to prepare thy way;
And coursly clad in *Norwich* Drugget came
To teach the nations in thy greater name.
My warbling Lute, the Lute I whilom strung
When to King *John* of *Portugal* I sung,
Was but the prelude to that glorious day,
When thou on silver *Thames* did'st cut thy way,
With well tim'd Oars before the Royal Barge,
Swell'd with the Pride of thy Celestial charge;
And big with Hymn, Commander of an Host,
The like was ne'er in *Epsom* Blankets tost.
Methinks I see the new *Arion* Sail,
The Lute still trembling underneath thy nail.
At thy well sharpned thumb from Shore to Shore
The Treble squeaks for fear, the Bases roar:
Echoes from *Pissing-Ally*, *Shadwell* call,
And *Shadwell* they resound from *Aston Hall*.
About thy boat the little Fishes throng,
As at the Morning Toast, that Floats along.
Sometimes as Prince of thy Harmonious band
Thou weild'st thy Papers in thy threshing hand.
St *Andre*'s feet ne'er kept more equal time,
Not ev'n the feet of thy own *Psyche*'s rhime:
Though they in number as in sense excell;
So just, so like tautology they fell,
That, pale with envy, *Singleton* forswore
The Lute and Sword which he in Triumph bore,

And vow'd he ne'er would act *Villerius* more.
Here stopt the good old *Syre*; and wept for joy
In silent raptures of the hopefull boy.
· · · · · · · · · · · · · · · · · · ·

    Now Empress *Fame* had publisht the Renown
Of *Shadwell*'s Coronation through the Town.
Rows'd by report of Fame, the Nations meet,
From near *Bun-Hill*, and distant *Watling-street*.
No *Persian* Carpets spread th' Imperial way,
But scatter'd Limbs of mangled Poets lay:
From dusty shops neglected Authors come,
Martyrs of Pies, and Reliques of the Bum.
Much *Heywood*, *Shirly*, *Ogleby* there lay,
But loads of *Shadwell* almost choakt the way.
Bilk't *Stationers* for Yeomen stood prepar'd,
And *Herringman* was Captain of the Guard.
The hoary Prince in Majesty appear'd,
High on a Throne of his own Labours rear'd.
At his right hand our young *Ascanius* sate
Rome's other hope, and pillar of the State.
His Brows thick fogs, instead of glories, grace,
And lambent dullness plaid arround his face.
As *Hannibal* did to the Altars come,
Sworn by his *Syre* a mortal Foe to *Rome*;
So *Shadwell* swore, nor should his Vow bee vain,
That he till Death true dullness would maintain;
And in his father's Right, and Realms defence,
Ne'er to have peace with Wit, nor truce with Sense.
The King himself the sacred Unction made,
As King by Office, and as Priest by Trade:
In his sinister hand, instead of Ball,
He plac'd a mighty Mug of potent Ale;
Love's Kingdom to his right he did convey,
At once his Sceptre and his rule of Sway;
Whose righteous Lore the Prince had practis'd young,
And from whose Loyns recorded *Psyche* sprung.
His Temples last with Poppies were o'erspread,
That nodding seem'd to consecrate his head:
Just as that point of time, if Fame not lye,
On his left hand twelve reverend *Owls* did fly.
So *Romulus*, 'tis sung, by *Tyber*'s *Brook*,
Presage of Sway from twice six Vultures took.

Th' admiring throng loud acclamations make,
And Omens of his future Empire take.
The *Syre* then shook the honours of his head,
And from his brows damps of oblivion shed
Full on the filial dullness: long he stood,
Repelling from his Breast the raging God;
At length burst out in this prophetick mood:
    Heavens bless my Son, from *Ireland* let him reign
To farr *Barbadoes* on the Western main;
Of his Dominion may no end be known,
And greater than his Father's be his Throne.
Beyond loves Kingdom let him stretch his Pen;
He paus'd, and all the people cry'd *Amen*.
Then thus, continu'd he, my Son advance
Still in new Impudence, new Ignorance.
Success let others teach, learn thou from me
Pangs without birth, and fruitless Industry.
Let *Virtuoso's* in five years be Writ;
Yet not one thought accuse thy toyl of wit.
. . . .

Nor let false friends seduce thy mind to fame,
By arrogating *Johnson*'s Hostile name.
Let Father *Fleckno* fire thy mind with praise,
And Uncle *Ogleby* thy envy raise.
Thou art my blood, where *Johnson* has no part;
What share have we in Nature or in Art?
Where did his wit on learning fix a brand,
And rail at Arts he did not understand?
Where made he love in Prince *Nicander*'s vein,
Or swept the dust in *Psyche*'s humble strain?
Where sold he Bargains, Whip-stitch, kiss my Arse,
Promis'd a Play and dwindled to a Farce?
When did his Muse from *Fletcher* scenes purloin,
As thou whole *Eth'ridg* dost transfuse to thine?
But so transfus'd as Oyl on Waters flow,
His always floats above, thine sinks below.
This is thy Province, this thy wondrous way,
New Humours to invent for each new Play:
This is that boasted Byas of thy mind,
By which one way, to dullness, 'tis inclin'd.
Which makes thy writings lean on one side still,
And in all changes that way bends thy will.

Nor let thy mountain belly make pretence
Of likeness; thine's a tympany of sense.
A Tun of Man in thy Large bulk is writ,
But sure thou'rt but a Kilderkin of wit.
Like mine thy gentle numbers feebly creep,
Thy Tragick Muse gives smiles, thy Comick sleep.
With whate'er gall thou sett'st thy self to write,
Thy inoffensive Satyrs never bite.
In thy fellonious heart, though Venom lies,
It does but touch thy *Irish* pen, and dyes.
Thy Genius calls thee not to purchase fame
In keen Iambicks, but mild Anagram:
Leave writing Plays, and chuse for thy command
Some peacefull Province in Acrostick Land.
There thou maist wings display and Altars raise,
And torture one poor word Ten thousand ways.
Or if thou would'st thy diff'rent talents suit,
Set thy own Songs, and sing them to thy lute.
He said, but his last words were scarcely heard,
For *Bruce* and *Longvil* had a *Trap* prepar'd,
And down they sent the yet declaiming Bard.
Sinking he left his Drugget robe behind,
Born upwards by a subterranean wind.
The Mantle fell to the young Prophet's part,
With double portion of his Father's Art.

ANONYMOUS
1705

Ignotum per Ignotius, or a Furious Hodge-Podge of Nonsense. A Pindaric

Or yield or die's the word, what could he mean,
   That tempted the corroborated scene?
      Though frying-pans to bite their nails,
Let fritters pass in ancient heraldry,
     And pudding boast its pedigree:
      When toads do fight with bankrupt quails,
Green cheese in embryo and lockram shirts
     Do poll for Knights o' the Shire,
     All buttoned down the skirts,
And quibble votes for the intoxicated year.

The semicircular excursions ran
   Forth to monopolise the three-legged can;
     When Justice Lickspit kembed his head,
Triumphant hieroglyphic thrummed the law,
     And spouting cataracts foresaw
     That magazines on bulks lay dead.
The scouring eggshells all besmeared with blood,
     Invelopèd in damned dry blows,
     Detached the sudorific mud,
And brewed a pair of stiff mustachios.

It galled the winching brush to hear them say
   That rigid southern hog-troughs danced the hay;
     Though porringers themselves do beat,
And flyblown crow, on vane of weathercock,
     Does threshing floors from hinges knock,
     And squeamish bellows loathe their meat.
Yet grinning oaks still show their butter-teeth,
     And fiery hogos from their sties
     Do limping legacies bequeath,
And jest upon their blind forefathers' eyes.

The Rum Mort's Praise of
her Faithless Maunder
1707

I

Now my kinching-cove is gone,
    By the rum-pad maundeth none,
Quarrons both for stump and bone,
    Like my clapperdogeon.

II

Dimber damber fare thee well,
    Palliards all thou didst excel,
And thy jockum bore the Bell,
    Glimmer on it never fell.

III

Thou the cramprings ne'er did scowre,
    Harmans had on thee no power,
Harmanbecks did never toure;
    For thee, the drawers still had loure.

IV

Duds and cheats thou oft hast won,
    Yet the cuffin quire couldst shun;
And the deuseaville didst run,
    Else the chates had thee undone.

V

Crank and dommerar thou couldst play,
    Or rum-maunder in one day,
And like an Abram-cove couldst pray,
    Yet pass with gybes well jerk'd away.

VI

When the darkmans have been wet,
    Thou the crackmans down didst beat
For glimmer, whilst a quaking cheat,
    Or tib-o'-th'-buttry was our meat.

VII

Red shanks then I could not lack,
 Ruff peck still hung on my Back,
Grannam ever fill'd my sack
 With lap and poplars held I tack.

VIII

To thy bugher and thy skew,
 Filch and gybes I bid adieu,
Though thy togeman was not new,
 In it the rogue to me was true.

The Maunder's Praise of his Strowling Mort

I

Doxy, oh! thy glaziers shine
 As glimmar; by the Salomon!
No gentry mort hath prats like thine,
 No cove e'er wap'd with such a one.

II

White thy fambles, red thy gan,
 And thy quarrons dainty is;
Couch a hogshead with me then,
 And in the darkmans clip and kiss.

III

What though I no togeman wear,
 Nor commission, mish, or slate;
Store of strammel we'll have here,
 And ith' skipper lib in state.

IV

Wapping thou I know does love,
Else the ruffin cly the mort;
From thy stampers then remove,
 Thy drawers, and let's prig in sport.

V

When the lightman up does call,
  Margery prater from her nest,
And her Cackling cheats withal,
  In a boozing ken we'll feast.

VI

There if lour we want; I'll mill
  A gage, or nip for thee a bung;
Rum booze thou shalt booze thy fill,
  And crash a grunting cheat that's young.

MATTHEW PRIOR
1664–1721

Bibo

AN EPIGRAM

When BIBO thought fit from the world to retreat,
As full of Champagne as an egg's full of meat,
He wak'd in the boat; and to CHARON he said,
He wou'd be row'd back, for he was not yet dead.
Trim the boat, and sit quiet, stern CHARON reply'd:
You may have forgot, you were drunk when you dy'd.

EDWARD WARD
1667–1731

The Extravagant Drunkard's Wish

Had I my wish, I would distend my guts
  As wide as from the north to southern skies,
And have at once as many mouths and throats
  As old Briareus arms, or Argos eyes.
The raging sea's unpalatable brine,
  That drowns so many thousands in a year,
I'd turn into an ocean of good wine,

And for my cup would choose the hemisphere;
Would then perform the wager Xanthus laid,
   In spite of all the river's flowing streams,
Swill till I pissed a deluge, then to bed,
   And please my thirsty soul with small-beer dreams.
Thus drink and sleep and, waking, swill again,
   Till I had drunk the sea-gods' cellar dry,
Then rob the niggard Neptune, and his train
   Of Tritons, of that wealth they now enjoy;
Kiss the whole Nerides and make the jades
   Sing all their charming songs to please my ear,
And whether flesh or fish, thornbacks or maids,
   I'd make the gypsies kind through love or fear.
And when thus wicked and thus wealthy grown,
   For nothing good, I'd turn rebellious Whig,
Pull ev'ry monarch headlong from his throne,
   And with the Prince of Darkness make a league,
That he and I, and all the Whigs beside,
   Might rend down churches, crowns in pieces tear,
Exert our malice, gratify our pride,
   And settle Satan's kingdom ev'rywhere.

JONATHAN SWIFT
1667–1745

I walk before no man (composed while asleep)

I walk before no man, a hawk in his fist;
Nor am I brilliant, whenever I list.

Anglo-Latin Verses

AS SONATA IN PRAES O MOLLI

Mollis abuti,
Has an acuti
No lasso finis;
Molli dii vinis
O mi de armistris,
Imi na Dis tres;
Cantu disco ver
Meas alo ver.

A LOVE SONG FROM DICK BETTESWORTH
TO MISS MOLLY WHITEWAY

Mi de armis molli,
Ure mel an colli,
It is a folli;
Fori alo ver,
A ram lingat Do ver,
Ure Dick mecum o ver.

AN EPIGRAM

A sui ne is abuti cum par ito Dic
A site offis fis it mite me cacat sic
Re diri no at es ter a quarto fine ale
Fora ringat his nos e an da stringat his tale.

A LOVE SONG

Apud in is almi des ire
Mimis tres Ine ver re qui re
Alo veri findit a gestis
His mi seri ne ver at restis.

'IN MY COMPANY'

In mi cum pani praedixit:
Claret finis ne ver mixit.
Cantu tellus Dicas tori;
Cingat super Tori rori.
Aleto claret adit basis;
Tosta Laedi, fieri faces.

A Riddling Letter

Sir,
Pray discruciate what follows:

A long-eared beast, and a field-house for cattle,
Among the coals does often rattle.
A long-eared beast, a bird that prates,
The bridegrooms' first gift to their mates,
Is by all pious Christians thought,
In clergymen the greatest fault.
A long-eared beast, and woman of Endor,
If your wife be a scold, that will mend her.
With a long-eared beast, and medicines use,
Cooks make their fowl look tight and spruce.
A long-eared beast and holy fable,
Strengthens the shoes of half the rabble.
A long-eared beast, and Rhenish wine,
Lies in the lap of ladies fine.
A long-eared beast and Flanders college,
Is Dr Tisdall to my knowledge.
A long-eared beast, and building knight;
Censorious people do in spite.
A long-eared beast, and bird of night,
We sinners are too apt to slight.
A long-eared beast, and shameful vermin,
A judge will eat, though clad in ermine.
A long-eared beast, and Irish cart,
Can leave a mark and give a smart.
A long-eared beast, in mud to lie,
No bird in air so swift can fly.
A long-eared beast, and a sputtering old Whig,
I wish he were in it dancing a jig.
A long-eared beast, and liquor to write,
Is a damnable smell both morning and night.
A long-eared beast, and the child of a sheep,
At whist they will make a desperate sweep.
A beast long-eared, and till midnight you stay,
Will cover a house much better than clay.
A long-eared beast, and the drink you love best
You call him a sloven in earnest or jest.

[134]

A long-eared beast, and the sixteenth letter,
I'd not look at all, unless I looked better.
    A long-eared beast give me, and eggs unsound,
Or else I will not ride one inch of ground.
    A long-eared beast, another name for jeer,
To ladies' skins there's nothing comes so near.
    A long-eared beast, and kind noise of a cat,
Is useful in journeys, take notice of that.
    A long-eared beast, and what seasons your beef,
On such an occasion the law gives relief.
    A long-eared beast, the thing that force must drive in,
Bears up his house, that's of his own contriving.

Behold! A Proof of Irish Sense!

Behold! a proof of Irish sense!
    Here Irish wit is seen!
When nothing's left, that's worth defence,
    We build a magazine.

A Cantata

In harmony would you excel,
Suit your words to music well, music well,
Suit your words to your music well,
Suit your words to music well,
For Pegasus runs, runs every race
By gal-lal-lal-lal-laloping high, or level pace,
Or ambling or sweet Canterbury,
Or with a down, a high down derry.
No, no victory, victory he ever got,
By jo-o-o-o-ogling, jo-o-o-o-ogling trot.
No muse harmonious entertains,
Rough roistering, rustic, roar-oar-oaring strains,
Nor shall you twine the cra-a-a-ackling, crackling bays,
By sneaking, snivelling rou-ou-oun-oundelays.

Now slowly move your fiddle stick,
Now, tantantantantantantivi,
Now tantantantantantivi quick, quick.

Now trembling, shivering, quivering, quaking,
Set hoping, hoping, hoping hearts of lovers aching,
Fly, fly-y-y-y
Above the sky,
Rambling, gambolling, ra-a-a-a-a-ambling, gambolling,
Trolloping, lolloping, galloping,
Trolloping, lolloping, galloping, trollop,
Lolloping, trolloping, galloping,
Lolloping, trolloping, galloping, lollop,
Now cree-ee-eep, sweep, sweep, sweep the deep,
See, see, Celia, Celia dies,
Dies, dies, dies, dies, dies, dies, dies,
While true lovers' eyes
Weeping sleep,
Sleeping weep,
Weeping sleep.
Bo peep, bo peep, bo peep,
Bo peep, peep, bo bo peep.

JOHN GAY

1685–1732

A New Song of New Similies

My passion is as mustard strong;
    I sit all sober sad;
Drunk as a piper all day long,
    Or like a March-hare mad.

Round as a hoop the bumpers flow;
    I drink, yet can't forget her;
For, though as drunk as David's sow,
    I love her still the better.

Pert as a pear-monger I'd be,
    If Molly were but kind;
Cool as a cucumber could see
    The rest of womankind.

Like a stuck pig I gaping stare,
    And eye her o'er and o'er;
Lean as a rake with sighs and care,
    Sleek as a mouse before.

Plump as a partridge was I known,
    And soft as silk my skin,
My cheeks as fat as butter grown;
    But as a groat now thin!

I, melancholy as a cat,
    And kept awake to weep;
But she, insensible of that,
    Sound as a top can sleep.

Hard is her heart as flint or stone,
    She laughs to see me pale;
And merry as a grig is grown,
    And brisk as bottled ale.

The God of Love at her approach
    Is busy as a bee;
Hearts, sound as any bell or roach,
    Are smit and sigh like me.

Ay me! as thick as hops or hail,
    The fine men crowd about her;
But soon as dead as a door nail
    Shall I be, if without her.

Straight as my leg her shape appears;
    O were we join'd together!
My heart would be scot-free from cares,
    And lighter than a feather.

As fine as fivepence is her mien,
    No drum was ever tighter;
Her glance is as the razor keen,
    And not the sun is brighter.

As soft as pap her kisses are,
    Methinks I taste them yet;

Brown as a berry is her hair,
    Her eyes as black as jet:

As smooth as glass, as white as curds,
    Her pretty hand invites;
Sharp as a needle are her words;
    Her wit, like pepper, bites:

Brisk as a body-louse she trips,
    Clean as a penny dress;
Sweet as a rose her breath and lips,
    Round as the globe her breast.

Full as an egg was I with glee;
    And happy as a king.
Good Lord! how all men envy'd me!
    She lov'd like any thing.

But false as hell! she, like the wind,
    Chang'd, as her sex must do;
Though seeming as the turtle kind,
    And like the gospel true.

If I and Molly could agree,
    Let who would take Peru!
Great as an emperor should I be,
    And richer than a Jew.

Till you grow tender as a chick,
    I'm dull as any post;
Let us, like burs, together stick,
    And warm as any toast.

You'll know me truer than a dye;
    And wish me better speed;
Flat as a flounder when I lie,
    And as a herring dead.

Sure as a gun, she'll drop a tear,
    And sigh, perhaps, and wish,
When I am rotten as a pear,
    And mute as any fish.

HENRY CAREY
1687?–1743

from *Namby-Pamby: or, A Panegyric on the New Versification (1725)*

Naughty-paughty Jack-a-Dandy,
Stole a piece of sugar candy
From the grocer's shoppy-shop,
And away did hoppy-hop.

All ye poets of the age,
All ye witlings of the stage,
Learn your jingles to reform,
Crop your numbers and conform.
Let your little verses flow
Gently, sweetly, row by row;
Let the verse the subject fit,
Little subject, little wit.
Namby-Pamby is your guide,
Albion's joy, Hibernia's pride.
Namby-Pamby Pilly-piss,
Rhimy pimed on Missy-Miss;
Tartaretta Tartaree,
From the navel to the knee;
That her father's gracy-grace
Might give him a placy-place.
He no longer writes of Mammy
Andromache and her lammy,
Hanging-panging at the breast
Of a matron most distressed.
Now the venal poet sings
Baby clouts and baby things,
Baby dolls and baby houses,
Little misses, little spouses,
Little playthings, little toys,
Little girls and little boys.
As an actor does his part,
So the nurses get by heart

[139]

Namby-Pamby's little rhymes,
Little jingle, little chimes,
To repeat to little miss,
Piddling ponds of pissy-piss;
Cacking-packing like a lady,
Or bye-bying in the crady.
Namby-Pamby ne'er will die
While the nurse sings lullaby.
Namby-Pamby's doubly mild,
Once a man, and twice a child;
To his hanging-sleeves restored,
Now he foots it like a lord;
Now he pumps his little wits,
Sh—ing writes, and writing sh—ts,
All by little tiny bits.
Now methinks I hear him say,
Boys and girls, come out to play!
Moon does shine as bright as day . . .

Roger and Dolly

Young Roger came tapping at Dolly's window,
    Tumpaty, tumpaty, tump.
He begged for admittance, she answered him, 'No',
    Glumpaty, glumpaty, glump.
'My Dolly, my dear, your true love is here',
    Dumpaty, dumpaty, dump.
'No, Roger, no, as you came you may go',
    Clumpaty, clumpaty, clump.

'O what is the reason, dear Dolly,' he cried,
    Pumpaty, pumpaty, pump.
'That thus I'm cast off and unkindly denied?'
    Frumpaty, frumpaty, frump.
'Some rival more dear I guess has been here',
    Crumpaty, crumpaty, crump.
'Suppose there's been two; pray, sir, what's that to you?'
    Numpaty, numpaty, nump.

O then with a sigh a sad farewell he took,
    Lumpaty, lumpaty, lump.

And all in despair he leaped into the brook,
  Flumpaty, flumpaty, flump.
His courage it cooled, he found himself fooled,
  Trumpaty, trumpaty, trump.
He swam to the shore and saw Dolly no more,
  Rumpaty, rumpaty, rump.

And then she recalled and recalled him again,
  Humpaty, humpaty, hump.
But he like a madman ran over the plain,
  Stumpaty, stumpaty, stump.
Determined to find a damsel more kind,
  Plumpaty, plumpaty, plump.
While Dolly's afraid she shall die an old maid,
  Mumpaty, mumpaty, mump.

ALEXANDER POPE
1688–1744

From *The Dunciad*

BOOK THE FIRST

Books and the Man I sing, the first who brings
The Smithfield Muses to the Ear of Kings.
Say great Patricians! (since your selves inspire
These wond'rous works; so Jove and Fate require)
Say from what cause, in vain decry'd and curst,
Still Dunce the second reigns like Dunce the first?
  In eldest time, e'er mortals writ or read,
E'er Pallas issued from the Thund'rer's head,
Dulnes o'er all possess'd her antient right,
Daughter of Chaos and eternal Night:
Fate in their dotage this fair idiot gave,
Gross as her sire, and as her mother grave,
Laborious, heavy, busy, bold, and blind,
She rul'd, in native Anarchy, the mind.
  Still her old empire to confirm, she tries,
For born a Goddess, Dulness never dies.
  O thou! whatever Title please thine ear,
Dean, Drapier, Bickerstaff, or Gulliver!
Whether thou chuse Cervantes' serious air,

Or laugh and shake in Rab'lais' easy Chair,
Or praise the Court, or magnify Mankind,
Or thy griev'd Country's copper chains unbind;
From thy Bæotia tho' Her Pow'r retires,
Grieve not at ought our sister realm acquires:
Here pleas'd behold her mighty wings out-spread,
To hatch a new Saturnian age of Lead.

Where wave the tatter'd ensigns of Rag-Fair,
A yawning ruin hangs and nods in air;
Keen, hollow winds howl thro' the bleak recess,
Emblem of Music caus'd by Emptiness:
Here in one bed two shiv'ring sisters lye,
The cave of Poverty and Poetry.
This, the Great Mother dearer held than all
The clubs of Quidnunc's, or her own Guild-hall.
Here stood her Opium, here she nurs'd her Owls,
And destin'd here th' imperial seat of Fools.
Hence springs each weekly Muse, the living boast
Of Curl's chaste press, and Lintot's rubric post,
Hence hymning Tyburn's elegiac lay,
Hence the soft sing-song on Cecilia's day,
Sepulchral lyes our holy walls to grace,
And New-year Odes, and all the Grubstreet race.

'Twas here in clouded majesty she shone;
Four guardian Virtues, round, support her Throne;
Fierce champion Fortitude, that knows no fears
Of hisses, blows, or want, or loss of ears:
Calm Temperance, whose blessings those partake
Who hunger, and who thirst, for scribling sake:
Prudence, whose glass presents th' approaching jayl:
Poetic Justice, with her lifted scale;
Where in nice balance, truth with gold she weighs,
And solid pudding against empty praise.

Here she beholds the Chaos dark and deep,
Where nameless somethings in their causes sleep,
'Till genial Jacob, or a warm Third-day
Call forth each mass, a poem or a play.
How Hints, like spawn, scarce quick in embryo lie,
How new-born Nonsense first is taught to cry,
Maggots half-form'd, in rhyme exactly meet,
And learn to crawl upon poetic feet.
Here one poor Word a hundred clenches makes,

And ductile dulness new meanders takes;
There motley Images her fancy strike,
Figures ill'pair'd, and Similes unlike.
She sees a Mob of Metaphors advance,
Pleas'd with the Madness of the mazy dance:
How Tragedy and Comedy embrace;
How Farce and Epic get a jumbled race;
How Time himself stands still at her command,
Realms shift their place, and Ocean turns to land.
Here gay description Ægypt glads with showers;
Or gives to Zembla fruits, to Barca flowers;
Glitt'ring with ice here hoary hills are seen,
There painted vallies of eternal green,
On cold December fragrant chaplets blow,
And heavy harvests nod beneath the snow.
    All these and more, the cloud-compelling Queen
Beholds thro' fogs that magnify the scene:
She, tinsel'd o'er in robes of varying hues,
With self-applause her wild creation views,
Sees momentary monsters rise and fall,
And with her own fool's colours gilds them all.

SAMUEL JOHNSON

1709–84

I put my hat upon my head

I put my hat upon my head
    And walk'd into the Strand,
And there I met another man
    Whose hat was in his hand

The tender infant, meek and mild

The tender infant, meek and mild,
    Fell down upon the stone;
The nurse took up the squealing child,
    But still the child squealed on.

I am Cassander come down from the sky

I am Cassander come down from the Sky,
To tell each Bystander – what none can deny
That I am Cassander come down from the sky.

If the man who Turneps cries

If the man who Turneps cries
Cry not when his Father dies;
'Tis a sign that he had rather
Have a Turnep than a Father.

A Song composed for Fanny Burney

She shall sing me a song,
Of two Days long
The woodcock and the sparrow;
Our little Dog has bit his Tail
And he'll be hanged to-morrow.

ANONYMOUS

Rhymes from *Tommy Thumb's Pretty Song Book* (c.1744)

Sing a Song of Sixpence

Sing a Song of Sixpence,
A bag full of Rye,
Four and twenty
Naughty boys,
Bak'd in a Pye.

When the pie was opened,
The birds began to sing;
Was not that a dainty dish,
To set before the king?

The king was in his counting-house,
Counting out his money;
The queen was in the parlor,
Eating bread and honey.

The maid was in the garden,
Hanging out the clothes,
There came a little blackbird,
And snapped off her nose.

There was an Old Woman

There was an Old Woman
Liv'd under a Hill,
And if she isn't gone,
She lives there still.

When I was a little boy

When I was a little boy,
I wash'd my
Mother's Dishes.
I put my finger in my
Ear, and pull'd out
Little fishes.

My Mother call'd me
Good boy,
And bid me pull out more,
I put my Finger
In my Ear,
And pull'd out fourscore.

Cock Robin

Who did kill Cock Robbin?
I, said the Sparrow,
With my bow & Arrow,
And I did kill Cock Robbin.

Who did see him die?
I, said the Fly,
With my little Eye,
And I did see him die.

And who did catch his blood?
I, said the Beetle,
With my little Dish,
And I did catch his blood.

And who did make his shroud?
I, said the Fish,
With my little Needle,
And I did make his shroud.

Who'll dig his grave?
I, said the Owl,
With my pick and shovel,
I'll dig his grave.

Who'll be the parson?
I, said the Rook,
With my little book,
I'll be the parson.

Who'll be the clerk?
I, said the Lark,
If it's not in the dark,
I'll be the clerk.

Who'll carry the link?
I, said the Linnet,
I'll fetch it in a minute,
I'll carry the link.

Who'll be chief mourner?
I, said the Dove,
I mourn for my love,
I'll be chief mourner.

Who'll carry the coffin?
I, said the Kite,
If it's not through the night,
I'll carry the coffin.

Who'll bear the pall?
We, said the Wren,
Both the cock and the hen,
We'll bear the pall.

Who'll sing a psalm?
I, said the Thrush,
As she sat on a bush,
I'll sing a psalm.

Who'll toll the bell?
I, said the Bull,
Because I can pull,
I'll toll the bell.

All the birds of the air
Fell a-sighing and a-sobbing,
When they heard the bell toll
For poor Cock Robbin.

There was a Mad Man

There was a Mad Man,
And he had a Mad Wife,
And they lived in a Mad town,
They had three Children
All at a Birth,
And they were Mad
Every One.

The Father was Mad,
The Mother was Mad,
The Children all Mad besides,
And they all got
Upon a Mad Horse,
And Madly they did ride.

They rode by night and they rode by day,
Yet never a one of them fell,
They rode so madly all the way,
Till they came to the gates of hell.

Old Nick was glad to see them so mad,
And gladly let them in:
But he soon grew sorry to see him so merry,
And let them out again.

There was a Man so Wise

There was a Man so Wise,
He jumpt into
A Bramble Bush,
And scratcht out both his eyes.
And when he saw,
His Eyes were out,
And reason to Complain,
He jumpt into a Quickset Hedge,
And Scracht them in again.

London Bridge

London Bridge is broken down,
        Dance o'er my lady lee,
London Bridge is broken down,
        With a gay lady.

How shall we build it up again?
        Dance o'er my lady lee,
How shall we build it up again?
        With a gay lady.

Build it up with silver and gold,
 Dance o'er my lady lee,
Build it up with silver and gold,
 With a gay lady.

Silver and gold will be stole away,
 Dance o'er my lady lee,
Silver and gold will be stole away,
 With a gay lady.

Build it up with iron and steel,
 Dance o'er my lady lee,
Build it up with iron and steel,
 With a gay lady.

Iron and steel will bend and bow,
 Dance o'er my lady lee,
Iron and steel will bend and bow,
 With a gay lady.

Build it up with wood and clay,
 Dance o'er my lady lee,
Build it up with wood and clay,
 With a gay lady.

Wood and clay will wash away,
 Dance o'er my lady lee,
Wood and clay will wash away,
 With a gay lady.

Build it up with stone so strong,
 Dance o'er my lady lee,
Huzza! 'twill last for ages long,
 With a gay lady.

London Bells

Gay go up, and gay go down,
To ring the bells of London town.

Bull's eyes and targets,
Say the bells of St Marg'ret's.

Brickbats and tiles,
Say the bells of St Giles'.

Halfpence and farthings
Say the bells of St Martin's.

Oranges and lemons,
Say the bells of St Clement's.

Pancakes and fritters,
Say the bells of St Peter's.

Two sticks and an apple,
Say the bells at Whitechapel.

Old Father Baldpate,
Say the slow bells at Aldgate.

Maids in white aprons,
Say the bells of St Cath'rine's.

Pokers and tongs,
Say the bells at St John's.

Kettles and pans,
Say the bells at St Ann's.

You owe me ten shillings,
Say the bells at St Helen's.

When will you pay me?
Say the bells at Old Bailey.

When I grow rich,
Say the bells at Fleetditch.

When will that be?
Say the bells at Stepney.

I am sure I don't know,
Says the great bell at Bow.

When I am old,
Say the bells at St Paul's.

Here comes a candle to light you to bed,
And here comes a chopper to chop off your head.

ANONYMOUS

A Man in the Wilderness asked of me,
How many red Strawberries growed in the sea?
I answered him again as well as I could,
So many red herrings as swimmed in the wood.

ANONYMOUS

The Oath of the Canting Crew

1749

I, Crank Cuffin, swear to be
True to this fraternity;
That I will in all obey
Rule and order of the lay.
Never blow the gab or squeak;
Never snitch to bum or beak;
But religiously maintain
Authority of those who reign
Over Stop Hole Abbey green,
Be their tawny king, or queen.
In their cause alone will fight;

Think what they think, wrong or right;
Serve them truly, and no other,
And be faithful to my brother;
Suffer none, from far or near,
With their rights to interfere;
No strange Abram, ruffler crack,
Hooker of another pack,
Rogue or rascal, frater, maunderer,
Irish toyle, or other wanderer;
No dimber, dambler, angler, dancer,
Prig of cackler, prig of prancer;
No swigman, swaddler, clapper-dudgeon;
Cadge-gloak, curtal, or curmudgeon;
No whip-jack, palliard, patrico;
No jarkman, be he high or low;
No dummerar, or romany;
No member of *the family*;
No ballad-basket, bouncing buffer,
Nor any other, will I suffer;
But stall-off now and for ever
All outtiers whatsoever;
And as I keep to the foregone,
So may help me Salamon!

JEAN-JOSEPH VADÉ
1719–1757

Three Amphigouris

I

AIR: *Du Menuet d'Exaudet.*

Alaric
A Dantzic
Vit Pégase
Qui jouait avec Brébeuf
Au volant dans un œuf
Au pied du Mont Caucase,
Sûr du fait,

Dom Japhet
Court chez Pline,
Et puis s'en va de Goa
Boire à Guipuscoa
Chopine;
Mais la reine Cléopàtre
Faisait cuire dans son âtre
Un marron
Que Baron
Jette aux Poules,
Dans le temps que Jézabel
Mangeait en Israël
Des moules.
Alors Job
Chez Jacob
Prit un masque,
Et s'en fut à Loyola
Chanter Alleluia
Sur un tambour de basque.
Phaëton,
Au toton,
Fut la dupe,
En jouant contre Psyché
Qui perdit au marché
Sa jupe.

Translation

Alaric
At Danzig
Saw Pegasus
Playing with Long Meg
Flying in an egg
At the foot of the Caucasus.
Assured of it
Dom Japhet
Ran to Pliny,
And thence to Goa
To drink at Guipuscoa
Pink gin;
But Queen Cleopatra

[153]

In a culinary disaster
  Cooked *marron*
  That the Baron
  Flung to the *Poules*
At the time when Jezebel
Was eating in Israel
  Some *moules.*
  Then Job
  Chez Jacob
  Took a mask
And went off to Loyola
To sing Halleluia
On a drum from *le pays Basque.*
  Phaeton
  At teetotum
  Was made a dupe,
While playing against Psyche;
Then riding her bike she
  Lost her *jupe.*

II

Sur le même air que le précédent.

  Sarpédon,
  Coridon
  Et Boccace
S'entretenaient tous les trois
  Une veille des Rois
  Sur la Grâce Efficace;
  Quand Platon
  Suit Milton
  En Alsace
Pour y barder un dindon
Dont leur avait fait don
  Ignace;
Mais que leur veut Artémise
Sur la porte d'une Église?
  Elle entend
  Et prétend
  Qu'on la frise.
Pour honorer son époux,
Que Goliath à genoux

Lui dise:
Si Glaucus
Aux Cocus
Fait la nique,
Prenez vous-en à Hector
Qui perdit son castor
Dans le conseil aulique;
C'est à tort
Que Nestor
Le critique,
Car sur le champ Ménélas
M'en écrivit sur l'as
De pique.

III

Sur le même air que le précédent.

Josaphat
Est un fat
Très-aride,
Qui croit être fort savant
Parce qu'il va souvent
Sous la Zone Torride,
Critiquant
Et piquant
Agrippine,
Pour avoir fait lire à Prau
Les ouvrages de Pro-
Serpine.
Si le Public lui pardonne
Tous les travers qu'il se donne,
Il faut donc
Que Didon
Ait pour elle
Le droit d'aller dans le parc
Qu'on destinait à Marc-
Aurèle:
En ce cas
Le fracas
D'abord cesse,
Chacun pourra sans respect
Persister à l'aspect

D'une auguste Princesse,
     Et malgré
      Le congré,
     Ariane
Pourra vendre au plus offrant
Une tourte de fran-
      Chipanne.

ANONYMOUS

This is the House that Jack Built

This is the farmer sowing his corn,
That kept the cock that crowed in the morn,
That waked the priest all shaven and shorn,
That married the man all tattered and torn,
That kissed the maiden all forlorn,
That milked the cow with the crumpled horn,
That tossed the dog,
That worried the cat,
That killed the rat,
That ate the malt
That lay in the house that Jack built.

ANONYMOUS

From *Mother Goose's Melody*:
or *Sonnets for the Cradle c.* 1765

A Dirge

Little Betty Winckle she had a pig,
It was a little pig not very big;
When he was alive he liv'd in clover,
But now he's dead and that's all over;
Johnny Winckle he

Sat down and cry'd,
Betty Winckle she
Laid down and dy'd;
So there was an end of one, two, and three,
Johnny Winckle he,
Betty Winckle she,
And Piggy Wiggie.

A dirge is a song made for the dead; but whether this was made for Betty Winckle or her pig, is uncertain; no notice being taken of it by Camden, or any of the famous antiquarians. WALL's System of Sense

Three Wise Men of Gotham

Three wise men of Gotham,
They went to sea in a bowl,
And if the bowl had been stronger,
My song had been longer.

It is long enough. Never lament the loss of what is not worth having. BOYLE

Great A, Little A

Great A, little A
 Bouncing B;
The cat's in the cupboard,
 And she can't see.

Yes, she can see that you are naughty, and don't mind your book.

See-saw Sacaradown

See-saw, sacaradown,
Which is the way to London town?
One foot up, the other foot down,
That is the way to London town.

Or to any other town upon the face of the earth. WICKLIFFE

High Diddle Diddle

High diddle diddle,
The cat and the fiddle,
   The cow jump'd over the moon;
The little dog laugh'd
To see such craft,
   And the dish ran away with the spoon.

It must be a little dog that laughed, for a great dog would be ashamed to laugh at such nonsense.

Jack and Jill

Jack and Jill
Went up the hill,
   To fetch a pail of water;
Jack fell down
And broke his crown,
   And Jill came tumbling after.

The more you think of dying, the better you will live. MAXIM

Aristotle's Story

There were two birds sat on a stone,
   Fa, la, la, la, lal, de;
One flew away, and then there was one,
   Fa, la, la, la, lal, de;
The other flew after,
And then there was none,
   Fa, la, la, la, lal, de;
And so the poor stone
Was left all alone,
   Fa, la, la, la, lal, de.

This may serve as a chapter of consequence in the next new book of logic. SAWMILL'S Reports

Alexander's Song

There was a man of Thessaly,
   And he was wondrous wise,
He jump'd into a quick-set hedge,
   And scratch'd out both his eyes:
And when he saw his eyes were out,
   With all his might and main
He jump'd into another hedge,
   And scratch'd them in again.

How happy it was for the man to scratch his eyes in again, when they were scratched out! But he was a blockhead or he would have kept himself out of the hedge, and not been scratched at all. WISEMAN's New Way to Wisdom

SAMUEL FOOTE

1720–77

The Great Panjandrum

So she went into the garden
to cut a cabbage-leaf
to make an apple-pie;
and at the same time
a great she-bear, coming down the street,
pops its head into the shop.
What! no soap?
     So he died,
and she very imprudently married the Barber:
and there were present
the Picninnies,
     and the Joblillies,
       and the Garyulies,
and the great Panjandrum himself,
with the little round button at top;
and they all fell to playing the game of catch-as-catch-can,
till the gunpowder ran out at the heels of their boots.

CHRISTOPHER SMART
1722–71

Verses Written in a London Churchyard

Maria now I'll cease to sing,
And all the op'ning sweets of spring:
The *Chop-house* in my verse shall ring,
　　Where lives my lovely *Jenny*.

Where antient cooks exert their art;
No youthful damsel bears a part:
Yet one has broil'd my very heart,
　　And that was lovely *Jenny*.

Brown as the walnut is her hair,
Her skin is like the napkin fair,
More blooming than red cabbage, are
　　The cheeks of lovely *Jenny*.

Each sav'ry dish to cit and fop
She bears, herself a nicer chop;
How far more elegant, to sop,
　　And feast on lovely *Jenny*.

More tempting than the smoaking stake,
Or sweetest tart her fingers make!
I'd lose my dinner for the sake
　　Of tasting lovely *Jenny*.

But when I pay for stake or tart,
I act a very miser's part;
At once the money and my heart,
　　I give to lovely *Jenny*.

Let *Jove* his fam'd ambrosia eat,
And youthful *Hebe* ever wait;
I envy not his joy or state,
　　While serv'd by lovely *Jenny*.

While *British* herrings *Britons* love,
Or city throats with custard move;
While nectar pleases mighty *Jove*,
   So long shall I love *Jenny*.

And when at length the beauty dies,
Oh! cut her into little pies!
Like jelly-stars she'll grace the skies,
   So bright is lovely *Jenny*.

St Clement's Church-yard, May 1, 1751

Reflections on Sounds and Language from *Jubilate Agno*

For the power of some animal is predominant in every language.

For the power and spirit of a CAT is in the Greek.

For the sound of a cat is in the most useful preposition κατ' ευχην.

For the pleasantry of a cat at pranks is in the language ten thousand times over.

For JACK UPON PRANCK is in the performance of περι together or separate.

For Clapperclaw is in the grappling of the words upon one another in all the modes of versification.

For the sleekness of a Cat in his αγλαιηφι.

For the Greek is thrown from heaven and falls upon its feet.

For the Greek when distracted from the line is sooner restored to rank and rallied into some form than any other.

For the purring of a Cat is his τρυζει.

For his cry is in ουαι, which I am sorry for.

For the Mouse (Mus) prevails in the Latin.

For Edi-mus, bibi-mus, vivi-mus – ore-mus.

For the Mouse is a creature of great personal valour.

For – this is a true case – Cat takes female mouse from the company of male – male mouse will not depart, but stands threatning and daring.

For this is as much as to challenge, if you will let her go, I will engage you, as prodigious a creature as you are.

For the Mouse is of an hospitable disposition.

For bravery and hospitality were said and done by the Romans rather than others.

For two creatures the Bull and the Dog prevail in the English.

For all the words ending in -ble are in the creature. Invisi-ble,
Incomprehensi-ble, ineffa-ble, A-ble.

For the Greek and Latin are not dead languages, but taken up and
accepted for the sake of him that spake them.

For can is (canis) is cause and effect a dog.

For the English is concise and strong. Dog and Bull again.

For Newton's notion of colours is αλογος unphilosophical.

For the colours are spiritual.

For God has given us a language of monosyllables to prevent our
clipping.

For a toad enjoys a finer prospect than another creature to compensate his
lack.

> Tho' toad I am the object of man's hate.
> Yet better am I than a reprobate.   (who has the worst of
> prospects).

For there are stones, whose constituent particles are little toads.

For the spiritual musick is as follows.

For there is the thunder-stop, which is the voice of God direct.

For the rest of the stops are by their rhimes.

For the trumpet rhimes are sound bound, soar more and the like.

For the Shawm rhimes are lawn fawn moon boon and the like.

For the harp rhimes are sing ring string and the like.

For the cymbal rhimes are bell well toll soul and the like.

For the flute rhimes are tooth youth suit mute and the like.

For the dulcimer rhimes are grace place beat heat and the like.

For the Clarinet rhimes are clean seen and the like.

For the Bassoon rhimes are pass, class and the like. God be gracious to
Baumgarden.

For the dulcimer are rather van fan and the like and grace place &c are of
the bassoon.

For beat heat, weep peep &c are of the pipe.

For every word has its marrow in the English tongue for order and for
delight.

Rhymes from *Gammer Gurton's Garland or the Nursery Parnassus* 1784

Kitty Alone

Quoth he, Miss Mouse, I'm come to thee,
   Kitty alone, Kitty alone,
Quoth he, Miss Mouse, I'm come to thee,
   Kitty alone and I.
Quoth he, Miss Mouse, I'm come to thee,
To see if thou can fancy me,
   Cock me cary, Kitty alone,
   Kitty alone and I.

Quoth she, answer I'll give you none,
   Kitty alone, Kitty alone,
Quoth she, answer I'll give you none,
   Kitty alone and I.
Quoth she, answer I'll give you none,
Until my uncle Rat come home,
   Cock me cary, Kitty alone,
   Kitty alone and I.

And when her uncle Rat came home,
   Kitty alone, Kitty alone,
And when her uncle Rat came home,
   Kitty alone and I.
And when her uncle Rat came home,
Who's been here since I've been gone?
   Cock me cary, Kitty alone,
   Kitty alone and I.

Sir, there's been a worthy gentleman,
   Kitty alone, Kitty alone,
Sir, there's been a worthy gentleman,
   Kitty alone and I.
Sir, there's been a worthy gentleman,

That's been here since you've been gone,
    Cock me cary, Kitty alone,
    Kitty alone and I.

The frog he came whistling through the brook,
    Kitty alone, Kitty alone,
The frog he came whistling through the brook,
    Kitty alone and I,
The frog he came whistling through the brook,
And there he met with a dainty duck,
    Cock me cary, Kitty alone,
    Kitty alone and I.

The duck she swallow'd him with a pluck,
    Kitty alone, Kitty alone,
The duck she swallow'd him with a pluck,
    Kitty alone and I.
The duck she swallow'd him with a pluck,
So there's an end of my history book,
    Cock me cary, Kitty alone,
    Kitty alone and I.

Can you make me a cambrick shirt

Can you make me a cambrick shirt,
    Parsley, sage, rosemary and thyme,
Without any seam or needle work?
    And you shall be a true lover of mine.

Can you wash it in yonder well,
    Parsley, sage, rosemary and thyme,
Where never spring water, nor rain ever fell?
    And you shall be a true lover of mine.

Can you dry it on yonder thorn,
    Parsley, sage, rosemary and thyme,
Which never bore blossom since Adam was born?
    And you shall be a true lover of mine.

Now you have ask'd me questions three,
    Parsley, sage, rosemary and thyme,
I hope you'll answer as many for me,
    And you shall be a true lover of mine.

Can you find me an acre of land,
    Parsley, sage, rosemary and thyme,
Between the salt water and the sea sand?
    And you shall be a true lover of mine.

Can you plow it with a ram's horn,
    Parsley, sage, rosemary and thyme,
And sow it all over with one pepper corn?
    And you shall be a true lover of mine.

Can you reap it with a sickle of leather,
    Parsley, sage, rosemary and thyme,
And bind it up with a peacock's feather?
    And you shall be a true lover of mine.

When you have done and finish'd your work,
    Parsley, sage, rosemary and thyme,
Then come to me for your cambrick shirt,
    And you shall be a true lover of mine.

A Man of Words

A man of words and not of deeds,
Is like a garden full of weeds;
And when the weeds begin to grow,
It's like a garden full of snow;
And when the snow begins to fall,
It's like a bird upon the wall;
And when the bird away does fly,
It's like an eagle in the sky;
And when the sky begins to roar,
It's like a lion at the door;
And when the door begins to crack,
It's like a stick across your back;
And when your back begins to smart,

It's like a penknife in your heart;
And when your heart begins to bleed,
You're dead, and dead, and dead indeed.

The man in the moon

The man in the moon
Came tumbling down,
And ask'd his way to Norwich.
He went by the south,
And burnt his mouth,
With supping hot pease porridge.

My father died

My father he died, but I can't tell you how,
He left me six horses to drive in my plough:
With my wing wang waddle oh,
Jack sing saddle oh,
Blowsey boys bubble oh,
Under the broom.

I sold my six horses and I bought me a cow,
I'd fain made a fortune, but did not know how:
With my wing wang waddle oh,
Jack sing saddle oh,
Blowsey boys bubble oh,
Under the broom.

I sold my cow, and I bought me a calf;
I'd fain made a fortune, but lost the best half:
With my wing wang waddle oh,
Jack sing saddle oh,
Blowsey boys bubble oh,
Under the broom.

I sold my calf, and I bought me a cat;
A pretty thing she was, in my chimney corner sat:
    With my wing wang waddle oh,
    Jack sing saddle oh,
    Blowsey boys bubble oh,
    Under the broom.

I sold my cat, and I bought me a mouse;
He carried fire in his tail, and burnt down my house:
    With my wing wang waddle oh,
    Jack sing saddle oh,
    Blowsey boys bubble oh,
    Under the broom.

THOMAS HOLCROFT
1745–1809

Fool's Song

When swallows lay their eggs in snow,
    And geese in wheat-ears build their nests;
When roasted crabs a-hunting go,
    And cats can laugh at gossips' jests;
When law and conscience are akin,
    And pigs are learnt by note to squeak;
Your worship then shall stroke your chin,
    And teach an owl to whistle Greek.

Till when let your wisdom be dumb;
    For say, man of Gotham,
        What is this world?
        A tetotum,
    By the finger of Folly twirled;
With a hey-go-up, and about we come;
While the sun a good post-horse is found,
So merrily we'll run round.

When frost, and snow, and hail, and rain,
    Are guided by the Almanack;
When Lapland wizards can explain

How many stars will fill a sack;
When courtiers hate to be preferred,
    And pearls are made of whitings' eyes;
Instructed by your worship's beard,
    The world shall merry be and wise.

Till when let your wisdom be dumb, *etc.*

WOLFGANG AMADEUS MOZART
1756–91

Kanonentext

bona nox; bist a rechter ox;
bona notte, liebe Lotte;
bonne nuit, pfui, pfui;
good night, good night,
heut müss ma no weit;
gute Nacht, gute Nacht,
sch . . . ins Bett, dass's kracht;
gute Nacht; schlaf fei g'sund
und reck'n A . . . zum Mund.

Translation

bona nox; you're an ox;
bona notte, darling Lotte;
bonne nuit, pfui pfui;
gute Nacht, gute Nacht,
today's over, that's a fact;
good night, good night,
s. . . . in the bed, it's cracked;
good night; sleep tight;
and stretch out A . . . to mouth.

WILLIAM BLAKE

1757–1827

An Island in the Moon

FROM CHAPTER 6

'Hang that,' said Suction; 'let us have a song.'
Then the Cynic sang –

'When old corruption first begun,
　　Adorn'd in yellow vest,
He committed on flesh a whoredom –
　　O, what a wicked beast!

From them a callow babe did spring,
　　And old corruption smil'd
To think his race should never end.
　　For now he had a child.

He call'd him surgery, & fed
　　The babe with his own milk,
For flesh & he could ne'er agree,
　　She would not let him suck.

And this he always kept in mind,
　　And form'd a crooked knife,
And ran about with bloody hands
　　To seek his mother's life.

And as he ran to seek his mother
　　He met with a dead woman,
He fell in love & married her,
　　A deed which is not common.

She soon grew pregnant & brought forth
　　Scurvy & spott'd fever.
The father grin'd & skipt about,
　　And said, 'I'm made for ever!

'For now I have procur'd these imps
   'I'll try experiments.'
With that he tied poor scurvy down
    & stopt up all its vents.

And when the child began to swell,
   He shouted out aloud,
'I've found the dropsy out, & soon
   'Shall do the world more good.'

He took up fever by the neck
   And cut out all its spots,
And thro' the holes which he had made
   He first discover'd guts.'

FROM CHAPTER 9

'I say, this evening we'll all get drunk – I say – dash! an Anthem, an Anthem!' said Suction.
           'Lo the Bat with Leathern wing,
           Winking & blinking,
           Winking & blinking,
           Winking & blinking,
           Like Doctor Johnson.'

QUID. '"Oho", said Doctor Johnson
    To Scipio Africanus,
    "If you don't own me a Philosopher,
    I'll kick your Roman Anus".'

SUCTION. '"Aha", To Doctor Johnson
    Said Scipio Africanus,
    "Lift up my Roman Petticoat
    "And kiss my Roman Anus".'

'And the Cellar goes down with a step.' (Grand Chorus.)

'Ho, Ho, Ho, Ho, Ho, Ho, Ho, Hooooo, my poooooor siiiides! I I should die if I was to live here!' said Scopprell, 'Ho, Ho, Ho, Ho, Ho!'

1st VOICE 'Want Matches?'
2nd VOICE 'Yes, yes, yes.'
1st VOICE 'Want Matches?'
2nd VOICE 'No.'

1st VOICE 'Want Matches?'
2nd VOICE 'Yes, yes, yes.'
1st VOICE 'Want Matches?'
2nd VOICE 'No.'

Here was great confusion & disorder. Aradobo said that the boys in the street sing something very pretty & funny about London – O no, about Matches. Then Mrs Nannicantipot sung:

'I cry my matches as far as Guild hall;
God bless the duke & his aldermen all!'

Then sung Scopprell:

'I ask the Gods no more, –
no more, no more.'

'Then,' said Suction, 'come, Mr Lawgiver, your song'; and the Lawgiver sung:

'As I walk'd forth one may morning
To see the fields so pleasant & so gay,
O there did I spy a young maiden sweet,
Among the Violets that smell so sweet,
    Smell so sweet,
    Smell so sweet,
Among the Violets that smell so sweet.'

'Hang your Violets! Here's your Rum & water.' 'O ay,' said Tilly Lally, 'Joe Bradley & I was going along one day in the sugar-house. Joe Bradley saw – for he had but one eye – saw a treacle Jar. So he goes of his blind side & dips his hand up to the shoulder in treacle. "Here, lick, lick, lick!" said he. Ha! Ha! Ha! Ha! Ha! For he had but one eye. Ha! Ha! Ha! Ho!'
    Then sung Scopprell:

'And I ask the Gods no more, –
no more, no more,
no more, no more.

'Miss Gittipin,' said he, 'you sing like a harpsichord. Let your bounty
descend to our fair ears and favour us with a fine song.'
Then she sung:

'This frog he would a-wooing ride,
Kitty alone, – Kitty alone, –
This frog he would a-wooing ride, –
Kitty alone & I!
Sing cock I cary, Kitty alone,
Kitty alone, – Kitty alone, –
Cock I cary, Kitty alone, –
Kitty alone & I!'

'Charming! Truly elegant!' said Scopprell.

'And I ask the gods no more!'

'Hang your serious songs!' said Sipsop, & he sung as follows:

'Fa ra so bo ro
Fa ra bo ra
Sa ba ra ra ba rare roro
Sa ra ra ra bo ro ro ro
Radara
Sarapodo no flo ro.'

'Hang Italian songs! Let's have English!' said Quid. 'English genius for
ever! Here I go:

'Hail Matrimony, made of Love,
To thy wide gates how great a drove
On purpose to be yok'd do come!
Widows & maids & youths also,
That lightly trip on beauty's toe,
Or sit on beauty's bum.

[172]

Hail, fingerfooted lovely Creatures!
The females of our human Natures,
   Formed to suckle all Mankind.
'Tis you that come in time of need;
Without you we should never Breed,
   Or any Comfort find.

For if a Damsel's blind or lame,
Or Nature's hand has crooked her frame,
   Or if she's deaf, or is wall eyed,
Yet if her heart is well inclined,
Some tender lover she shall find
   That panteth for a Bride.

The universal Poultice this,
To cure whatever is amiss
   In damsel or in widow gay.
It makes them smile, it makes them skip,
Like Birds just cured of the pip,
   They chirp, & hop away.

Then come ye maidens, come ye swains,
Come & be eased of all your pains
   In Matrimony's Golden cage.'

'Go & be hanged!' said Scopprell. 'How can you have the face to make game of matrimony?'

Then Quid call'd upon Obtuse Angle for a Song, & he, wiping his face & looking on the corner of the ceiling, sang:

'To be, or not to be
Of great capacity,
   Like Sir Isaac Newton,
Or Locke, or Doctor South,
Or Sherlock upon death?
   I'd rather be Sutton.

For he did build a house
For aged men & youth,
   With walls of brick & stone.
He furnish'd it within
With whatever he could win,
   And all his own.

[173]

He drew out of the Stocks
His money in a box,
   And sent his servant
To Green the Bricklayer
And to the Carpenter:
He was so fervent.

The chimneys were three score,
The windows many more,
   And for convenience
He sinks & gutters made,
And all the way he pav'd
To hinder pestilence.

Was not this a good man,
Whose life was but a span,
   Whose name was Sutton, –
As Locke, or Doctor South,
Or Sherlock upon Death,
   Or Sir Isaac Newton?'

The World Turned Upside Down
OR,
No News, and Strange News

Here you may see what's very rare,
   The world turn'd upside down;
A tree and castle in the air,
   A man walk on his crown.

To see a butcher kill a hog,
        is no news;
But to see a hare run after a dog,
        is strange indeed!

This hare hunts the dog,
   Tho' all of you know,
Most dogs hunt the hare –
   But here it's not so.

To see a poor man and a rich,
        is no news;
But to see the devil hugging a witch,
        is strange indeed!

Is your name Nick, sir,
   Or Old Harry,
I insist you tell before
   We marry.

To see a cat catching a mouse,
            is no news;
But to see a rat building a house,
            is strange indeed!

Some rats take delight to gnaw
    Houses down –
I want to build a good
    House of my own.

To see a bird picking at fruit,
            is no news;
But to see a dog playing the flute,
            is strange indeed!

You see I am playing here,
    Too, too, too, too;
When I've done with my flute,
    I'll give it to you.

To see a greyhound catch a hare,
　　　　is no news;
But to see a lamb hunting a bear,
　　　　is strange indeed!

The bear runs away, the
　　Lamb is pursuing;
If he catches the bear,
　　There'll be terrible doing.

To see an eagle spread her wings,
　　　　is no news;
But to see an old man in leading strings,
　　　　is strange indeed!

Take care, grandpapa, lest
　　You should fall,
And if you want your
　　Chair – pray call.

To see a weaver throw his shuttle,
        is no news;
But to see a man get in a quart bottle,
        is strange indeed!

You'll all be amazed to
  See me get in,
And much more surprised
  If I get out again.

To see a man get a boat,
        is no news;
But to see a man jump down his throat,
        is strange indeed!

If I once get my legs in
  As far as my knees,
The rest will slip down
  With a great deal of ease.

To see a dog baiting a bull,
      is no news;
But to see a ram spinning of wool,
      is strange indeed!

Good lack a daisy!
  How you grin,
To see a poor ram
  Try to spin.

To see a miller grinding corn,
      is no news;
But to see an ox blowing a horn,
      is strange indeed!

I blow and I run,
  And I run and I blow,
And which I do best,
  I'm sure I don't know.

To see a shoemaker hammer his leather,
  is no news;
But to see a hound and a buck drinking together,
  is strange indeed!

Mr Buck, I wish you luck.
Mr Hound, your most profound.

To see a good boy read his book,
  is no news;
But to see a goose roasting a cook,
  is strange indeed!

I'll roast ye, and baste ye,
But who will may taste ye.

To see a beau at his toilet dress,
        is no news;
But to see two horses playing at chess,
            is strange indeed!

Mr Horse, you don't play
    Fair, but cheat:
Mr Nag, you say so,
    Now you're beat.

To see a boy swim in a brook,
        is no news;
But to see a fish catch a man with a hook,
            is strange indeed!

Spare me, good Mr Fish,
    I didn't molest you.
I'll spare you no longer
    Than till I dress you.

To see a cat steal milk from a pan,
                is no news;
But to see a buck hunting a man,
                is strange indeed!

Hark forward, huzza,
He can't get away:
And he's not buck enough
To stand at a bay.

To see a cobbler mending a shoe,
                is no news;
But to see a goat cry old clothes like a jew,
                is strange indeed!

'Tis alvays my vay,
To cheat ven I can,
Yet for all that I be
A very goot man.

To see a haymaker using of rakes,
    is no news;
But to see a bear making plum cakes,
    is strange indeed!

What I have got in the pan,
    I shall eat if I can,
And this cake on the shelf,
    I shall keep for myself.

To see a barrel made by a cooper,
    is no news,
But to see a goat act the part of a trooper,
    is strange indeed!

Hur will fight hur foes
    For the honour of Wales,
And if the French come,
    They shall turn their tails.

To see wrestlers kicking shins,
                    is no news;
But to see cats playing at nine pins,
                    is strange indeed!

I'll lay a penny, you don't get many.
I'll knock down all, and swallow the ball.

To hear a parrot say, pretty Poll,
                    is no news;
But to see a sow with a parasol,
                    is strange indeed!

Like a lady I shine,
    I'm so fat and so fine;
I've a right I suppose,
    To a shade for my nose.

ANONYMOUS

The Comic Adventures of
Old Mother Hubbard and her Dog
1805

Old Mother Hubbard
Went to the cupboard,
To fetch her poor dog a bone;
But when she came there
The cupboard was bare
And so the poor dog had none.

She went to the baker's
To buy him some bread;
But when she came back
The poor dog was dead.

She went to the undertaker's
To buy him a coffin;
But when she came back
The poor dog was laughing.

She took a clean dish
To get him some tripe:
But when she came back
He was smoking a pipe.

She went to the alehouse
To get him some beer;
But when she came back
The dog sat in a chair.

She went to the tavern
For white wine and red;
But when she came back
The dog stood on his head.

She went to the fruiterer's
  To buy him some fruit;
But when she came back
  He was playing the flute.

She went to the tailor's
  To buy him a coat;
But when she came back
  He was riding a goat.

She went to the hatter's
  To buy him a hat;
But when she came back
  He was feeding the cat.

She went to the barber's
  To buy him a wig;
But when she came back
  He was dancing a jig.

She went to the cobbler's
  To buy him some shoes:
But when she came back
  He was reading the news.

She went to the seamstress
  To buy him some linen;
But when she came back
  The dog was a-spinning.

She went to the hosier's
  To buy him some hose;
But when she came back
  He was dressed in his clothes.

The dame made a curtsey,
  The dog made a bow;
The dame said, Your servant,
  The dog said, Bow-wow.

ANONYMOUS

As I walked by myself, I said to myself,
  And myself said again to me,
Look well to thyself, take care of thyself,
  For nobody cares for thee.

Then I answered to myself, and said to myself,
  With the self-same repartee,
Look well to thyself, or not to thyself,
  It's the selfsame thing to me.

SAMUEL TAYLOR COLERIDGE
1772–1834

The Devil's Thoughts

From his brimstone bed at break of day
A walking the Devil is gone,
To visit his snug little farm the earth,
And see how his stock goes on.

Over the hill and over the dale,
And he went over the plain,
And backward and forward he switched his long tail
As a gentleman switches his cane.

And how then was the Devil drest?
Oh! he was in his Sunday's best:
His jacket was red and his breeches were blue,
And there was a hole where the tail came through.

He saw a Lawyer killing a Viper
On a dunghill hard by his own stable;
And the Devil smiled, for it put him in mind
Of Cain and his brother, Abel.

He saw an Apothecary on a white horse
    Ride by on his vocations,
And the Devil thought of his old Friend
    Death in the Revelations.

He saw a cottage with a double coach-house,
    A cottage of gentility;
And the Devil did grin, for his darling sin
    Is pride that apes humility.

He peep'd into a rich bookseller's shop,
    Quoth he! we are both of one college!
For I sate myself, like a cormorant, once
    Hard by the tree of knowledge.

Down the river did glide, with wind and tide,
    A pig with vast celerity;
And the Devil look'd wise as he saw how the while,
It cut its own throat. 'There!' quoth he with a smile,
    'Goes "England's commercial prosperity."'

As he went through Cold-Bath Fields he saw
    A solitary cell;
And the Devil was pleased, for it gave him a hint
    For improving his prisons in Hell.

He saw a Turnkey in a trice
    Fetter a troublesome blade;
'Nimbly,' quoth he, 'do the fingers move
    If a man be but used to his trade.'

He saw the same Turnkey unfetter a man,
    With but little expedition,
Which put him in mind of the long debate
    On the Slave-trade abolition.

He saw an old acquaintance
    As he passed by a Methodist meeting; –
She holds a consecrated key,
    And the devil nods her a greeting.

She turned up her nose, and said,
　'Avaunt! my name's Religion,'
And she looked to Mr ——
　And leered like a love-sick pigeon.

He saw a certain minister
　(A minister to his mind)
Go up into a certain House,
　With a majority behind.

The Devil quoted Genesis
　Like a very learnéd clerk,
How 'Noah and his creeping things
　Went up into the Ark.'

He took from the poor,
　And he gave to the rich,
And he shook hands with a Scotchman,
　For he was not afraid of the ——

General —— burning face
　He saw with consternation,
And back to hell his way did he take,
For the Devil thought by a slight mistake
　It was general conflagration.

The House that Jack Built

And this reft house is that the which he built,
Lamented Jack! and here his malt he piled.
Cautious in vain! these rats that squeak so wild,
Squeak not unconscious of their father's guilt.
Did he not see her gleaming through the glade?
Belike 'twas she, the maiden all forlorn.
What though she milked no cow with crumpled horn,
Yet, *aye* she haunts the dale where *erst* she strayed:
And *aye* before her stalks her amorous knight!
Still on his thighs their wonted brogues are worn,
And through those brogues, still tattered and betorn,
His hindward charms gleam an unearthly white;
As when through broken clouds at night's high noon
Peeps in fair fragments forth the full-orbed harvest-moon.

The Madman and the Lethargist

Quoth Dick to me, as once at College
We argued on the use of knowledge; –

'In old King Olim's reign, I've read,
There lay two patients in one bed.
The one in fat lethargic trance,
Lay wan and motionless as lead:
The other, (like the Folks in France),
Possess'd a different disposition –
In short, the plain truth to confess,
The man was madder than Mad Bess!
But both diseases, none disputed,
Were unmedicinably rooted;
Yet, so it chanc'd, by Heaven's permission,
Each prov'd the other's true physician.

'Fighting with a ghostly stare
Troops of Despots in the air,
Obstreperously Jacobinical,
The madman froth'd, and foam'd, and roar'd:
The other, snoring octaves cynical,
Like good John Bull, in posture clinical,
Seem'd living only when he snor'd.
The *Citizen* enraged to see
This fat Insensibility,
Or, tir'd with solitary labour,
Determin'd to convert his neighbour;
So up he sprang and to 't he fell,
Like devil piping hot from hell,
With indefatigable fist
Belabr'ing the poor Lethargist;
Till his own limbs were stiff and sore,
And sweat-drops roll'd from every pore: –
Yet, still, with flying fingers fleet,
Duly accompanied by feet,
With some short intervals of biting,
He executes the self-same strain,

Till the Slumberer woke for pain,
And half-prepared himself for fighting –
That moment that his mad Colleague
Sunk down and slept thro' pure fatigue.
So both were cur'd – and this example
Gives demonstration full and ample –
That *Chance* may bring a thing to bear,
Where *Art* sits down in blank despair.'

'That's true enough, Dick,' answer'd I,
'But as for the *Example*, 'tis a lie.'

The Angel's like a Flea

'The angel's like a flea,
The devil is a bore; –'
No matter for that! quoth S. T. C.,
I love him the better therefore.

CHARLES LAMB
1775–1834

Nonsense Verses

Lazy-bones, lazy-bones, wake up and peep!
The cat's in the cupboard, your mother's asleep.
There you sit snoring, forgetting her ills;
Who is to give her her Bolus and Pills?
Twenty fine Angels must come into town,
All for to help you to make your new gown:
Dainty aerial Spinsters and Singers;
Aren't you ashamed to employ such white fingers?
Delicate hands, unaccustom'd to reels,
To set 'em working a poor body's wheels?
Why they came down is to me all a riddle,
And left Hallelujah broke off in the middle;
Jove's court, and the Presence angelical, cut –
To eke out the work of a lazy young slut.

Angel-duck, Angel-duck, winged and silly,
Pouring a watering-pot over a lily,
Gardener gratuitous, careless of pelf,
Leave her to water her lily herself,
Or to neglect it to death if she chuse it:
Remember the loss is her own, if she lose it.

THOMAS LOVE PEACOCK
1785–1866

From *Sir Proteus, A Satirical Ballad*

II
DIVERSE LINGUE, ORRIBILI FAVELLE

Even while he sung Sir Proteus rose,
    That wight of ancient fun,
With salmon-scales instead of clothes,
    And fifty shapes in one.

He first appeared a folio thick,
    A glossary so stout,
Of modern language politic,
    Where conscience was left out.

He next appeared in civic guise,
    Which C—s could not flout,
With forced-meat balls instead of eyes,
    And, for a nose, a snout.

And then he seemed a patriot *braw*,
    Who, o'er a pot of froth,
Was very busy, stewing straw,
    To make the *people* broth.

In robes collegiate, loosely spread,
    His form he seemed to wrap:
Much Johnny mused to see no head
    Between the gown and cap.

Like grave logician, next he drew
   A tube from garment mystic;
And bubbles blew, which Johnny knew
   Were *anti-hyloistic*.

Like *doughty* critic next he sped,
   Of fragrant Edinbroo':
A yellow cap was on his head;
   His jacket was sky-blue:

He wore a cauliflower wig,
   With bubble filled, and squeak;
Where hung behind, like *tail of pig*,
   Small lollypop of Greek.

With rusty knife he seemed prepared
   Poor poet's blood to fetch:
In speechless horror Johnny stared
   Upon the ruthless wretch.

Like washing-tub he next appeared
   O'er W—'s sea that scuds;
Where poor John Bull stood all besmeared,
   Up to the neck in suds.

Then three wise men he seemed to be,
   Still sailing in the tub;
Whose white wigs looked upon the sea,
   Like bowl of syllabub.

The first he chattered, chattered still,
   With meaning none at all,
Of Jack and Jill, and Harry Gill,
   And Alice Fell so small.

The second of three graves did sing,
   And in such doggrel strains,
You might have deemed the Elfin King
   Had charmed away his brains.

Loud sang the third of Palmy Isle,
　　Mid oceans vast and wild,
Where he had won a mermaid's smile,
　　And got a fairy child.

Like rueful wanderer next he shewed,
　　Much posed with pious qualm;
And first he roared a frantic ode,
　　And then he sung a psalm.

Like farmer's man, he seemed to rear
　　His form in smock-frock dight;
And screeched in poor Apollo's ear,
　　Who ran with all his might.

And, even while Apollo ran,
　　Arose the Bellman there,
And clapped the crack-voiced farmer's man
　　Into his vacant chair.

Next, like Tom Thumb, he skipped along
　　In merry Irish jig:
And now he whined an amorous song,
　　And now he pulled a wig,

Whose frizzles, firing at his rage,
　　Like Indian crackers flew,
Each wrapped in party-coloured page
　　Of some profound review.

In jaunting car, like tourist brave,
　　Full speed he seemed to rush;
And chaunted many a clumsy stave,
　　Might make the Bellman blush.

Like grizzly monk, on spectral harp
　　Deep dole he did betoken;
And strummed one strain, 'twixt flat and sharp,
　　Till all the strings were broken.

Like modish bard, intent to please
    The sentimental fair,
He strung conceits and similes,
    Where feeling had no share.

At last, in cap with border red,
    A Minstrel seemed to stand,
With heather bell upon his head,
    And fiddle in his hand;

And such a shrill and piercing scrape
    Of hideous discord gave,
That none but Johnny's ear could scape
    Unfractured by the stave.

Old Poulter's mare, in sudden fright,
    Forgot all John had taught her;
And up she reared, a furious height,
    And soused him in the water.

III
OR CHI SEI TU?

Ten thousand thousand fathoms down
    Beneath the sea he popped:
At last a coral cracked his crown,
    And Johnny Raw was stopped.

Sir Proteus came, and picked him up,
    With grim and ghastly smile;
And asked him to walk in and sup,
    And fiddled all the while.

So up he got, and felt his head,
    And feared his brain was diddled;
While still the ocean o'er him spread,
    And still Sir Proteus fiddled.

And much surprised he was to be
    Beneath the ocean's root;
Which then he found was one great tree,
    Where grew odd fish for fruit.

And there were fish both young and old,
    And fish both great and small;
And some of them had heads of gold,
    And some no heads at all.

And now they came, where Neptune sate,
    With beard like any Jew,
With all his Tritons round in state,
    And all his Nereids too:

And when poor Johnny's bleeding sconce
    The moody king did view,
He stoutly bellowed, all at once:
    'Pray who the deuce are you?

'That thus dare stalk, and walk, and talk,
    Beneath my tree, the sea, sir,
And break your head on coral bed,
    Without the leave of me, sir?'

IV

ΟΜΑΔΟΣ Δ' ΑΛΙΑΣΤΟΣ ΟΡΩΡΕΙ.

Poor Johnny looked exceeding blue,
    As blue as Neptune's self;
And cursed the jade, his skull that threw
    Upon the coral shelf;

And thrice he cursed the jarring strain,
    That scraping Proteus sung,
Which forced his mare to rear amain,
    And got her rider flung.

His clashing thoughts, that flocked so quick,
    He strove in vain to clear;
For still the ruthless fiddlestick
    Was shrieking at his ear,

A piercing modulated shriek,
    So comically sad,
That oft he strove in vain to speak,
    He felt so wondrous mad.

But seeing well, by Neptune's phiz,
    He deemed the case no joke,
In spite of all the diz and whiz,
    Like parish-clerk he spoke

A wondrous speech, and all in rhyme,
    As long as *Chevy Chase,*
Which made Sir Proteus raise his chime,
    While Glaucus fled the place.

He sung of men, who nature's law
    So little did redoubt,
They flourished when the life was raw,
    And when the brain was out;

Whose arms were iron spinning-wheels,
    That twirled when winds did puff,
And forced Old Scratch to ply his heels,
    By dint of usage rough.
Grim Neptune bade him stop the peals
    Of such infernal stuff.

But when once in, no art could win
    To silence Johnny Raw:
For Nereid's grin, or Triton's fin,
    He did not care a straw;
So still did spin his rhyming din,
    Without one hum or haw,
Though still the crazy violin
    Kept screaming: 'Hoot awa'!'

Till all the Tritons gave a yell,
    And fled, in rout inglorious,
With all the Nereids, from the spell
    Of Johnny's stave laborious,
And Neptune scouted in his shell,
    And left stout Raw victorious.

The Wise Men of Gotham

Εκιᾶς ὄυαρ

PINDAR

In a bowl to sea went wise men three,
    On a brilliant night of June:
They carried a net, and their hearts were set
    On fishing up the moon.

The sea was calm, the air was balm,
    Not a breath stirred low or high,
And the moon, I trow, lay as bright below,
    And as round as in the sky.

The wise men with the current went,
    Nor paddle nor oar had they,
And still as the grave they went on the wave,
    That they might not disturb their prey.

Far, far at sea, were the wise men three,
    When their fishing-net they threw;
And at the throw, the moon below
    In a thousand fragments flew.

The sea was bright with the dancing light
    Of a million million gleams,
Which the broken moon shot forth as soon
    As the net disturbed her beams.

They drew in their net: it was empty and wet,
    And they had lost their pain,
Soon ceased the play of each dancing ray,
    And the image was round again.

Three times they threw, three times they drew,
    And all the while were mute;
And evermore their wonder grew,
    Till they could not but dispute.

Their silence they broke, and each one spoke
   Full long, and loud, and clear;
A man at sea their voices three
   Full three leagues off might hear.

The three wise men got home again
   To their children and their wives:
But touching their trip, and their net's vain dip,
   They disputed all their lives.

The wise men three could never agree,
   Why they missed the promised boon;
They agreed alone that their net they had thrown,
   And they had not caught the moon.

I have thought myself pale o'er this ancient tale,
   And its sense I could not ken;
But now I see that the wise men three
   Were paper-money men.

'Rub-a-dub-dub, three men in a tub,'
   Is a mystic burthen old,
Which I've pondered about till my fire went out,
   And I could not sleep for cold.

I now divine each mystic sign,
   Which robbed me oft of sleep,
Three men in a bowl, who went to troll,
   For the moon in the midnight deep.

Three men were they who science drank
   From Scottish fountains free;
The cash they sank in the Gotham bank,
   Was the moon beneath the sea.

The breaking of the imaged moon,
   At the fishing-net's first splash,
Was the breaking of the bank as soon
   As the wise men claimed their cash.

The dispute which lasted all their lives,
    Was the economic strife,
Which the son's son's son of every one
    Will maintain through all his life.

The son's son's sons will baffled be,
    As were their sires of old;
But they only agree, like the wise men three,
    That they could not get their gold.

And they'll build systems dark and deep,
    And systems broad and high;
But two of three will never agree
    About the reason why.

And he who at this day will seek
    The Economic Club,
Will find at least three sages there,
As ready as any that ever were
    To go to sea in a tub.

HENRY COGGESWELL KNIGHT
1789–1835

Lunar Stanzas

Night saw the crew like pedlers with their packs
    Altho' it were too dear to pay for eggs;
Walk crank along with coffin on their backs
    While in their arms they bow their weary legs.

And yet 't was strange, and scarce can one suppose
    That a brown buzzard-fly should steal and wear
His white jean breeches and black woollen hose,
    But thence that flies have souls is very clear.

But, Holy Father! what shall save the soul,
    When cobblers ask three dollars for their shoes?
When cooks their biscuits with a shot-tower roll,
    And farmers rake their hay-cocks with their hoes.

Yet, 't were profuse to see for pendant light,
    A tea-pot dangle in a lady's ear;
And 't were indelicate, although she might
    Swallow two whales and yet the moon shine clear.

But what to me are woven clouds, or what,
    If dames from spiders learn to warp their looms?
If coal-black ghosts turn soldiers for the State,
    With wooden eyes, and lightning-rods for plumes?

Oh! too, too shocking! barbarous, savage taste!
    To eat one's mother ere itself was born!
To gripe the tall town-steeple by the waste,
    And scoop it out to be his drinking-horn.

No more: no more! I'm sick and dead and gone;
    Boxed in a coffin, stifled six feet deep;
Thorns, fat and fearless, prick my skin and bone,
    And revel o'er me, like a soulless sheep.

JOHN KEATS
1795–1821

There was a naughty boy:
A song about myself

I

There was a naughty boy,
    A naughty boy was he,
He would not stop at home,
    He could not quiet be –
        He took
        In his knapsack

A book
Full of vowels
And a shirt
With some towels,
A slight cap
For night-cap,
A hair brush,
Comb ditto,
New stockings,
For old ones
Would split O!
This knapsack
Tight at's back
He rivetted close
And followed his nose
To the north,
To the north,
And followed his nose
To the north.

II

There was a naughty boy,
And a naughty boy was he,
For nothing would he do
But scribble poetry –
He took
An inkstand
In his hand,
And a pen
Big as ten
In the other.
And away
In a pother
He ran
To the mountains
And fountains
And ghostès
And postès
And witches
And ditches,
And wrote
In his coat

When the weather
Was cool –
Fear of gout –
And without
When the weather
Was warm.
Och, the charm
When we choose
To follow one's nose
To the north,
To the north,
To follow one's nose
To the north!

III

There was a naughty boy,
And a naughty boy was he,
He kept little fishes
In washing tubs three.
In spite
Of the might
Of the maid,
Nor afraid
Of his granny-good,
He often would
Hurly burly
Get up early
And go,
By hook or crook,
To the brook
And bring home
Miller's thumb,
Tittlebat
Not over fat,
Minnows small
As the stall
Of a glove,
Not above
The size
Of a nice
Little baby's
Little finger –

Oh, he made
('Twas his trade)
Of fish a pretty kettle –
A kettle,
A kettle,
Of fish a pretty kettle,
A kettle!

IV

There was a naughty boy,
And a naughty boy was he,
He ran away to Scotland
The people for to see –
Then he found
That the ground
Was as hard,
That a yard
Was as long,
That a song
Was as merry,
That a cherry
Was as red,
That lead
Was as weighty,
That fourscore
Was as eighty,
That a door
Was as wooden
As in England –
So he stood in his shoes
And he wondered,
He wondered,
He stood in his shoes
And he wondered.

Two or three posies

Two or three posies
With two or three simples –
Two or three noses
With two or three pimples –

Two or three wise men
And two or three ninnies –
Two or three purses
And two or three guineas –
Two or three raps
At two or three doors –
Two or three naps
Of two or three hours –
Two or three cats
And two or three mice –
Two or three sprats
At a very great price –
Two or three sandies
And two or three tabbies –
Two or three dandies
And two Mrs —— mum!
Two or three smiles
And two or three frowns –
Two or three miles
To two or three towns –
Two or three pegs
For two or three bonnets –
Two or three dove's eggs
To hatch into sonnets.

Pensive they sit, and roll their languid eyes

Pensive they sit, and roll their languid eyes,
Nibble their toasts and cool their tea with sighs;
Or else forget the purpose of the night,
Forget their tea, forget their appetite.
See, with crossed arms they sit – Ah! hapless crew,
The fire is going out and no one rings
For coals, and therefore no coals Betty brings.
A fly is in the milk-pot – must he die
Circled by a Humane Society?
No, no; there, Mr Werter takes his spoon,
Inverts it, dips the handle, and lo! soon
The little struggler, saved from perils dark,
Across the teaboard draws a long wet mark.
Romeo! Arise! take snuffers by the handle,

There's a large cauliflower in each candle.
A winding-sheet – ah, me! I must away
To No. 7, just beyond the Circus gay.
'Alas, my friend, your coat sits very well;
Where may your tailor live?' 'I may not tell.
O pardon me – I'm absent now and then.
Where *might* my tailor live? I say again
I cannot tell. Let me no more be teased –
He lives in Wapping, *might* live where he pleased.'

Two Undated Fragments

I

I am as brisk
As a bottle of Wisk –
Ey and as nimble
As a Milliner's thimble.

II

O grant that like to Peter I
May like to Peter B,
And tell me, lovely Jesus, Y
This Peter went to C.

O grant that like to Peter I
May like to Peter B,
And tell me, lovely Jesus, Y
Old Jonah went to C.

ANONYMOUS
(Irish traditional)

The Song of Lies

'Twas a comical sight that I saw by the roadside,
An eel with the pipes, and he playing a broadside,
The trout with fine shoes in the pool by the heather,
And the sheep cutting turf in this black winter weather!

> *Mangalum die dero, dow dero, dear is he,*
> *Stir your foot, shake your foot, come now*
> *and dance with me.*

A troutlet was hauling a rabbit so frisky,
And a lark had her nest in a gander's grey whiskers,
The coot had a jew's-harp on which she was strumming,
Reynard lay on the hearth, and the cricket was humming.

A crow in the marsh gathered cress with great zeal,
And a horse had a quart-pot for measuring meal,
A hen and a drake took a voyage to Spain,
And a trousered hare drank as he sailed o'er the main.

I saw a blackthorn tree with never a thorn,
A fox with no ears and no tail, all forlorn,
A church that was dancing and waving its spires –
If you say you believe me, we're none of us liars!

translated from The Irish by Donal O'Sullivan

ANONYMOUS

There was an old man of Tobago,
Who lived on rice, gruel, and sago;
    Till, much to his bliss,
    His physician said this –
To a leg, sir, of mutton you may go.

ANONYMOUS

In the Dumps

We're all in the dumps,
  For diamonds are trumps,
The kittens are gone to St Paul's,
  The babies are bit,
  The Moon's in a fit,
And the houses are built without walls.

THOMAS HOOD
1799–1844

Sally Simpkin's Lament, or
John Jones's Kit-Cat-astrophe

  'He left his body to the sea,
  And made the shark his legatee'.
    BRYAN AND PERENNE

'Oh! what is that comes gliding in,
  And quite in middling haste?
It is the picture of my Jones,
  And painted to the waist.

'It is not painted to the life,
  For where's the trowsers blue?
Oh Jones, my dear! – Oh dear! my
    Jones,
  What is become of you?'

'Oh! Sally dear, it is too true, –
  The half that you remark
Is come to say my other half
  Is bit off by a shark!

'Oh! Sally, sharks do things by
    halves,
  Yet most completely do!
A bite in one place seems enough,
  But I've been bit in two.

'You know I once was all your own,
  But now a shark must share!
But let that pass – for now to you
  I'm neither here nor there.

'Alas! death has a strange divorce
  Effected in the sea,
It has divided me from you,
  And even me from me!

'Don't fear my ghost will walk 'o
    nights
  To haunt as people say;
My ghost *can't* walk, for, oh! my legs
  Are many leagues away!

'Lord! think when I am swimming
    round,
  And looking where the boat is,
A shark just snaps away a *half*,
  Without 'a *quarter's* notice.'

'One half is here, the other half
  Is near Columbia placed;
Oh! Sally, I have got the whole
  Atlantic for my waist.

'But now, adieu – a long adieu!
  I've solved death's awful riddle,
And would say more, but I am doomed
  To break off in the middle.'

Epicurean Reminiscences of a Sentimentalist

'My *Tables*! *Meat* it is, *I set it* down!' HAMLET

I think it was Spring – but not certain I am –
    When my passion began first to work;
But I know we were certainly looking for lamb,
    And the season was over for pork.

'Twas at Christmas, I think, when I met with Miss Chase,
    Yes, – for Morris had asked me to dine, –
And I thought I had never beheld such a face,
    Or so noble a turkey and chine.

Placed close to her side, it made others quite wild,
    With sheer envy to witness my luck;
How she blushed as I gave her some turtle, and smiled
    As I afterwards offered some duck.

I looked and I languished, alas, to my cost,
    Through three courses of dishes and meats;
Getting deeper in love – but my heart was quite lost,
    When it came to the trifle and sweets!

With a rent-roll that told of my houses and land
    To her parents I told my designs –
And then to herself I presented my hand,
    With a very fine pottle of pines!

I asked her to have me for weal or for woe,
    And she did not object in the least:
I can't tell the date – but we married, I know,
    Just in time to have game at the feast.

We went to –, it certainly was the seaside;
    For the next, the most blessed of morns,
I remember how fondly I gazed at my bride,
    Sitting down to a plateful of prawns.

Oh, never may mem'ry lose sight of that year,
 But still hallow the time as it ought,
That season the 'grass' was remarkably dear,
 And the peas at a guinea a quart.

So happy, like hours, all our days seemed to haste,
 A fond pair, such as poets have drawn,
So united in heart – so congenial in taste,
 We were both of us partial to brawn!

A long life I looked for of bliss with my bride,
 But then Death – I ne'er dreamt about that!
Oh, there's nothing certain in life, as I cried,
 When my turbot eloped with the cat!

My dearest took ill at the turn of the year,
 But the cause no physician could nab;
But something it seemed like consumption, I fear,
 It was just after supping on crab.

In vain she was doctored, in vain she was dosed,
 Still her strength and her appetite pined;
She lost relish for what she had relished the most,
 Even salmon she deeply declined.

For months still I lingered in hope and in doubt,
 While her form it grew wasted and thin;
But the last dying spark of existence went out,
 As the oysters were just coming in!

She died, and she left me the saddest of men
 To indulge in a widower's moan;
Oh, I felt all the power of solitude then,
 As I ate my first natives alone!

But when I beheld Virtue's friends in their cloaks,
 And with sorrowful crape on their hats,
Oh, my grief poured a flood! and the out-of-door folks
 Were all crying – I think it was sprats!

The Lament of Toby the Learned Pig

'A little learning is a dangerous thing' POPE

O heavy day! oh day of woe!
　　To misery a poster,
Why was I ever farrow'd – why
　　Not spitted for a roaster?

In this world, pigs, as well as men,
　　Must dance to fortune's fiddlings,
But must I give the classics up,
　　For barley-meal and middlings?

Of what avail that I could spell
　　And read, just like my betters,
If I must come to this at last,
　　To litters, not to letters?

O, why are pigs made scholars of?
　　It baffles my discerning,
What griskins, fry, and chitterlings
　　Can have to do with learning.

Alas! my learning once drew cash,
　　But public fame's unstable,
So I must turn a pig again,
　　And fatten for the table.

To leave my literary line
　　My eyes get red and leaky;
But Giblett doesn't want me *blue*,
　　But red and white, and streaky.

Old Mullins used to cultivate
　　My learning like a gard'ner;
But Giblett only thinks of lard,
　　And not of Doctor Lardner.

He does not care about my brain
    The value of two coppers,
All that he thinks about my head
    Is, how I'm off for choppers.

Of all my literary kin
    A farewell must be taken.
Goodbye to the poetic Hogg!
    The philosophic Bacon!

Day after day my lessons fade,
    My intellect gets muddy;
A trough I have, and not a desk,
    A sty – and not a study!

Another little month, and then
    My progress ends, like Bunyan's;
The seven sages that I loved
    Will be chopp'd up with onions!

Then over head and ears in brine
    They'll souse me, like a salmon,
My mathematics turn'd to brawn,
    My logic into gammon.

My Hebrew will all retrograde,
    Now I'm put up to fatten,
My Greek, it will all go to grease;
    The Dogs will have my Latin!

Farewell to Oxford! – and to Bliss!
    To Milman, Crowe, and Glossop, –
I now must be content with chats,
    Instead of learned gossip!

Farewell to 'Town!' farewell to
    'Gown!'
    I've quite outgrown the latter, –
Instead of Trencher-cap my head
    Will soon be in a platter!

O why did I at Brazen-Nose
  Rout up the roots of knowledge?
A butcher that can't read will kill
  A pig that's been to college!

For sorrow I could stick myself,
  But conscience is a clasher;
A thing that would be rash in man
  In me would be a rasher!

One thing I ask – when I am dead,
  And past the Stygian ditches –
And that is, let my schoolmaster
  Have one of my two flitches:

'Twas he who taught my letters so
  I ne'er mistook or miss'd 'em,
Simply by *ringing* at the nose,
  According to *Bell's* system.

A Flying Visit

'A Calendar! A Calendar! look in the Almanac,
find out moonshine – find out moonshine!'
A MIDSUMMER NIGHT'S DREAM

The by-gone September,
  As folks may remember,
At least if their memory saves but an ember.
  One fine afternoon,
  There went up a Balloon,
Which did not return to the Earth very soon.

  For, nearing the sky,
  At about a mile high,
The Aeronaut bold had resolved on a fly;
  So cutting his string,
  In a Parasol thing
Down he came in a field like a lark from the wing.

[215]

Meanwhile, thus adrift,
The Balloon made a shift
To rise very fast, with no burden to lift;
It got very small,
Then to nothing at all;
And then rose the question of where it would fall?

Some thought that, for lack
Of the man and his pack,
'Twould rise to the Cherub that watches Poor Jack;
Some held, but in vain,
With the first heavy rain
'Twould surely come down to the Gardens again!

But still not a word
For a month could be heard
Of what had become of the Wonderful Bird:
The firm Gye and Hughes,
Wore their boots out and shoes
In running about and inquiring for news.

Some thought it must be
Tumbled into the Sea;
Some thought it had gone off to High Germanie;
For Germans, as shown
By their writings, 'tis known
Are always delighted with what is high-flown.

Some hinted a bilk,
And that maidens who milk,
In far distant Shires would be walking in silk:
Some swore that it must,
'As they said at the *fust*,
Have gone agin flashes of lightning and *bust*!'

However, at last,
When six weeks had gone past,
Intelligence came of a plausible cast;
A wondering clown,
At a hamlet near town,
Had seen 'like a moon of green cheese' coming down.

Soon spread the alarm,
    And from cottage and farm,
The natives buzz'd out like the bees when they swarm;
    And off ran the folk, –
    It is such a good joke
To see the descent of a bagful of smoke.

    And lo! the machine,
    Dappled yellow and green,
Was plainly enough in the clouds to be seen:
    'Yes, yes,' was the cry,
    'It's the old one, sure*ly*,
Where *can* it have been such a time in the sky?

    Lord! where will it fall
    It can't find out Vauxhall,
Without any pilot to guide it at all!
    Some wager'd that Kent
    Would behold the event,
Debrett had been posed to *predict* its descent.

    Some thought it would pitch
    In the old Tower Ditch,
Some swore on the Cross of St Paul's it would hitch;
    And Farmers cried 'Zounds!
    If it drops on our grounds,
We'll try if Balloons can't be put into pounds!'

    But still to and fro
    It continued to go
As if looking out for soft places below;
    No difficult job,
    It had only to bob
Slap-dash down at once on the heads of the mob:

    Who, too apt to stare
    At some castle in air,
Forget that the earth is their proper affair;
    Till, watching the fall
    Of some soap-bubble ball
They tumble themselves with a terrible sprawl.

Meanwhile, from its height
      Stooping downward in flight,
The Phenomenon came more distinctly in sight:
      Still bigger and bigger,
      And strike me a nigger
Unfreed, if there was not a live human figure!

      Yes, plain to be seen,
      Underneath the machine,
There dangled a mortal – some swore it was Green;
      Some Mason could spy;
      Others named Mr Gye;
Or Hollond, compell'd by the Belgians to fly.

      'Twas Graham the flighty,
      Whom the Duke high and mighty
Resign'd to take care of his own lignum-vitae;
      'Twas Hampton, whose whim
      Was in Cloudland to swim,
Till e'en Little Hampton looked little to him!

      But all were at fault;
      From the heavenly vault
The falling balloon came at last to a halt;
      And bounce! with the jar
      Of descending so far,
An outlandish Creature was thrown from the car!

      At first with the jolt
      All his wits made a bolt,
As if he'd been flung by a mettlesome colt:
      And while in his faint,
      To avoid all complaint,
The muse shall endeavour his portrait to paint.

      The face of this elf,
      Round as platter of delf,
Was pale as if only a cast of itself:
      His head had a rare
      Fleece of silvery hair,
Just like the Albino at Bartlemy Fair.

His eyes they were odd,
     Like the eyes of a cod,
And gave him the look of a watery God.
     His nose was a snub;
     Under which, for his grub,
Was a round open mouth like to that of a chub.

     His person was small,
     Without figure at all,
A plump little body as round as a ball;
     With two little fins,
     And a couple of pins,
With what has been christened a bow in the shins.

     His dress it was new,
     A full suit of sky-blue –
With bright silver buckles in each little shoe –
     Thus painted complete,
     From his head to his feet,
Conceive him laid flat in Squire Hopkins's wheat.

     Fine text for the crowd!
     Who disputed aloud
What sort of a creature had droppd from the cloud –
     'He's come from o'er seas,
     He's a Cochin Chinese –
By jingo! he's one of the wild Cherokees!'

     'Don't nobody know?'
     'He's a young Esquimaux,
Turn'd white like the hares by the Arctical snow.'
     'Some angel, my dear,
     Sent from some upper *spear*
For Plumtree or Agnew, too good for this-here!'

     Meanwhile, with a sigh,
     Having open'd one eye,
The Stranger rose up on his seat by and by;
     And finding his tongue,
     Thus he said, or he sung,
'Mi criky bo biggamy kickery bung!'

'Lord! what does he speak?'
'It's Dog-Latin – it's Greek!'
'It's some sort of slang for to puzzle a Beak!'
'It's no like the Scotch,'
Said a Scot on the watch,
'Phoo! it's nothing at all but a kind of hotch-potch!'

'It's not parly voo,'
Cried a schoolboy or two,
'Nor Hebrew at all,' said a wandering Jew.
Some held it was sprung
From the Irvingite tongue,
The same that is used by a child very young.

Some guess'd it high Dutch,
Others thought it had much
In sound of the true Hoky-poky-ish touch;
But none could be poz,
What the Dickins! (not Boz)
No mortal could tell what the Dickins it was!

When who should come pat,
In a moment like that,
But Bowring, to see what the people were at –
A Doctor well able,
Without any fable,
To talk and translate all the babble of Babel.

So just drawing near,
With a vigilant ear,
That took ev'ry syllable in, very clear,
Before one could sip
Up a tumbler of flip,
He knew the whole tongue, from the root to the tip!

Then stretching his hand,
As you see Daniel stand,
In the Feast of Belshazzar, that picture so grand!
Without more delay,
In the Hamilton way
He English'd whatever the Elf had to say.

'*Krak kraziboo ban,*
I'm the Lunatick Man,
Confined in the Moon since creation began –
Sit muggy bigog,
Whom except in a fog
You see with a Lanthorn, a Bush, and a Dog.

'*Lang sinery lear,*
For this many a year,
I've longed to drop in at your own little sphere, –
Och, pad-mad aroon
Till one fine afternoon,
I found that Wind-Coach on the horns of the Moon.

'*Cush quackery go,*
But, besides you must know,
I'd heard of a profiting Prophet below;
Big botherum blether,
Who pretended to gather
The tricks that the Moon meant to play with the weather.

'*So Crismus an crash,*
Being shortish of cash,
I thought I'd a right to partake of the hash –
Slik mizzle an smak,
So I'm come with a pack,
To sell to the trade, of My Own Almanack.

'*Fiz bobbery pershal*
Besides aims commercial,
Much wishing to honour my friend Sir John Herschel,
Cum puddin and tame,
It's inscribed to his name,
Which is now at the full in celestial fame.

'*Wept wepton wish wept,*
Pray this Copy accept!' –
But here on the Stranger some Kidnappers leapt:
For why? a shrewd man
Had devis'd a sly plan
The Wonder to grab for a show Caravan.

So plotted, so done –
With a fight as in fun,
While mock pugilistical rounds were begun,
  A knave who could box,
  And give right and left knocks,
Caught hold of the Prize by his silvery locks.

  And hard he had fared,
  But the people were scared
By what the Interpreter roundly declared:
  'You ignorant Turks!
  You will be your own Burkes –
He holds all the keys of the lunary works!

  'You'd best let him go –
  If you keep him below,
The Moon will not change, and the tides will not flow;
  He left her at full,
  And with such a long pull,
Zounds! ev'ry man Jack will run mad like a bull!'

  So awful a threat
  Took effect on the set;
The fight, tho', was more than their guest could forget;
  So taking a jump,
  In the car he came plump,
And threw all the ballast right out in a lump.

  Up soar'd the machine,
  With its yellow and green;
But still the pale face of the Creature was seen,
  Who cried from the car,
  Dam in ʒooman bi gar!'
That is, – 'What a sad set of villains you are!'

  Howbeit, at some height,
  He threw down quite a flight
Of Almanacks wishing to set us all right –
  And, thanks to the boon,
  We shall see very soon
If Murphy knows most, or the Man in the Moon!

THOMAS LOVELL BEDDOES

1803–49

The Legend of St Gingulph's Relict

Whoever has heard of St Gingo
  Must know that the gipsy
  He married was tipsy
Every day of her life with old Stingo.

And after the death of St Gingo
  The wonders he did do
  Th' incredulous widow
Denied with unladylike lingo.

'For St Gingo a fig's and feather-end!
  He no more can work wonder
  Than a clyster-pipe thunder
Or I sing a psalm with my nether-end.'

As she said it, her breakfast beginning on
  A tankard of home-brewed inviting ale,
Lo! the part she was sitting and sinning on
  Struck the old hundredth up like a nightingale.

Loud as psophia in an American forest, or
  The mystic Memnonian marble in
A desart at daybreak, that chorister
  Breathed forth his Æolian warbling.

That creature seraphic and spherical,
Her firmament, kept up its clerical
  Thanksgivings, until she did aged die,
Cooing and praising and chirping alert in
Her petticoats, swung like a curtain
  Let down o'er the tail of a Tragedy.

Therefore, ladies, repent and be sedulous
  In praising your lords, lest, ah! well a day!
Such judgement befall the incredulous
  And your latter ends melt into melody.

The New Dodo: Isabrand's Song

What is the night-bird's tune, wherewith she startles
The bee out of his dream and the true lover,
And both in the still moonshine turn and kiss
The flowery bosoms where they rest, and murmuring
Sleep smiling and more happily again?
What is the lobster's tune when he is boiled?
I hate your ballads that are made to come
Round like a squirrel's cage, and round again.
We nightingales sing boldly from our hearts:
So listen to us.

SONG

Squats on a toad-stool under a tree
   A bodiless childfull of life in the gloom,
Crying with frog voice, 'What shall I be?
Poor unborn ghost, for my mother killed me
   Scarcely alive in her wicked womb.
What shall I be? shall I creep to the egg
   That's cracking asunder yonder by Nile,
     And with eighteen toes,
     And a snuff-taking nose,
   Make an Egyptian crocodile?
Sing, "Catch a mummy by the leg
And crunch him with an upper jaw,
Wagging tail and clenching claw;
Take a bill-full from my craw,
Neighbour raven, caw, O caw,
Grunt, my crocky, pretty maw!"

'Swine, shall I be one? 'Tis a dear dog;
   But for a smile, and kiss, and pout,
   I much prefer *your* black-lipped snout,
     Little, gruntless, fairy hog,
     Godson of the hawthorn hedge.
For, when Ringwood snuffs me out,
     And 'gins my tender paunch to grapple,
     sing, "'Twixt your ancles visage wedge,
     And roll up like an apple."

'Serpent Lucifer, how do you do?
Of your worms and your snakes I'd be one or two
   For in this dear planet of wool and of leather
'Tis pleasant to need no shirt, breeches or shoe,
    And have arm, leg, and belly together.
    Then aches your head, or are you lazy?
    Sing, "Round your neck your belly wrap,
    Tail-a-top, and make your cap
      Any bee and daisy."

'I'll not be a fool, like the nightingale
Who sits up all midnight without any ale,
   Making a noise with his nose;
Nor a camel, although 'tis a beautiful back;
Nor a duck, notwithstanding the music of quack
   And the webby, mud-patting toes.
I'll be a new bird with the head of an ass,
   Two pigs' feet, two men's feet, and two of a hen;
Devil-winged; dragon-bellied; grave-jawed, because grass
  Is a beard that's soon shaved, and grows seldom again
    Before it is summer; so cow all the rest;
    The new Dodo is finished. O! come to my nest.'

The Oviparous Tailor

    Wee, wee tailor,
Nobody was paler
   Than wee, wee tailor;
And nobody was thinner.
Hast thou mutton-chops for dinner,
My small-beer sinner,
My starveling rat, – but haler, –
   Wee, wee tailor?

Below his starving garret
Lived an old witch and a parrot, –
   Wee, wee tailor, –
Cross, horrid and uncivil,
For her grandson was the Devil
Or a chimney-sweeper evil;
She was sooty too, but paler, –
   Wee, wee tailor.

[225]

Her sooty hen laid stale eggs,
And then came with his splay legs
 Wee, wee tailor,
And stole them all for dinner.
Then would old witch begin her
Damnations on the sinner, –
'May the thief lay eggs, – but staler;'
 Wee, wee tailor.

Wee, wee tailor,
Witch watched him like a jailor.
 Wee, wee tailor
Did all his little luck spill.
Tho' he swallowed many a muck's pill,
Yet his mouth grew like a duck's bill,
Crowed like a hen, – but maler, –
 Wee, wee tailor.

Near him did cursed doom stick,
As he perched upon a broomstick, –
 Wee, wee tailor.
It lightened, rained and thundered,
And all the doctors wondered
When he laid above a hundred
Gallinaceous eggs, – but staler, –
 Wee, wee tailor.

A hundred eggs laid daily;
No marvel he looked palely, –
 Wee, wee tailor.
Witch let folks in to see some
Poach'd tailor's eggs; to please 'em
He must cackle on his besom,
Till Fowl-death did prevail o'er
 Wee, wee tailor.

ANONYMOUS

The Lover's Arithmetic

In love to be sure what disasters we meet,
    what torment what grief and vexation;
I've crosses encountered my hopes to defeat,
    will scarcely admit NUMERATION.
I courted a maid, and I called her divine,
    and begged she would change her condition;
For I thought that her fortune united to mine,
    would make a most handsome ADDITION.
        Heigho, dot and go one,
        Fal lal de ral de ra, &c.

When married, a plaguy SUBTRACTION I found,
    her debts wanted much liquidation;
And we couldn't, so badly our wishes were crowned,
    get forward in MULTIPLICATION.
DIVISION in wedlock in common they say,
    and both being fond of the suction;
I very soon had to exclaim 'Lack-a-day!
    my fortune's got into REDUCTION.'
        Heigho, dot and go one, &c.

The RULES OF PROPORTION Dame Nature forgot
    when my Deary she formed – so the fact is,
And she had a tongue to embitter my lot,
    which she never could keep out of PRACTICE,
One day after breaking my head with a stool,
    said I, 'Ma'am, if these are your actions,
I'm off; for you know I've been so long at school
    I don't want to learn VULGAR FRACTIONS.'
        Heigho, dot and go one, &c.

ANONYMOUS

Rumble, rumble in the pot
One-erzoll, two-erzoll, zickerzoll zan
Bobtail vinegar, little tan tan;
Harum squarum virgin marum
Zinctum, zanctum buck.

EDUARD MÖRIKE
1804–75

The Prisoner
From *The Wispeliads*

Elegiac balladière,
Written in the Stuttgart Prison,
5 April 1837

Down among the smelly dungeons
    Shivering I sit,
Caught for jabbadizing onions,
    Royal ones, to wit.

My intent in onion-stealing
    Was to splice our soup
With onions of far finer feeling
    Than the common weepful group.*

And I crept to the king's garden,
    Where the silverthruster† swims,
Where the afrikaaners†† quaaken
    And the tulip glims.

* My cooking to improve somewhat
    Was also what I meant,
  This field of knowledge to unclot
    My mind is restless bent.**
** The author aimed to publish a cookbook using his original ideas, which his brother was going to print.
† The swan.
†† A sort of foreign duck, very beautiful, but with an ugly screech.

'Help me now your bulb to hoe
    Up, O Cypris, ††† please!
No one possibly can know,
    Not a person sees!'

Soon a sloping hole I grub,
    Soon my plea she hears,
When suddenly from out the shrub
    A pesky man appears.

Flowerily I said, uprisen,
    What had brought me here.
But would the braided donzel*** listen?
    He did not lend me ear.

Sure as little chickens poke
    From eggs to find release,
Crimes of any kind provoke
    Action by police.

Down among the smelly dungeons
    Shivering I sit,
Caught for jabbadizing onions,
    Royal ones, to wit.

translated from the German by Christopher Middleton

A. C. SWINBURNE
1807–1909

The Higher Pantheism in a Nutshell

One, who is not, we see; but one, whom we see not, is;
Surely, this is not that; but that is assuredly this.

What, and wherefore, and whence: for under is over and under;
If thunder could be without lightning, lightning could be without
    thunder.

††† Goddess of Botanique.
*** Ancient term for 'porter'.

Doubt is faith in the main; but faith, on the whole, is doubt;
We cannot believe by proof; but could we believe without?

Why, and whither, and how? for barley and rye are not clover;
Neither are straight lines curves; yet over is under and over.

One and two are not one; but one and nothing is two;
Truth can hardly be false, if falsehood cannot be true.

Parallels all things are; yet many of these are askew;
You are certainly I; but certainly I am not you.

One, whom we see not, is; and one, who is not, we see;
Fiddle, we know, is diddle; and diddle, we take it, is dee.

W. M. THACKERAY
1811–63

Foreign Literature

TO THE EDITOR OF THE NATIONAL STANDARD

Sir,

   I was much pleased with the following pretty pastoral in the Breton dialect, which I found lately in some numbers of the French Literary Journal . . .

W.M.T.

Choeses me boue er plach yoang,
   Hi e garau perpet,
Mas helas! me halon paûr
   Hi des me zileset.

Pi greden en em hare,
   Contant oue me halon,
Bourmen he don didrompet
   Ia gole glaharet on.

Na me chahuet me'en, doucic,
   Ne zelet quit do'heign;
Zel er haranté tromp lus
   Ne de quet ehiu teign.

Ma me guelet m'en, doucic,
    Ha pe veign me hunon;
Dahlet hon comzan gwen oh
    Drouc e rand dem halon.

Ha pe glehuan en druhumel
    Da geneign ar er bar;
Me lar gahus e li halon,
    Neh quet pel doh hi far.

Ha re veign marhue, doucic,
    Hui lareign ar me be
Che tu be en deu yoang
    Marhue quet carante!

FROM *The Nursery Rhymes of England,
collected chiefly from Oral Tradition by
James Orchard Halliwell*, 1842, 1853

There was a King

There was a King and he had three daughters,
And they all lived in a basin of water;
    The basin bended,
    My story's ended.
If the basin had been stronger
My story would have been longer.

Rock, Ball, Fiddle

He that lies at the stock,
Shall have the gold rock;
He that lies at the wall,
Shall have the gold ball;
He that lies in the middle,
Shall have the gold fiddle.

This is the key

This is the key of the kingdom:
In that kingdom there is a city.
In that city there is a town.
In that town there is a street.
In that street there is a lane.
In that lane there is a yard.
In that yard there is a house.
In that house there is a room.
In that room there is a bed.
On that bed there is a basket.
In that basket there are some flowers.

Flowers in a basket.
Basket in the bed.
Bed in the room.
Room in the house.
House in the yard.
Yard in the lane.
Lane in the street.
Street in the town.
Town in the city.
City in the kingdom.
Of the kingdom this is the key.

Solomon Grundy

Solomon Grundy,
Born on a Monday,
Christened on Tuesday,
Married on Wednesday,
Took ill on Thursday,
Worse on Friday,
Died on Saturday,
Buried on Sunday.
This is the end
Of Solomon Grundy.

As I went to Bonner

As I went to Bonner,
  I met a pig
    Without a wig,
Upon my word and honour.

There was a crooked man

There was a crooked man, and he went a crooked mile,
He found a crooked sixpence against a crooked stile:
He bought a crooked cat which caught a crooked mouse,
And they all lived together in a little crooked house.

There were three jovial Welshmen

There were three jovial Welshmen,
  As I have heard men say,
And they would go a-hunting
  Upon St David's Day.

All the day they hunted
  And nothing could they find,
But a ship a-sailing,
  A-sailing with the wind.

One said it was a ship,
  The other he said, Nay.
The third said it was a house,
  With the chimney blown away.

And all the night they hunted
  And nothing could they find
But the moon a-gliding,
  A-gliding with the wind.

One said it was the moon,
  The other he said, Nay.
The third said it was a cheese,
  And half of it cut away.

And all the day they hunted
  And nothing could they find,
But a hedgehog in a bramble bush,
  And that they left behind.

The first said it was a hedgehog,
  The second he said, Nay.
The third said it was a pincushion,
  And the pins stuck in wrong way.

One-ery, two-ery

One-ery, two-ery,
  Ziccary zan;
Hollow bone, crack a bone,
  Ninery, ten;
Spittery spot,
  It must be done;
Twiddleum twaddleum,
  Twenty-one.

Mr Punchinello

Oh! mother, I shall be married to Mr Punchinello.
  To Mr Punch,
  To Mr Joe,
  To Mr Nell,
  To Mr Lo,
  Mr Punch, Mr Joe,
  Mr Nell, Mr Lo,
  To Mr Punchinello.

A game on the fingers

Heetum peetum penny pie,
Populorum gingum gie;
East, West, North, South,
Kirby, Kendal, Cock him out!

One Old Oxford Ox

One old Oxford ox opening oysters;
Two tee-totums totally tired of trying to trot to Tadbury;
Three tall tigers tippling tenpenny tea;
Four fat friars fanning fainting flies;
Five frippy Frenchmen foolishly fishing for flies;
Six sportsmen shooting snipes;

Seven Severn salmons swallowing shrimps;
Eight Englishmen eagerly examining Europe;
Nine nimble noblemen nibbling nonpareils;
Ten tinkers tinkling upon ten tin tinder-boxes with ten ten-
     penny tacks;
Eleven elephants elegantly equipt;
Twelve typographical typographers typically translating types.

Flowers, Flowers

A game to alarm children.

Flowers, flowers, high-no!
Sheeny, greeny, rino! –
   Sheeny greeny,
   Sheeny greeny,
Rum tum fra!

EDWARD LEAR
1812–88

To Ann Lear

To Miss Lear on her Birthday
17 January 1826

Dear, and very dear relation,
Time, who flies without cessation, –
Who ne'er allows procrastination, –
Who never yields to recubation
Nor ever stops for respiration,
Has brought again in round rotation,
The once a yearly celebration
Of the day of thy creation, –
When another augmentation
Of a whole year in numeration
Will be joined in annexation
To thy former glomeration
Of five seven-years incalculation.
And in this very blest occasion
A thought had crossed my imagination,
That I 'neath an obligation
To make to thee a presentation,
(So 'tis the custom of our nation)
Of any trifling small donation,
Just to express my gratulation
Because of thy safe peragration
To one more long year's termination;
But having made an indagation
As to my moneyed situation,
What must have been my indignation
Mortification, and vexation. –
I tell you sans equivocation,
– I found – through dire depauperation,
A want of power – my sweet relation,
To practise my determination! –

So as the fates ordained frustration
I shortly ceased my lamentation

[236]

And, though it caused much improbation,
I set to work with resignation
To torture my imagination,
To spin some curious dication
To merit p'raps thine approbation, –
At least to meet thine acceptation,
And – after much deliberation
And 'mongst my thoughts much altercation,
I fixed that every termination
To every line should end in -ation! –
Now – since I've given this explanation,
Deign to receive my salutation
And let me breathe an aspiration
To thee – this day of thy creation.

First then, I wish thee, dear relation,
Many a sweet reduplication
Of this thy natal celebration:
And may'st thou from this first lunation
Unto thy vital termination
Be free from every derogation
By fell disease's contamination,
Whose catalogic calculation
Completely thwarts enumeration, –
Emaciation, fomentation,
With dementation – deplumation,
And many more in computation
For these are but an adumberation: –
– And may'st thou never have occasion
For any surgic operation
Or medical administration, –
Sanguification, – defalcation, –
Cauterization – amputation –
Rhabarbaration – scarification
And more of various designation: –
May'st thou be kept in preservation
From every sort of vitiation
By evils dark depreciation: –
Intoxication – trucidation, –
From Malversation – desecration –
From giving way to execration,
And every sinful machination: –

And in thy daily occupation –
Whether it be discalceation,
Or any other ministration
May'st thou not meet the least frustration;
May'st thou withstand all obtrectation
Thrown out to mar thy reputation; –
May'st thou be free from altercations
Or with thy word or thy relations; –
And (though it wants corroberation,
Yet nor quite void of confirmation, –)
If as report gives intimation
You are about to change your station,
May every peaceful combination
Of bliss await your situation
In matrimonial elevation –
May'st thou be loved with veneration; –
– By none be held in detestation, –
And towards thy life's advesperation,
When most are prone to
Their feeble limbs to desiccation, –
Their strength through years to deliquation, –
Their minds and brains to conquassation, –
Their failing speech to aberration, –
Their wearied taste to nauseation, –
                              then,
Then, may'st thou, – Oh dear relation,
Always receive refulerlation, –
Thy frame imbibe reanimation, –
Thy reason hold her wonted station
And keep her prudent scintillation,
Till thou descend'st by slow gradation
Unto thy final destination –
The long last home of all creation.
– This is my birthday aspiration; –
– Believe it, ever dear relation
Sincere without exaggeration –
In every individual ation! –
Sanguine – in each anticipation –
And kindly meant in perpetration.

                                        17th Jan 1826.

To Lady Wyatt

[Villa Emily, San Remo] | 16. April. 1875.

Dear Lady Wyatt,

If I a*M int*erupting you please excuse me
as I *mint* to have asked you a question the other day
but forgot to *mint*=ion it. Can you tell me how to make
preserved or dry *mint*? I have got a
mint of
mint in my garden, but although I
a*m int*=erested in getting some of it dried for
peasoup, I a*m in t*errible ignorance of how to dry it,
and a*m in t*orture till I know how. On cutting | the
leaves, should they be *mint*'sd up small like
mint'sd meat? – or should I put
the*m into* Gin & Tarragon vinegar? Or place them
in a jar of *Mint*on pottery, & expose them to the
ele*mint*s in a
her*mint*ically sealed bottle? If Mr Disraeli,
who is now Prime *mint*=stir, could teach us how to stir
the *mint*,
I a*m int*ernally convinced we could manage it.
This is as plain as that the *Mint*cio is a large River in Italy, or that
Lord *Mint*o was once Governor Genl. of India. Perhaps
at the risingof Parlia*mint*, he may help us. After all would the
success be com*mint*surate with the trouble?
What com*mint* can be made on this except
that Mrs Wyatt should send To*m into* the country if he is unwell in town?
One thing is sure, all ver*mint* must be carefully excluded
from the bottle, & I a*m int*ending to get one really well
made, for I a*m int*oxicated with the idea of getting good dry
mint. Please if you have a receipt, give it me
which will be a monu*mint* of your good nature.
*Mint*ime I
a *mint*oo much haste to write any
more, so will leave off im*mint*iately.

Your's sincerely
Edward Lear.

Limericks from *The Book of Nonsense* (1846)

There was an Old Man with a beard,
Who said, 'It is just as I feared! –
Two Owls and a Hen, four Larks and a Wren,
Have all built their nests in my beard!'

There was an Old Man in a boat,
Who said, 'I'm afloat! I'm afloat!'
When they said, 'No! you ain't!' he was ready to faint,
That unhappy Old Man in a boat.

There was an Old Person of Cadiz,
Who was always polite to the ladies;
But in handing his daughter, he fell into the water,
Which drowned that Old Person of Cadiz.

There was an Old Person of Basing,
Whose presence of mind was amazing;
He purchased a steed, which he rode at full speed,
And escaped from the people of Basing.

There was an Old Person of Philæ,
Whose conduct was scroobious and wily;
He rushed up a Palm, when the weather was calm,
And observed all the ruins of Philæ.

There was a Young Lady of Lucca,
Whose lovers completely forsook her;
She ran up a tree, and said, 'Fiddle-de-dee!'
Which embarrassed the people of Lucca.

There was an Old Man of Cape Horn,
Who wished he had never been born;
So he sat on a chair, till he died of despair,
That dolorous Man of Cape Horn.

There was an Old Man of Whitehaven;
Who danced a quadrille with a Raven;
But they said – 'It's absurd, to encourage this bird!'
So they smashed that Old Man of Whitehaven.

There was a Young Lady of Sweden,
Who went by the slow train to Weedon;
When they cried, 'Weedon Station!' she made no observation,
But thought she should go back to Sweden.

There was an Old Person of Ems,
Who casually fell in the Thames;
And when he was found, they said he was drowned,
That unlucky Old Person of Ems.

The Owl and the Pussy-cat

I

The Owl and the Pussy-cat went to sea
   In a beautiful pea-green boat;
They took some honey, and plenty of money,
   Wrapped up in a five-pound note.
The Owl looked up to the stars above,
   And sang to a small guitar,
'O lovely Pussy! O Pussy, my love,
     What a beautiful Pussy you are,
       You are,
       You are!
   What a beautiful Pussy you are!'

II

Pussy said to the Owl, 'You elegant fowl!
   How charmingly sweet you sing!
O let us be married! too long we have tarried:
   But what shall we do for a ring?'
They sailed away, for a year and a day,
   To the land where the Bong-tree grows,
And there in a wood a Piggy-wig stood
   With a ring at the end of his nose,
       His nose,
       His nose,
   With a ring at the end of his nose.

'Dear Pig, are you willing to sell for one shilling
    Your ring?' Said the Piggy, 'I will.'
So they took it away, and were married next day
    By the Turkey who lives on the hill.
They dined on mince, and slices of quince,
    Which they ate with a runcible spoon;
And hand in hand, on the edge of the sand,
    They danced by the light of the moon,
        The moon,
        The moon,
They danced by the light of the moon.

The Daddy Long-legs and the Fly

I

Once Mr Daddy Long-legs,
    Dressed in brown and gray,
Walked about upon the sands
Upon a summer's day;
And there among the pebbles,
    When the wind was rather cold,
He met with Mr Floppy Fly,
    All dressed in blue and gold.
And as it was too soon to dine,
They drank some Periwinkle-wine,
And played an hour two, or more,
At battlecock and shuttledore.

II

Said Mr Daddy Long-legs
    To Mr Floppy Fly,
'Why do you never come to court?
    I wish you'd tell me why.
All gold and shine, in dress so fine,
    You'd quite delight the court.
Why do you never go at all?
    I really think you *ought!*
And if you went, you'd see such sights!
Such rugs! and jugs! and candle-lights!

And more than all, the King and Queen.
One in red, and one in green!'

III

'O Mr Daddy Long-legs,'
   Said Mr Floppy Fly,
'It's true I never go to court,
   And I will tell you why.
If I had six long legs like yours,
   At once I'd go to court!
But oh! I can't, because *my* legs
   Are so extremely short.
And I'm afraid the King and Queen
(One in red, and one in green)
Would say aloud, "You are not fit,
You Fly, to come to court a bit!"'

IV

'O Mr Daddy Long-legs,'
   Said Mr Floppy Fly,
'I wish you'd sing one little song!
   One mumbian melody!
You used to sing so awful well
   In former days gone by,
But now you never sing at all;
   I wish you'd tell me why:
For if you would, the silvery sound
Would please the shrimps and cockles round,
And all the crabs would gladly come
To hear you sing, "Ah, Hum di Hum!"'

V

Said Mr Daddy Long-legs,
   'I can never sing again!
And if you wish, I'll tell you why,
   Although it gives me pain.
For years I could not hum a bit,
   Or sing the smallest song;
And this the dreadful reason is,
   My legs are grown too long!
My six long legs, all here and there,
Oppress my bosom with despair;

[245]

And if I stand, or lie, or sit,
I cannot sing one single bit!"

VI

So Mr Daddy Long-legs
 And Mr Floppy Fly
Sat down in silence by the sea,
 And gazed upon the sky.
They said, 'This is a dreadful thing!
 The world has all gone wrong,
Since one has legs too short by half,
 The other much too long!
One never more can go to court,
Because his legs have grown too short;
The other cannot sing a song,
Because his legs have grown too long!'

VII

Then Mr Daddy Long-legs
 And Mr Floppy Fly
Rushed downward to the foaming sea
 With one sponge-taneous cry;
And there they found a little boat,
 Whose sails were pink and gray;
And off they sailed among the waves,
 Far, and far away.
They sailed across the silent main,
And reached the great Gromboolian plain;
And there they play for evermore
At battlecock and shuttledore.

The Jumblies

I

They went to sea in a Sieve, they did,
   In a Sieve they went to sea:
In spite of all their friends could say,
On a winter's morn, on a stormy day,
   In a Sieve they went to sea!
And when the Sieve turned round and round,
And every one cried, 'You'll all be drowned!'
They called aloud, 'Our Sieve ain't big,
But we don't care a button! we don't care a fig!
   In a Sieve we'll go to sea!'
     Far and few, far and few,
       Are the lands where the Jumblies live;
       Their heads are green, and their hands are blue,
       And they went to sea in a Sieve.

II

They sailed away in a Sieve, they did,
   In a Sieve they sailed so fast,
With only a beautiful pea-green veil
Tied with a ribbon by way of a sail,
   To a small tobacco-pipe mast;
And every one said, who saw them go,
'O won't they be soon upset, you know!

For the sky is dark, and the voyage is long,
And happen what may, it's extremely wrong
  In a Sieve to sail so fast!'
    Far and few, far and few,
      Are the lands where the Jumblies live;
     Their heads are green, and their hands are blue,
      And they went to sea in a Sieve.

III

The water it soon came in, it did,
  The water it soon came in;
So to keep them dry, they wrapped their feet
In a pinky paper all folded neat,
  And they fastened it down with a pin.
And they passed the night in a crockery-jar,
And each of them said, 'How wise we are!
Though the sky be dark, and the voyage be long,
Yet we never can think we were rash or wrong,
  While round in our Sieve we spin!'
    Far and few, far and few,
      Are the lands where the Jumblies live;
     Their heads are green, and their hands are blue,
      And they went to sea in a Sieve.

IV

And all night long they sailed away;
  And when the sun went down,
They whistled and warbled a moony song
To the echoing sound of a coppery gong,
  In the shade of the mountains brown.
'O Timballoo! How happy we are,
When we live in a sieve and a crockery-jar,
And all night long in the moonlight pale,
We sail away with a pea-green sail,
  In the shade of the mountains brown!'
    Far and few, far and few,
      Are the lands where the Jumblies live;
     Their heads are green, and their hands are blue,
      And they went to sea in a Sieve.

They sailed to the Western Sea, they did,
    To a land all covered with trees,
And they bought an Owl, and a useful Cart,
And a pound of Rice, and a Cranberry Tart,
    And a hive of silvery Bees.
And they bought a Pig, and some green Jack-daws,
And a lovely Monkey with lollipop paws,
And forty bottles of Ring-Bo-Ree,
    And no end of Stilton Cheese.
      Far and few, far and few,
        Are the lands where the Jumblies live;
      Their heads are green, and their hands are blue,
        And they went to sea in a Sieve.

VI

And in twenty years they all came back,
    In twenty years or more,
And every one said, 'How tall they've grown!
For they've been to the Lakes, and the Torrible Zone,
    And the hills of the Chankly Bore.'
And they drank their health, and gave them a feast
Of dumplings made of beautiful yeast;
And every one said, 'If we only live,
We too will go to sea in a Sieve, –
    To the hills of the Chankly Bore!'
      Far and few, far and few,
        Are the lands where the Jumblies live;
      Their heads are green, and their hands are blue,
        And they went to sea in a Sieve.

More Nonsense

There was an Old Man whose despair
Induced him to purchase a hare:
Whereon one fine day, he rode wholly away,
Which partly assuaged his despair.

There was an Old Person of Bree,
Who frequented the depths of the sea;
She nurs'd the small fishes, and washed all the dishes,
And swam back again into Bree.

There was an Old Man who screamed out
Whenever they knocked him about;
So they took off his boots, And fed him with fruits,
And continued to knock him about.

There was an Old Person of Slough,
Who danced at the end of a bough;
But they said, 'If you sneeze, You might damage the trees,
You imprudent old person of Slough.'

There was an Old Person of Grange,
Whose manners were scroobious and strange;
He sailed to St Blubb, in a waterproof tub,
That aquatic old person of Grange.

There was a Young Person of Kew,
Whose virtues and vices were few;
But with blameable haste, she devoured some hot paste,
Which destroyed that young person of Kew.

There was an Old Person of Bow,
Whom nobody happened to know;
So they gave him some soap, and said coldly, 'We hope
You will go back directly to Bow!'

There was an Old Person of Brigg,
Who purchased no end of a wig;
So that only his nose, and the end of his toes,
Could be seen when he walked about Brigg.

There was an Old Man in a tree,
Whose whiskers were lovely to see;
But the birds of the air, pluck'd them perfectly bare,
To make themselves nests in that tree.

Twenty-Six Nonsense Rhymes
[without their Pictures]

A   The Absolutely Abstemious Ass,
who resided in a Barrel, and only lived on
Soda Water and Pickled Cucumbers.

B   The Bountiful Beetle,
who always carried a Green Umbrella when it didn't rain,
and left it at home when it did.

C   The Comfortable Confidential Cow,
who sate in her Red Morocco Armchair and
toasted her own Bread at the parlour Fire.

D   The Dolomphious Duck,
who caught spotted frogs for her dinner
with a Runcible Spoon.

E   The Enthusiastic Elephant,
who ferried himself across the water with the
Kitchen Poker and a New pair of Ear-rings.

F   The Fizzgiggious Fish,
who always walked about upon Stilts,
because he had no legs.

G   The Good-natured Gray Gull,
who carried the Old Owl, and his Crimson Carpetbag,
across the river, because he could not swim.

H   The Hasty Higgledypiggledy Hen,
who went to market in a Blue Bonnet and Shawl,
and bought a Fish for Supper.

I   The Inventive Indian,
who caught a Remarkable Rabbit in a
Stupendous Silver Spoon.

J   The Judicious Jubilant Jay,
who did up her Back Hair every morning with a Wreath of
    Roses,
Three feathers, and a Gold Pin.

K   The Kicking Kangaroo,
who wore a Pale Pink Muslin dress
with Blue spots.

L   The Lively Learned Lobster,
who mended his own Clothes with
a Needle and Thread.

M   The Melodious Meritorious Mouse,
who played a merry minuet on the
Pianoforte.

N   The Nutritious Newt,
who purchased a Round Plum-pudding,
for his granddaughter.

O   The Obsequious Ornamental Ostrich,
who wore boots to keep his
feet quite dry.

P   The Perpendicular Purple Polly,
        who read the Newspaper and ate Parsnip Pie
        with his Spectacles.

Q   The Queer Querulous Quail,
        who smoked a pipe of tobacco on the top of
        a Tin Tea-kettle.

R   The Rural Runcible Raven,
        who wore a White Wig and flew away
        with the Carpet Broom.

S   The Scroobious Snake,
        who always wore a Hat on his Head, for
        fear he should bite anybody.

T   The Tumultuous Tom-tommy Tortoise,
        who beat a Drum all day long in the
        middle of the wilderness.

U   The Umbrageous Umbrella-maker,
        whose Face nobody ever saw, because it was always covered by
            his Umbrella.

V   The Visibly Vicious Vulture,
        who wrote some verses to a Veal-cutlet in a
        Volume bound in Vellum.

W   The Worrying Whizzing Wasp,
        who stood on a Table, and played sweetly on a
        Flute with a Morning Cap.

X   The Excellent Double-extra XX
        imbibing King Xerxes, who lived a
        long while ago.

Y   The Yonghy-Bonghy-Bo
        whose Head was ever so much bigger than his
        Body, and whose Hat was rather small.

Z   The Zigzag Zealous Zebra,
        who carried five Monkeys on his back all
        the way to Jellibolee.

The Dong with a Luminous Nose

When awful darkness and silence reign
Over the great Gromboolian plain,
  Through the long, long wintry nights; –
When the angry breakers roar
As they beat on the rocky shore; –
  When Storm-clouds brood on the towering heights
Of the Hills of the Chankly Bore: –

Then, through the vast and gloomy dark,
There moves what seems a fiery spark,
  A lonely spark with silvery rays
  Piercing the coal-black night, –
  A Meteor strange and bright: –
Hither and thither the vision strays,
  A single lurid light.

Slowly it wanders, – pauses, – creeps, –
Anon it sparkles, – flashes and leaps;
And ever as onward it gleaming goes
A light on the Bong-tree stems it throws.
And those who watch at that midnight hour
From Hall or Terrace, or lofty Tower,
Cry, as the wild light passes along, –
    'The Dong! – the Dong!
  'The wandering Dong through the forest goes!
    'The Dong! the Dong!
  'The Dong with a luminous Nose!'

Long years ago
The Dong was happy and gay,
Till he fell in love with a Jumbly Girl
Who came to those shores one day.
For the Jumblies came in a sieve, they did, –
Landing at eve near the Zemmery Fidd
Where the Oblong Oysters grow,
And the rocks are smooth and gray.
And all the woods and the valleys rang
With the Chorus they daily and nightly sang, –
'Far and few, far and few,
Are the lands where the Jumblies live;
Their heads are green, and their hands are blue
And they went to sea in a sieve.'

Happily, happily passed those days!
While the cheerful Jumblies staid;
They danced in circlets all night long,
To the plaintive pipe of the lively Dong,
In moonlight, shine, or shade.
For day and night he was always there
By the side of the Jumbly Girl so fair,
With her sky-blue hands, and her sea-green hair.
Till the morning came of that hateful day
When the Jumblies sailed in their sieve away,
And the Dong was left on the cruel shore
Gazing – gazing for evermore, –
Ever keeping his weary eyes on
That pea-green sail on the far horizon, –
Singing the Jumbly Chorus still
As he sate all day on the grassy hill, –
'Far and few, far and few,
Are the lands where the Jumblies live;
Their heads are green, and their hands are blue,
And they went to sea in a sieve.'

But when the sun was low in the West,
The Dong arose and said, –
– 'What little sense I once possessed
Has quite gone out of my head!' –
And since that day he wanders still

By lake and forest, marsh and hill,
Singing – 'O somewhere, in valley or plain
'Might I find my Jumbly Girl again!
'For ever I'll seek by lake and shore
'Till I find my Jumbly Girl once more!'

Playing a pipe with silvery squeaks,
Since then his Jumbly Girl he seeks,
And because by night he could not see,
He gathered the bark of the Twangum Tree
    On the flowery plain that grows.
    And he wove him a wondrous Nose, –
A Nose as strange as a Nose could be!
Of vast proportions and painted red,
And tied with cords to the back of his head.
    – In a hollow rounded space it ended
    With a luminous Lamp within suspended,
        All fenced about
        With a bandage stout
        To prevent the wind from blowing it out; –
    And with holes all round to send the light,
    In gleaming rays on the dismal night.

And now each night, and all night long,
Over those plains still roams the Dong;
And above the wail of the Chimp and Snipe
You may hear the squeak of his plaintive pipe
While ever he seeks, but seeks in vain
To meet with his Jumbly Girl again;
Lonely and wild – all night he goes, –
The Dong with a luminous Nose!
And all who watch at the midnight hour,
From Hall or Terrace, or lofty Tower,
Cry, as they trace the Meteor bright,
Moving along through the dreary night, –
    'This is the hour when forth he goes,
    'The Dong with a luminous Nose!
    'Yonder – over the plain he goes;
        'He goes!
        'He goes;
    'The Dong with a luminous Nose!'

The Pobble who has no Toes

The Pobble who has no toes
   Had once as many as we;
When they said, 'Some day you may lose them all;' –
   He replied, – 'Fish fiddle de-dee!'
And his Aunt Jobiska made him drink,
Lavender water tinged with pink,
For she said, 'The World in general knows
     There's nothing so good for a Pobble's toes!'

II

The Pobble who has no toes,
   Swam across the Bristol Channel;
But before he set out he wrapped his nose,
   In a piece of scarlet flannel.
For his Aunt Jobiska said, 'No harm
'Can come to his toes if his nose is warm;
'And it's perfectly known that a Pobble's toes
'Are safe, – provided he minds his nose.'

III

The Pobble swam fast and well
   And when boats or ships came near him
He tinkledy-binkledy-winkled a bell
   So that all the world could hear him.
And all the Sailors and Admirals cried,
When they saw him nearing the further side, –
'He has gone to fish, for his Aunt Jobiska's
'Runcible Cat with crimson whiskers!'

IV

But before he touched the shore,
   The shore of the Bristol Channel,
A sea-green Porpoise carried away
   His wrapper of scarlet flannel.
And when he came to observe his feet
Formerly garnished with toes so neat
His face at once became forlorn
On perceiving that all his toes were gone!

And nobody ever knew
   From that dark day to the present,
Whoso had taken the Pobble's toes,
   In a manner so far from pleasant.
Whether the shrimps or crawfish gray,
Or crafty Mermaids stole them away –
Nobody knew; and nobody knows
How the Pobble was robbed of his twice five toes!

VI

The Pobble who has no toes
   Was placed in a friendly Bark,
And they rowed him back, and carried him up,
   To his Aunt Jobiska's Park.
And she made him a feast at his earnest wish
Of eggs and buttercups fried with fish; –
And she said, – 'It's a fact the whole world knows,
'That Pobbles are happier without their toes.'

The Quangle Wangle's Hat

I

On the top of the Crumpetty Tree
   The Quangle Wangle sat,
But his face you could not see,
   On account of his Beaver Hat.

For his Hat was a hundred and two feet wide,
With ribbons and bibbons on every side
And bells, and buttons, and loops, and lace,
So that nobody ever could see the face
        Of the Quangle Wangle Quee.

II

The Quangle Wangle said
    To himself on the Crumpetty Tree, –
'Jam, and jelly, and bread,
    'Are the best of food for me!
'But the longer I live on this Crumpetty Tree
'The plainer than ever it seems to me
'That very few people come this way
'And that life on the whole is far from gay!'
        Said the Quangle Wangle Quee.

III

But there came to the Crumpetty Tree,
    Mr and Mrs Canary;
And they said, – 'Did you ever see
    'Any spot so charmingly airy?
'May we build a nest on your lovely Hat?
'Mr Quangle Wangle, grant us that!
'O please let us come and build a nest
'Of whatever material suits you best,
        'Mr Quangle Wangle Quee!'

IV

And besides, to the Crumpetty Tree
    Came the Stork, the Duck, and the Owl;
The Snail, and the Bumble-Bee,
    The Frog, and the Fimble Fowl;
(The Fimble Fowl, with a Corkscrew leg;)
And all of them said, – 'We humbly beg,
'We may build our homes on your lovely Hat, –
'Mr Quangle Wangle, grant us that!
        'Mr Quangle Wangle Quee!'

V

And the Golden Grouse came there,
    And the Pobble who has no toes, –

And the small Olympian bear, –
 And the Dong with a luminous nose.
And the Blue Baboon, who played the flute, –
And the Orient Calf from the Land of Tute, –
And the Attery Squash, and the Bisky Bat, –
All came and built on the lovely Hat
  Of the Quangle Wangle Quee.

VI

And the Quangle Wangle said
 To himself on the Crumpetty Tree, –
'When all these creatures move
 'What a wonderful noise there'll be!'
And at night by the light of the Mulberry moon
They danced to the Flute of the Blue Baboon,
On the broad green leaves of the Crumpetty Tree,
And all were as happy as happy could be,
  With the Quangle Wangle Quee.

The Akond of Swat

Who, or why, or which, or *what*, Is the Akond of SWAT?
Is he tall or short, or dark or fair?
Does he sit on a stool or a sofa or chair,   or SQUAT,
      The Akond of Swat?

Is he wise or foolish, young or old?
Does he drink his soup and his coffee cold,   or HOT,
      The Akond of Swat?

Does he sing or whistle, jabber or talk,
And when riding abroad does he gallop or walk   or TROT,
      The Akond of Swat?

Does he wear a turban, a fez, or a hat?
Does he sleep on a mattress, a bed, or a mat,   or a COT,
      The Akond of Swat?

When he writes a copy in round-hand size,
Does he cross his T's and finish his I's   with a DOT,
      The Akond of Swat?

Can he write a letter concisely clear
Without a speck or a smudge or smear
              or BLOT,
          The Akond of Swat?

Do his people like him extremely well?
Or do they, whenever they can, rebel,
              or PLOT,
        At the Akond of Swat?

If he catches them then, either old or young,
Does he have them chopped in pieces or hung,
              or *shot*,
          The Akond of Swat?

Do his people prig in the lanes or park?
Or even at times, when days are dark,
              GAROTTE?
         O the Akond of Swat!

Does he study the wants of his own dominion?
Or doesn't he care for public opinion
              a JOT,
          The Akond of Swat?

To amuse his mind do his people show him
Pictures, or any one's last new poem,
              or WHAT,
        For the Akond of Swat?

At night if he suddenly screams and wakes,
Do they bring him only a few small cakes,
              or a LOT,
        For the Akond of Swat?

Does he live on turnips, tea, or tripe?
Does he like his shawl to be marked with a stripe,
        or a DOT,
         The Akond of Swat?

Does he like to lie on his back in a boat
Like the lady who lived in that isle remote,
        SHALLOTT,
        The Akond of Swat?

Is he quiet, or always making a fuss?
Is his steward a Swiss or a Swede or a Russ,
        or a SCOT,
        The Akond of Swat?

Does he like to sit by the calm blue wave?
Or to sleep and snore in a dark green cave,   or a GROTT,
        The Akond of Swat?

Does he drink small beer from a silver jug?
Or a bowl? or a glass? or a cup? or a mug?   or a POT.
        The Akond of Swat?

Does he beat his wife with a gold-topped pipe,
When she lets the gooseberries grow too ripe,   or ROT,
        The Akond of Swat?

Does he wear a white tie when he dines with friends,
And tie it neat in a bow with ends,   or a KNOT,
        The Akond of Swat?

Does he like new cream, and hate mince-pies?
When he looks at the sun does he wink his eyes,   or NOT,
        The Akond of Swat?

Does he teach his subjects to roast and bake?
Does he sail about on an inland lake,   in a YACHT,
        The Akond of Swat?

Some one, or nobody, knows I wot
Who or which or why or what
        Is the Akond of Swat!

Incidents in the Life of my Uncle Arly

I

O my agèd Uncle Arly!
Sitting on a heap of Barley
    Thro' the silent hours of night, –
Close beside a leafy thicket: –
On his nose there was a Cricket, –
In his hat a Railway-Ticket; –
    (But his shoes were far too tight.)

[263]

II

Long ago, in youth, he squander'd
All his goods away, and wander'd
  To the Tiniskoop-hills afar.
There on golden sunsets blazing,
Every evening found him gazing, –
Singing, – 'Orb! you're quite amazing!
  'How I wonder what you are!'

III

Like the ancient Medes and Persians,
Always by his own exertions
  He subsisted on those hills; –
Whiles, – by teaching children spelling, –
Or at times by merely yelling, –
Or at intervals by selling
  'Propter's Nicodemus Pills.'

IV

Later, in his morning rambles
He perceived the moving brambles –
  Something square and white disclose; –
'Twas a First-class Railway-Ticket;
But, on stooping down to pick it
Off the ground, – a pea-green Cricket
  Settled on my uncle's Nose.

V

Never – never more, – oh! never,
Did that Cricket leave him ever, –
  Dawn or evening, day or night; –
Clinging as a constant treasure, –
Chirping with a cheerious measure, –
Wholly to my uncle's pleasure, –
  (Though his shoes were far too tight.)

VI

So for three-and-forty winters,
Till his shoes were worn to splinters,
  All those hills he wander'd o'er, –
Sometimes silent; – sometimes yelling; –

Till he came to Borley-Melling,
Near his old ancestral dwelling; –
 (But his shoes were far too tight.)

VII

On a little heap of Barley
Died my agèd uncle Arly,
 And they buried him one night; –
Close beside the leafy thicket; –
There, – his hat and Railway-Ticket; –
There, – his ever-faithful Cricket; –
 (But his shoes were far too tight.)

How Pleasant to know Mr Lear!

How pleasant to know Mr Lear!
 Who has written such volumes of stuff!
Some think him ill-tempered and queer,
 But a few think him pleasant enough.

His mind is concrete and fastidious,
 His nose is remarkably big;
His visage is more or less hideous,
 His beard it resembles a wig.

He has ears, and two eyes, and ten fingers,
 Leastways if you reckon two thumbs;
Long ago he was one of the singers,
 But now he is one of the dumbs.

He sits in a beautiful parlour,
 With hundreds of books on the wall;
He drinks a great deal of Marsala,
 But never gets tipsy at all.

He has many friends, laymen and clerical;
 Old Foss is the name of his cat;
His body is perfectly spherical,
 He weareth a runcible hat.

When he walks in a waterproof white,
   The children run after him so!
Calling out, 'He's come out in his night-
   Gown, that crazy old Englishman, oh!'

He weeps by the side of the ocean,
   He weeps on the top of the hill;
He purchases pancakes and lotion,
   And chocolate shrimps from the mill.

He reads but he cannot speak Spanish,
   He cannot abide ginger-beer:
Ere the days of his pilgrimage vanish,
   How pleasant to know Mr Lear!

1895

Cold are the Crabs

Cold are the crabs that crawl on yonder hills,
Colder the cucumbers that grow beneath,
And colder still the brazen chops that wreathe
   The tedious gloom of philosophic pills!
For when the tardy film of nectar fills
The ample bowls of demons and of men,
There lurks the feeble mouse, the homely hen,
   And there the porcupine with all her quills.
Yet much remains – to weave a solemn strain
That lingering sadly – slowly dies away,
Daily departing with departing day.
A pea green gamut on a distant plain
When wily walrusses in congress meet –
   Such such is life –
                                 .

A Sample of *Teapots and Quails*

Teapots and Quails,
Snuffers and snails,
Set him a sailing
and see how he sails!

Volumes and Pigs,
Razors and Figs,
Set him a jigging
and see how he jigs!

Hurdles and Mumps,
Poodles and pumps,
Set it a jumping
and see how it jumps!

Houses and Kings,
Oysters and Rings,
Set him a singing
and see how he sings!

Scissors and Fowls
Filberts and Owls,
Set him a howling
and see how he howls!

The Scroobious Pip *

The Scroobious Pip went out one day
When the grass was green, and the sky was grey.
Then all the beasts in the world came round
When the Scroobious Pip sat down on the ground.
   The cat and the dog and the kangaroo
   The sheep and the cow and the guineapig too –
   The wolf he howled, the horse he neighed
   The little pig squeaked and the donkey brayed,
   And when the lion began to roar
   There never was heard such a noise before.
   And every beast he stood on the tip
   Of his toes to look at the Scroobious Pip.

*The phrases in square brackets are mine, makeshift metrical bridges to cross holes in t
original text in the Harvard Library collection.

At last they said to the Fox – 'By far,
You're the wisest beast! You know you are!
Go close to the Scroobious Pip and say,
Tell us all about yourself we pray –
For as yet we can't make out in the least
If you're Fish or Insect, or Bird or Beast.'
The Scroobious Pip looked vaguely round
And sang these words with a rumbling sound –
      Chippetty Flip; Flippetty Chip; –
My only name is the Scroobious Pip.

2

The Scroobious Pip from the top of a tree
Saw the distant Jellybolee, –
And all the birds in the world came there,
Flying in crowds all through the air.
      The Vulture and Eagle, the cock and the hen
      The Ostrich the Turkey the Snipe and the Wren;
      The Parrot chattered, the Blackbird sung
      And the owl looked wise but held his tongue,
      And when the Peacock began to scream
      The hullabaloo was quite extreme.
      And every bird he fluttered the tip
      Of his wing as he stared at the Scroobious Pip.
At last they said to the owl – 'By far,
You're the wisest Bird – you know you are!
Fly close to the Scroobious Pip and say,
Explain all about yourself we pray –
For as yet we have neither seen nor heard
If you're fish or insect, beast or bird!'
The Scroobious Pip looked gaily round
And sang these words with a chirpy sound –
      Flippetty chip – Chippetty flip –
My only name is the Scroobious Pip.

3

The Scroobious Pip went into the sea
By the beautiful shore of the Jellybolee –
All the Fish in the world swam round
With a splashing squashy spluttering sound.
      The sprat, the herring, the turbot too
      The shark the sole and the mackerel blue,

[268]

The flounder sputtered, the porpoise puffed
[The pickerel piped and the bloater bluffed]
And when the whale began to spout
[The ocean green turned inside out]
And every fish he shook the tip
Of his tail as he gazed on the Scroobious Pip.
At last they said to the whale – 'By far
You're the biggest Fish – you know you are!
Swim close to the Scroobious Pip and say –
Tell us all about yourself we pray! –
For to know you yourself is our only wish;
Are you beast or insect, bird or fish?'
The Scroobious Pip looked softly round
And sung these words with a liquid sound –
  Pliffity flip, Pliffity flip –
My only name is the Scroobious Pip.

4

The Scroobious Pip sat under a tree
By the silent shores of the Jellybolee;
All the insects in all the world
About the Scroobious Pip entwirled.
  Beetles and [ants] with purple eyes
  Gnats and buzztilential flies –
  Grasshoppers, butterflies, spiders too,
  Wasps and bees and dragon-flies blue,
  And when the gnats began to hum
  [The grey shore] bounced like a dismal drum,
  And every insect curled the tip
  Of his snout, and looked at the Scroobious Pip.
At last they said to the Ant – 'By far
You're the wisest insect, you know you are!
Creep close to the Scroobious Pip and say –
Tell us all about yourself we pray,
For we can't find out, and we can't tell why –
If you're beast or fish or a bird or a fly.'
The Scroobious Pip turned quickly round
And sang these words with a whistly sound
  Wizzeby wip – wizzeby wip –
My only name is the Scroobious Pip.

Then all the beasts that walk on the ground
Danced in a circle round and round –
And all the birds that fly in the air
Flew round and round in a circle there,
And all the fish in the Jellybolee
Swum in a circle about the sea,
And all the insects that creep or go
Buzzed in a circle to and fro.
And they roared and sang and whistled and cried
Till the noise was heard from side to side –
      Chippetty tip! Chippetty tip!
It's only name is the Scroobious Pip.

CHARLES BAUDELAIRE
1821–67

Le Pauvre Diable

Père	Songe
Las!	Vain …
Mère	Ronge
Pas.	Frein.
Erre	Couche
Sur	Froid,
Terre …	Mouche
Dur! …	Doigt;
Maigre	Chaque
Flanc,	Vent
Nègre	Claque
Blanc,	Dent.
Blême!	Rude
Pas	Jeu …
Même	Plus de
Gras.	Feu!

Rêve	Couve
Pain	Port
Crève	Trouve
Faim . . .	Mort!
Cherche	Bière . . .
Rôt,	Trou . . .
Perche	Pierre
Haut,	Où
Trotte	Sale
Loin,	Chien
Botte	Pâle
Point.	Vient,
Traîne	Sur le
Sa	Bord,
Gêne,	Hurle
Va,	Fort
Pâle	Clame
Fou,	Geint
Pas le	Brame . . .
Sou!	Fin!

MUMMERS' PLAY

c. 1864

from Weston-sub-Edge, Gloucestershire

Final Scene

DOCTOR. Now boys, a long pull short pull, pull all together boys. Oh, we've got him this time, John Finney. Ladies and gentlemen, all this large wolf's tooth has been growing in this man's head ninety-nine years before his great grandmother was born: if it had n't have been taken out to-day, he would have died yesterday. I've a little bottle by my side called Eelgumpane, one spot on the roof of this man's tongue, another on his tooth, will quickly bring him to life again. Rise up, bold fellow, and fight again.

[271]

KING GEORGE *and the* TURKISH KNIGHT *fight.*

FATHER CHRISTMAS. Peace, peace, peace. Walk in Beelzebub.

BEELZEBUB. In comes I old Belzebub
And on my back I carries my club
And in my hand the dripping-pan,
I thinks myself a jolly old man.
Round hole, black as a coal,
Long tail and little hole.

I went up a straight crooked lane. I met a bark and he dogged at me. I went to the stick and cut a hedge, gave him a rallier over the yud jud killed him round stout stiff and bold from Lancashire I came, if Doctor has n't done his part, John Finney wins the game.

Last Christmas night I turned the spit,
I burnt me finger and felt it itch,
The sparks flew over the table,
The pot-lid kicked the ladle,
Up jumped spit jack
Like a mansion man
Swore he'd fight the dripping pan
With his long tail,
Swore he'd send them all to jail.
In comes the grid iron, if you can't agree
I'm the justice, bring um to me.
As I was going along, as I was standing still,
I saw a wooden church built on a wooden hill,
Nineteen leather bells a going without a clapper
That made me wonder what was the matter.

I went on a bit further, I came to King Charles up a cast iron pear tree. He asked I the way to get down. I said put thee feet in the stirrup iron and pitchee poll headfust into a marl pit where ninety-nine parish churches had been dug out besides a few odd villages. I went on a bit further, I came to a little big house, I knocked at the door and the maid fell out. She asked if I could eat a cup of her cider and drink a hard crust of her bread and cheese. I said 'No thanks, yes if yer please.' So I picked up me latters and went me ways. I went on a bit further.

I came to two old women winnowing butter,
That made me mum mum mummer and stutter.

I went on a little bit further: I came to two little whipper snappers thrashing canary seeds: one gave a hard cut, the tother gen a driving cut, cut a sid through a wall nine foot wide killed a little jed dog tother side. I went of the morroe about nine days after, picks up this little jied dog, romes my arm down his throat, turned him inside outards, sent him down Buckle Street barking ninety miles long and I followed after him.

JOHN FINNEY. Now my lads we've come to the land of plenty, rost stones, plum puddings, houses thatched with pancakes, and little pigs running about with knives and forks stuck in their backs crying 'Who'll eat me, who'll eat me?'

FATHER CHRISTMAS. Walk in clever legs.

CLEVERLEGS. In comes I ain't been hit.
With me big hump and little wit.
Me chump's so big, me wit's so small,
But I can play you a tune to please yer all.

FATHER CHRISTMAS. What tune's that then?

CLEVERLEGS. One of our old favourites tunes Ran tan tinder box Cat in the fiddle bag Jonnie up up the orchard.

FATHER CHRISTMAS. Let's have him the.

Now the three-handed reel takes place.

FATHER CHRISTMAS. If this old frying pan had but a tongue,
He'd say 'chuck in yer money and think it no wrong.'

EMILY DICKINSON
1830–86

I'm Nobody

I'm Nobody! Who are you?
Are you – Nobody – Too?
Then there's a pair of us?
Don't tell! they'd advertise – you know!

How dreary – to be – Somebody!
How public – like a Frog –
To tell one's name – the livelong June –
To an admiring Bog!

ANONYMOUS

Chequered Poem, or
Verse for a chess-piece

très	ce	en-	bruit	guer-	pour	té	sim-
tout	un	re	sur-	sci-	qu'un	la	j'ai
ren-	peu	tra-	ce	pré	re	ple	ber-
re	par-	fé-	la	tout	plo-	truit	me
c'est	vail	gloi-	dé-	co-	paix	li-	dé-
plus	l'en	la	qui	re	dé-	j'ai	arts
ter-	que	vaut	la	ne	dé-	boi-	mais
jeu	que	re	de	re	ja-	qu'on	Si

To read the verse, you have to start at the bottom right corner and travel across the board in the style of a knight in chess, as indicated below:

7	38	45	24	5	34	43	26
48	23	6	39	44	25	4	33
37	8	49	46	35	54	27	42
22	47	36	55	40	61	32	3
9	50	21	60	53	56	41	28
18	15	12	54	62	31	2	57
13	10	17	20	59	52	29	64
16	19	14	11	30	63	58	1

The result is the following little poem:

Si j'aime la guerre
    Très peu,
C'est que de la terre
    L'enjeu

Vaut plus que la gloire, –
    Un bruit
Qu'un simple déboire
    Détruit.
J'ai pour préférence
    Surtout

Liberté, science
    Partout,
Travail qui décore
    La paix,
Arts qu'on ne déplore
    Jamais.

[275]

LEWIS CARROLL
1832–98

My Fairy
1845

I have a fairy by my side
   Which says I must not sleep,
When once in pain I loudly cried
   It said 'You must not weep'.

If, full of mirth, I smile and grin,
   It says 'You must not laugh';
When once I wished to drink some gin
   It said 'You must not quaff'.

When once a meal I wished to taste
   It said 'You must not bite';
When to the wars I went in haste
   It said 'You must not fight'.

'What may I do?' at length I cried,
   Tired of the painful task.
The fairy quietly replied,
   And said 'You must not ask'.

   Moral: 'You mustn't.'

Melodies

There was an old farmer of Readall,
Who made holes in his face with a needle,
   Then went *far* deeper in
   Than to pierce through the skin,
And yet strange to say he was made beadle.

There was once a young man of Oporta,
Who daily got shorter and shorter,
    The reason he said
    Was the hod on his head,
Which was filled with the *heaviest* mortar.

His sister, named Lucy O'Finner,
Grew constantly thinner and thinner;
    The reason was plain,
    She slept out in the rain,
And was never allowed any dinner.

The Palace of Humbug

I dreamt I dwelt in marble halls,
And each damp thing that creeps and crawls
Went wobble-wobble on the walls.

Faint odours of departed cheese,
Blown on the dank, unwholesome breeze,
Awoke the never-ending sneeze.

Strange pictures decked the arras drear,
Strange characters of woe and fear,
The humbugs of the social sphere.

One showed a vain and noisy prig,
That shouted empty words and big
At him that nodded in a wig.

And one, a dotard grim and gray,
Who wasteth childhood's happy day
In work more profitless than play.

Whose icy breast no pity warms,
Whose little victims sit in swarms,
And slowly sob on lower forms.

And one, a green thyme-honoured Bank,
Where flowers are growing wild and rank,
Like weeds that fringe a poisoned tank.

All birds of evil omen there
Flood with rich Notes the tainted air,
The witless wandered to snare.

The fatal Notes neglected fall,
No creature heeds the treacherous call,
For all those goodly Strawn Baits Pall.

The wandering phantom broke and fled,
Straightway I saw within my head
A vision of a ghostly bed,

Where lay two worn decrepit men,
The fictions of a lawyer's pen,
Who never more might breathe again.

The serving-man of Richard Roe
Wept, inarticulate with woe:
She wept, that waited on John Doe.

'Oh rouse', I urged, 'the waning sense
With tales of tangled evidence,
Of suit, demurrer, and defence.'

'Vain', she replied, 'such mockeries:
For morbid fancies, such as these,
No suits can suit, no plea can please.'

And bending o'er that man of straw,
She cried in grief and sudden awe,
Not inappropriately, 'Law!'

The well-remembered voice he knew,
He smiled, he faintly mutter 'Sue!'
(Her very name was legal too.)

The night was fled, the dawn was nigh:
A hurricane went raving by,
And swept the Vision from mine eye.

Vanished that dim and ghostly bed,
(The hangings, tape; the tape was red:)
'Tis o'er, and Doe and Roe are dead!

Oh, yet my spirit inly crawls,
What time it shudderingly recalls
That horrid dream of marble halls!

The Mad Hatter's Concert Song

Twinkle, twinkle, little bat!
How I wonder what you're at!
Up above the world you fly
Like a tea-tray in the sky.
         Twinkle, twinkle –

The Mouse's Tale

Fury said to
a mouse, That
he met in the
house, 'Let
us both go
to law: *I*
will prose-
cute *you*.
Come, I'll
take no de-
nial; We
must have
a trial:
For really
this morn-
ing I've
nothing
to do.'
Said the
mouse to
the cur,
'Such a
trial, dear
Sir, With
no jury
or judge,
would
be wast-
ing our
breath.'
'I'll be
judge,
I'll be
jury,'
Said
cun-
ning
old
Fury:
'I'll
try
the
whole
cause,
and
con-
demn
you to
death.'

Father William

'You are old, Father William,' the young man said,
   'And your hair has become very white;
And yet you incessantly stand on your head –
   Do you think, at your age, it is right?'

'In my youth,' Father William replied to his son,
   'I feared it might injure the brain;
But, now that I'm perfectly sure I have none,
   Why, I do it again and again.'

'You are old,' said the youth, 'as I mentioned before.
   And have grown most uncommonly fat;
Yet you turned a back-somersault in at the door –
   Pray, what is the reason of that?'

'In my youth,' said the sage, as he shook his grey locks,
   'I kept all my limbs very supple
By the use oft his ointment – one shilling the box –
   Allow me to sell you a couple?'

'You are old,' said the youth, 'and your jaws are too weak
    For anything tougher than suet;
Yet you finished the goose, with the bones and the beak –
    Pray, how did you manage to do it?'

'In my youth,' said his father, 'I took to the law,
    And argued each case with my wife;
And the muscular strength, which it gave to my jaw
    Has lasted the rest of my life.'

'You are old,' said the youth, 'one would hardly suppose
    That your eye was as steady as ever;
Yet you balanced an eel on the end of your nose –
    What made you so awfully clever?'

'I have answered three questions, and that is enough,'
    Said his father, 'Don't give yourself airs!
Do you think I can listen all day to such stuff?
    Be off, or I'll kick you down-stairs!'

Verses from the Trial of the Knave of Hearts

They told me you had been to her,
    And mentioned me to him:
She gave me a good character,
    But said I could not swim.

He sent them word I had not gone
    (We know it to be true):
If she should push the matter on,
    What would become of you?

I gave her one, they gave him two,
    You gave us three or more;
They all returned from him to you,
    Though they were mine before.

If I or she should chance to be
    Involved in this affair,
He trusts to you to set them free,
    Exactly as we were.

[282]

My notion was that you had been
    (Before she had this fit)
An obstacle that came between
    Him, and ourselves, and it.

Don't let him know she liked them best,
    For this must ever be
A secret, kept from all the rest,
    Between yourself and me.'

The Duchess's Lullaby

Speak roughly to your little boy,
    And beat him when he sneezes:
He only does it to annoy,
    Because he knows it teases.
      Chorus
    Wow! wow! wow!

I speak severely to my boy,
    I beat him when he sneezes;
For he can thoroughly enjoy
    The pepper when he pleases!
      Chorus
    Wow! wow! wow!

How doth the Little Crocodile

How doth the little crocodile
    Improve his shining tail,
And pour the waters of the Nile
    On every golden scale!

How cheerfully he seems to grin,
    How neatly spreads his claws,
And welcomes little fishes in,
    With gently smiling jaws.

The Mock Turtle's Song

'Will you walk a little faster?' said a whiting to a snail,
'There's a porpoise close behind us, and he's treading on my tail.
See how eagerly the lobsters and the turtles all advance!
They are waiting on the shingle – will you come and join the dance?
    Will you, wo'n't you, will you, wo'n't you, will you join the dance?
    Will you, wo'n't you, will you, wo'n't you, wo'n't you join the dance?

'You can really have no notion how delightful it will be
'When they take us up and throw us, with the lobsters, out to sea!'
But the snail replied 'Too far, too far!' and gave a look askance –
Said he thanked the whiting kindly, but he would not join the dance.
    Would not, could not, would not, could not, would not join the dance.
    Would not, could not, would not, could not, could not join the dance.

'What matters it how far we go?' his scaly friend replied.
'There is another shore, you know, upon the other side.
The further off from England the nearer is to France –
Then turn not pale, beloved snail, but come and join the dance.
    Will you, wo'n't you, will you, wo'n't you, will you join the dance?
    Will you, wo'n't you, will you, wo'n't you, wo'n't you join the dance?'

'Tis the Voice of the Lobster

'Tis the voice of the Lobster: I heard him declare
'You have baked me too brown, I must sugar my hair.'
As a duck with his eyelids, so he with his nose
Trims his belt and his buttons, and turns out his toes.
When the sands are all dry, he is gay as a lark,
And will talk in contemptuous tones of the Shark:
But, when the tide rises and sharks are around,
His voice has a timid and tremulous sound.

I passed by his garden, and marked, with one eye,
How the Owl and the Panther were sharing a pie:
The Panther took pie-crust, and gravy, and meat,
While the Owl had the dish as its share of the treat.
When the pie was all finished, the Owl, as a boon,
Was kindly permitted to pocket the spoon:
While the Panther received knife and fork with a growl,
And concluded the banquet by –

Jabberwocky

'Twas brillig, and the slithy toves
   Did gyre and gimble in the wabe;
All mimsy were the borogoves,
    And the mome raths outgrabe.

'Beware the Jabberwock, my son!
   The jaws that bite, the claws that catch!
Beware the Jubjub bird, and shun
    The frumious Bandersnatch!'

He took his vorpal sword in hand:
   Long time the manxome foe he sought –
So rested he by the Tumtum tree,
    And stood awhile in thought.

And as in uffish thought he stood,
   The Jabberwock, with eyes of flame,
Came whiffling through the tulgey wood,
    And burbled as it came!

One, two! One, two! And through and through
   The vorpal blade went snicker-snack!
He left it dead, and with its head
    He went galumphing back.

'And hast thou slain the Jabberwock?
   Come to my arms, my beamish boy!
O frabjous day! Callooh! Callay!'
    He chortled in his joy.

'Twas brillig, and the slithy toves
   Did gyre and gimble in the wabe;
All mimsy were the borogoves,
    And the mome raths outgrabe.

The Walrus and the Carpenter

The sun was shining on the sea,
   Shining with all his might:
He did his very best to make
   The billows smooth and bright –
And this was odd, because it was
   The middle of the night.

The moon was shining sulkily,
   Because she thought the sun
Had got no business to be there
   After the day was done –
'It's very rude of him,' she said,
   'To come and spoil the fun!'

The sea was wet as wet could be,
   The sands were dry as dry.
You could not see a cloud, because
   No cloud was in the sky:
No birds were flying overhead –
   There were no birds to fly.

The Walrus and the Carpenter
  Were walking close at hand:
They wept like anything to see
  Such quantities of sand:
'If this were only cleared away,'
  They said, 'it *would* be grand!'

'If seven maids with seven mops
  Swept it for half a year,
Do you suppose', the Walrus said,
  'That they could get it clear?'
'I doubt it,' said the Carpenter,
  And shed a bitter tear.

'O Oysters, come and walk with us!'
  The Walrus did beseech.
'A pleasant walk, a pleasant talk,
  Along the briny beach:
We cannot do with more than four,
  To give a hand to each.'

The eldest Oyster looked at him,
  But never a word he said:
The eldest Oyster winked his eye,
  And shook his heavy head –
Meaning to say he did not choose
  To leave the oyster-bed.

But four young Oysters hurried up,
  All eager for the treat:
Their coats were brushed, their faces washed,
  Their shoes were clean and neat –
And this was odd, because, you know,
  They hadn't any feet.

Four other Oysters followed them,
  And yet another four;
And thick and fast they came at last,
  And more, and more, and more –
All hopping through the frothy waves,
  And scrambling to the shore.

The Walrus and the Carpenter
   Walked on a mile or so,
And then they rested on a rock
   Conveniently low:
And all the little Oysters stood
   And waited in a row.

'The time has come', the Walrus said,
   'To talk of many things:
Of shoes – and ships – and sealing wax –
   Of cabbages – and kings –
And why the sea is boiling hot –
   And whether pigs have wings.'

'But wait a bit,' the Oysters cried,
   'Before we have our chat;
For some of us are out of breath,
   And all of us are fat!'
'No hurry!' said the Carpenter.
   They thanked him much for that.

'A loaf of bread,' the Walrus said,
   'Is what we chiefly need:
Pepper and vinegar besides
   Are very good indeed –
Now, if you're ready, Oysters dear,
   We can begin to feed.'

'But not on us!' the Oysters cried,
   Turning a little blue.
'After such kindness, that would be
   A dismal thing to do!'
'The night is fine,' the Walrus said.
   'Do you admire the view?

'It was so kind of you to come!
   And you are very nice!'
The Carpenter said nothing but
   'Cut us another slice.
I wish you were not quite so deaf –
   I've had to ask you twice!'

'It seems a shame,' the Walrus said,
  'To play them such a trick.
After we've brought them out so far,
  And made them trot so quick!'
The Carpenter said nothing but
  'The butter's spread too thick!'

'I weep for you,' the Walrus said:
  'I deeply sympathize.'
With sobs and tears he sorted out
  Those of the largest size,
Holding his pocket-handkerchief
  Before his streaming eyes.

'O Oysters,' said the Carpenter,
  'You've had a pleasant run!
Shall we be trotting home again?'
  But answer came there none –
And this was scarcely odd, because
  They'd eaten every one.

Humpty Dumpty's Poetic Recitation

In winter, when the fields are white,
I sing this song for your delight –

In spring, when woods are getting green,
I'll try and tell you what I mean:

In summer, when the days are long,
Perhaps you'll understand the song:

In autumn, when the leaves are brown,
Take pen and ink, and write it down.

I sent a message to the fish:
I told them 'This is what I wish.'

The little fishes of the sea,
They sent an answer back to me.

The little fishes' answer was
'We cannot do it, Sir, because –'

I sent to them again to say
'It will be better to obey'.

The fishes answered, with a grin,
'Why, what a temper you are in!'

I told them once, I told them twice:
They would not listen to advice.

I took a kettle large and new,
Fit for the deed I had to do.

My heart went hop, my heart went thump:
I filled the kettle at the pump.

Then some one came to me and said,
'The little fishes are in bed.'

I said to him, I said it plain,
'Then you must wake them up again.'

I said it very loud and clear:
I went and shouted in his ear.

But he was very stiff and proud:
He said, 'You needn't shout so loud!'

And he was very proud and stiff:
He said 'I'd go and wake them, if –'

I took a corkscrew from the shelf:
I went to wake them up myself.

And when I found the door was locked,
I pulled and pushed and kicked and knocked.

And when I found the door was shut,
I tried to turn the handle, but –

The White Knight's Song
or Haddock's Eyes,
or The Aged Aged Man,
or Ways and Means,
or A-sitting On A Gate

I'll tell thee everything I can;
   There's little to relate.
I saw an aged aged man,
   A-sitting on a gate.
'Who are you, aged man?' I said.
   'And how is it you live?'
And his answer trickled through my head
   Like water through a sieve.

He said 'I look for butterflies
   That sleep among the wheat:
I make them into mutton-pies,
   And sell them in the street.
I sell them unto men,' he said,
   'Who sail on stormy seas;
And that's the way I get my bread –
   A trifle, if you please.'

But I was thinking of a plan
    To dye one's whiskers green,
And always use so large a fan
    That they could not be seen.
So, having no reply to give
    To what the old man said,
I cried 'Come, tell me how you live!'
    And thumped him on the head.

His accents mild took up the tale:
    He said 'I go my ways,
And when I find a mountain-rill,
    I set it in a blaze;
And thence they make a stuff they call
    Rowland's Macassar Oil —
Yet twopence-halfpenny is all
    They give me for my toil.'

But I was thinking of a way
    To feed oneself on batter,
And so go on from day to day
    Getting a little fatter.
I shook him well from side to side,
    Until his face was blue:
'Come, tell me how you live,' I cried
    'And what it is you do!'

He said 'I hunt for haddocks' eyes
    Among the heather bright,
And work them into waistcoat-buttons
    In the silent night.
And these I do not sell for gold
    Or coin of silvery shine,
But for a copper halfpenny,
    And that will purchase nine.

'I sometimes dig for buttered rolls,
    Or set limed twigs for crabs;
I sometimes search the grassy knolls
    For wheels of hansom-cabs.

And that's the way' (he gave a wink)
    'By which I get my wealth –
And very gladly will I drink
    Your Honour's noble health.'

I heard him then, for I had just
    Completed my design
To keep the Menai bridge from rust
    By boiling it in wine.
I thanked him much for telling me
    The way he got his wealth.
But chiefly for his wish that he
    Might drink my noble health.

And now, if e'er by chance I put
    My fingers into glue,
Or madly squeeze a right-hand foot
    Into a left-hand shoe
Or if I drop upon my toe
    A very heavy weight,
I weep, for it reminds me so
Of that old man I used to know –
Whose look was mild, whose speech was slow,
Whose hair was whiter than the snow,
Whose face was very like a crow,
With eyes, like cinders, all aglow,
Who seemed distracted with his woe,
Who rocked his body to and fro,
And muttered mumblingly and low,
As if his mouth were full of dough,
Who snorted like a buffalo –
That summer evening long ago
    A-sitting on a gate.

The Hunting of the Snark

An Agony in Eight Fits

Fit the First
THE LANDING

'Just the place for a Snark!' the Bellman cried,
    As he landed his crew with care;
Supporting each man on the top of the tide
    By a finger entwined in his hair.

'Just the place for a Snark! I have said it twice:
    That alone should encourage the crew.
Just the place for a Snark! I have said it thrice:
    What I tell you three times is true.'

The crew was complete: it included a Boots –
    A maker of Bonnets and Hoods –
A Barrister, brought to arrange their disputes –
    And a Broker, to value their goods.

A Billiard-marker, whose skill was immense,
    Might perhaps have won more than his share –
But a Banker, engaged at enormous expense,
    Had the whole of their cash in his care.

There was also a Beaver, that paced on the deck,
    Or would sit making lace in the bow:
And had often (the Bellman said) saved them from wreck,
    Though none of the sailors knew how.

There was one who was famed for the number of things
    He forgot when he entered the ship:
His umbrella, his watch, all his jewels and rings,
    And the clothes he had bought for the trip.

He had forty-two boxes, all carefully packed,
    With his name painted clearly on each:
But, since he omitted to mention the fact,
    They were all left behind on the beach.

Supporting each man on the top of the tide

The loss of his clothes hardly mattered, because
    He had seven coats on when he came,
With three pair of boots – but the worst of it was,
    He had wholly forgotten his name.

He would answer to 'Hi!' or to any loud cry,
    Such as 'Fry me!' or 'Fritter my wig!'
To 'What-you-may-call-um!' or 'What-was-his-name!'
    But especially 'Thing-um-a-jig!'

While, for those who preferred a more forcible word,
    He had different names from these:
His intimate friends called him 'Candle-ends,'
    And his enemies 'Toasted-cheese.'

'His form is ungainly – his intellect small –'
    (So the Bellman would often remark)
'But his courage is perfect! And that, after all,
    Is the thing that one needs with a Snark.'

He would joke with hyænas, returning their stare
    With an impudent wag of the head:
And he once went a walk, paw-in-paw, with a bear,
    'Just to keep up its spirits,' he said.

He came as a Baker: but owned when too late –
    And it drove the poor Bellman half-mad –
He could only bake Bridecake – for which, I may state,
    No materials were to be had.

The last of the crew needs especial remark,
    Though he looked an incredible dunce:
He had just one idea – but, that one being 'Snark,'
    The good Bellman engaged him at once.

He came as a Butcher: but gravely declared,
    When the ship had been sailing a week,
He could only kill Beavers. The Bellman looked scared,
    And was almost too frightened to speak:

But at length he explained, in a tremulous tone,
  There was only one Beaver on board;
And that was a tame one he had of his own,
  Whose death would be deeply deplored.

The Beaver, who happened to hear the remark,
  Protested, with tears in its eyes,
That not even the rapture of hunting the Snark
  Could atone for that dismal surprise!

It strongly advised that the Butcher should be
  Conveyed in a separate ship:
But the Bellman declared that would never agree
  With the plans he had made for the trip:

Navigation was always a difficult art,
  Though with only one ship and one bell:
And he feared he must really decline, for his part,
  Undertaking another as well.

The Beaver's best course was, no doubt, to procure
  A second-hand dagger-proof coat –
So the Baker advised it – and next, to insure
  Its life in some Office of note:

This the Baker suggested, and offered for hire
  (On moderate terms), or for sale,
Two excellent Policies, one Against Fire,
  And one Against Damage From Hail.

Yet still, ever after that sorrowful day,
  Whenever the Butcher was by,
The Beaver kept looking the opposite way,
  And appeared unaccountably shy.

Fit the Second
THE BELLMAN'S SPEECH

The Bellman himself they all praised to the skies –
  Such a carriage, such ease and such grace!
Such solemnity, too! One could see he was wise,
  The moment one looked in his face!

He had bought a large map representing the sea,
  Without the least vestige of land:
And the crew were much pleased when they found it to be
  A map they could all understand.

'What's the good of Mercator's North Poles and Equators,
  Tropics, Zones, and Meridian Lines?'
So the Bellman would cry: and the crew would reply,
  'They are merely conventional signs!

'Other maps are such shapes, with their islands and capes!
  But we've got our brave Captain to thank'
(So the crew would protest) 'that he's bought *us* the best –
  A perfect and absolute blank!'

This was charming, no doubt: but they shortly found out
  That the Captain they trusted so well
Had only one notion for crossing the ocean,
  And that was to tingle his bell.

He was thoughtful and grave – but the orders he gave
  Were enough to bewilder a crew.
When he cried, 'Steer to starboard, but keep her head larboard!'
  What on earth was the helmsman to do?

Then the bowsprit got mixed with the rudder sometimes:
  A thing, as the Bellman remarked,
That frequently happens in tropical climes,
  When a vessel is, so to speak, 'snarked.'

But the principal failing occurred in the sailing,
  And the Bellman, perplexed and distressed,
Said he *had* hoped, at least, when the wind blew due East,
  That the ship would *not* travel due West!

But the danger was past – they had landed at last,
    With their boxes, portmanteaus, and bags:
Yet at first sight the crew were not pleased with the view,
    Which consisted of chasms and crags.

The Bellman perceived that their spirits were low,
    And repeated in musical tone
Some jokes he had kept for a season of woe –
    But the crew would do nothing but groan.

He served out some grog with a liberal hand,
    And bade them sit down on the beach:
And they could not but own that their Captain looked grand,
    As he stood and delivered his speech.

'Friends, Romans, and countrymen, lend me your ears!'
    (They were all of them fond of quotations:
So they drank to his health, and they gave him three cheers,
    While he served out additional rations.)

'We have sailed many months, we have sailed many weeks
    (Four weeks to the month you may mark),
But never as yet ('tis your Captain who speaks)
    Have we caught the least glimpse of a Snark!

'We have sailed many weeks, we have sailed many days
    (Seven days to the week I allow),
But a Snark, on the which we might lovingly gaze,
    We have never beheld till now!

'Come, listen, my men, while I tell you again
    The five unmistakable marks
By which you may know, wheresoever you go,
    The warranted genuine Snarks.

'Let us take them in order. The first is the taste,
    Which is meagre and hollow, but crisp:
Like a coat that is rather too tight in the waist,
    With a flavour of Will-o'-the-wisp.

'Its habit of getting up late you'll agree
    That it carries too far, when I say
That it frequently breakfasts at five-o'clock tea,
    And dines on the following day.

'The third is its slowness in taking a jest,
    Should you happen to venture on one,
It will sigh like a thing that is deeply distressed:
    And it always looks grave at a pun.

'The fourth is its fondness for bathing-machines,
    Which it constantly carries about,
And believes that they add to the beauty of scenes –
    A sentiment open to doubt.

'The fifth is ambition. It next will be right
    To describe each particular batch:
Distinguishing those that have feathers, and bite,
    From those that have whiskers, and scratch.

'For, although common Snarks do no manner of harm,
    Yet, I feel it my duty to say,
Some are Boojums – ' The Bellman broke off in alarm,
    For the Baker had fainted away.

Fit the Third
THE BAKER'S TALE

They roused him with muffins – they roused him with ice –
    They roused him with mustard and cress –
They roused him with jam and judicious advice –
    They set him conundrums to guess.

When at length he sat up and was able to speak,
    His sad story he offered to tell;
And the Bellman cried 'Silence! not even a shriek!'
    And excitedly tingled his bell.

There was silence supreme! Not a shriek, not a scream,
    Scarcely even a howl or a groan,
As the man they called 'Ho!' told his story of woe
    In an antediluvian tone.

[301]

'My father and mother were honest, though poor –'
  'Skip all that!' cried the Bellman in haste.
'If it once becomes dark, there's no chance of a Snark –
  We have hardly a minute to waste!'

'I skip forty years,' said the Baker, in tears,
  'And proceed without further remark
To the day when you took me aboard of your ship
  To help you in hunting the Snark.

'A dear uncle of mine (after whom I was named)
  Remarked, when I bade him farewell –'
'Oh, skip your dear uncle!' the Bellman exclaimed,
  As he angrily tingled his bell.

'He remarked to me then,' said that mildest of men,
  '"If your Snark be a Snark, that is right:
Fetch it home by all means – you may serve it with greens,
  And it's handy for striking a light.

'"You may seek it with thimbles – and seek it with care;
  You may hunt it with forks and hope;
You may threaten its life with a railway-share;
  You may charm it with smiles and soap –"'

('That's exactly the method,' the Bellman bold
  In a hasty parenthesis cried,
'That's exactly the way I have always been told
  That the capture of Snarks should be tried!')

'"But oh, beamish nephew, beware of the day,
  If your Snark be a Boojum! For then
You will softly and suddenly vanish away,
  And never be met with again!"

'It is this, it is this that oppresses my soul,
  When I think of my uncle's last words:
And my heart is like nothing so much as a bowl
  Brimming over with quivering curds!

'It is this, it is this——' 'We have had that before!'
  The Bellman indignantly said.
And the Baker replied, 'Let me say it once more.
  It is this, it is this that I dread!

'I engage with the Snark – every night after dark –
  In a dreamy delirious fight:
I serve it with greens in those shadowy scenes,
  And I use it for striking a light;

'But if ever I meet with a Boojum, that day,
  In a moment (of this I am sure),
I shall softly and suddenly vanish away –
  And the notion I cannot endure!'

Fit the Fourth
THE HUNTING

The Bellman looked uffish, and wrinkled his brow.
  'If only you'd spoken before!
It's excessively awkward to mention it now,
  With the Snark, so to speak, at the door!

'We should all of us grieve, as you well may believe,
  If you never were met with again –
But surely, my man, when the voyage began,
  You might have suggested it then?

'It's excessively awkward to mention it now –
  As I think I've already remarked.'
And the man they called 'Hi!' replied, with a sigh,
  'I informed you the day we embarked.

'You may charge me with murder – or want of sense –
  (We are all of us weak at times):
But the slightest approach to a false pretence
  Was never among my crimes!

'I said it in Hebrew – I said it in Dutch –
  I said it in German and Greek;
But I wholly forgot (and it vexes me much)
  That English is what you speak!'

[303]

''Tis a pitiful tale, ' said the Bellman, whose face
 Had grown longer at every word;
'But, now that you've stated the whole of your case,
 More debate would be simply absurd.

'The rest of my speech' (he explained to his men)
 'You shall hear when I've leisure to speak it.
But the Snark is at hand, let me tell you again!
 'Tis your glorious duty to seek it!

'To seek it with thimbles, to seek it with care;
 To pursue it with forks and hope;
To threaten its life with a railway-share;
 To charm it with smiles and soap!

'For the Snark's a peculiar creature, that won't
 Be caught in a commonplace way.
Do all that you know, and try all that you don't:
 Not a chance must be wasted to-day!

'For England expects – I forbear to proceed:
 'Tis a maxim tremendous, but trite:
And you'd best be unpacking the things that you need
 To rig yourselves out for the fight.'

Then the Banker endorsed a blank cheque (which he crossed),
 And changed his loose silver for notes.
The Baker with care combed his whiskers and hair,
 And shook the dust out of his coats.

The Boots and the Broker were sharpening a spade –
 Each working the grindstone in turn;
But the Beaver went on making lace, and displayed
 No interest in the concern:

Though the Barrister tried to appeal to its pride,
 And vainly proceeded to cite
A number of cases, in which making laces
 Had been proved an infringement of right.

The maker of Bonnets ferociously planned
　　A novel arrangement of bows:
While the Billiard-marker with quivering hand
　　Was chalking the tip of his nose.

But the Butcher turned nervous, and dressed himself fine,
　　With yellow kid gloves and a ruff –
Said he felt it exactly like going to dine,
　　Which the Bellman declared was all 'stuff.'

'Introduce me, now there's a good fellow,' he said,
　　'If we happen to meet it together!'
And the Bellman, sagaciously nodding his head,
　　Said, 'That must depend on the weather.'

The Beaver went simply galumphing about,
　　At seeing the Butcher so shy:
And even the Baker, though stupid and stout,
　　Made an effort to wink with one eye.

'Be a man!' said the Bellman in wrath, as he heard
　　The Butcher beginning to sob.
'Should we meet with a Jubjub, that desperate bird,
　　We shall need all our strength for the job!'

Fit the Fifth
THE BEAVER'S LESSON

They sought it with thimbles, they sought it with care;
　　They pursued it with forks and hope;
They threatened its life with a railway-share;
　　They charmed it with smiles and soap.

Then the Butcher contrived an ingenious plan
　　For making a separate sally;
And had fixed on a spot unfrequented by man,
　　A dismal and desolate valley.

But the very same plan to the Beaver occurred:
　　It had chosen the very same place;
Yet neither betrayed, by a sign or a word,
　　The disgust that appeared in his face.

Each thought he was thinking of nothing but 'Snark'
    And the glorious work of the day;
And each tried to pretend that he did not remark
    That the other was going that way.

But the valley grew narrow and narrower still,
    And the evening got darker and colder,
Till (merely from nervousness, not from goodwill)
    They marched along shoulder to shoulder.

Then a scream, shrill and high, rent the shuddering sky,
    And they knew that some danger was near:
The Beaver turned pale to the tip of its tail,
    And even the Butcher felt queer.

He thought of his childhood, left far behind –
    That blissful and innocent state –
The sound so exactly recalled to his mind
    A pencil that squeaks on a slate!

''Tis the voice of the Jubjub!' he suddenly cried.
    (This man, that they used to call 'Dunce.')
'As the Bellman would tell you,' he added with pride,
    'I have uttered that sentiment once.

''Tis the note of the Jubjub! Keep count, I entreat;
    You will find I have told it you twice.
'Tis the song of the Jubjub! The proof is complete,
    If only I've stated it thrice.'

The Beaver had counted with scrupulous care,
    Attending to every word:
But it fairly lost heart, and outgrabe in despair,
    When the third repetition occurred.

It felt that, in spite of all possible pains,
    It had somehow contrived to lose count,
And the only thing now was to rack its poor brains
    By reckoning up the amount.

The Beaver brought paper, portfolio, pens

'Two added to one – if that could but be done,'
  It said, 'with one's fingers and thumbs!'
Recollecting with tears how, in earlier years,
  It had taken no pains with its sums.

'The thing can be done,' said the Butcher, 'I think.
  The thing must be done, I am sure.
The thing shall be done! Bring me paper and ink,
  The best there is time to procure.'

The Beaver brought paper, portfolio, pens,
  And ink in unfailing supplies:
While strange creepy creatures came out of their dens,
  And watched them with wondering eyes.

So engrossed was the Butcher, he heeded them not,
  As he wrote with a pen in each hand,
And explained all the while in a popular style
  Which the Beaver could well understand.

'Taking Three as the subject to reason about –
  A convenient number to state –
We add Seven, and Ten, and then multiply out
  By One Thousand diminished by Eight.

'The result we proceed to divide, as you see,
  By Nine Hundred and Ninety and Two:
Then subtract Seventeen, and the answer must be
  Exactly and perfectly true.

'The method employed I would gladly explain,
  While I have it so clear in my head,
If I had but the time and you had but the brain –
  But much yet remains to be said.

'In one moment I've seen what has hitherto been
  Enveloped in absolute mystery,
And without extra charge I will give you at large
  A Lesson in Natural History.'

In his genial way he proceeded to say
   (Forgetting all laws of propriety,
And that giving instruction, without introduction,
   Would have caused quite a thrill in Society),

'As to temper the Jubjub's a desperate bird,
   Since it lives in perpetual passion:
Its taste in costume is entirely absurd –
   It is ages ahead of the fashion:

'But it knows any friend it has met once before:
   It never will look at a bribe:
And in charity-meetings it stands at the door,
   And collects – though it does not subscribe.

'Its flavour when cooked is more exquisite far
   Than mutton, or oysters, or eggs:
(Some think it keeps best in an ivory jar,
   And some, in mahogany kegs:)

'You boil it in sawdust: you salt it in glue:
   You condense it with locusts and tape:
Still keeping one principal object in view –
   To preserve its symmetrical shape.'

The Butcher would gladly have talked till next day,
   But he felt that the Lesson must end,
And he wept with delight in attempting to say
   He considered the Beaver his friend.

While the Beaver confessed, with affectionate looks
   More eloquent even than tears,
It had learnt in ten minutes far more than all books
   Would have taught it in seventy years.

They returned hand-in-hand, and the Bellman, unmanned
   (For a moment) with noble emotion,
Said, 'This amply repays all the wearisome days
   We have spent on the billowy ocean!'

Such friends, as the Beaver, and Butcher became,
    Have seldom if ever been known;
In winter or summer, 'twas always the same –
    You could never meet either alone.

And when quarrels arose – as one frequently finds
    Quarrels will, spite of every endeavour –
The song of the Jubjub recurred to their minds,
    And cemented their friendship for ever!

Fit the Sixth
THE BARRISTER'S DREAM

They sought it with thimbles, they sought it with care;
    They pursued it with forks and hope;
They threatened its life with a railway-share;
    They charmed it with smiles and soap.

But the Barrister, weary of proving in vain
    That the Beaver's lace-making was wrong,
Fell asleep, and in dreams saw the creature quite plain
    That his fancy had dwelt on so long.

He dreamed that he stood in a shadowy Court,
    Where the Snark, with a glass in its eye,
Dressed in gown, bands, and wig, was defending a pig
    On the charge of deserting its sty.

The Witnesses proved, without error or flaw,
    That the sty was deserted when found:
And the Judge kept explaining the state of the law
    In a soft under-current of sound.

The indictment had never been clearly expressed,
    And it seemed that the Snark had begun,
And had spoken three hours, before any one guessed
    What the pig was supposed to have done.

The Jury had each formed a different view
    (Long before the indictment was read),
And they all spoke at once, so that none of them knew
    One word that the others had said.

'You must know –' said the Judge: but the Snark exclaimed, 'Fudge!
    That statute is obsolete quite!
Let me tell you, my friends, the whole question depends
    On an ancient manorial right.

'In the matter of Treason the pig would appear
    To have aided, but scarcely abetted:
While the charge of Insolvency fails, it is clear,
    If you grant the plea "never indebted."

'The fact of Desertion I will not dispute:
    But its guilt, as I trust, is removed
(So far as relates to the costs of this suit)
    By the Alibi which has been proved.

'My poor client's fate now depends on your votes.'
    Here the speaker sat down in his place,
And directed the Judge to refer to his notes
    And briefly to sum up the case.

But the Judge said he never had summed up before;
    So the Snark undertook it instead,
And summed it so well that it came to far more
    Than the Witnesses ever had said!

When the verdict was called for, the Jury declined,
    As the word was so puzzling to spell;
But they ventured to hope that the Snark wouldn't mind
    Undertaking that duty as well.

So the Snark found the verdict, although, as it owned,
    It was spent with the toils of the day:
When it said the word 'GUILTY!' the Jury all groaned,
    And some of them fainted away.

Then the Snark pronounced sentence, the Judge being quite
    Too nervous to utter a word:
When it rose to its feet, there was silence like night,
    And the fall of a pin might be heard.

'Transportation for life' was the sentence it gave,
  'And *then* to be fined forty pound.'
The Jury all cheered, though the Judge said he feared
  That the phrase was not legally sound.

But their wild exultation was suddenly checked
  When the jailer informed them, with tears,
Such a sentence would have not the slightest effect,
  As the pig had been dead for some years.

The Judge left the Court, looking deeply disgusted:
  But the Snark, though a little aghast,
As the lawyer to whom the defence was intrusted,
  Went bellowing on to the last.

Thus the Barrister dreamed, while the bellowing seemed
  To grow every moment more clear:
Till he woke to the knell of a furious bell,
  Which the Bellman rang close at his ear.

Fit the Seventh
THE BANKER'S FATE

They sought it with thimbles, they sought it with care;
  They pursued it with forks and hope;
They threatened its life with a railway-share;
  They charmed it with smiles and soap.

And the Banker, inspired with a courage so new
    It was matter for general remark,
Rushed madly ahead and was lost to their view
    In his zeal to discover the Snark.

But while he was seeking with thimbles and care,
    A Bandersnatch swiftly drew nigh
And grabbed at the Banker, who shrieked in despair,
    For he knew it was useless to fly.

He offered large discount – he offered a cheque
    (Drawn 'to bearer') for seven-pounds-ten:
But the Bandersnatch merely extended its neck
    And grabbed at the Banker again.

Without rest or pause – while those frumious jaws
    Went savagely snapping around –
He skipped and he hopped, and he floundered and flopped,
    Till fainting he fell to the ground.

The Bandersnatch fled as the others appeared:
    Led on by that fear-stricken yell:
And the Bellman remarked, 'It is just as I feared!'
    And solemnly tolled on his bell.

He was black in the face, and they scarcely could trace
    The least likeness to what he had been:
While so great was his fright that his waistcoat turned white –
    A wonderful thing to be seen!

To the horror of all who were present that day,
    He uprose in full evening dress,
And with senseless grimaces endeavoured to say
    What his tongue could no longer express.

Down he sank in a chair – ran his hands through his hair –
    And chanted in mimsiest tones
Words whose utter inanity proved his insanity,
    While he rattled a couple of bones.

'Leave him here to his fate – it is getting so late!'
    The Bellman exclaimed in a fright.
'We have lost half the day. Any further delay,
    And we shan't catch a Snark before night!'

Fit the Eighth
THE VANISHING

They sought it with thimbles, they sought it with care;
    They pursued it with forks and hope;
They threatened its life with a railway-share;
    They charmed it with smiles and soap.

They shuddered to think that the chase might fail,
    And the Beaver, excited at last,
Went bounding along on the tip of its tail,
    For the daylight was nearly past.

'There is Thingumbob shouting!' the Bellman said.
    'He is shouting like mad, only hark!
He is waving his hands, he is wagging his head,
    He has certainly found a Snark!'

They gazed in delight, while the Butcher exclaimed,
    'He was always a desperate wag!'
They beheld him – their Baker – their hero unnamed –
    On the top of a neighbouring crag,

Erect and sublime, for one moment of time.
    In the next, that wild figure they saw
(As if stung by a spasm) plunge into a chasm,
    While they waited and listened in awe.

'It's a Snark!' was the sound that first came to their ears,
    And seemed almost too good to be true.
Then followed a torrent of laughter and cheers:
    Then the ominous words, 'It's a Boo –'

Then, silence. Some fancied they heard in the air
    A weary and wandering sigh
That sounded like '– jum!' but the others declare
    It was only a breeze that went by.

[314]

They hunted till darkness came on, but they found
  Not a button, or feather, or mark,
By which they could tell that they stood on the ground
  Where the Baker had met with the Snark.

In the midst of the word he was trying to say,
  In the midst of his laughter and glee,
He had softly and suddenly vanished away –
  For the Snark *was* a Boojum, you see.

SONGS FROM *Sylvie and Bruno*

The Mad Gardener's Song

He thought he saw an Elephant,
  That practised on a fife:
He looked again, and found it was
  A letter from his wife.
'At length I realise,' he said,
  'The bitterness of Life!'

He thought he saw a Buffalo
    Upon the chimney-piece:
He looked again, and found it was
    His Sister's Husband's Niece.
'Unless you leave this house,' he said,
    'I'll send for the Police!'

He thought he saw a Rattlesnake
    That questioned him in Greek:
He looked again, and found it was
    The Middle of Next Week.
'The one thing I regret,' he said,
    'Is that it cannot speak!'

He thought he saw a Banker's Clerk
    Descending from the bus:
He looked again, and found it was
    A Hippopotamus:
'If this should stay to dine,' he said,
    'There won't be much for us!'

He thought he saw a Kangaroo
    That worked a coffee-mill:
He looked again, and found it was
    A Vegetable-Pill.
'Were I to swallow this,' he said,
    'I should be very ill!'

He thought he saw a Coach-and-Four
    That stood beside his bed:
He looked again, and found it was
    A Bear without a Head.
'Poor thing,' he said, 'poor silly thing!
    It's waiting to be fed!'

He thought he saw an Albatross
    That fluttered round the lamp:
He looked again, and found it was
    A Penny-Postage-Stamp.
'You'd best be getting home,' he said:
    'The nights are very damp!'

He thought he saw a Garden-Door
    That opened with a key:
He looked again, and found it was
    A Double Rule of Three:
'And all its mystery,' he said,
    'Is clear as day to me!'

He thought he saw an Argument
    That proved he was the Pope:
He looked again, and found it was
    A Bar of Mottled Soap.
'A fact so dread,' he faintly said,
    'Extinguishes all hope!'

The Three Badgers

'There be three Badgers on a mossy stone,
    Beside a dark and covered way:
Each dreams himself a monarch on his throne,
    And so they stay and stay –
Though their old Father languishes alone,
    They stay, and stay, and stay.

There be three Herrings loitering around,
    Longing to share that mossy seat:
Each Herring tries to sing what she has found
    That makes Life seem so sweet.
Thus, with a grating and uncertain sound,
    They bleat, and bleat, and bleat.

The Mother-Herring, on the salt sea-wave,
    Sought vainly for her absent ones:
The Father-Badger, writhing in a cave,
    Shrieked out 'Return, my sons!
You shall have buns,' he shrieked, 'if you'll behave!
    Yea, buns, and buns, and buns!'

'I fear,' said she, 'your sons have gone astray?
    My daughters left me while I slept.'
'Yes'm,' the Badger said: 'it's as you say.'
    'They should be better kept.'
Thus the poor parents talked the time away,
    And wept, and wept, and wept.

The Badgers did not care to talk to Fish;
    They did not dote on Herrings's songs:
They never had experienced the dish
    To which that name belongs:
'And oh, to pinch their tails' (this was their wish),
    'With thongs, yea, tongs, and tongs!'

'And are not these the Fish,' the Eldest sighed,
    'Whose Mother dwells beneath the foam?'
'They *are* the Fish!' the Second one replied.
    'And they have left their home!'
'Oh wicked Fish,' the Youngest Badger cried,
    'To roam, yea, roam, and roam!'

Gently the Badgers trotted to the shore –
    The sandy shore that fringed the bay:
Each in his mouth a living Herring bore –
    Those aged ones waxed gay:
Clear rang their voices through the ocean's roar,
    'Hooray, hooray, hooray!'

The King-Fisher's Song

King Fisher courted Lady Bird –
Sing Beans, sing Bones, sing Butterflies!
  'Find me my match,' he said,
  'With such a noble head –
With such a beard, as white as curd –
  With such expressive eyes!'

'Yet pins have heads,' said Lady Bird –
Sing Prunes, sing Prawns, sing Primrose-Hill!
  'And, where you stick them in,
  They stay, and thus a pin
Is very much to be preferred
  To one that's never still!'

'Oysters have beards,' said Lady Bird –
Sing Flies, sing Frogs, sing Fiddle-strings!
  'I love them, for I know
  They never chatter so:
They would not say one single word –
  Not if you crowned them Kings!'

'Needles have eyes,' said Lady Bird –
Sing Cats, sing Corks, sing Cowslip-teal
  'And they are sharp – just what
  Your Majesty is *not*:
So get you gone – 'tis too absurd
  To come a-courting *me*!'

The Little Man that had a Little Gun

In stature the Manlet was dwarfish –
   No burly big Blunderbore he:
And he wearily gazed on the crawfish
   His Wifelet had dressed for his tea.
'Now reach me, sweet Atom, my gunlet,
   And hurl the old shoelet for luck:
Let me hie to the bank of the runlet,
              And shoot thee a Duck!'

She has reached him his minikin gunlet:
   She has hurled the old shoelet for luck:
She is busily baking a bunlet,
   To welcome him home with his Duck.
On he speeds, never wasting a wordlet,
   Though thoughtlets cling, closely as wax,
To the spot where the beautiful birdlet
              So quietly quacks.

Where the Lobsterlet lurks, and the Crablet
   So slowly and sleepily crawls:
Where the Dolphin's at home, and the Dablet
   Pays long ceremonious calls:
Where the Grublet is sought by the Froglet:
   Where the Frog is pursued by the Duck:
Where the Ducklet is chased by the Doglet –
            So runs the world's luck!

He has loaded with bullet and powder:
   His footfall is noiseless as air:
But the Voices grow louder and louder,
   And bellow, and bluster, and blare.
They bristle before him and after,
   They flutter above and below,
Shrill shriekings of lubberly laughter,
             Weird wailings of woe!

They echo without him, within him:
   They thrill through his whiskers and beard:

Like a teetotum seeming to spin him,
   With sneers never hitherto sneered.
'Avengement,' they cry, 'on our Foelet!
   Let the Manikin weep for our wrongs!
Let us drench him, from toplet to toelet,
                  With Nursery-Songs!

'He shall muse upon "Hey! Diddle! Diddle!"
   On the Cow that surmounted the Moon:
He shall rave of the Cat and the Fiddle,
   And the Dish that eloped with the Spoon:
And his soul shall be sad for the Spider,
   When Miss Muffet was sipping her whey,
That so tenderly sat down beside her,
                  And scared her away!

'The music of Midsummer-madness
   Shall sting him with many a bite,
Till, in rapture of rollicking sadness,
   He shall groan with a gloomy delight:
He shall swathe him, like mists of the morning,
   In platitudes luscious and limp,
Such as deck, with a deathless adorning,
                  The Song of the Shrimp!

'When the Ducklet's dark doom is decided,
   We will trundle him home in a trice:
And the banquet, so plainly provided,
   Shall round into rose-buds and rice:
In a blaze of pragmatic invention
   He shall wrestle with Fate, and shall reign:
But he has not a friend fit to mention,
                  So hit him again!'

He has shot it, the delicate darling!
   And the Voices have ceased from their strife:
Not a whisper of sneering or snarling,
   As he carries it home to his wife:
Then, cheerily champing the bunlet
   His spouse was so skilful to bake,
He hies him once more to the runlet,
                  To fetch her the Drake!

[321]

GEORGE DU MAURIER
1834–96

Vers Nonsensiques

1

'Cassez-vous, cassez-vous, cassez-vous,
O mer, sur vos froids gris cailloux!'
    Ainsi traduisait Laure
    Au profit d'Isidore,
(Beau jeune homme, et son futur époux).

2

Un Marin naufragé (de Doncastre)
Pour prière, au milieu du désastre,
    Répétait à genoux
    Ces mots simples et doux: –
'Scintillez, scintillez, petit astre!'

3

Il existe une Espinstère à Tours,
Un peu vite, et qui porte toujours
    Un ulsteur peau-de-phoque,
    Un chapeau bilicoque,
Et des nicrebocqueurs en velours.

4

A Cologne est un mâitre d'hôtel
Hors du centre du ventre duquel
    Se projette une sorte
    De tiroir qui supporte
La moutarde, et le poivre, et le sel.

5

Il était un Gendarme, à Nanteuil,
Qui n'avait qu'une dent et qu'un œil;
    Mais cet œil solitaire
    Était plein de mystère,
Cette dent, d'importance et d'orgueil.

THOMAS HOOD THE YOUNGER
1835–74

The Ballad of the Basking Shark

I'm the Beautiful Basking Shark,
    And I would not change my name,
For that of an asking bark,
    Or a basket of sparkling game.
So do not come to woo,
For I will not marry you!
Sang the Basking Shark to the sailor lad afloat on the ocean blue.

If I were but a nautilus,
    I might not so much object
To be called an omnibus,
    Or a wandering intellect.
I might just make them do.
Yet do not come to woo!
Sang the Basking Shark to the sailor lad afloat on the ocean blue.

Were I even a loin of pork –
    (And here it gave a sigh) –
You might call me a knife and fork,
    Or even a porcupie.
I might endorse that view.
But do not come to woo!
Sang the Basking Shark to the sailor lad afloat on the ocean blue.

I'm the Beautiful Basking Shark,
    And my name I would not change,
Save for one, a man of mark,
    In the whole world's mighty range.
For I'd marry the Stingaroo
If *he* would come to woo!
And the Basking Shark ate that sailor lad afloat on the ocean blue.

Song

He dreamt that he saw the Buffalant,
  And the spottified Dromedaraffe,
The blue Camelotamus, lean and gaunt,
  And the wild Tigeroceros calf.
      Yes, the Ca-amelotamus, le-ean and gaunt,
        And the Ti-ti-geroceros ca-a-a-alf,
        And the Ti-i-geroceros calf!

The maned Liodillo loudly roared,
  And the Peccarbok whistled its whine,
The Chinchayak leapt on the dewy sward,
  As it hunted the pale Baboopine.
      Yes, the Chi-inchayak on the dew-ewy sward,
        It hu-unted the pale Baboopi-i-i-ine,
        It hu-unted the Ba-aboopine!

He dreamt that he met the Crocoghau,
  As it swam in the Stagnolent Lake;
But everything that in dreams he saw
  Came of eating too freely of cake.
      Yes, e-everything that in dre-eams he saw
        Was e-eating too freely of ca-a-a-ake –
        From e-ating too-oo much cake!

Confounded Nonsense

Alpaca pictures of the previous past,
  Droop on the hovering confines of a snore,
And yet one further bloom, conversely vast,
  Springs bright in the perspective of the shore,

Where porphyry wings bear up an ardent pride,
  And rainbows drip from evanescent crags,
Where peaceful popinjays smile side by side,
  And immemorial franchise furls its flags.

So let it be: imperious tumbrils howl,
    And palpitating fixtures utter screeds;
Afar the murmurous aspens hoarsely scowl,
    And purple pageants echo frantic deeds.

Farewell! I see life's periphrastic orb
    Shiver to scantlings with a latent sound,
Dark ether pours, while shrinking minds absorb,
    And blatant wildernesses close around.

W. S. GILBERT
1836–1911

The Story of Prince Agib

Strike the concertina's melancholy string!
Blow the spirit-stirring harp like any thing!
    Let the piano's martial blast
    Rouse the Echoes of the Past,
For of Agib, Prince of Tartary, I sing!

Of Agib, who amid Tartaric scenes,
Wrote a lot of ballet-music in his teens:
    His gentle spirit rolls
    In the melody of souls –
Which is pretty, but I don't know what it means.

Of Agib, who could readily, at sight,
Strum a march upon the loud Theodolite:
        He would diligently play
        On the Zoetrope all day,
And blow the gay Pantechnicon all night.

One winter – I am shaky in my dates –
Came two starving minstrels to his gates,
        Oh, Allah be obeyed,
        How infernally they played!
I remember that they called themselves the 'Oiiaits.'

Oh! that day of sorrow, misery, and rage,
I shall carry to the Catacombs of Age,
        Photographically lined
        On the tablet of my mind,
When a yesterday has faded from its page!

Alas! Prince Agib went and asked them in!
Gave them beer, and eggs, and sweets, and scents, and tin.
        And when (as snobs would say)
        They 'put it all away,'
He requested them to tune up and begin.

Though its icy horror chill you to the core,
I will tell you what I never told before,
        The consequences true
        Of that awful interview,
For I listened at the key-hole in the door!

They played him a sonata – let me see!
'Medulla oblongata' – key of G.
        Then they began to sing
        That extremely lovely thing,
'Scherzando! ma non troppo, ppp.'

He gave them money, more than they could count,
Scent, from a most ingenious little fount,
        More beer, in little kegs,
        Many dozen hard-boiled eggs,
And goodies to a fabulous amount.

Now follows the dim horror of my tale,
And I feel I'm growing gradually pale,
For, even at this day,
Though its sting has passed away,
When I venture to remember it, I quail!

The elder of the brothers gave a squeal,
All-overish it made me for to feel!
'Oh Prince,' he says, says he,
'If a Prince indeed you be,
I've a mystery I'm going to reveal!

'Oh, listen, if you'd shun a horrid death,
To what the gent who's speaking to you, saith:
No "Oiiaits" in truth are we,
As you fancy that we be,
For (ter-remble) I am Aleck – this is Beth!'

Said Agib, 'Oh! accursed of your kind,
I have heard that you are men of evil mind!'
Beth gave a dreadful shriek –
But before he'd time to speak
I was mercilessly collared from behind.

In number ten or twelve or even more,
They fastened me, full length upon the floor.
On my face extended flat
I was walloped with a cat
For listening at the key-hole of the door.

Oh! the horror of that agonizing thrill!
(I can feel the place in frosty weather still).
For a week from ten to four
I was fastened to the floor,
While a mercenary wopped me with a will!

They branded me, and broke me on a wheel,
And they left me in a hospital to heal;
And, upon my solemn word,
I have never never heard
What those Tartars had determined to reveal.

[327]

But that day of sorrow, misery, and rage,
I shall carry to the Catacombs of Age,
Photographically lined
On the tablet of my mind,
When a yesterday has faded from its page!

The Chancellor's Nightmare

Love, unrequited, robs me of my rest:
Love, hopeless love, my ardent soul encumbers:
Love, nightmare-like, lies heavy on my chest:
And weaves itself into my midnight slumbers!

When you're lying awake with a dismal headache, and repose is taboo'd by
anxiety,
I conceive you may use any language you choose to indulge in, without
impropriety;
For your brain is on fire – the bedclothes conspire of usual slumber to
plunder you:
First your counterpane goes, and uncovers your toes, and your sheet slips
demurely from under you;
Then the blanketing tickles – you feel like mixed pickles – so terribly sharp
is the pricking.
And you're hot, and you're cross, and you tumble and toss till there's
nothing 'twixt you and the ticking.
Then the bedclothes all creep to the ground in a heap, and you pick 'em all
up in a tangle;
Next your pillow resigns and politely declines to remain at its usual angle!
Well, you get some repose in the form of a doze, with hot eyeballs and head
ever aching,
But your slumbering teems with such horrible dreams that you'd very much
better be waking;
For you dream you are crossing the Channel, and tossing about in a steamer
from Harwich –
Which is something between a large bathing machine and a very small
second-class carriage –
And you're giving a treat (penny ice and cold meat) to a party of friends and
relations –

They're a ravenous horde – and they all came on board at Sloane Square
and South Kensington Stations.

And bound on that journey you find your attorney (who started that
morning from Devon);

He's a bit undersized, and you don't feel surprised when he tells you he's
only eleven.

Well, you're driving like mad with this singular lad (by the by, the ship's
now a four-wheeler),

And you're playing round games, and he calls you bad names when you tell
him that 'ties pay the dealer';

But this you can't stand, so you throw up your hand, and you find you're as
cold as an icicle,

In your shirt and your socks (the black silk with gold clocks), crossing
Salisbury Plain on a bicycle:

And he and the crew are on bicycles too—which they've somehow or other
invested in –

And he's telling the tars all the particu*lars* of a company he's interested in –

It's a scheme of devices, to get at low prices all goods from cough mixtures
to cables

(Which tickled the sailors,) by treating retailers as though they were all
vege*t*ables –

You get a good spadesman to plant a small tradesman (first take off his
boots with a boot-tree),

And his legs will take root, and his fingers will shoot, and they'll blossom
and bud like a fruit-tree –

From the greengrocer tree you get grapes and green pea, cauliflower,
pineapple, and cranberries,

While the pastrycook plant cherry brandy will grant, apple puffs, and
three-corners, and Banburys –

The shares are a penny, and ever so many are taken by Rothschild and
Baring,

And just as a few are allotted to you, you awake with a shudder despairing –

You're a regular wreck, with a crick in your neck, and no wonder you snore,
for your head's on the floor, and you've needles and pins from your soles
to your shins, and your flesh is a-creep, for your left leg's asleep, and
you've cramp in your toes, and a fly on your nose, and a thirst that's
intense, and a general sense that you haven't been sleeping in clover;

But the darkness has passed, and it's daylight at last, and the night has been
long – ditto ditto my song – and thank goodness they're both of them
over!

ANONYMOUS

J'ai faim
Mange ta main
Garde l'autre pour demain
Et si tu n'as pas assez
Mange un de tes pieds
Et garde l'autre pour danser.

CHARLES CROS
1842–85

Le Hareng saur

Il était un grand mur blanc – nu, nu, nu,
Contre le mur une échelle – haute, haute, haute,
Et, par terre, un hareng saur – sec, sec, sec.

Il vient, tenant dans ses mains – sales, sales, sales,
Un marteau lourd, un grand clou – pointu, pointu, pointu,
Un peloton de ficelle – gros, gros, gros.

Alors il monte à l'échelle – haute, haute, haute,
Et plante le clou pointu – toc, toc, toc,
Tout en haut du grand mur blanc – nu, nu, nu.

Il laisse aller le marteau – qui tombe, qui tombe, qui tombe,
Attache au clou la ficelle – longue, longue, longue,
Et, au bout, le hareng saur – sec, sec, sec.

Il redescend de l'échelle – haute, haute, haute,
L'emporte avec le marteau – lourd, lourd, lourd;
Et puis, il s'en va ailleurs, – loin, loin, loin.

Et, depuis, le hareng saur – sec, sec, sec,
Au bout de cette ficelle – longue, longue, longue,
Très lentement se balance – toujours, toujours, toujours.

J'ai composé cette histoire, – simple, simple, simple,
Pour mettre en fureur les gens – graves, graves, graves,
Et amuser les enfants – petits, petits, petits.

Intérieur

'Joujou, pipi, caca, dodo.'
'Do, ré, mi, fa, sol, la, si, do.'
Le moutard gueule, et sa sœur tape
Sur un vieux clavecin de Pape.
Le père se rase au carreau
Avant de se rendre au bureau.
La mère émiette une panade
Qui mijote, gluante et fade,
Dans les cendres. Le fils aîné
Cire, avec un air étonné,
Les souliers de toute la troupe,
Car, ce soir même, après la soupe,
Ils iront autour de Musard
Et ne rentreront pas trop tard;
Afin que demain l'on s'éveille
Pour une existence pareille.
'Do, ré, mi, fa, sol, la, si, do.'
'Joujou, pipi, caca, dodo.'

WALTER HENLEY
1849–1903

Villon's Good-night

I

You bible-sharps that thump on tubs,
You lurkers on the Abram-sham,
You sponges miking round the pubs,
You flymy titters fond of flam,
You judes that clobber for the stramm,
You ponces good at talking tall,
With fawneys on your dexter famm –
A mot's good-night to one and all!

II

Likewise you molls that flash your bubs
For swells to spot and stand you sam,
You bleeding bonnets, pugs, and subs,
You swatchel-coves that pitch and slam.
You magsmen bold that work the cram,
You flats and joskins great and small,
Gay grass-widows and lawful-jam –
A mot's good-night to one and all!

III

For you, you coppers, narks, and dubs,
Who pinched me when upon the snam,
And gave me mumps and mulligrubs
With skilly and swill that made me clam,
At you I merely lift my gam –
I drink your health against the wall!
That is the sort of man I am,
A mot's good-night to one and all!

The Farewell

Paste 'em, and larrup 'em and lamm!
Give Kennedy, and make 'em crawl!
I do not care one bloody damn,
A mot's good-night to one and all.

Villon's Straight Tip to all Cross Coves

'Tout aux tavernes et aux filles'

I

Suppose you screeve, or go cheap-jack?
Or fake the broads? or fig a nag?
Or thimble-rig? or knap a yack?
Or pitch a snide? or smash a rag?
Suppose you duff? or nose and lag?
Or get the straight, and land your pot?
How do you melt the multy swag?
Booze and the blowens cop the lot.

Fiddle, or fence, or mace, or mack;
Or moskeneer, or flash the drag;
Dead-lurk a crib, or do a crack;

Pad with a slang, or chuck a mag;
Bonnet, or tout, or mump and gag;
Rattle the tats, or mark the spot
You cannot bank a single stag:
Booze and the blowens cop the lot.

III

Suppose you try a different tack,
And on the square you flash your flag?
At penny-a-lining make your whack,
Or with the mummers mug and gag?
For nix, for nix the dibbs you bag
At any graft, no matter what!
Your merry goblins soon stravag:
Booze and the blowens cop the lot.

The Moral

It's up-the-spout and Charley-Wag
With wipes and tickers and what not!
Until the squeezer nips your scrag,
Booze and the blowens cop the lot.

ARTHUR RIMBAUD
1854–91

Fêtes de la Faim

Ma faim, Anne, Anne,
Fuis sur ton âne.

Si j'ai du *goût*, ce n'est guère
Que pour la terre et les pierres.
Dinn! dinn! dinn! dinn! Mangeons l'air,
Le roc, les charbons, le fer.

Mes faims, tournez. Paissez, faims,
Le pré des sons!

Attirez le gai venin
    Des liserons;

Mangez
    Les cailloux qu'un pauvre brise,
    Les vieilles pierres d'église,
    Les galets, fils des déluges,
    Pains couchés aux vallées grises!

Mes faims, c'est les bouts d'air noir;
    L'azur sonneur;
– C'est l'estomac qui me tire.
    C'est le malheur.

Sur terre ont paru les feuilles!
Je vais aux chairs de fruits blettes.
Au sein du sillon je cueille
La doucette et la violette.

    Ma faim, Anne, Anne!
    Fuis sur ton âne.

    O saisons, ô châteaux,
    Quelle âme est sans défauts?

O Saisons, O Châteaux

    O saisons, ô châteaux,

    J'ai fait la magique étude
    Du Bonheur, que nul n'élude.

    O vive lui, chaque fois
    Que chante son coq gaulois.

    Mais! je n'aurai plus d'envie,
    Il s'est chargé de ma vie.

    Ce Charme! il prit âme et corps,
    Et dispersa tous efforts.

    Que comprendre à ma parole?
    Il fait qu'elle fuie et vole!

    O saisons, ô châteaux!

A. E. HOUSMAN
1859–1936

'Hallelujah!' was the only observation
That escaped Lieutenant-Colonel Mary Jane,
When she tumbled off the platform in the station,
And was cut in little pieces by the train.
   Mary Jane, the train is through yer:
   Hallelujah, Hallelujah!
We will gather up the fragments that remain.

The African Lion

To meet a bad lad on the African waste
   Is a thing that a lion enjoys;
But he rightly and strongly objects to the taste
   Of good and uneatable boys.

When he bites off a piece of a boy of that sort
   He spits it right out of his mouth,
And retires with a loud and dissatisfied snort
   To the east, or the west, or the south.

So lads of good habits, on coming across
   A lion, need feel no alarm,
For they know they are sure to escape with the loss
   Of a leg, or a head, or an arm.

Purple William or
The Liar's Doom

The hideous hue which William is
Was not originally his:
So long as William told the truth
He was a usual-coloured youth.

[335]

He now is purple. One fine day
His tender father chanced to say
'What colour is a whelp, and why?'
'Purple' was William's false reply.

'Pooh,' said his Pa, 'You silly elf,
It's no more purple than yourself.
Dismiss the notion from your head.'
'I, too, am purple,' William said.

And he *was* purple. With a yell
His mother off the sofa fell
Exclaiming 'William's purple! Oh!'
William replied 'I told you so.'

His parents, who could not support
The pungency of this retort,
Died with a simultaneous groan.
The purple orphan was alone.

Aunts and Nieces or
Time and Space

Some nieces won't, some nieces can't
Imbibe instruction from an aunt.
Eliza scorned her good Aunt Clare.
Where is Eliza now? Ah, where?
'Avoid, at the approach of dark,
Eliza, the umbrageous park.
During the daytime, lairs and dens
Conceal its direr denizens.
But when that brilliant orb, the Sun,
His useful journey nearly done,
Approaches the horizon's verge,
They will, my dearest niece, emerge;
And forth the cockatrice will frisk,
And out will bounce the basilisk,
And the astoundingly absurd
Yet dangerous cockyoly-bird
Will knock you, with its baneful beak,

Into the middle of next week.'
'Pooh,' said Eliza, 'that it can't.
Still, if you think so, thank you, Aunt.
Now, after this exhausting talk,
I think that I will take a walk'.
She therefore fetched her parasol,
Her gloves and reticule and all,
And need I specify the spot
Which drew her footsteps? I need not.

                *   *   *

'Eliza,' said her aunt, 'is late.
Jane, place the crumpets by the grate.
What was that distant crow I heard?
Was it the cockyoly-bird?
I think so. There it goes again.
You may remove the crumpets, Jane.'
Meanwhile Eliza took the air.
(Shall I? – I will not – mention where),
And as the afternoon progressed
She sat upon the grass to rest,
Drew from her reticule a bun,
And bit it in the setting sun.
Soon, with her mouth full, she perceives
Movements and rustlings in the leaves
Which spoil the situation's charm
And tend to substitute alarm.
She dropped the bun and said 'Dear me!
I fear I shall be late for tea.'
Then, from behind, a vicious peck
Descended on Eliza's neck.
Eliza into the azure distance
Followed the line of least resistance.

                *   *   *

In the middle of next week
There will be heard a piercing shriek,
And looking pale and weak and thin
Eliza will come flying in.

PAUL SCHEERBART

1863–1915

Monologue of the Crazed Mastodon

Zépke! Zépke!
Mekkimápsi – muschibróps.
Okosôni! Mamimûne . . .
Epakróllu róndima sêka, inti . . . windi . . . nakki; pakki
                    salône hepperéppe – hepperéppe!!
Lakku – Zakku – Wakku – Quakku – – muschibróps.
Mamimûne – lesebesebímbera – roxróx – roxróx!!!

Quilliwaûke?
Lesebesebímbera – surû – huhû ∴ .

Kikakokú!
Ekoraláps!

Wîso kollipánda opolôsa.
Ipasátta îh fûo.
Kikakokú proklínthe petêh.
Nikifilí mopaléxio intipáschi benakáffro – própsa
                    pî! própsa pî!
Jasóllu nosaressa flípsei.
Aukarótto passakrússar Kikakokú.
Núpsa púsch?
Kikakokú bulurú?
Futupúkke – própsa pî!
Jasóllu . . .

ANONYMOUS

I saw Shandon steeple a needle for a tailor to sew,
And I saw the New Bridge making wigs for the County Mayo
I saw Enniskillen distilling strong whisky in Athy
And the Empress of Greece plucking geese in a village close by.

OLIVER HERFORD
1863–1935

Metaphysics

Why and Wherefore set out one day
    To hunt for a wild Negation.
They agreed to meet at a cool retreat
    On the Point of Interrogation.

But the night was dark and they missed their mark,
    And, driven well-nigh to distraction,
They lost their ways in a murky maze
    Of utter abstruse abstraction.

Then they took a boat and were soon afloat
    On a sea of Speculation,
But the sea grew rough, and their boat, though tough,
    Was split into an Equation.

As they floundered about in the waves of doubt
    Rose a fearful Hypothesis,
Who gibbered with glee as they sank in the sea,
    And the last they saw was this:

On a rock-bound reef of Unbelief
    There sat the wild Negation;
Then they sank once more and were washed ashore
    At the Point of Interrogation.

ANONYMOUS

Christian

Christian hat Hosen an,
26 Knöpfe dran.
Hätt' er keine Knöpfe dran,
Hiess' er auch nicht Christian.

Translation

Christian has trousers on,
26 buttons thereupon.
Had he not those buttons on,
He would not be Christian.

W. B. YEATS
1865–1939

The Collarbone of a Hare

Would I could cast a sail on the water
Where many a king has gone
And many a king's daughter,
And alight at the comely trees and the lawn,
The playing upon pipes and the dancing,
And learn that the best thing is
To change my loves while dancing
And pay but a kiss for a kiss.

I would find by the edge of that water
The collarbone of a hare
Worn thin by the lapping of water,
And pierce it through with a gimlet, and stare
At the old bitter world where they marry in churches,
And laugh over the untroubled water
At all who marry in churches,
Through the white thin bone of a hare.

High Talk

Processions that lack high stilts have nothing that catches the eye.
What if my great-granddad had a pair that were twenty foot high,

And mine were but fifteen foot, no modern stalks upon higher,
Some rogue of the world stole them to patch up a fence or a fire.
Because piebald ponies, led bears, caged lions, make but poor shows,
Because children demand Daddy-long-legs upon his timber toes,
Because women in the upper storeys demand a face at the pane,
That patching old heels they may shriek, I take to chisel and plane.

Malachi Stilt-Jack am I, whatever I learned has run wild,
From collar to collar, from stilt to stilt, from father to child.
All metaphor, Malachi, stilts and all. A barnacle goose
Far up in the stretches of night; night splits and the dawn breaks loose;
I, through the terrible novelty of light, stalk on, stalk on;
Those great sea-horses bare their teeth and laugh at the dawn.

ANONYMOUS

A Chronicle

Once – but no matter when –
  There lived – no matter where –
A man, whose name – but then
  I need not that declare.

He – well, he had been born,
  And so he was alive;
His age – I details scorn –
  Was somethingty and five.

He lived – how many years
  I truly can't decide;
But this one fact appears
  He lived – until he died.

'He died,' I have averred,
　　But cannot prove 't was so,
But that he was interred,
　　At any rate, I know.

I fancy he'd a son,
　　I hear he had a wife:
Perhaps he'd more than one,
　　I know not, on my life!

But whether he was rich,
　　Or whether he was poor,
Or neither – both – or which,
　　I cannot say, I'm sure.

I can't recall his name,
　　Or what he used to do:
But then – well, such is fame!
　　'T will so serve me and you.

And that is why I thus,
　　About this unknown man
Would fain create a fuss,
　　To rescue, if I can

From dark oblivion's blow,
　　Some record of his lot:
But, ah! I do not know
　　Who – where – when – why – or what.

MORAL

In this brief pedigree
　　A moral we should find –
But what it ought to be
　　Has quite escaped my mind!

GELETT BURGESS
1866–1951

Psycholophon

Supposed to be Translated from the Old Parsee

Twine then the rays
　　Round her soft Theban tissues!
All will be as She says,
　　When that dead past reissues.
Matters not what nor where,
　　Hark, to the moon's dim cluster!
How was her heavy hair
　　Lithe as a feather duster!
Matters not when nor whence;
　　Flittertigibbet!
Sounds make the song, not sense,
　　Thus I inhibit!

The Purple Cow

I never saw a Purple Cow,
I never hope to see one;
But I can tell you, any how,
I'd rather see than be one.

HILAIRE BELLOC
1870–1953

Sarah Byng who could not read and was tossed into a thorny hedge by a bull. A Cautionary Tale.

Of Sarah Byng the tale is told
How when the child was twelve years old
She could not read or write a line.

[343]

Her sister Jane, though barely nine,
Could spout the Catechism through
And parts of Matthew Arnold too,
While little Bill who came between
Was quite unnaturally keen
On 'Athalie' by Jean Racine.
But not so Sarah! Not so Sal!
She was a most uncultured girl
Who didn't care a pinch of snuff
For any literary stuff
And gave the classics all a miss.
Observe the consequence of this!
As she was walking home one day,
Upon the fields across her way
A gate, securely padlocked, stood,
And by its side a piece of wood
On which was painted plain and full,
BEWARE THE VERY FURIOUS BULL.
Alas! The young illiterate
Went blindly forward to her fate,
And ignorantly climbed the gate!
Now happily the bull that day
Was rather in the mood for play
Than goring people through and through
As Bulls so very often do;
He tossed her lightly with his horns
Into a prickly bush of thorns,
And stood by laughing while she strode
And pushed and struggled to the road.
The lesson was not lost upon
The child, who since has always gone
A long way round to keep away
From signs, whatever they may say,
And leaves a padlocked gate alone.
Moreover she has wisely grown
Confirmed in her instinctive guess
That literature breeds distress.

JOHN SYNGE

1871–1909

*The ending to Old Mourteen's story recounted in
John Synge's* The Aran Islands, *1911*

They found the path and I found the puddle
They were drowned and I was found,
If it's all one to me tonight,
It was all one to them the next night.
Yet if it wasn't itself, not a thing did they lose
But an old back tooth
or some such gibberish.

CHRISTIAN MORGENSTERN

1871–1914

The Great Lalula

Kroklokwafzi? Seṁemeṁi!
Seiokrontro – prafriplo:
Bifzi, bafzi; hulaleṁi:
quasti basti bo . . .
Lalu lalu lalu lalu la!

Hontraruru miromente
zasku zes rü rü?
Entepente, leiolente
klekwapufzi lü?
lalu lalu lalu lalu la!

Simarar kos malzipempu
silzuzankunkrei (;)!
Marjomar dos: Quempu Lempu
Siri Suri Sei [ ]!
Lalu lalu lalu lalu la!

The Fish's Night Song

The Police Inquiry

Korf gets a police chief's questionnaire,
written in a stiff, official way,
asking who he is and how and where.

At what other places did he stay,
what professional life he claims to lead,
and when born, exactly, year and day.

Furthermore, was he indeed
licensed here to live? And would he check
where he banks, and what his race and creed?

Otherwise he'll get it in the neck
and be jailed. Below are two
signatures: Borowsky, Heck.

Korf replies in short, without ado:
'Honorable gracious Sir,
after thorough personal review

it is necessary to aver
that the party signed below
does not actually occur

in conventional reality, although
he himself by self-same fact is vexed.
Korf. (To County Office so-and-so.)'

The concerned police chief reads, perplexed.

translated from the German by Max Knight

Korf's Clock

Korf a kind of clock invents
where two pairs of hands go round:
one the current hour presents,
one is always backward bound.

When it's two – it's also ten;
when it's three – it's also nine.
You just look at it, and then
time gets never out of line,

for in Korf's astute invention
with its Janus-kindred stride
(which, of course, was his intention)
time itself is nullified.

translated from the German by Max Knight

The Midnightmouse

It midnights, not a moon is out.
No star lives in the heavenhouse.
Runs twelve times through the heavenhouse
    The Midnightmouse.

She pipes upon her little jaws.
The hellhorse from his nightmare roars . . .
Runs quietly, her allotted course,
        The Midnightmouse.

Her Lord, the Spirit great and white,
Has gone abroad on such a night.
She keeps watch in his heaven; all's right.
        The Midnightmouse.

translated from the German by W. D. Snodgrass and Lore Segal

The Knee

There wanders through the world, a knee
It's just a knee, no more.
It's not a tent; it's not a tree;
Only a knee, no more.

There was a man once in a war
Overkilled, killed fatally.
Alone, unhurt, remained the knee
Like a saint's relics, pure.

Since then it roams the whole world, lonely.
It is a knee, now, only.
It's not a tent; it's not a tree;
Only a knee, no more.

translated from the German by W. D. Snodgrass and Lore Segal

The Nosobame

Upon his noses strides
about, the Nosobame,
his children at his sides.
He's not yet got to Thame.

He's not yet got to Shire,
nor even yet to Wight.
He's just stepped from my lyre
for the first time into light.

Upon his noses strides
(as said above) since then,
his children at his sides,
the stately Nosobame.

The Pearl-hen

The pearl-hen counts; one, two, three, four.
What is it counting, the patient creature
  below the darkening alder?

It's counting with a scientific air
(which to it and us seems charming there)
  its pearls; their precise number.

translated from the German by H.H.

The Moonsheep

The moonsheep stands on the huge lawn.
It's patiently waiting to be shorn.
  The moonsheep.

The moonsheep plucks himself a blade
And then goes home to his alpine shade.
  The moonsheep.

The moonsheep mumbles in his dream:
'I am the Worldsoul's darker theme'.
  The moonsheep.

The moonsheep in the morn lies dead.
His body is white, the sun is red.
  The moonsheep.

translated from the German by H.H.

Palmstroem in Animal Costume

Palmstroem loves to ape the animals.
He has therefore trained two youthful tailors
to specialise in animal costumes.

Thus, e.g., he likes to perch as a raven
on the upper branches of an oak
and observe the heavens.

Often he plays the St Bernard
laying shaggy head on trusty paws,
barking in sleep as he dreams of spectacular rescues.

Or he spins a web in his garden
out of twine, and sits as a spider
for days long at its centre.

Or he swims as a goggle-eyed carp,
around the fountain in his fishpond,
and allows the children to throw him crumbs.

Or he hangs, dressed in a stork suit,
below an airship's gondola,
and journeys thus to Egypt.

translated from the German by H.H.

ALFRED JARRY

(1873–1907)

La Chanson du Décervelage

from Ubu Cocu

A cabinet-maker was I for many a long year,
Rue du Champs de Mars in All Saints' Parish;
My dear wife was a dressmaker designing lady's wear,
And the style in which we lived was pretty lavish.

Every blooming Sunday if it wasn't raining,
We'd put on our best clothes and toddle down
To join the mob who came for the Debraining,
Rue de l'Echaudé, the greatest show in town.
One, two, watch the wheels go round,
Snip, snap, the brains fly all around,
My oh my the Rentier's in a stew!
CHORUS: *Hip hip arse-over-tip! Hurrah for Old Ubu!*

With our two beloved nippers, clutching us jammily
And waving paper dolls, as happy as can be,
Upstairs on the bus we're a well-adjusted family
As we roll off merrily towards the Echaudé.
Crowding to the barrier, risking broken bones,
Regardless of the blows, we push to the front row.
Then yours truly climbs up on a pile of stones
To protect my turn-ups when the claret starts to flow,
One, two, etc.
CHORUS: *Hip hip arse-over-tip! Hurrah for Old Ubu!*

Soon with brains we're plastered, the old girl and me,
Our two kids lap it up and we're all jubilating
As we watch the Palcontent display his cutlery –
The first incision's made and the numbered coffins waiting.
Suddenly I notice right up by the machine
The half-familiar phiz of a chap I used to know.
Hey, there! I shout to him, So much for you, old bean!
You tried to cheat me once, am I glad to see you go!
One, two, etc.
CHORUS: *Hip hip arse-over-tip! Hurrah for Old Ubu!*

A plucking at my sleeve, it's my spouse as I perceive.
Come on, you slob, she screeches, Take a crack!
Chuck a man-sized wad of dung at the lying bastard's tongue,
The Palcontent's just turned his ruddy back!
Such excellent advice won't allow me to think twice,
I summon all my courage and let fly –
An enormous lump of pschitt meant to score the winning hit,
Got the Palcontent instead full in the eye.
CHORUS: *Hip hip arse-over-tip! Hurrah for Old Ubu!*

Toppled from my heap of stone, on the barrier I'm thrown,
As the Palcontent turns round to see who nicked him:
Down the hole of no return, pulped like butter in a churn,
And The People's justice claims another victim.
So that is what you cop for a little Sunday hop,
Rue de l'Echaudé where necks are craning –
You set out like a lord and they return you on a board,
Just because you fancied a debraining.
WITH CHORUS: *One, two, see the wheels go round,*
Snip, snap, the brains fly all around,
My oh my the Rentier's in a stew!
Hip hip arse-over-tip! Hurrah for Old Ubu!
from the translation of the play, Ubu Cuckolded,
by Cyril Connolly and Simon Watson Taylor

Le Homard et la Boîte
de Corned-Beef que Portait
Le Docteur Faustroll en Sautoir

FABLE

(*to A. F. Hérold*)

Une boîte de corned-beef, enchaînée comme une lorgnette,
Vit passer un homard qui lui ressemblait fraternellement.
Il se cuirassait d'une carapace dure
Sur laquelle était écrit qu'à l'intérieur, comme elle, il était sans arêtes,
(Boneless and economical);
Et sous sa queue repliée
Il cachait vraisemblablement une clé destinée à l'ouvrir.
Frappé d'amour, le corned-beef sédentaire

Déclara à la petite boîte automobile de conserves vivante
Que si elle consentait à s'acclimater,
Près de lui, aux devantures terrestres,
Elle serait décorée de plusieurs médailles d'or.

WALTER DE LA MARE
1873–1956

Kiph

My Uncle Ben, who's been
To Bisk, Bhir, Biak –
Been, and come back:
To Tab, Tau, Tze, and Tomsk,
And home, by Teneriffe:
Who, brown as desert sand,
Gaunt, staring, slow and stiff,
Has chased the Unicorn
And Hippogriff,
Gave me a smooth, small, shining stone,
Called *Kiph*.

'Look'ee, now, Nevvy mine,'
He told me – '*If*
You'd wish a wish,
Just rub this smooth, small, shining stone,
Called *Kiph*.'

Hide it did I,
In a safe, secret spot;
Slept, and the place
In dreams forgot.

One wish *alone*
Now's mine: Oh, if
I could but find again
That stone called *Kiph!*

Jim Jay

Do diddle di do,
  Poor Jim Jay
Got stuck fast
  In Yesterday.
Squinting he was,
  On cross-legs bent,
Never heeding
  The wind was spent.
Round veered the weathercock,
  The sun drew in –
And stuck was Jim
  Like a rusty pin . . .
We pulled and we pulled
  From seven till twelve,
Jim, too frightened
  To help himself.
But all in vain.
  The clock struck one,
And there was Jim
  A little bit gone.
At half-past five
  You scarce could see
A glimpse of his flapping
  Handkerchee.
And when came noon,
  And we climbed sky-high,
Jim was a speck
  Slip – slipping by.
Come to-morrow,
  The neighbours say,
He'll be past crying for:
  Poor Jim Jay.

G. K. CHESTERTON
1874–1936

The Oneness of the Philosopher with Nature

I love to see the little Stars
  all dancing to one tune;
I think quite highly of the Sun,
  and kindly of the Moon.

The million forests of the Earth
  come trooping in to tea.
The great Niagara waterfall
  is never shy with me.

I am the Tiger's confidant,
  and never mention names:
the Lion drops the formal 'Sir,'
  and lets me call him James.

Into my ear the blushing Whale
  stammers his love. I know
why the Rhinoceros is sad,
  – ah, child! 'twas long ago.

I am akin to all the Earth
  by many a tribal sign:
the aged Pig will often wear
  that sad, sweet smile of mine.

My niece, the Barnacle, has got
  my piercing eyes of black;
the Elephant has got my nose,
  I do not want it back.

I know the strange tale of the Slug;
  the Early Sin – the Fall –
the Sleep – the Vision – and the Vow –
  the Quest – the Crown – the Call.

And I have loved the Octopus,
   since we were boys together.
I love the Vulture and the Shark:
   I even love the weather.

I love to bask in sunny fields,
   and when that hope is vain,
I go and bask in Baker Street,
   all in the pouring rain.

Come snow! where fly, by some strange law,
   hard snowballs – without noise –
through streets untenanted, except
   by good unconscious boys.

Come fog! Exultant mystery –
   where, in strange darkness rolled,
the end of my own nose becomes
   a lovely legend old.

Come snow, and hail, and thunderbolts,
   sleet, fire, and general fuss;
come to my arms, come all at once –
   oh photograph me thus!

HARRY GRAHAM
1874–1936

The Stern Parent

Father heard his Children scream,
So he threw them in the stream,
Saying, as he drowned the third,
'Children should be seen, *not* heard!'

Tender-Heartedness

Billy, in one of his nice new sashes,
Fell in the fire and was burnt to ashes;
Now, although the room grows chilly,
I haven't the heart to poke poor Billy.

L'Enfant Glacé

When Baby's cries grew hard to bear
I popped him in the Frigidaire.
I never would have done so if
I'd known that he'd be frozen stiff.
My wife said: 'George, I'm so unhappé!
Our darling's now completely *frappé*!'

The Englishman's Home

I was playing golf the day
   That the Germans landed;
All our troops had run away,
   All our ships were stranded;
And the thought of England's shame
Altogether spoilt my game.

Compensation

Weep not for little Léonie,
Abducted by a French *Marquis*!
Though loss of honour was a wrench,
Just think how it's improved her French!

EDMUND CLERIHEW BENTLEY

1875–1956

Clerihews

GEORGE III

George the Third
Ought never to have occurred.
One can only wonder
At so grotesque a blunder.

SAVONAROLA

Savonarola
Declined to wear a bowler
Expressing the view that it was gammon
To talk of serving God and Mammon.

WALLACE STEVENS

1879–1955

The Emperor of Ice-Cream

Call the roller of big cigars,
The muscular one, and bid him whip
In kitchen cups concupiscent curds.
Let the wenches dawdle in such dress
As they are used to wear, and let the boys
Bring flowers in last month's newspapers.
Let be be finale of seem.
The only emperor is the emperor of ice-cream.

Take from the dresser of deal
Lacking the three glass knobs, that sheet
On which she embroidered fantails once
And spread it so as to cover her face.
If her horny feet protrude, they come
To show how cold she is, and dumb.
Let the lamp affix its beam.
The only emperor is the emperor of ice-cream.

Disillusionment of Ten O'Clock

The houses are haunted
By white night-gowns.
None are green,
Or purple with green rings,
Or green with yellow rings,
Or yellow with blue rings.
None of them are strange,
With socks of lace
And beaded ceintures.
People are not going
To dream of baboons and periwinkles.
Only, here and there, an old sailor,
Drunk and asleep in his boots,
Catches tigers
In red weather.

PAUL KLEE

1879–1940

Der Herr weis was der wil
(In the style of Klee's favourite cat, Bimbo)

Der Herr weis was der wil.
der kan.

Aber hat ain Laster, nicht rauchen.
Aber grazt mit ain Harpeitsche auf den Gaige,
das tu den Bimbo so weh in or.

Translation

The Master knows what he want.
he can.

But he has one vice, not smoking.
He skrattches on his fiddle with a hairwhip.
It make Bimbo's ears go tingle.

GUILLAUME APOLLINAIRE
1880–1918

Le Phoque

J'ai des yeux d'un vrai veau marin
Et de Madame Ygrec l'allure.
On me voit dans tous nos meetings
Je fais de la littérature
Je suis phoque de mon état
Et comme il faut qu' on se marie
Un beau jour j'épouserai Lota
Du matin au soir L'Otarie
   Papa Maman
Pipi et tabac crachoir caf' conc'
   Laï Tou

Translation

The Seal

I have the eyes of a real sea calf
and Madame Y's allure
I am present at all our soirées
I am involved in Literature
I am a seal by nature
And as one has to marry
One fine day I'll wed my Lota
From dawn to dusk the Otary
   Daddy mummy
Wee-wee and tobacco spittoon caf' conc'
   Lai Tou

Chapeau-tombeau

On a niché
Dans son tombeau
L'oiseau perché
Sur ton chapeau
Il a vécu
En Amérique
Le petit cul
   Or
nithologique
   Or
J'en ai assez
Je vais pisser.

Translation

Hat-tomb

Something's nested
In his tomb
The bird perched
On your hat
He has lived
In America
The wee
   Or
nithological
Shit
And/
   Or
That's it.
I'm off for a pee.

From *Nursery Songs of the Appalachian Mountains,*
Collected by Cecil Sharp (1923)

ANONYMOUS

The Derby Ram

As I was going to Derby,
    'Twas on a market day,
I saw the finest ram, sir,
    That ever was fed on hay.
This ram was fat behind, sir,
    This ram was fat before,
This ram was ten yards high, sir,
    If he wasn't a little more.
      That's a lie, that's a lie,
      That's a tid i fa la lie.

Now the inside of this ram, sir,
    Would hold ten sacks of corn,
And you could turn a coach and six
    On the inside of his horn.
Now the wool upon his back, sir,
    It reached up to the sky,
And in it was a crow's nest,
    For I heard the young ones cry.
      That's a lie, that's a lie,
      That's a tid i fa la lie.

Now the wool upon his belly, sir,
    Went draggling on the ground,
And that was took to Derby, sir,
    And sold for ten thousand pound.
Now the wool upon his tail, sir,
    Was ten inches and an ell,
And that was took to Derby, sir,
    To toll the old market-bell.
      That's a lie, that's a lie,
      That's a tid i fa la lie.

Now the man that fed this ram, sir,
   He fed him twice a day,
And each time that he fed him, sir,
   He ate a rick of hay.
Now the man that watered this ram, sir,
   He watered him twice a day,
And each time that he watered him
   He drank the river dry.
     That's a lie, that's a lie,
     That's a tid i fa la lie.

Now the butcher that killed the ram, sir,
   Was up to his knees in blood,
And the boy that held the bowl, sir,
   Got washed away in the flood.
Now all the boys in Derby, sir,
   Went begging for his eyes,
They kicked them up and down the street,
   For they were a good football size.
     That's a lie, that's a lie,
     That's a tid i fa la lie.

Now all the women of Derby, sir,
   Went begging for his ears,
To make their leather aprons of
   That lasted them forty years.
And the man that fatted the ram, sir,
   He must be very rich,
And the man that sung this song, sir,
   Is a lying son of a bitch.
     That's the truth, that's the truth,
     That's the tid i fa la truth.

ANONYMOUS

Nottamun Town

In Nottamun Town not a soul would look up,
Not a soul would look up, not a soul would look down,
Not a soul would look up, not a soul would look down,
To tell me the way to Nottamun Town.

I rode a big horse that was called a grey mare,
Grey mane and tail, grey stripes down his back,
Grey mane and tail, grey stripes down his back,
There weren't a hair on him but what was called black.

She stood so still, she threw me to the dirt,
She tore my hide and bruised my shirt;
From stirrup to stirrup I mounted again
And on my ten toes I rode over the plain.

Met the King and the Queen and a company of men
A-walking behind and a-riding before.
A stark naked drummer came walking along
With his hands in his bosom a-beating his drum.

Sat down on a hot and cold frozen stone,
Ten thousand stood round me yet I was alone.
Took my heart in my hand to keep my head warm.
Ten thousand got drowned that never were born.

ANONYMOUS
TWO IRISH BALLADS

Brian O Linn

Brian O Linn had no breeches to wear
He got an old sheepskin to make him a pair
With the fleshy side out and the woolly side in,
'They'll be pleasant and cool,' says Brian O Linn.

Brian O Linn had no shirt to his back,
He went to a neighbour's, and borrowed a sack,
Then he puckered the meal bag in under his chin –
'Sure they'll take them for ruffles,' says Brian O Linn.

Brian O Linn was hard up for a coat,
So be borrowed the skin of a neighbouring goat,
With the horns sticking out from his oxsters, and then,
'Sure they'll take them for pistols,' says Brian O Linn.

Brian O Linn had no hat to put on,
So he got an old beaver to make him a one,
There was none of the crown left and less of the brim,
'Sure there's fine ventilation,' says Brian O Linn.

Brian O Linn had no brogues for his toes,
He hopped in two crab-shells to serve him for those.
Then he split up two oysters that match'd like a twin,
'Sure they'll shine out like buckles,' says Brian O Linn.

Brian O Linn had no watch to put on,
So he scooped out a turnip to make him a one.
Then he placed a young cricket in-under the skin –
'Sure they'll think it is ticking,' says Brian O Linn.

Brian O Linn to his house had no door,
He'd the sky for a roof, and the bog for a floor;
He'd a way to jump out, and a way to swim in,
''Tis a fine habitation,' says Brian O Linn.

Brian O Linn weant a-courting one night,
He set both the mother and daughter to fight;
To fight for his hand they both stripped to the skin,
'Sure! I'll marry you both,' says Brian O Linn.

Brian O Linn, his wife and wife's mother,
They all lay down in the bed together,
The sheets they were old and the blankets were thin,
'Lie close to the wall,' says Brian O Linn.

Brian O Linn, his wife and wife's mother,
Were all going home o'er the bridge together,
The bridge it broke down, and they all tumbled in,
'We'll go home by the water,' says Brian O Linn.

Finnegan's Wake

Tim Finnegan liv'd in Walkin Street,
A gentleman Irish mighty odd.
He had a tongue both rich and sweet,
An' to rise in the world he carried a hod,
Now Tim had a sort of a tipplin' way
With the love of the liquor he was born,
An' to help him on with his work each day,
He'd a drop of the craythur ev'ry morn.

> *Whack fol the dah, dance to your partner*
> *Welt the flure, yer trotters shake,*
> *Wasn't it the truth I told you,*
> *Lots of fun at Finnegan's Wake.*

One morning Tim was rather full,
His head felt heavy which made him shake,
He fell from the ladder and broke his skull,
So they carried him home his corpse to wake,
They rolled him up in a nice clean sheet,
And laid him out upon the bed,
With a gallon of whisky at his feet,
And a barrel of porter at his head.

His friends assembled at the wake,
And Mrs Finnegan called for lunch,
First they brought in tay and cake,
Then pipes, tobacco, and whiskey punch.
Miss Biddy O'Brien began to cry,
'Such a neat clean corpse, did you ever see,
Arrah, Tim avourneen, why did you die?'
'Ah, hould your gab,' said Paddy McGee.

Then Biddy O'Connor took up the job,
'Biddy,' says she, 'you're wrong, I'm sure,'
But Biddy gave her a belt in the gob,
And left her sprawling on the floor;
Oh, then the war did soon enrage;
'Twas woman to woman and man to man,
Shillelagh law did all engage,
And a row and a ruction soon began.

Then Mickey Maloney raised his head,
When a noggin of whiskey flew at him,
It missed and falling on the bed,
The liquor scattered over Tim;
Bedad he revives, see how he rises,
And Timothy rising from the bed,
Says, 'Whirl your liquor round like blazes,
Thanam o'n dhoul, do ye think I'm dead?'
    Whack fol the dah, dance to your partner
    Welt the flure, yer trotters shake,
    Wasn't it the truth I told you,
    Lots of fun at Finnegan's Wake.

JAMES JOYCE
1882–1941

An advertisement for Finnegans Wake

Humpty Dump Dublin squeaks through his norse;
Humpty Dump Dublin hath a horrible vorse;
But for all his kinks English, plus his irismanx brogues
Humpty Dump Dublin's grandada of all rogues.

The Ballad of Persse O'Reilly
From *Finnegans Wake*

Have you heard of one Humpty Dumpty
How he fell with a roll and a rumble
And curled up like Lord Olofa Crumple
By the butt of the Magazine Wall,
    (Chorus) Of the Magazine Wall,
        Hump, helmet and all?

He was one time our King of the Castle
Now he's kicked about like a rotten old parsnip.
And from Green street he'll be sent by order of His Worship
To the penal jail of Mountjoy
    (Chorus) To the jail of Mountjoy!
        Jail him and joy.

He was fafafather of all schemes for to bother us
Slow coaches and immaculate contraceptives for the populace,
Mare's milk for the sick, seven dry Sundays a week,
Openair love and religion's reform,
    (Chorus) And religious reform,
        Hideous in form.

Arrah, why, says you, couldn't he manage it?
I'll go bail, my fine dairyman darling,
Like the bumping bull of the Cassidys
All your butter is in your horns.
    (Chorus) His butter is in his horns.
        Butter his horns!

(Repeat) Hurrah there, Hosty, frosty Hosty, change that shirt on ye,
Rhyme the rann, the king of all ranns!

          Balbaccio, balbuccio!
We had chaw chaw chops, chairs, chewing gum, the chicken-pox and
   china chambers
Universally provided by this soffsoaping salesman.
Small wonder He'll Cheat E'erawan our local lads nicknamed him
When Chimpden first took the floor
    (Chorus) With his bucketshop store
        Down Bargainweg, Lower.

So snug he was in his hotel premises sumptuous
But soon we'll bonfire all his trash, tricks and trumpery
And 'tis short till sheriff Clancy'll be winding up his unlimited company
With the bailiff's bom at the door,
    (Chorus) Bimbam at the door.
        Then he'll bum no more.

Sweet bad luck on the waves washed to our island
The hooker of that hammerfast viking

And Gall's curse on the day when Eblana bay
Saw his black and tan man-o'-war.
    (Chorus) Saw his man-o'-war.
           On the harbour bar.

Where from? roars Poolbeg. Cookingha'pence, he bawls Donnez-moi
    scampitle, wick an wipin'fampiny
Fingal Mac Oscar Onesine Bargearse Boniface
Thok's min gammelhole Norveegickers moniker
Og as ay are at gammelhore Norveegickers cod.
    (Chorus) A Norwegian camel old cod.
           He is, begod.

Lift it, Hosty, lift it, ye devil ye! up with the rann, the rhyming rann!

It was during some fresh water garden pumping
Or, according to the *Nursing Mirror*, while admiring the monkeys
That our heavyweight heathen Humpharey
Made bold a maid to woo
    (Chorus) Woohoo, what'll she doo!
           The general lost her maidenloo!

He ought to blush for himself, the old hayheaded philosopher,
For to go and shove himself that way on top of her.
Begob, he's the crux of the catalogue
Of our antediluvial zoo,
    (Chorus) Messrs. Billing and Coo.
           Noah's larks, good as noo.

He was joulting by Wellinton's monument
Our rotorious hippopopotamuns
When some bugger let down the backtrap of the omnibus
And he caught his death of fusiliers,
    (Chorus) With his rent in his rears.
           Give him six years.

'Tis sore pity for his innocent poor children
But look out for his missus legitimate!
When that frew gets a grip of old Earwicker
Won't there be earwigs on the green?
    (Chorus) Big earwigs on the green,
           The largest ever you seen.

Suffoclose! Shikespower! Seudodanto! Anonymoses!

Then we'll have a free trade Gaels' band and mass meeting
For to sod the brave son of Scandiknavery.
And we'll bury him down in Oxmanstown
Along with the devil and Danes,
      (Chorus) With the deaf and dumb Danes,
            And all their remains.

And not all the king's men nor his horses
Will resurrect his corpus
For there's no true spell in Connacht or hell
      (bis) That's able to raise a Cain.

A. A. MILNE
1882–1956

Cottleston Pie from Winnie the Pooh

'Good morning, Eeyore,' said Pooh.

'Good morning, Pooh Bear,' said Eeyore gloomily. 'If it *is* a good morning,' he said. 'Which I doubt,' said he.

'Why, what's the matter?'

'Nothing, Pooh Bear, nothing. We can't all, and some of us don't. That's all there is to it.'

'Can't all *what*?' said Pooh, rubbing his nose.

'Gaiety. Song-and-dance. Here we go round the mulberry bush.'

'Oh!' said Pooh. He thought for a long time, and then asked, 'What mulberry bush is that?'

'Bon-hommy,' went on Eeyore gloomily. 'French word meaning bonhommy,' he explained. 'I'm not complaining, but There It Is.'

Pooh sat down on a large stone, and tried to think this out. It sounded to him like a riddle, and he was never much good at riddles, being a Bear of Very Little Brain. So he sang *Cottleston Pie* instead:

      Cottleston, Cottleston, Cottleston Pie.
      A fly can't bird, but a bird can fly.
      Ask me a riddle and I reply:
      'Cottleston, Cottleston, Cottleston Pie.'

That was the first verse. When he had finished it, Eeyore didn't actually say that he didn't like it, so Pooh very kindly sang the second verse to him:

> Cottleston, Cottleston, Cottleston Pie,
> A fish can't whistle and neither can I.
> Ask me a riddle and I reply:
> *'Cottleston, Cottleston, Cottleston Pie.'*

Eeyore still said nothing at all, so Pooh hummed the third verse quietly to himself:

> Cottleston, Cottleston, Cottleston Pie,
> Why does a chicken, I don't know why.
> Ask me a riddle and I reply:
> *'Cottleston, Cottleston, Cottleston Pie.'*

'That's right,' said Eeyore. 'Sing. Umty-tiddly, umty-too. Here we go gathering Nuts and May. Enjoy yourself.'
'I am,' said Pooh.
'Some can,' said Eeyore.

VELIMIR KHLEBNIKOV
1885–1922

Incantation by Laughter

> O laugh it out, you laughsters!
> O laugh it up, you laughsters!
> So they laugh with laughters, so they laugherize delaughly.
> O laugh it up belaughably!
> O the laughingstock of the laughed-upon – the laugh of belaughed
>   laughsters!
> O laugh it out roundlaughingly, the laugh of laughed-at laughians!
>   Laugherino, laugherino,
>   Laughify, laughicate, laugholets, laugholets,
>   Laughikins, laughikins,
>   O laugh it out, you laughsters!
>   O laugh it up, you laughsters!

translated from the Russian by Gary Kern

'We chant and enchant'

We chant and enchant,
Oh charming enchantment!
No raving, no ranting,
No canting enchantment!
This ranting enchantress
Has cast her enchantment –
We see what her chant meant!
Here rant! There cant!
You charming enchanter,
Cast out her enchantment,
Uncast it, uncant it,
Discast it, discant it,
Descant: Decant! Recant!
He can't. She can't.
Why can't she recant?
Why can't he uncant?
Ranting chanting,
No recanting.
Discant, descant.

The law of the see-saw argues
That your shoes will be loose or tight,
That the hours will be day or night,
And the ruler of earth the rhinoceros
Or us.

translated from the Russian by Paul Schmidt

The opening scenes of Zangesi

A Supersaga in 20 planes

PLANE ONE: THE BIRDS

(These are the birds' morning speeches to the rising sun.)

Chaffinch (from the very top of the fir tree, puffing out its silver throat) Peet páte tveechan! Peet pate tveechan! Peets páte tveechan!

Yellow Bunting (quietly, from the top of a walnut tree) Kree-tee-tee-tee-tee-ee – tsuey-tsuey-tsuey-ssueyee.

Tree Swallow Vyer-vyór veéroo syek-syek-syek! Ver-ver veéroo sek-sek-sék!

Mountain Sparrow Tyortee yedeégredee *(he sees people and hops into the tall fir tree)*. Tyorteé yedeegredee!

Yellow Bunting (rocking back and forth on a branch) Tsuey-tsuey-tsuey-sssueyeé.

Green Chiff-Chaff (alone, flitting over the green sea of the pine grove, grazing waves that the wind keeps forever in motion) Pruéyn! ptseerép-ptseerép! Ptseérep!—tsehsehséh.

Yellow Bunting Tsuey-suey-suey-ssuéy *(rocks back and forth on a twig)*.

Blue Jay Peéoo! Peéoo! pyak, pyak, pyak!

Barn Swallow Tseeveéts! Tseezeéts!

Black-Banded Warbler Behbot éh-oo-véhvyats!

Cuckoo Koo-koó! koo-koo! *(rocks back and forth on a treetop)*.

(Silence. A young birdcatcher passes, with a cage on his back.)

PLANE TWO: THE GODS

(Little by little, the mist clears. Sheer cliff faces appear: they resemble the faces of men who have led harsh, uncompromising lives; clearly, this is the nesting place of the gods. Swanwings hover upon transparent bodies, and the grasses murmur and bend beneath invisible footsteps. And in truth, the gods are at hand! Louder and louder their voices resound; this is the assembly of the gods of all nations, their great gathering, their encampment in the mountains.

Tien stands; his long hair touches the ground; it forms his only garment. With a flat iron he smoothes away wrinkles.

Shang-ti wipes from his face the soot of Western cities. 'Little better so, maybe.' Two snowy wisps of hair, like little rabbits, perch above his ears. He has a long Chinese moustache.

White Juno is draped in green hopvines: she scrapes at her snow-white shoulder with a diligent metal file, cleaning scales from the white stone.

Unkulunkulu listens attentively to the sound of a beetle tunneling its way through the beam of his wooden body.)

Eros Mara-róma
  Be'ebah-bo'ol
  Oook, kooks, ell!
  Rede de'edee dee-dee-de'e!
  Pe'eree, pépee, pa-pa-pe'e!
  Chógi, go'ona, géni-gan
  Ahl, Ell, Eeell!
  Ahlee, Ellee, Eelee!
  Ek, ak, oook!
  Gamch, gemch, ee-ó!
  rrr-pee! rrr-pee!

The Gods Respond Na-no-na!
  Echee, oochee, ochee
  Kézee, nézee, dzee-ga-gá!
  Neezare'ezee ozeere'e
  Mayahmo'ora zeemoró!
  Peeps!
  Mazacheecheecheemoro!
  Plyan!

Veles Broovoo ro'o roo roo ro'o!
  Pe'etse tsápe seh seh séh!
  Broovoo ro'oroo roo-roo-ro'o!
  Se'etsee, le'etsee tsee-tsee-tse'e!
  Painch, panch, painnch!

Eros Emch, amch, oomch!
  Do'omchee dámchee dómchee,
  Makaráko keeochérk!
  Tseetseeleetsee tsee-tsee-tse'e!

[374]

Kookareékee keekeekoó.
Reéchee cheéchee tsee-tsee-tseé.
Olga, Elga, Alga.
Peets, patch, pótch! Ekhamcheé!

Juno   Peerarára peerooroóroo!
Layo lólo Booaroh-óh
Beechehólo seh-seh-séh.
Béechee! Béechee! eébee beé!
Zeezazeéza, eezazó!
Eps, Aps, Eps!
Moóree-goóree reekokó!
Mio, Máo, Moom!
Ep!

Unkulunkulu   Rapt, grapt, apr! zhar!
Kaf! Bzuey! Kaf!
Zhrap, gap, bokv kook
Rrrtoopt! Toopt!

(The gods rise up into the air. Once more the mist thickens and burns blue upon the rockface.)

translated from the Russian by Paul Schmidt

ALEKSEI KRUCHENYKH
1886–1968

Heights

(Universal Language)

e u w
i a o
o a
o a e e i e w
o a
e u i e i
i e e
i i y i e i i y

dyr bul shchyl

dyr bul shchyl
uleshshchur
skum
vy so bu
r l èz.

Battle of India and Europe

driving
ruffian
fluff
so
baby
reason
rat
unshoed the armchair

translated from the Russian by Vladimir Markov

HUGO BALL

1886–1927

Karawane

jolifanto bambla ô falli bambla
grossiga m'pfa habla horem
égiga goramen
higo bloiko russula huju
hollaka hollala
anlogo bung
blago bung
blago bung
bosso fataka
ü üü ü
schampa wulla wussa ólobo
hej tatta gôrem
eschige zunbada
wulubu ssubudu uluw ssubudu
tumba ba- umf
kusagauma
ba - umf

[376]

MARIANNE MOORE
1887–1972

To Victor Hugo of My Crow Pluto

'Even when the bird is walking we know that it has wings.'
VICTOR HUGO

Of:
my crow
Pluto,

the true
Plato,

azzurro-
negro

green-blue
rainbow –

Victor Hugo,
it is true

we know
that the crow

'has wings,' how-
ever pigeon-toe-

inturned on grass. We do.
   (adagio)

Vivo-
rosso

'corvo,'
although

con dizio-
nario

io parlo
Italiano –

this pseudo
Esperanto

which, savio
uccello

you speak too –
my vow and motto

(botto e totto)
io giuro

è questo
credo:

lucro
è peso morto.

And so
dear crow –

gioièllo
mio –

I have to
let you go;

a bel bosco
generoso,

tuttuto
vagabondo,

serafino
uvaceo

Sunto,
oltremarino

verecondo
Plato, addio.

Impromptu equivalents for *esperanto madinusa* (made in USA) for those who might not resent them.

azzurro-negro: blue-black
vivorosso: lively
con dizionario: with dictionary
savio uccello: knowing bird
botto e totto: vow and motto
io giuro: I swear
è questo credo: is this credo
lucro è peso morto: profit is a
   dead weight

gioièllo mio: my jewel
a bel bosco: to lovely woods
tuttuto vagabondo: complete gyp-
   sy
serafino uvaceo: grape-black
   seraph
sunto: in short
verecondo: modest

HANS ARP
1887–1966

Opus Nil

1

I am the mighty He-she-it
the great unbending regiment
the ozone stalk called prima Qua
and the anonymous One per cent.

The P.P.Tit. and also Tro
trombone without a mouth or hole
the famous outfit Hercules
left ankle of the right-hand cook.

I am the lanky Wholelifelong
twelfth sense within the ovary
the entire Augustine top to toes
in radiant frock of cellulose.

2

From his black coffin he pulls out
coffin on coffin like a tape.
He blubbers with his forward end
and wraps himself in mourning crêpe.

Half conjuror and half conductor
without an alpenstock beats time
a grass-green dial on his hat
and tumbles from his coachman's seat.

So doing knocks the ghetto fish
from off its furnished easel frame.
His long square stocking tears in two
twice tears in two and thrice in three.

3

Sits in a circle with himself.
In its own flesh the circle sits.
A sack that holds an upright comb
serves him as sofa and as wife.

His very flesh his very sack.
The ofof and his left-hand skin
and tip and tap and tick and tock
out of his bride his body slips.

As pound found in his stone he swings
his very own bride in his sack.
In its own circle his own flesh
slips nude a sofa from his frock.

4

With his steam engine now he drives
hat after hat from out his hat
and in small rounds disposes them
as one would soldiers – just like that.

Then every hat he fills with blood
anoints himself with banner fat
says cockatoo to cockathree
and with his rifle goes to bed.

In bed he dreams of hat and blood
and of a reddish allthesame.
Around him there's a whirl a surge
moved by an evil melody.

translated from the German by Michael Hamburger

The Domestic Stones

(FRAGMENT)

The feet of morning the feet of noon and the feet of evening
walk ceaselessly round pickled buttocks
on the other hand the feet of midnight remain motionless
in their echo-woven baskets

consequently the lion is a diamond

on the sofas made of bread
are seated the dressed and the undressed
the undressed hold leaden swallows between their toes
the dressed hold leaden nests between their fingers
at all hours the undressed get dressed again
and the dressed get undressed
and exchange the leaden swallows for the leaden nests

consequently the tail is an umbrella

a mouth opens within another mouth
and within this mouth another mouth
and within this mouth another mouth
and so on without end
it is a sad perspective
which adds an I-don't-know-what
to another I-don't-know-what

consequently the grasshopper is a column

the pianos with heads and tails
place pianos with heads and tails
on their heads and their tails

consequently the tongue is a chair

translated from the French by David Gascoyne

EDITH SITWELL

1887–1964

Polka

'Tra la la la –
      See me dance the polka,'
Said Mr Wagg like a bear,
'With my top hat
And my whiskers that –
(Tra la la la) trap the Fair.

Where the waves seem chiming haycocks
I dance the polka; there
Stand Venus' children in their gay frocks –
Maroon and marine – and stare

To see me fire my pistol
Through the distance blue as my coat;
Like Wellington, Byron, the Marquis of Bristol,
Buzbied great trees float.

While the wheezing hurdy-gurdy
Of the marine wind blows me
To the tune of Annie Rooney, sturdy,
Over the sheafs of the sea;

And bright as a seedsman's packet
With zinnias, candytufts chill,
Is Mrs Marigold's jacket
As she gapes at the inn door still,

Where at dawn in the box of the sailor,
Blue as the decks of the sea,
Nelson awoke, crowed like the cocks,
Then back to dust sank he.

And Robinson Crusoe
Rues so
The bright and foxy beer –
But he finds fresh isles in a Negress' smiles –
The poxy doxy dear,

As they watch me dance the polka,'
Said Mr Wagg like a bear,
'In my top hat and my whiskers that –
Tra la la la, trap the Fair.

Tra la la la la –
Tra la la la la –
Tra la la la la la la la la
                    La
                    La
                    La!'

T. S. ELIOT
1888–1965

The Hippopotamus

*And when this epistle is read among you, cause that
it be read also in the church of the Laodiceans.*

The broad-backed hippopotamus
Rests on his belly in the mud;
Although he seems so firm to us
He is merely flesh and blood.

Flesh and blood is weak and frail,
Susceptible to nervous shock;
While the True Church can never fail
For it is based upon a rock.

The hippo's feeble steps may err
In compassing material ends,
While the True Church need never stir
To gather in its dividends.

[383]

The 'potamus can never reach
The mango on the mango-tree;
But fruits of pomegranate and peach
Refresh the Church from over sea.

At mating time the hippo's voice
Betrays inflexions hoarse and odd,
But every week we hear rejoice
The Church, at being one with God.

The hippopotamus's day
Is passed in sleep; at night he hunts;
God works in a mysterious way –
The Church can sleep and feed at once.

I saw the 'potamus take wing
Ascending from the damp savannas,
And quiring angels round him sing
The praise of God, in loud hosannas.

Blood of the Lamb shall wash him clean
And him shall heavenly arms enfold,
Among the saints he shall be seen
Performing on a harp of gold.

He shall be washed as white as snow,
By all the martyr'd virgins kist,
While the True Church remains below
Wrapt in the old miasmal mist.

Mr Mistoffelees

You ought to know Mr Mistoffelees!
The Original Conjuring Cat –
(There can be no doubt about that).
Please listen to me and don't scoff. All his
Inventions are off his own bat.
There's no such Cat in the metropolis;
He holds all the patent monopolies
For performing surprising illusions
And creating eccentric confusions.

At prestidigitation
      And at legerdemain
He'll defy examination
      And deceive you again.
The greatest magicians have something to learn
From Mr Mistoffelees' Conjuring Turn.
Presto!
      Away we go!
            And we all say: OH!
                  Well I never!
                  Was there ever
                  A Cat so clever
                        As Magical Mr Mistoffelees!

He is quiet and small, he is black
From his ears to the tip of his tail;
He can creep through the tiniest crack,
He can walk on the narrowest rail.
He can pick any card from a pack,
He is equally cunning with dice;
He is always deceiving you into believing
That he's only hunting for mice.
      He can play any trick with a cork
            Or a spoon and a bit of fish-paste;
      If you look for a knife or a fork
            And you think it is merely misplaced –
You have seen it one moment, and then it is *gawn*!
But you'll find it next week lying out on the lawn.
      And we all say: OH!
            Well I never!
            Was there ever
            A Cat so clever
                  As Magical Mr Mistoffelees!

His manner is vague and aloof,
You would think there was nobody shyer –
But his voice has been heard on the roof
When he was curled up by the fire.
And he's sometimes been heard by the fire
When he was about on the roof –
(At least we all *heard* that somebody purred)

Which is incontestable proof
  Of his singular magical powers:
    And I have known the family to call
  Him in from the garden for hours,
    While he was asleep in the hall.

And not long ago this phenomenal Cat
Produced *seven kittens* right out of a hat!
    And we all said: OH!
      Well I never!
      Did you ever
      Know a Cat so clever
        As Magical Mr Mistoffelees!

JOHN CROWE RANSOM
1888–1974

Captain Carpenter

Captain Carpenter rose up in his prime
Put on his pistols and went riding out
But had got wellnigh nowhere at that time
Till he fell in with ladies in a rout.

It was a pretty lady and all her train
That played with him so sweetly but before
An hour she'd taken a sword with all her main
And twined him of his nose for evermore.

Captain Carpenter mounted up one day
And rode straightaway into a stranger rogue
That looked unchristian but be that as may
The Captain did not wait upon prologue.

But drew upon him out of his great heart
The other swung against him with a club
And cracked his two legs at the shinny part
And let him roll and stick like any tub.

Captain Carpenter rode many a time
From male and female took he sundry harms
He met the wife of Satan crying 'I'm
The she-wolf bids you shall bear no more arms.'

Their strokes and counters whistled in the wind
I wish he had delivered half his blows
But where she should have made off like a hind
The bitch bit off his arms at the elbows.

And Captain Carpenter parted with his ears
To a black devil that used him in this wise
O Jesus ere his threescore and ten years
Another had plucked out his sweet blue eyes.

Captain Carpenter got up on his roan
And sallied from the gate in hell's despite
I heard him asking in the grimmest tone
If any enemy yet there was to fight?

'To any adversary it is fame
If he risk to be wounded by my tongue
Or burnt in two beneath my red heart's flame
Such are the perils he is cast among.

'But if he can he has a pretty choice
From an anatomy with little to lose
Whether he cut my tongue and take my voice
Or whether it be my round red heart he choose.'

It was the neatest knave that ever was seen
Stepping in perfume from his lady's bower
Who at this word put in his merry mien
And fell on Captain Carpenter like a tower.

I would not knock old fellows in the dust
But there lay Captain Carpenter on his back
His weapons were the old heart in his bust
And a blade shook between rotten teeth alack.

The rogue in scarlet and grey soon knew his mind
He wished to get his trophy and depart
With gentle apology and touch refined
He pierced him and produced the Captain's heart.

God's mercy rest on Captain Carpenter now
I thought him Sirs an honest gentleman
Citizen husband soldier and scholar enow
Let Jangling kites eat of him if they can.

But God's deep curses follow after those
That shore him of his goodly nose and ears
His legs and strong arms at the two elbows
And eyes that had not watered seventy years.

The curse of hell upon the sleek upstart
That got the Captain finally on his back
And took the red red vitals of his heart
And made the kites to whet their beaks clack clack.

ANONYMOUS

The Billboard Song

Come smoke a coca-cola,
Drink catsup cigarettes
See Lilian Brussels wrestle
With a box of castanets.

Pork and beans will meet tonight
And have a finished fight
Chauncey de Pew will lecture on
Sopolio tonight

Bay rum is good for horses
It is the best in town
Vastoria cures the measles
If you pay five dollars down

Teeth extracted without pain
At the cost of half a dime
Overcoats are selling now
A little out of time
Do me a favour – drop dead.

ANONYMOUS

Do you carrot all for me?
My heart beets for you.
With your turnip nose
And your radish face
You are a peach.
If we cantaloupe
Lettuce marry.
Weed make a swell pear.

ANONYMOUS

Why are Fire Engines red?

Two and two is four
Three times four is twelve
Twelve inches is a ruler
Queen Mary was a ruler
Queen Mary ruled the sea
There are fish in the sea
The fish have fins
The Finns fought the Russians
The Russians are Red
Fire engines are always rushin'
That's why fire engines are red.

ANONYMOUS

Down in the meadow
Where the corn cobs grow,
Flea jumped on the elephant's toe
Elephant cried, with tears in his eyes,
Why don't you pick on someone your size?

ROBERT GRAVES
1895–1985

Warning to Children

Children, if you dare to think
Of the greatness, rareness, muchness,
Fewness of this precious only
Endless world in which you say
You live, you think of things like this:
Blocks of slate enclosing dappled
Red and green, enclosing tawny
Yellow nets, enclosing white
And black acres of dominoes,
Where a neat brown paper parcel
Tempts you to untie the string.
In the parcel a small island,
On the island a large tree,
On the tree a husky fruit.
Strip the husk and pare the rind off:
In the kernel you will see
Blocks of slate enclosed by dappled
Red and green, enclosed by tawny
Yellow nets, enclosed by white
And black acres of dominoes,
Where the same brown paper parcel –
Children, leave the string alone!
For who dares undo the parcel
Finds himself at once inside it,
On the island, in the fruit,
Blocks of slate about his head,
Finds himself enclosed by dappled
Green and red, enclosed by yellow
Tawny nets, enclosed by black
And white acres of dominoes,
With the same brown paper parcel
Still unopened on his knee.
And, if he then should dare to think

[390]

Of the fewness, muchness, rareness,
Greatness of this endless only
Precious world in which he says
He lives – he then unties the string.

Welsh Incident

'But that was nothing to what things came out
From the sea-caves of Criccieth yonder.'
'What were they? Mermaids? dragons? ghosts?'
'Nothing at all of any things like that.'
'What were they, then?'
                     'All sorts of queer things,
Things never seen or heard or written about,
Very strange, un-Welsh, utterly peculiar
Things. Oh, solid enough they seemed to touch,
Had anyone dared it. Marvellous creation,
All various shapes and sizes and no sizes,
All new, each perfectly unlike his neighbour,
Though all came moving slowly out together.'
'Describe just one of them.'
                   'I am unable.'
'What were their colours?'
                    'Mostly nameless colours,
Colours you'd like to see; but one was puce
Or perhaps more like crimson, but not purplish.
Some had no colour.'
                'Tell me, had they legs?'
'Not a leg nor foot among them that I saw.'
'But did these things come out in any order?
What o'clock was it? What was the day of the week?
Who else was present? How was the weather?'
'I was coming to that. It was half-past three
On Easter Tuesday last. The sun was shining.
The Harlech Silver Band played *Marchog Jesu*
On thirty-seven shimmering instruments,
Collecting for Carnarvon's (Fever) Hospital Fund.
The populations of Pwllheli, Criccieth,
Portmadoc, Borth, Tremadoc, Penrhyndeudraeth,
Were all assembled. Criccieth's mayor addressed them
First in good Welsh and then in fluent English,

[391]

Twisting his fingers in his chain of office,
Welcoming the things. They came out on the sand,
Not keeping time to the band, moving seaward
Silently at a snail's pace. But at last
The most odd, indescribable thing of all,
Which hardly one man there could see for wonder
Did something recognisably a something.'
'Well, what?'
           'It made a noise.'
                      'A frightening noise?'
'No, no.'
       'A musical noise? A noise of scuffling?'
'No, but a very loud, respectable noise –
Like groaning to oneself on Sunday morning
In Chapel, close before the second psalm.'
'What did the mayor do?'
                  'I was coming to that.'

PHILIPPE SOUPAULT
1897–

Chassé-Croisé

Un certain monsieur
Loup Pou ou Hibou
une jolie demoiselle
Estelle Cruelle et Hirondelle
un grand petit garçon
Guy Goutran ou Gaston
un roquet nauséabond
Dick Médor ou Azor
un affreux gros maton
Pompon Minet ou Minon
un stupide canari
Serin Coco ou Kiki
Tous ensemble
devant la fenêtre
quand s'épanouit
le crépuscule
Ne vous croyez pas
plus malins
que ne vous êtes.

Toute la Vie

De quoi croyez-vous qu'il vivait
(de victuailles et de boisson)
cet homme mûr cet homme
qui n'avait qu'une tête
qu'une tête et qu'un tronc
sur des jambes de coton

LOUIS ARAGON
1897–1982

Translations from the French

The Phoenix Reborn from Its Ashes

On love was written
Emergency exit forbidden in case of fire
On the sky was written
You are mistaken it is not here
And on the night was written
Nothing at all was written on the night.

Mimosas

The government had just been overthrown
In a hawthorn bush
A general strike was discovered in the far distance
Under the combined influences of the moon and cephalogy
The assassins were fleeing in a perspective of air currents
The victim was hanging on the grill like a beefsteak
A heat to applaud
Must also see if the barracks had heard anything funny
The alcohol was flowing in floods over the skylights on the roofs
The Metro came above ground to breathe
When suddenly there appeared
At the corner of the street
A little donkey dragging a carriage
Decorated for battle with flowers
First Prize for the entire town
And the neighbouring towns.

[393]

E. L. T. MESENS
1898–1957

Le moyen d'en finir

Dans l'oeil du roi il y avait un timbre-poste
Et dans l'oeil du roi figurant sur le timbre-poste
Il y avait encore un roi qui avait un oeil
Dans lequel il y avait un timbre-poste
Avec ou sans roi
Avec ou sans oeil . . .

Mort au roi
À bas le timbre-poste
Vive l'oeil.

Faits divers intraduisibles Statistique et Critique

Un homme
Deux fois plus grand que nature
Trois heures avant sa mort voit
Quatre personnages au lieu de
Cinq apparaître vers les
Six heures du matin et il n'est qu'à
Sept heures que
Huit policiers arrivent n'apportant rien de
Neuf

TOTAL: 45

Statistique: Hommes: Un.
                    Heures: Seize.
                    Personnages: Neuf.
                    Policiers: Huit.

$1 + 16 + 9 + 8 = 34.$

Vérification: Quarante-cinq moins trente-quatre égale NEUF.

Critique: Facile à faire.
              Difficile à défaire.
              Impossible à refaire.

NB. Les erreurs sont à votre mesure.

The way to finish it off

In the eye of the king there was a postage stamp
And in the eye of the king figured on the postage stamp
There was another king who had an eye
In which there was a postage stamp
With or without a king
With or without an eye . . .

Death to the king
Down with the postage stamp
Long live the eye.

Untranslatable factual items

One man
Two times larger than life
Three hours before his death saw
Four characters instead of
Five appear towards
Six in the morning and it wasn't till
Seven that
Eight policemen arrived bearing
Nigh no news.

TOTAL: 45

Statistical breakdown: Men: One.
     Hours: Sixteen.
     Characters: Nine.
     Policemen: Eight.

$1 + 16 + 9 + 8 = 34.$

Verification: Forty-five minus thirty-four equals NINE.

Criticism: Easy to do.
     Difficult to undo.
     Impossible to redo.

NB. Mistakes are to your measurements.

FEDERICO GARCIA LORCA

1898–1936

Translations from the Spanish

Shell

They have brought me a shell.

Inside it sings
a map of sea.
My heart
fills with water
with fishlets
of shadow and silver.

They have brought me a shell.

Corridor

In the high corridors
two gentlemen stroll
    (New
    sky.
    Blue
    sky!)
... two gentlemen stroll
who were formerly friars
    (Middle
    sky.
    Purple
    sky!)
... two gentlemen stroll
who were formerly hunters
    (Old
    sky.
    Gold
    sky!)
... two gentlemen stroll
who were formerly ...
Night.

Girl by the River

(with an accompaniment of bells)

They say you have the face
(balalin)
of the full moon.
(balalan).

How many bells do you hear?
(balalin)
They never leave me.
(balalan).
But your eyes . . . Ah!
(balalin)
. . . sorry, your eye-rings . . .
(balalan)
and that golden laugh
(balalin)
and that . . . I can't, that . . .
(balalan).

The bells strike
their hard crinoline.

Oh! your secret charm! . . . , Your . . .
(balalin
lin
lin
lin . . .)

Pardon.

Tío-Vivo, or the Merry-go-round

The days of fiesta
pass by in a whirl.
The merry-go-round brings them
and bears them away.

Blue Corpus Christi
White Christmas Eve.

[397]

The days all abandon
their skins, like snakes,
with the sole exception
of fiesta days.

They stay the same
as for our mothers,
their noons long trains
of sequins and silks.

Blue Corpus Christi
White Christmas Eve.

The merry-go-round spins
hung from a star.
A tulip of the five
parts of the earth.

On little horses
disguised as panthers
the children eat the moon up
as if it were a cherry.

O rage, rage, Marco Polo!
On a fantastic wheel
the children see horizons
unknown to all the earth.

Blue Corpus Christi
White Christmas Eve.

BENJAMIN PÉRET
1899–1959

Les Yeux du Vent

La banlieue est bleue
quand passe le juge
Si le juge n'était pas juge
on verrait un phénomène
Quatre veaux
debout sur un paratonnerre
et criant
Liberté Liberté chérie
Et madame répondrait
Chéri
et monsieur
Bibi

Devenu Vieux
Le Diable se fait Ermite

Louis-Philippe est grand pour son âge
Donne-lui quelques sous
son chapeau sera trop petit
Donne-lui deux cravates
il mentira tous les jours
Donne-lui une autre pipe
sa mère pleurera
Donne-lui une paire de gants
il perdra ses chaussures
Donne-lui du café
il aura des ampoules
Donne-lui un corset
il portera un collier
Donne-lui des bretelles
il soignera des souris
Donne-lui un battoir

il montera en avion
Donne-lui un potage
il en fera une statue
Donne-lui des lacets
il mangera des groseilles
C'est Monsieur Louis-Philippe
qui vit de pilules et de buvards
mange sa mère
et perd l'heure en marchant

ROBERT DESNOS
1900–45

Rrose Sélavy, etc.

Rose aisselle a vit.
Rr'ose, essaie là, vit.
Rôts et sel à vie.
Rose S, L, have I.
Rosée, c'est la vie.
Rrose scella vît.
Rrose sella vît.
Rrose sait la vie.
Rose, est-ce, hélas, vie?
Rrose aise héla vît.
Rrose est-ce aile, est-ce elle?
    Est celle

AVIS

*

S. E.
E. C.

★

/C. /Q. /F. /D.
harles/ uint/ aux/ éfunt

(10 décembre 1923)

[400]

P'Oasis

Nous sommes les pensées arborescentes qui fleurissent sur les chemins des jardins cérébraux.

– Sœur Anne, ma Sainte Anne, ne vois-tu rien venir ... vers Sainte-Anne?

– Je vois les pensées odorer les mots.

– Nous sommes les mots arborescents qui fleurissent sur les chemins des jardins cérébraux.

De nous naissent les pensées.

– Nous sommes les pensées arborescentes qui fleurissent sur les chemins des jardins cérébraux.

Les mots sont nos esclaves.

– Nous sommes

– Nous sommes

– Nous sommes les lettres arborescentes qui fleurissent sur les chemins des jardins cérébraux.

Nous n'avons pas d'esclaves.

– Sœur Anne, ma sœur Anne, que vois-tu venir vers Sainte-Anne?

– Je vois les Pan C

– Je vois les crânes K C

– Je vois les mains D C D

– Je les M

– Je vois les pensées B C et les femmes M E et les poumons qui en ont A C de l'R L O

poumons noyés des ponts N M I.

Mais la minute précédente est déjà trop A G.

– Nous sommes les arborescences qui fleurissent sur les déserts des jardins cérébraux.

★

Art rythmé tic

Lit temps nie.

Prenez vos 16
litanies
n'italie
Inde œuf, un deux, la muscadence
Troie, qu'âtre neuf dans les seins (les siens) sise
les seins, cet étui pour le 9

Troie m'Ilion
　　　　　zéro
　　　　　rosée rose si 12
　　　　　réseau
　　　navigateurs traversez les 2–3
　　　　　　　à toute 8-S
11 ondes jusqu'à vos bouches portent l'odeur marine
　　　　　des 13 fraises
Par nos amours décuplées nous devenons vains
　　　　　mais 10-20-2-20

quand je vins vous mourûtes

dans vos cerveaux

trop 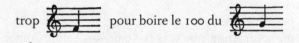 pour boire le 100 du

　　　　En somme, F M R F I J
sommes-nous des cow-boys de l'Arizona dans un laboratoire
ou des cobayes prenant l'horizon pour un labyrinthe?

Les Hiboux

Ce sont les mères des hiboux
Qui désiraient chercher les poux
De leurs enfants, leurs petits choux,
En les tenant sur les genoux.

Leurs yeux d'or valent des bijoux
Leur bec est dur comme cailloux,
Ils sont doux comme des joujoux,
Mais aux hiboux point de genoux!

Votre histoire se passait où?
Chez les Zoulous? Les Andalous?
Ou dans la cabane bambou?
A Moscou? Ou à Tombouctou?
En Anjou ou dans le Poitou?
Au Pérou ou chez les Mandchous?

Hou! Hou!
Pas du tout, c'était chez les fous.

Le Brochet

Le brochet
Fait des projets.
J'irai voir, dit-il,
Le Gange et le Nil,
Le Tage et le Tibre
Et le Yang-Tse-Kiang.
J'irai, je suis libre
D'user mon temps.

Et la lune?
Iras-tu voir la lune?
    Brochet voyageur,
Brochet mauvais coeur,
    Brochet de fortune.

CHARLIE JORDAN

Keep It Clean

I went to the river: couldn't get across,
I jumped on your papa 'cause I thought he was a horse;
        Now I
        rode him on over,
        give him a Coca-Coly,
        lemon sody,
        saucer of ice cream;
        takes soap and water
        for to keep it clean.

Up she jumped, down she fell,
Her mouth flew open like a mushry shell;
        Now
        ride her over,
        give her a Coca-Coly,
        lemon sody,
        saucer of ice cream;
        takes soap and water
        for to keep it clean.

Your sister was a teddy, your daddy was a bear,
Put the muzzle on your mama 'cause she had bad hair;
        Now
        ride her on over,
        give her a Coca-Coly,
        lemon sody,
        saucer of ice cream;
        takes soap and water
        for to keep it clean.

If you want to hear that elephant laugh,
Take him down to the river and wash his yes yes yes;
            Now
            ride him over,
            give him a Coca-Coly,
            lemon sody,
            saucer of ice cream;
            takes soap and water
            for to keep it clean.

If you want to go to heaven when you d / i / e,
You got to put on your collar and your t / i / e;
            Now
            ride him over,
            give him a Coca-Coly,
            lemon sody,
            saucer of ice cream;
            takes soap and water
            for to keep it clean.

If you want to get the rabbits out the l / o / g,
You got to put on the stump like a d / o / g;
            Now
            ride him over,
            give him a Coca-Coly,
            lemon sody,
            saucer of ice cream;
            takes soap and water
            for to keep it clean.

Run here doctor, run here fast,
See what's the matter with his yes yes yes;
            Now
            ride him over,
            give him a Coca-Coly,
            lemon sody,
            saucer of ice cream;
            takes soap and water
            for to keep it clean.

BLIND BLAKE

Diddie Wa Diddie

There's a great big mystery
And it surely is worrying me
      This diddie wa diddie
      This diddie wa diddie
      I wish somebody would tell me what diddie wa diddie means

The little girl about four feet four:
'Come on papa and give me some more
      Of your diddie wa diddie
      Your diddie wa diddie'
      I wish somebody would tell me what diddie wa diddie means

I went out and walked around
Somebody yelled, said: 'Look who's in town –
      Mister diddie wa diddie
      Mister diddie wa diddie'
      I wish somebody would tell me what diddie wa diddie means

Went to church, put my hand on the seat
Lady sat on it, said: 'Daddy you sure is sweet,
      Mister diddie wa diddie
      Mister diddie wa diddie'
      I wish somebody would tell me what diddie wa diddie means

I said: 'Sister I'll soon be gone
Just gimme that thing you setting on
      My diddie wa diddie
      My diddie wa diddie'
      I wish somebody would tell me what diddie wa diddie means

Then I got put out of church
'Cause I talk about diddie wa diddie too much
      Mister diddie wa diddie
      Mister diddie wa diddie
      I wish somebody would tell me what diddie wa diddie means

GEORGE SEFERIS

1900–71

Limericks

A young girl in remote Samarkand
had buried one hand in the sand
stretched the other out far
and took hold of a star,
that young girl in remote Samarkand.

There was an old woman of Wales
who carried a douche and two pails
full of eau de cologne,
and by rock, stock and stone
she went running, poor lady of Wales.

There was a young lady of Graz
who fished with a trident for sprats,
when a pink spotted sow
jumped in over the bow
and she drowned the young lady of Graz.

translated from the Greek by Peter Levi

There was a black girl from Pretoria
Who spun round like a top in euphoria.
When at last she grew peckish
She ate fifty crayfish,
That gluttonous girl from Pretoria.

There once was a girl from the Congo
Who in a bush went as far as one can go.
As she looked round to see
Where an exit could be,
Her fingers toyed with a mango.

There was an old dame from Jerusalem
Who ate a huge bowl of sweet rose jam.
When it started to rain
She rushed homewards again
And suddenly burst in Jerusalem.

translated by Hugh Haughton

JACQUES PRÉVERT
1900–77

Pour faire le Portrait d'un oiseau

À Elsa Henriquez

Peindre d'abord une cage
avec une porte ouverte
peindre ensuite
quelque chose de joli
quelque chose de simple
quelque chose de beau
quelque chose d'utile
pour l'oiseau
placer ensuite la toile contre un arbre
dans un jardin
dans un bois
ou dans une forêt
se cacher derrière l'arbre
sans rien dire
sans bouger . . .
Parfois l'oiseau arrive vite
mais il peut aussi bien mettre de longues années
avant de se décider
Ne pas se décourager
attendre
attendre s'il le faut pendant des années
la vitesse ou la lenteur de l'arrivée de l'oiseau
n'ayant aucun rapport
avec la réussite du tableau
Quand l'oiseau arrive

s'il arrive
observer le plus profond silence
attendre que l'oiseau entre dans la cage
et quand il est entré
fermer doucement la porte avec le pinceau
puis
effacer un à un tous les barreaux
en ayant soin de ne toucher aucune des plumes de l'oiseau
Faire ensuite le portrait de l'arbre
en choisissant la plus belle de ses branches
pour l'oiseau
peindre aussi le vert feuillage et la fraîcheur du vent
la poussière du soleil
et le bruit des bêtes de l'herbe dans la chaleur de l'été
et puis attendre que l'oiseau se décide à chanter
Si l'oiseau ne chante pas
c'est mauvais signe
signe que le tableau est mauvais
mais s'il chante c'est bon signe
signe que vous pouvez signer
Alors vous arrachez tout doucement
une des plumes de l'oiseau
et vous écrivez votre nom dans un coin du tableau.

Translation

To paint a portrait of a bird

First paint a cage
with an open door
then paint
something pretty
something simple
something beautiful
something useful
for the bird
then place the canvas against a tree
in a garden
in a wood
or in a forest
hide behind the tree

[409]

without speaking
without moving . . .
Sometimes the bird arrives quickly
but he might also wait long years
before deciding
Do not be discouraged
wait
wait if necessary for years
the speed or slowness of the bird's arrival
has absolutely no connection
with the success or failure of the picture
When the bird arrives
if he arrives
observe the most solemn silence
wait until the bird enters the cage
and when he enters
gently close the door with the brush
then erase the bars one by one
making sure not to touch the feathers of the bird
Then paint a portrait of the tree
choosing the prettiest of its branches
for the bird
and then paint the green foliage and the freshness of the breeze
the dust of the sun
and the noise of the creatures in the grass in the summer heat
and then wait until the bird decides to sing
If the bird does not sing
it is a bad sign
a sign the picture is bad
but if he sings it's a good sign
a sign you can sign
Now very gently pluck
one of the bird's feathers
and write your name in a corner of the picture.

ALEKSANDER WAT

1900–

From Notes Written in Obory

X was asked
          if he believed in the objective existence of Parzota.
– To believe in the objective existence of Parzota –
                    that smacks of mysticism,
I am an old horse, you know, and a staunch
rationalist
answered X.
The sequel was more interesting.

X persisted in his refusal to believe in the objective existence of Parzota.
Who, the said Parzota, placed him in a dungeon, put him to torture.
Yet everything would have been in perfect order
if not for one sad circumstance:
the stupid man of principle was so obstinate that he died in the dungeon.
Poor Parzota! Condemned to eternal doubt.
Now he will never find out
if he existed objectively.

                              translated from the Polish by Czeslaw Milosz

LAURA RIDING

1901–

The Sad Boy

Ay, his mother was a mad one
And his father was a bad one:
The two begot this sad one.

Alas for the single boot
The Sad Boy pulled out of the rank green pond,
Fishing for happiness
On the gloomy advice
Of a professional lover of small boys.

[411]

Pity the lucky Sad Boy
With but a single happy boot
And an extra foot
With no boot for it.

This was how the terrible hopping began
That wore the Sad Boy down
To a single foot
And started the great fright in the province
Where the Sad Boy became half of himself.

Wherever he went thumping and hopping,
Pounding a whole earth into a half-heaven,
Things split all around
Into a left side for the left magic,
Into no side for the missing right boot.

Mercy be to the Sad Boy,
Mercy be to the melancholy folk
On the Sad Boy's right.

It was not for clumsiness
He lost the left boot
And the knowledge of his left side,
But because one awful Sunday
This dear boy dislimbed
Went back to the old pond
To fish up the other boot
And was quickly (being too light for his line)
Fished in.

Gracious how he kicks now –
And the almost-ripples show
Where the Sad Boy went in
And his mad mother
And his bad father after him.

OGDEN NASH

1902–71

Oh To Be Odd!

Hypochondriacs
Spend the winter at the bottom of Florida and the summer on top of the
    Adirondriacs.
You go to Paris and live on champagne wine and cognac
If you're a dipsomognac.
If you're a manic-depressive
You don't go anywhere where you won't be cheered up, and people say
    'There, there!' if your bills are excessive.
But you stick around and work day and night and night and day with
    your nose to the sawmill.
If you're nawmill.

The Wombat

> The wombat lives across the seas,
> Among the far Antipodes.
> He may exist on nuts and berries,
> Or then again, on missionaries;
> His distant habitat precludes
> Conclusive knowledge of his moods.
> But I would not engage the wombat
> In any form of mortal combat.

The Grackle

> The grackle's voice is less than mellow,
> His heart is black, his eye is yellow,
> He bullies more attractive birds
> With hoodlum deeds and vulgar words,
> And should a human interfere,
> Attacks that human in the rear.
> I cannot help but deem the grackle
> An ornithological debacle.

[413]

The Shrimp

A shrimp who sought his lady shrimp
Could catch no glimpse,
Not even a glimp.
At times, translucence
Is rather a nuisance.

The City

Here men walk alone
For most of their lives,
What with hydrants for dogs,
And windows for wives.

STEVIE SMITH
1902–71

My Hat

Mother said if I wore this hat
I should be certain to get off with the right sort of chap
Well look where I am now, on a desert island
With so far as I can see no one at all on hand

I know what has happened though I suppose Mother wouldn't see
This hat being so strong has completely run away with me
I had the feeling it was beginning to happen the moment I put it on
What a moment that was as I rose up, I rose up like a flying swan
As strong as a swan too, why see how far my hat has flown me away
It took us a night to come and then a night and a day
And all the time the swan wing in my hat waved beautifully
Ah, I thought, How this hat becomes me.
First the sea was dark but then it was pale blue
And still the wing beat and we flew and we flew
A night and a day and a night, and by the old right way
Between the sun and the moon we flew until morning day.
It is always early morning here on this peculiar island
The green grass grows into the sea on the dipping land
Am I glad I am here? Yes, well, I am,
It's nice to be rid of Father, Mother and the young man
There's just one thing causes me a twinge of pain,
If I take my hat off, shall I find myself home again?
So in this early morning land I always wear my hat
Go home, you see, well I wouldn't run a risk like that.

My Cats

I like to toss him up and down
A heavy cat weighs half a Crown
With a hey do diddle my cat Brown.

I like to pinch him on the sly
When nobody is passing by
With a hey do diddle my cat Fry.

I like to ruffle up his pride
And watch him skip and turn aside
With a hey do diddle my cat Hyde.

Hey Brown and Fry and Hyde my cats
That sit on tombstone for your mats.

Who Killed Lawless Lean?

The parrot
Is eating a carrot
In his cage in the garret

Why is the parrot's
Cage in the garret?
He is not a sage
Parrot: his words enrage.

Downstairs
In his bed
Lies the head
Of the family
He is dead.

And the brothers gather
Mutter utter would rather
Forget
The words the parrot
Said.

When high in his cage swinging
From the lofty ceiling
Sat the pet screaming:
'Who killed Lawless Lean?'
It was not at all fitting.

So they put the parrot
In his cage in the garret
And gave him a carrot
To keep him quiet.
He should be glad they did not wring his neck.

Our Bog is Dood

Our Bog is dood, our Bog is dood,
They lisped in accents mild,
But when I asked them to explain
They grew a little wild.
How do you know your Bog is dood
My darling little child?

We know because we wish it so
That is enough, they cried,
And straight within each infant eye
Stood up the flame of pride,
And if you do not think it so
You shall be crucified.

Then tell me, darling little ones,
What's dood, suppose Bog is?
Just what we think, the answer came,
Just what we think it is.
They bowed their head. Our Bog is ours
And we are wholly his.

But when they raised them up again
They had forgotten me
Each one upon each other glared
In pride and misery
For what was dood, and what their Bog
They never could agree.

Oh sweet it was to leave them then,
And sweeter not to see,
And sweetest of all to walk alone
Beside the encroaching sea,
The sea that soon should drown them all,
That never yet drowned me.

Charlie's Sad Date

My necktie, my gloves.
My gloves, my necktie.

The butterfly knows nothing about the death of the tailors,
about wardrobes conquering the sea.
Sirs, my age is 900,000 years.
Oh!

I was a boy when fish didn't swim,
when geese didn't say mass
or the snail attack the cat.
Miss, let's play at cat and mouse.

The saddest thing, sir, is a watch:
11, 12, 1, 2.

At three on the dot a passerby will drop dead.
You, moon, moon of late taxis,
smoky moon of firemen,
do not be frightened.

The city is burning in the sky,
clothing like mine is hated in the country.
My age is suddenly 25.

Because it snows, it snows
and my body turns into a wooden shack.
Wind, I invite you to rest.
It is too late to dine on stars.

But we can dance, lost tree,
a waltz for wolves,
for the sleep of the hen without fox's claws.

I have mislaid my cane.
It is very sad to think of it alone in the world.
My cane!

My hat, my cuffs,
my gloves, my shoes.

The bone that hurts most, my love, is the watch:
11, 12, 1, 2.

3 on the dot.
In the pharmacy a nude cadaver evaporates.
translated from the Spanish by Mark Strand

DANIIL KHARMS
1905–41

See the house took flight

I

See the house took flight
See the dog took flight.
See the dream took flight.
See the mother took flight.
See the garden took flight.
The steed took flight.
The bath took flight.
The globe took flight.
See the stone take flight.
See the foam take flight.
See the moment take flight.
See the circle take flight.
The house flies.
The mother flies.
The garden flies.
The clock to fly.
The hand to fly.
The eagles to fly.
The spear to fly.
And the steed to fly.

[419]

And the house to fly.
And the point to fly.
Forehead flies.
Chest flies.
Stomach flies.
Oh hold me – the ear is flying!
Oh look – the nose is flying!
Oh monks, the mouth is flying!

II

The house chimes.
The water chimes.
The stone around chimes.
The book around chimes.
Mother and son and garden chimes.
A chimes.
B chimes.
THAT flies and THAT chimes.
Forehead chimes and flies.
Chest chimes and flies.
Hey monks, the mouth is chiming!
Hey monks, the forehead's flying!
What to fly but not to ring?
Sound is flying and to chime.
THERE is flying and ringing.
Hey monks! We to be flying!
We to fly and there to be flying.
Hey monks! We to ring!
We to ring and THERE to chime.

translated from The Russian *by Alice Stone Nakhamovsky*

(a railroad happening)

Once when Grandma moved her hand
the train stopped immediately
for the children – and it said,
'drink your porridge and valise'.
In the morning they came back.
Children sat down on the fence
and they said, 'You, raven-horse,
You may work but I will not,
Mary's not like that at all
As you like it and perhaps
it's all right; we'll lick the sand
something that the sky expressed
here's the station, let's get off
hello Georgia! hello Georgia!
how can we get out of here?
Simply go on past the big one –
o you children – not the fence
there a polyandra grew
and alighting on the cars
she kept scrubbing the wrong man
who surrounded out of fright
one catfish with seven oxen
he took money from his pockets
Money pale gray in the face.

well that's that, and so they simmered
all the soups – the old aunt said
all the sparrows – said the dead man
and the body sank down lower
with a chirping that was pleasant
but a little boring too
moving backward – as it seemed.

children went to hear a mass
putting it upon a shoulder
mousey ran into an apron
tearing shoulders all apart

[421]

Georgian woman on the threshold
kept repeating. Georgian man
by the hill was bending over
groped for something in the mud.

translated from The Russian by Vladimir Markov and Merrill Sparks

ANONYMOUS

Cocaine Lil

Did you ever hear about Cocaine Lil?
She lived in Cocaine town on Cocaine hill,
She had a cocaine dog and a cocaine cat,
They fought all night with the cocaine rat.

She had cocaine hair on her cocaine head.
She wore a snowbird hat and sleigh-riding clothes.
She had a cocaine dress that was poppy red.
On her coat she wore a crimson, cocaine rose.

Big gold chariots on the Milky Way,
Snakes and elephants silver and gray,
O the cocaine blues they make me sad,
O the cocaine blues make me feel bad.

Lil went to a 'snow' party one cold night,
And the way she 'sniffed' was sure a fright.
There was Hophead Mag with Dopey Slim,
Kankakee Liz with Yen Shee Jim.

There was Hasheesh Nell and the Poppy Face Kid,
Climbed up snow ladders and down they slid;
There was Stepladder Kit, stood six feet,
And The Sleighriding Sisters that are hard to beat.

Along in the morning about half-past three
They were all lit up like a Christmas tree;
Lil got home and started to go to bed,
Took another 'sniff' and it knocked her dead.

[422]

They laid her out in her cocaine clothes.
She wore a snowbird hat and a crimson rose;
On her headstone you'll find this refrain:
'She died as she lived sniffing cocaine.'

LUIS D'ANTIN VAN ROOTEN
1906–73

from *Mots d'Heures; Gousses, Rames*

Un petit d'un petit[1]
S'étonne aux Halles[2]
Un petit d'un petit
Ah! degrés te fallent[3]
Indolent qui ne sort cesse[4]
Indolent qui ne se mène[5]
Qu'importe un petit d'un petit
Tout Gai de Reguennes.[6]

[1] The inevitable result of a child marriage.

[2] The subject of this epigrammatic poem is obviously from the provinces, since a native Parisian would take this famous old market for granted.

[3] Since this personage bears no titles, we are led to believe that the poet writes of one of those unfortunate idiot-children that in olden days existed as a living skeleton in their family's closet. I am inclined to believe, however, that this is a fine piece of misdirection and that the poet is actually writing of some famous political prisoner, or the illegitimate offspring of some noble house. The Man in the Iron Mask, perhaps?

[4,5] Another misdirection. Obviously it was not laziness that prevented this person's going out and taking himself places.

[6] He was obviously prevented from fulfilling his destiny, since he is compared to Gai de Reguennes. This was a young squire (to one of his uncles, a Gaillard of Normandy) who died at the tender age of twelve of a surfeit of Saracen arrows before the walls of Acre in 1191.

'Pousse y gâte, pousse y gâte,
Et Arabe, yeux bine?'[1]
'A ben, tout l'on donne
Toluca de couenne.'[2]
'Pousse y gâte, pousse y gâte,
Oh, a dit Dieu d'hère?'[3]
'Y fraternelle Lydie, Moïse,
Honneur de chair.'[4]

[1] Although the dialogue form of versifying is very ancient and quite common, this is one of the few fragments so written. In the first speech, an Arab is chided for planting a crop, then allowing it to spoil, while merely eyeing his hoe. The Arabs are a traditionally nomadic people, not given to agriculture.

[2] In his reply, our hero admits he was building castles in Spain, dreaming of a pigskin from Toluca (famous market town, capital of the State of Mexico, Mexico). These pigskins make excellent water bags – an item of great interest to a desert-dweller.

[3] 'What sayeth the poor man's God?' *Hère*, in medieval times, a serf, bound to the lord of a manor.

[4] 'There will be brotherhood in Lydia, Moses, blood is thicker than water.' Lydia, Middle East region bordering on the Aegean Sea.

> Papa, blague chipe
> À vieux inouï houle[1]
> Y est-ce art? Y est-ce art? Trépas que se foulent[2]
> Aune format masure, en nouant format thème[3]
> En nouant fleur-de-lis de bois de solive en délienne.[4]

[1] Stealing, even in fun, my father, can disturb a mature man to unheard-of depths. Note how *houle*, the swell and stir of the sea, is used in a highly poetic simile.

[2] 'Where is art?' We are dealing with total destruction.

[3] Huts are built of alders or wattles, tightly forming the theme.

[4] Knotted fleur-de-lis carved in old beams after the manner of Delos. As Shakespeare said, 'So may the outward shows of earth be least themselves, the world is still deceived with ornament.' Here the poet cries anathema to cheap builders and cheating contractors.

WILLIAM EMPSON
1906–84

> Mother, saying Anne good night,
> Feared the dark would cause her fright.
> 'Four angels guard you,' low she said,
> 'One at the foot and one at the head –'
>
> 'Mother – quick – the pillow!! – There!!!
> Missed that angel, skimmed his hair.
> Never mind, we'll get the next.
> Ooh! but angels make me vexed!!'
>
> Mother, shocked, gasped feebly 'Anne!!!'
> (A pillow disabled the water-can.)
> Said Anne, 'I won't have things in white
> Chant prayers about my bed all night.'

Empson's first recorded poem, written by 29 June 1920, aetat 13; text taken from the autograph book of a school contemporary, J. A. Simson.

Two Centos

[1926; annotations by Empson]

i

At Algezir,[1] and will in overplus,[2]
Their herdsmen,[3] well content to think thee page,[4] divided.[3]
Tell Isabel the queen, I looked not[5] thus
Leander, Mr Ekenhead, and I did.[6]

ii

of them that are overcome with. Woe[1]
stay me with flagons,[2] civilly delight.[3]
So lovers contracts, images of those,[4]
so be I equalled with,[5] as dark as night.[6]

Do thy worst, blind Cupid,[7] dark amid the blaze of.[8] Woe
to the crown of pride,[1] and Phineus prophets old,[5]
did cry To-whoo To-whoo, and the sun did shine so[9]
(the lords and owners of,[10] poor Toms-a)[11] cold.

1. Chaucer Prologue l. 57.
2. Shakespeare Sonnet no. cxxxv.
3. Genesis, chapter 13.
4. Donne Elegy xvi.
5. Marlowe Ed II.
6. Don Juan, canto 2, stanza 105.

1. Isaiah. xxviii.i.
2. Song of Solomon. ii.5.
3. Pope. Arbuthnot. 313.
4. Donne. Songs and Sonnets. Woman's constancy.
5. Paradise Lost. iii.34.
6. Shakespeare Sonnet cxlvii.
7. Lear. Act IV scene vi.
8. Sams. Ag. 80.
9. Wordsworth. Idiot Boy.
10. Shakespeare Sonnet xciv.
11. Lear. Act IV scene i.

Poem about a Ball in the Nineteenth Century

Feather, feather, if it was a feather, feathers for fair, or to be fair, aroused. Round to be airy, feather, if it was airy, very, aviary, fairy, peacock, and to be well surrounded. Well-aired, amoving, to peacock, cared-for, share dancing inner to be among aware. Peacock around, peacock to care for dancing, an air, fairing, will he become, to stare. Peacock around, rounded, to turn the wearer, turning in air, peacock and I declare, to wear for dancing, to be among, to have become preferred. Peacock, a feather, there, found together, grounded, to bearer share turned for dancing, among them peacock a feather feather, dancing and to declare for turning, turning a feather as it were for dancing, turning for dancing, dancing being begun turning together, together to become, barely a feather being, beware, being a peacock only on the stair, staring at, only a peacock to be coming, fairly becoming for a peacock, be fair together being around in air, peacock to be becoming lastly, peacock around to be become together, peacock a very peacock to be there.

Moving and to make one the pair, to wear for asking of all there, wearing and to be one for wearing, to one by moving of all there.

Reproof, recovered, solitaire.

Grounded and being well surrounded, so feathered that if a peacock sounded, rounded and with an air for wearing, aloof and grounded to beware.

Aloof, overt, to stare.

Will he be there, can he be there, be there?

Being a feathered peacock.

Only a feathered peacock on the stair.

SAMUEL BECKETT
1906–

Vladimir's Song from Waiting for Godot

A dog came in the kitchen
And stole a crust of bread.
Then cook up with a ladle
And beat him till he was dead.

Then all the dogs came running
And dug the dog a tomb –
He stops, broods, resumes:

[426]

Then all the dogs came running
And dug the dog a tomb
And wrote upon the tombstone
For the eyes of dogs to come:

A dog came in the kitchen
And stole a crust of bread.
Then cook up with a ladle
And beat him till he was dead.

Then all the dogs came running
And dug the dog a tomb –
He stops, broods, resumes:

Then all the dogs came running
And dug the dog a tomb –
He stops, broods. Softly.

And dug the dog a tomb . . .

W. H. AUDEN
1907–73

As I Walked out one Evening

As I walked out one evening,
     Walking down Bristol Street,
The crowds upon the pavement
     Were fields of harvest wheat.

And down by the brimming river
     I heard a lover sing
Under an arch of the railway:
     'Love has no ending.

'I'll love you, dear, I'll love you
     Till China and Africa meet
And the river jumps over the mountain
     And the salmon sing in the street.

'I'll love you till the ocean
        Is folded and hung up to dry
And the seven stars go squawking
        Like geese about the sky.

'The years shall run like rabbits
        For in my arms I hold
The Flower of the Ages
        And the first love of the world.'

But all the clocks in the city
        Began to whirr and chime:
'O let not Time deceive you,
        You cannot conquer Time.

'In the burrows of the Nightmare
        Where Justice naked is,
Time watches from the shadow
        And coughs when you would kiss.

'In headaches and in worry
        Vaguely life leaks away,
And Time will have his fancy
        To-morrow or to-day.

'Into many a green valley
        Drifts the appalling snow;
Time breaks the threaded dances
        And the diver's brilliant bow.

'O plunge your hands in water,
        Plunge them in up to the wrist;
Stare, stare in the basin
        And wonder what you've missed.

'The glacier knocks in the cupboard,
        The desert sighs in the bed,
And the crack in the tea-cup opens
        A lane to the land of the dead.

'Where the beggars raffle the banknotes
  And the Giant is enchanting to Jack,
And the Lily-white Boy is a Roarer
  And Jill goes down on her back.

'O look, look in the mirror,
  O look in your distress;
Life remains a blessing
  Although you cannot bless.

'O stand, stand at the window
  As the tears scald and start;
You shall love your crooked neighbour
  With your crooked heart.'

It was late, late in the evening,
  The lovers they were gone;
The clocks had ceased their chiming
  And the deep river ran on.

November 1937

Alice is gone and I'm alone,
  Nobody understands
How lovely were her Fire Alarms,
  How fair her German Bands.

O how I cried when Alice died
  The day we were to have wed.
We never had our Roasted Duck
  And now she's a Loaf of Bread.

At nights I weep, I cannot sleep:
  Moonlight to me recalls
I never saw her Waterfront
  Nor she my Waterfalls.

GUNTER EICH
1907–72

Timetable

Those aeroplanes
between Boston and Düsseldorf.
It's up to hippopotamuses
to pronounce decisions.
I prefer
to lay lettuce leaves
on a sandwich and
remain in the wrong.

translated from the German by Michael Hamburger

THEODORE ROETHKE
1908–63

Mips and ma the mooly moo,
The likes of him is biting who,
A cow's a care and who's a coo? –
What footie does is final.

My dearest dear my fairest fair,
Your father tossed a cat in air,
Though neither you nor I was there, –
What footie does is final.

Be large as an owl, be slick as a frog,
Be good as a goose, be big as a dog,
Be sleek as a heifer, be long as a hog, –
What footie will do will be final.

OLIVIER MESSIAEN
1908

Doundou Tchil (from HARAWI)

Doundou tchil.
Piroutcha te voilà, ô mon àmoi,
la danse des étoiles, doundou tchil.
Piroutcha te voilà, ô mon àmoi,
miroir d'oiseau familiėr, doundou tchil.
Arc-en-ciel, mon souffle, mon écho,
ton regard est revenu, tchil.
Piroutcha, te voilà, ô mon àmoi,
mon fruit léger dans la lumière, doundou tchil.
Toungou, mapa, nama, mapa, kahipipas.

Syllabes

Colombe verte,
Le chiffre cinq à toi,
La violette double doublera,
Très loin, tout bas.
O mon ciel tu fleuris,
Piroutcha mia!
O déplions du ciel,
Piroutcha mia!
Kahpipas, mahipipas.
Pia pia pia doundou tchil . . .

NORMAN MACCAIG
1910–

After his Death

FOR HUGH MACDIARMID

It turned out
that the bombs he had thrown
raised buildings:

[431]

that the acid he had sprayed
had painfully opened
the eyes of the blind.

Fishermen hauled
prizewinning fish
from the water he had polluted.

We sat with astonishment
enjoying the shade
of the vicious words he had planted.

The government decreed that
on the anniversary of his birth
the people should observe
two minutes pandemonium.

KENNETH PATCHEN

1911–1972

Because it's Good to Keep Things Straight

Now the little green blackbird liked a mouse
And a Malayan sunbear and a horse
And a beetle and a mouse and a horse
And a mouse and a leopard and a beaver
And a black fox and a fox squirrel and a lion
And a buffalo and a beaver and a donkey
And a tiger and a gorilla and a panther
And a salamander and a periwinkle and an ox
And an elephant and an alligator and an armadillo
And a mouse and a mule and a beetle
And a moonfish and a buffalo and a snail
And a horse and a lion and a butterfly
And a horse and a tiger and a mouse;
And the leopard and the donkey and the horse
And the buffalo and the ox and the elephant
And the mouse and the beetle and the gorilla
And the horse and the periwinkle and the mouse
And the panther and the lion and the tiger

And the butterfly and the beaver and the snail
Also liked the little green blackbird;
But the horse and the armadillo and the lion
And the buffalo were quite indifferent to him;
While the beetle and the mouse and the moonfish
And the salamander and the mule and the beaver
Didn't care one way or the other about him;
Whereas the mouse and the horse and the mouse
And the tiger didn't even know he existed.

Because his Sister Saw
Shakespeare in the Moon

The little green blackbird decided to study
Some history and geography; now, this meant going
To places like Portugal and Ayr Moor Gullibaad;
So he had some cards printed and
Handed them out. This of course started
A war, because the cards were printed
With ink. And the little green blackbird
Arrived in Portugal not only without cards,
But without a head, or arms, or legs,
Or even a little toe. This might not have been
So bad had he been feeling all right.
And it was no better in Ayr Moor Gullireet either;
In fact, it was just as sad really. 'So much
For history and geography,' he reflected
Ruefully; 'but at least I'm a lot luckier
Than those poor unfortunates who still have heads
Left to think about what's going to happen to them.'

MERVYN PEAKE
1911–68

The Frivolous Cake

A freckled and frivolous cake there was
    That sailed on a pointless sea,
Or any lugubrious lake there was,
    In a manner emphatic and free.

[433]

How jointlessly, and how jointlessly
    The frivolous cake sailed by
On the waves of the ocean that pointlessly
    Threw fish to the lilac sky.

Oh, plenty and plenty of hake there was
    Of a glory beyond compare,
And every conceivable make there was
    Was tossed through the lilac air.

Up the smooth billows and over the crests
    Of the cumbersome combers flew
The frivolous cake with a knife in the wake
    Of herself and her curranty crew.

Like a swordfish grim it would bounce and skim
    (This dinner knife fierce and blue),
And the frivolous cake was filled to the brim
    With the fun of her curranty crew.

Oh, plenty and plenty of hake there was
    Of a glory beyond compare –
And every conceivable make there was
    Was tossed through the lilac air.

Around the shores of the Elegant Isles
    Where the cat-fish bask and purr
And lick their paws with adhesive smiles
    And wriggle their fins of fur,
They fly and fly 'neath the lilac sky –
    The frivolous cake and the knife
Who winketh his glamorous indigo eye
    In the wake of his future wife.

The crumbs blow free down the pointless sea
    To the beat of a cakey heart
And the sensitive steel of the knife can feel
    That love is a race apart.
In the speed of the lingering light are blown
    The crumbs to the hake above,
And the tropical air vibrates to the drone
    Of a cake in the throes of love.

[434]

ELIZABETH BISHOP
1911–79

*The Man-Moth**

Here, above,
cracks in the buildings are filled with battered moonlight.
The whole shadow of Man is only as big as his hat.
It lies at his feet like a circle for a doll to stand on,
and he makes an inverted pin, the point magnetized to the moon.
He does not see the moon; he observes only her vast properties,
feeling the queer light on his hands, neither warm nor cold,
of a temperature impossible to record in thermometers.

But when the Man-Moth
pays his rare, although occasional, visits to the surface,
the moon looks rather different to him. He emerges
from an opening under the edge of one of the sidewalks
and nervously begins to scale the faces of the buildings.
He thinks the moon is a small hole at the top of the sky,
proving the sky quite useless for protection.
He trembles, but must investigate as high as he can climb.

Up the façades,
his shadow dragging like a photographer's cloth behind him,
he climbs fearfully, thinking that this time he will manage
to push his small head through that round clean opening
and be forced through, as from a tube, in black scrolls on the light.
(Man, standing below him, has no such illusions.)
But what the Man-Moth fears most he must do, although
he fails, of course, and falls back scared but quite unhurt.

Then he returns
to the pale subways of cement he calls his home. He flits,
he flutters, and cannot get aboard the silent trains
fast enough to suit him. The doors close swiftly.
The Man-Moth always seats himself facing the wrong way
and the train starts at once at its full, terrible speed,
without a shift in gears or a gradation of any sort.
He cannot tell the rate at which he travels backwards.

Each night he must
be carried through artificial tunnels and dream recurrent dreams.
Just as the ties recur beneath his train, these underlie
his rushing brain. He does not dare look out the window,
for the third rail, the unbroken draught of poison,
runs there beside him. He regards it as a disease
he has inherited the susceptibility to. He has to keep
his hands in his pockets, as others must wear mufflers.

If you catch him,
hold up a flashlight to his eye. It's all dark pupil,
an entire night itself, whose haired horizon tightens
as he stares back, and closes up the eye. Then from the lids
one tear, his only possession, like the bee's sting, slips.
Slyly he palms it, and if you're not paying attention
he'll swallow it. However, if you watch, he'll hand it over,
cool as from underground springs and pure enough to drink.

* Newspaper misprint for 'mammoth.'

Twelfth Morning;
or What You Will

Like a first coat of whitewash when it's wet,
the thin gray mist lets everything show through:
the black boy Balthazár, a fence, a horse,
    a foundered house,

– cement and rafters sticking from a dune.
(The Company passes off these white but shopworn
dunes as lawns.) 'Shipwreck,' we say; perhaps
    this is a housewreck.

The sea's off somewhere, doing nothing. Listen.
An expelled breath. And faint, faint, faint
(or are you hearing things), the sandpipers'
    heart-broken cries.

The fence, three-strand, barbed-wire, all pure rust,
three dotted lines, comes forward hopefully
across the lots; thinks better of it; turns
    a sort of corner . . .

[436]

Don't ask the big white horse, *Are you supposed*
to be inside the fence or out? He's still
asleep. Even awake, he probably
     remains in doubt.

He's bigger than the house. The force of
personality, or is perspective dozing?
A pewter-colored horse, an ancient mixture,
     tin, lead, and silver,

he gleams a bit. But the four-gallon can
approaching on the head of Balthazár
keeps flashing that the world's a pearl, *and I,*
     I am

its highlight! You can hear the water now,
inside, slap-slapping. Balthazár is singing.
'Today's my Anniversary,' he sings,
     'the Day of Kings.'

Cabo Frio

Visits to St Elizabeths

1950

This is the house of Bedlam.

This is the man
that lies in the house of Bedlam.

This is the time
of the tragic man
that lies in the house of Bedlam.

This is a wristwatch
telling the time
of the talkative man
that lies in the house of Bedlam.

This is a sailor
wearing the watch
that tells the time
of the honored man
that lies in the house of Bedlam.

This is the roadstead all of board
reached by the sailor
wearing the watch
that tells the time
of the old, brave man
that lies in the house of Bedlam.

These are the years and the walls of the ward,
the winds and clouds of the sea of board
sailed by the sailor
wearing the watch
that tells the time
of the cranky man
that lies in the house of Bedlam.

This is a Jew in a newspaper hat
that dances weeping down the ward
over the creaking sea of board
beyond the sailor
winding his watch
that tells the time
of the cruel man
that lies in the house of Bedlam.

This is a world of books gone flat.
This is a Jew in a newspaper hat
that dances weeping down the ward
over the creaking sea of board
of the batty sailor
that winds his watch
that tells the time
of the busy man
that lies in the house of Bedlam.

This is a boy that pats the floor
to see if the world is there, is flat,
for the widowed Jew in the newspaper hat
that dances weeping down the ward
waltzing the length of a weaving board
by the silent sailor
that hears his watch
that ticks the time
of the tedious man
that lies in the house of Bedlam.

These are the years and the walls and the door
that shut on a boy that pats the floor
to feel if the world is there and flat.
This is a Jew in a newspaper hat
that dances joyfully down the ward
into the parting seas of board
past the staring sailor
that shakes his watch
that tells the time
of the poet, the man
that lies in the house of Bedlam.

This is the soldier home from the war.
These are the years and the walls and the door
that shut on a boy that pats the floor
to see if the world is round or flat.
This is a Jew in a newspaper hat
that dances carefully down the ward,
walking the plank of a coffin board
with the crazy sailor
that shows his watch
that tells the time
of the wretched man
that lies in the house of Bedlam.

FRITZ GRASSHOFF
1913–

Juego de Picasso

EINE SCHÜTTEL-SERIE

Picasso ist ein Picoass

ein Ipsosac ein Aspicos

ein Posicas ein Socisap

ein Osipacs ein Ossapic

ein Bapicos ein Pissoac

ein Isocaps ein Caopiss

ein Saopics ein Passico

ein Cosaips ein Cassiop

ein Asocips ein Ocsipas

ein Piasocs ein Biposac

ein Opaicss ein Sacsipo

ein Isospac ein Pisacos

ein Aposisc ein Isascop

ein Coisaps ein Possaic

ein Icsosap ein Spasico

ein Asiposc ein Sciasop

Picasso ist ein Opsicas

Picasso ist Aspic. S. o.

[440]

DYLAN THOMAS
1914–53

I, the First Named

I, the first named, am the ghost of this sir and Christian friend
Who writes these words I write in a still room in a spellsoaked house:
I am the ghost in this house that is filled with the tongue and eyes
Of a lack-a-head ghost I fear to the anonymous end.

JOHN BERRYMAN
1914–72

Dream Song

1

Huffy Henry hid the day,
unappeasable Henry sulked.
I see his point, – a trying to put things over.
It was the thought that they thought
they could *do* it made Henry wicked & away.
But he should have come out and talked.

All the world like a woolen lover
once did seem on Henry's side.
Then came a departure.
Thereafter nothing fell out as it might or ought.
I don't see how Henry, pried
open for all the world to see, survived.

What he has now to say is a long
wonder the world can bear & be.
Once in a sycamore I was glad
all at the top, and I sang.
Hard on the land wears the strong sea
and empty grows every bed.

LAWRENCE FERLINGHETTI
1919–

Don't Let that Horse

Don't let that horse
                    eat that violin
   cried Chagall's mother

                        But he
         kept right on
                 painting

And became famous

And kept on painting
                 The Horse With Violin In Mouth
And when he finally finished it
he jumped up upon the horse
                   and rode away
     waving the violin

And then with a low bow gave it
to the first naked nude he ran across

And there were no strings
               attached

ROBERT DUNCAN
1919–88

Turning into

turning into a restful roomfull;
turning into a guide to the book;
turning into a man-naked memory;
turning into a long avenue;
turning into a lady reclining;

turning into a mother declining;
turning into a vegetable declaiming;
turning into a yesterday for tomorrow;
turning into an age old sorrow;
turning into a cat fit for fiddling;
turning into a wheel withering;
turning into a god whose heart's at ease;
turning into an hour of sore dis-ease;
turning into an eagle bottle January;
turning into a hairy baby song;
turning into an all nite long;
turning into a doctor's office;
turning into a rubber grimace;
turning into a snail's pace,
    a rail's distance, a long face;
turning into a turn with grace.

D. J. ENRIGHT

1920–

A Child's Guide to Welfare

The babe insures the teat
The hope insures the ray
The pot insures the teatray

The driver insures the car
The mistress insures the pet
The housewife insures the carpet

The cat insures its purr
The model insures her pose
The planner insures his purpose

The college insures its don
The composer insures his key
The cart insures the donkey

The glutton insures his tum
The cow insures her bull
The rough insures the tumble

The slaver insures his dhow
The lawyer insures the *re*
The bride insures her dowry

The bank insures its cod
The master insures his piece
The lover insures his codpiece

The merchant insures his wreck
The hangman insures the cord
The runner insures his record

The hand insures the arm
The I insures the Me
The state insures the army

The consumptive insures his cough
The shark insures its fin
The corpse insures its coffin.

PAUL CELAN

1920–70

Großes Geburtstagsblaublau mit Reimzeug und Assonanz

In der R-Mitage,
da hängt ein blauer Page.
Da hängt er, im Lasso:
Er stammt von Pik-As(so?).
Wer hängt ihn ab?
Das Papperlapapp.
Wo tut es ihn hin?
Nach Neuruppin.
In den Kuchen.
Da könnt ihr ihn suchen.
Da könnt ihr ihn finden,
bei den Korinthen
aus der époque bleue,

links von der Kö,
rechts von der Düssel,
in einer blauen Schüssel.
Er hockt auf der Kante
und schwört aufs Blümerante.

Translation

Great Birthday Blaublau
with Rhymework and Assonance

In the R-Mitage
there hangs a page.
He hangs there in a lassoo
and stems from Picasso.
Who will pick him up?
Papparlappup.
Where will he be thrown?
Newropeone.
In a biscuit
if you'll risk it
he'll be found
with currants ground
from the *époque bleue*
left of the Kö
right of the Düssel
on a blue dishle.
He perches on the rim
and swears on the bloomerim.

EDWIN MORGAN

1920–

The First Men on Mercury

– We come in peace from the third planet.
Would you take us to your leader?

– Bawr stretter! Bawr. Bawr. Stretterhawl?

– This is a little plastic model
of the solar system, with working parts.
You are here and we are there and we
are now here with you, is this clear?

– Gawl horrop. Bawr. Abawrhannahanna!

– Where we come from is blue and white
with brown, you see we call the brown
here 'land', the blue is 'sea', and the white
is 'clouds' over land and sea, we live
on the surface of the brown land,
all round is sea and clouds. We are 'men'.
Men come –

– Glawp men! Gawrbenner menko. Menhawl?

– Men come in peace from the third planet
which we call 'earth'. We are earthmen.
Take us earthmen to your leader.

– Thmen? Thmen? Bawr. Bawrhossop.
Yuleeda tan hanna. Harrabost yuleeda.

– I am the yuleeda. You see my hands,
we carry no benner, we come in peace.
The spaceways are all stretterhawn.

– Glawn peacemen all horrobhanna tantko!
Tan come at'mstrossop. Glawp yuleeda!

– Atoms are peacegawl in our harraban.
Menbat worrabost from tan hannahanna.

– ou men we know bawrhossoptant. Bawr.
We know yuleeda. Go strawg backspetter quick.

– We cantantabawr, tantingko backspetter now!

– Banghapper now! Yes, third planet back.
Yuleeda will go back blue, white, brown
nowhanna! There is no more talk.

– Gawl han fasthapper?

– No. You must go back to your planet.
Go back in peace, take what you have gained
but quickly.

– Stretterworra gawl, gawl . . .

– Of course, but nothing is ever the same,
now is it? You'll remember Mercury.

VASKO POPA

1922–

Translated from the Serbo-Croat

He

Some bite off the others'
Arm or leg or whatever

Take it between their teeth
Run off as quick as they can
Bury it in the earth

The others run in all directions
Sniff search sniff search
Turn up all the earth

If any are lucky enough to find their arm
Or leg or whatever
It's their turn to bite

The game goes on briskly

As long as there are arms
As long as there are legs
As long as there is anything whatever

A Wise Triangle

Once upon a time there was a triangle
It had three sides
The fourth it hid
In its glowing centre

By day it would climb to its three vertices
And admire its centre
By night it would rest
In one of its three angles

At dawn it would watch its three sides
Turned into three glowing wheels
Disappear into the blue of no return

It would take out its fourth side
Kiss it break it three times
And hide it once more in its former place

And again it had three sides

And again by day it would climb
To its three vertices
And admire its centre
And by night it would rest
In one of its three angles

The Story of a Story

Once upon a time there was a story

It ended
Before its beginning
And it began
After its end

Its heroes entered it
After their death
And left it
Before their birth

Its heroes talked
About some earth about some heaven
They said all sorts of things

Only they didn't say
What they themselves didn't know
That they are only heroes in a story

In a story that ends
Before its beginning
And that begins
After its end

The Little Box

The little box grows her first teeth
And her little length grows
Her little width her little emptiness
And everything she has

The little box grows and grows
And now inside her is the cupboard
That she was in before

And she grows and grows and grows
And now inside her is the room
And the house and town and land
And the world she was in before

The little box remembers her childhood
And by most great yearning
Becomes a little box again

Now inside the little box
Is the whole world tiny small
It's easy to put in your pocket
Easy to steal easy to lose

Take care of the little box

translated from the Serbo-Croat by Anne Pennington

MIROSLAV HOLUB

1923–

A Boy's Head

In it there is a space-ship
and a project
for doing away with piano lessons.

And there is
Noah's ark,
which shall be first.

And there is
an entirely new bird,
an entirely new hare,
an entirely new bumble-bee.

There is a river
that flows upwards.

There is a multiplication table.

There is anti-matter.

And it just cannot be trimmed.

I believe
that only what cannot be trimmed
is a head.

There is much promise
in the circumstance
that so many people have heads.

translated from the Czech by Ian Milner and George Theiner

Brief Reflection on Cats Growing in Trees

When moles still had their annual general meetings
    and when they still had better eyesight it befell
    that they expressed a wish to discover what
    was above.
So they elected a commission to ascertain what was above.
The commission despatched a sharp-sighted fleet-footed
    mole. He, having left his native mother earth,
    caught sight of a tree with a bird on it.

Thus a theory was put forward that up above
    birds grew on trees. However,
    some moles thought this was
    too simple. So they despatched another
    mole to ascertain if birds did grow on trees.

By then it was evening and on the tree
    some cats were mewing. Mewing cats,
    the second mole announced, grew on the tree.
Thus an alternative theory emerged about cats.

The two conflicting theories bothered an elderly
    neurotic member of the commission. And he
    climbed up to see for himself.
By then it was night and all was pitch-black.

Both schools are mistaken, the venerable mole declared.
    Birds and cats are optical illusions produced
    by the refraction of light. In fact, things above

Were the same as below, only the clay was less dense and
    the upper roots of the trees were whispering something,
    but only a little.

And that was that.

Ever since the moles have remained below ground:
    they do not set up commissions
    or presuppose the existence of cats.

Or if so only a little.

translated from the Czech by Ewald Osers

Biodrama

The puppet king
stages a mounted hunt
for sausages.
Terrified boiling wursts
and bewildered frankfurters
scuttle through thickets,
their fat little bellies
pierced by arrows.

They are close to extinction.
The last specimens
are kept
in refrigerated cages
at the Babylon zoo.

The balance of nature
has again been upset. The knell
has been sounded for the invertebrates.

A few foolish children
are crying.

translated from the Czech by Ewald Osers

EDWARD GOREY

1925–

from *The Listing Attic*

A gift was delivered to Laura
From a cousin who lived in Gomorrah;
   Wrapped in tissue and crepe,
   It was peeled, like a grape,
And emitted a pale, greenish aura.

There's a rather odd couple in Herts
Who are cousins (or so each asserts);
    Their sex is in doubt
    For they're never without
Their moustaches and long, trailing skirts.

From Number Nine, Penwiper Mews,
There is really abominable news:
    They've discovered a head
    In the box for the bread,
But nobody seems to know whose.

The Utter Zoo Alphabet

The Ampoo is intensely neat;
Its head is small, likewise its feet.

The Boggerslosh conceals itself
In back of bottles on a shelf.

The Crunk is not unseldom drastic
And must be hindered by elastic.

The Dawbis is remote and shy;
It shuns the gaze of passers-by.

The Epitwee's inclined to fits
Until at last it falls to bits.

The Fidknop is devoid of feeling;
It drifts about beneath the ceiling.

The Gawdge is understood to save
All sorts of objects in its cave.

The Humglum crawls along the ground
And never makes the slightest sound.

The Ippagoggy has a taste
For every kind of glue and paste.

The Jelbislup cannot get far
Because it's kept inside a jar.

The Kwongdzu has enormous claws;
Its character is full of flaws.

The Limplig finds it hard to keep
From spending all its life asleep.

The Mork proceeds with pensive grace
And no expression on its face.

The Neapse's sufferings are chronic;
It lives exclusively on tonic.

The Ombledroom is vast and white
And therefore visible by night.

The Posby goes into a trance
In which it does a little dance.

The Quingawaga squeaks and moans
While dining off of ankle bones.

The Raitch hangs downward from its tail
By knotting it around a nail.

The Scrug's extremely nasty-looking
And is unusable for cooking.

The Twibbit on occasion knows
A difficulty with its toes.

The Ulp is very, very small;
It hardly can be seen at all.

The Veazy makes a creaking noise;
It has no dignity or poise.

The Wambulus has floppy ears
With which it wipes away its tears.

The Xyke stands up at close of day,
And then it slowly walks away.

The Yawfle stares, and stares, and stares,
And stares, and stares, and stares, and stares.

About the Zote what can be said?
There was just one, and now it's dead.

JACK SPICER

1925–65

The Territory is not the Map

What is a half-truth the lobster declared
You have sugared my groin and have sugared my hair
What correspondence except my despair?
What is my crime but my youth?

Truth is a map of it, oily eyes said
Half-truth is half of a map instead
Which you will squint at until you are dead
Putting to sea with the truth.

Hisperica Famina

Joan of Arc
Built an ark
In which she placed
Three peas
– Can you imagine translating this poem into New English –
In the ark
Were three ghosts
Named Hymen, Simon, and Bynem
– Can you imagine ghosts like that translating these poems into New
    English –
I, they, him, it, her
I, they, him, it, ourselves, her.

Fort Wayne

The messages come through at last:
'We are the ghosts of Christmas past

Our bodies are a pudding boiled
With sixteen serpents and a narrow blade.'

I asked my silly messengers to sing it again
'We are the advantages that hate all men

Our bodies are a pudding boiled
With sixteen serpents and a narrow blade.'

For there are poems and Christmas pies
And loves like ours while you blink your eyes
And love rises up like a butterfly

'Our bodies are a pudding boiled
With sixteen serpents and a narrow blade.'

ERNST JANDL
1925–

A TRANSLATION OF WORDSWORTH'S

*My heart leaps up when I behold
a rainbow in the sky*

mai hart lieb zapfen eibe hold
er renn bohr in sees kai
so was sieht wenn mai läuft begehen
so es sieht nahe emma mähen
so biet wenn ärschel grollt
hor leck mit ei!
scht steil dies fader rosse mähen
in teig kurt wisch mai desto bier
baum deutsche deutsch bajonett schur alp eiertier.

FRANK O'HARA
1926–66

Poem

At night Chinamen jump
on Asia with a thump

while in our willful way
we, in secret, play

affectionate games and bruise
our knees like China's shoes.

The birds push apples through
grass the moon turns blue,

these apples roll beneath
our buttocks like a heath

full of Chinese thrushes
flushed from China's bushes.

As we love at night
birds sing out of sight,

Chinese rhythms beat
through us in our heat,

the apples and the birds
move us like soft words,

we couple in the grace
of that mysterious race.

A Terrestrial Cuckoo

What a hot day it is! for
Jane and me above the scorch
of sun on jungle waters to be
paddling up and down the Essequibo
in our canoe of war-surplus gondola parts.

We enjoy it, though: the bats squeak
in our wrestling hair, parakeets
bungle lightly into gorges of blossom,
the water's full of gunk and
what you might call waterlilies if you're

silly as we. Our intuitive craft
our striped T shirts and shorts
cry out to vines that are feasting
on flies to make straight the way
of tropical art. 'I'd give a lempira or two

to have it all slapped onto a
canvas' says Jane. 'How like
lazy flamingos look the floating
weeds! and the infundibuliform
corolla on our right's a harmless Charybdis!

or am I seduced by its ambient
mauve?' The nose of our vessel sneezes
into a bundle of amaryllis, quite
artificially tied with ribbon.
Are there people nearby? and postcards?

We, essentially travellers, frown
and backwater. What will the savages
think if our friends turn up? with
sunglasses and cuneiform decoders!
probably. Oh Jane, is there no more frontier?

We strip off our pretty blazers
of tapa and dive like salamanders
into the vernal stream. Alas! they
have left the jungle aflame, and in
friendly chatter of Kotzebue and Salonika our

friends swiftly retreat downstream
on a flowery float. We strike through
the tongues and tigers hotly, towards
orange mountains, black taboos, dada!
and clouds. To return with absolute treasure!

our only penchant, that. And a red-
billed toucan, pointing t'aurora highlands
and caravanserais of junk, cries out
'New York is everywhere like Paris!
go back when you're rich, behung with lice!'

How poecile and endearing is the porch

How poecile and endearing is the Porch
it lingers there in the dying light
a school of fish, scared and wise
Sappho is teaching Socrates is
teaching Virgil is teaching Nadia
and Ned everyone is teaching someone
This is Greek civilisation! Come on in

JOHN ASHBERY

1927–

He

He cuts down the lakes so they appear straight
He smiles at his feet in their tired mules.
He turns up the music much louder.
He takes down the vaseline from the pantry shelf.

He is the capricious smile behind the colored bottles.
He eats not lest the poor want some.
He breathes of attitudes the piney altitudes.
He indeed is the White Cliffs of Dover.

He knows that his neck is frozen.
He snorts in the vale of dim wolves.
He writes to say, 'If ever you visit this island,
He'll grow you back to your childhood.

'He is the liar behind the hedge
He grew one morning out of candor.
He is his own consolation prize.
He has had his eye on you from the beginning.'

He hears the weak cut down with a smile.
He waltzes tragically on the spitting housetops.
He is never near. What you need
He cancels with the air of one making a salad.

[459]

He is always the last to know.
He is strength you once said was your bonnet.
He has appeared in 'Carmen.'
He is after us. If you decide

He is important, it will get you nowhere.
He is the source of much bitter reflection.
He used to be pretty for a rat.
He is now over-proud of his Etruscan appearance.

He walks in his sleep into your life.
He is worth knowing only for the children
He has reared as savages in Utah.
He helps his mother take in the clothes-line.

He is unforgettable as a shooting star.
He is known as 'Liverlips.'
He will tell you he has had a bad time of it.
He will try to pretend his pressagent is a temptress.

He looks terrible on the stairs.
He cuts himself on what he eats.
He was last seen flying to New York.
He was handing out cards which read:

'He wears a question in his left eye.
He dislikes the police but will associate with them.
He will demand something not on the menu.
He is invisible to the eyes of beauty and culture.

'He prevented the murder of Mistinguett in Mexico.
He has a knack for abortions. If you see
He is following you, forget him immediately:
He is dangerous even though asleep and unarmed.'

Farm Implements and Rutabagas
in a Landscape

The first of the undecoded messages read: 'Popeye sits in thunder,
Unthought of. From that shoebox of an apartment,
From livid curtain's hue, a tangram emerges: a country.'
Meanwhile the Sea Hag was relaxing on a green couch: 'How pleasant
To spend one's vacation *en la casa de Popeye*,' she scratched
Her cleft chin's solitary hair. She remembered spinach

And was going to ask Wimpy if he had bought any spinach.
'M'love,' he intercepted, 'the plains are decked out in thunder
Today, and it shall be as you wish.' He scratched
The part of his head under his hat. The apartment
Seemed to grow smaller. 'But what if no pleasant
Inspiration plunge us now as to the stars? *For this is my country*.'

Suddenly they remembered how it was cheaper in the country.
Wimpy was thoughtfully cutting open a number 2 can of spinach
When the door opened and Swee'pea crept in. 'How pleasant!'
But Swee'pea looked morose. A note was pinned to his bib. 'Thunder
And tears are unavailing,' it read. 'Henceforth shall Popeye's apartment
Be but remembered space, toxic or salubrious, whole or scratched.'

Olive came hurtling through the window; its geraniums scratched
Her long thigh. 'I have news!' she gasped. 'Popeye, forced as you know to
    flee the country
One musty gusty evening, by the schemes of his wizened, duplicate
    father, jealous of the apartment
And all that it contains, myself and spinach
In particular, heaves bolts of loving thunder
At his own astonished becoming, rupturing the pleasant

Arpeggio of our years. No more shall pleasant
Rays of the sun refresh your sense of growing old nor the scratched
Tree-trunks and mossy foliage, only immaculate darkness and thunder.'

She grabbed Swee'pea. 'I'm taking the brat to the country.'
'But you can't do that – he hasn't even finished his spinach,'
Urged the Sea Hag, looking fearfully around at the apartment.

But Olive was already out of earshot. Now the apartment
Succumbed to a strange new hush. 'Actually it's quite pleasant
Here,' thought the Sea Hag. 'If this is all we need fear from spinach
Then I don't mind so much. Perhaps we could invite Alice the Goon over'
   – she scratched
One dug pensively – 'but Wimpy is such a country
Bumpkin, always burping like that.' Minute at first, the thunder

Soon filled the apartment. It was domestic thunder,
The color of spinach. Popeye chuckled and scratched
His balls: it sure was pleasant to spend a day in the country.

W. S. MERWIN
1927–

The Diggers

If a man with a shovel came down the road

if two men
with shovels came down the road
if eight men with shovels
came down the road

if seventeen men with shovels came down the road
and I wanted to hide
I would see then that everything here
is transparent

yes that is what I would see but I would feel myself
then like my hand in front of my eyes
like this hand just as it is
in front of my eyes

and I would try to take it down
before they saw through it and found me

GUILLERMO CABRERA INFANTE

1929–

I Want-a-name-'ere La Guantanamera

... Marryling my self and Cuba and Martí and the Wanton nightmare I
Want-a-name-'ere La Guantanamera, that Martían song with its tropsical
rhythm that goes wroughly like thus, dedicated to the one I hate:

(instant pretension or interpoleation or inpernetration by M.S.)

> *Yo soy un hombre sincero*
> I'm a man without a zero
> *De donde crece la palma*
> From the land of the pawn-trees
> *Y antes de morirme quiero*
> And 'fore lay-dying I xerox
> *Hechar mil voces del alma.*
> One thousand copies of me.

> *Con los sobres de la piedra*
> With the sour sickle of this hearse
> *Quiero yo mi muerte hinchar*
> I want to share man Mao
> *El apoyo de la Sierra*
> The reivers of the Sierra
> *Más compras hace que el mal*
> I like butter, then some tea.

> *Mi anverso es un verde claro*
> My grin is a dear sun-tan
> *En un jardín encendido*
> Gotten in a flaming garden
> *Mi reverso un muerto herido*
> My torso is a wounded fountain
> *Que luce en el norte un faro.*
> That looks for shells in a maiden.

translated from The Spanish by Donald Gardner and Suzanne Jill Levine

TED HUGHES

1930–

Wodwo

What am I? Nosing here, turning leaves over
Following a faint stain on the air to the river's edge
I enter water. What am I to split
The glassy grain of water looking upward I see the bed
Of the river above me upside down very clear
What am I doing here in mid-air? Why do I find
this frog so interesting as I inspect its most secret
interior and make it my own? Do these weeds
know me and name me to each other have they
seen me before, do I fit in their world? I seem
separate from the ground and not rooted but dropped
out of nothing casually I've no threads
fastening me to anything I can go anywhere
I seem to have been given the freedom
of this place what am I then? And picking
bits of bark off this rotten stump gives me
no pleasure and it's no use so why do I do it
me and doing that have coincided very queerly
But what shall I be called am I the first
have I an owner what shape am I what
shape am I am I huge if I go
to the end on this way past these trees and past these trees
till I get tired that's touching one wall of me
for the moment if I sit still how everything
stops to watch me I suppose I am the exact centre
but there's all this what is it roots
roots roots roots and here's the water
again very queer but I'll go on looking

ANDREAS OKOPENKO
1930–
Translation from the German

Interview with Herr Limerick

How long have you suffered from this tick?
For ever, said Herr Limerick.

Is it a tick or is it a trick?
A trick tick, said Herr Limerick.

Do you always get it in the neck?
It wanders, said Herr Limerick.

Do you limmer when your eyelids flick?
Outdoors too, said Herr Limerick.

And if they sent you to the Nick?
It would stink like hell, said Herr Limerick.

Do you find quartz and mica chic?
Only feldspar, said Herr Limerick.

When is a swimmer's torso thick?
When he's a sea-horse, said Herr Limerick.

Do you read Newsweek or Quick?
Mainly Shakespeare, said Herr Limerick.

What do you think about a fic-
tional being, Herr Limerick?

Ah, Vaihinger's 'As if' magic
I love it, said Herr Limerick.

And how about the Body Politic?
I hate it, said Herr Limerick.

Between bric-à-brac and brac-à-bric
which would you chose, Herr Limerick?

I would chose cognac with shashlik
and drink to the health of Herr Limerick.

But aren't you worried when all's done
stupidity's increasing because of your fun?

Any increase in dumbness isn't partic-
ularly traceable to me, said Herr Limerick.

KONRAD BAYER

1932–1964

Franz War

franz war.
war franz?
franz.
war.
wahr.
war wahr.
wirr.
wir.
franz, wir!
wir, franz.
ihr.
franz war wirr.
war franz irr?
wirrwarr.

JOHN UPDIKE

1932–

Upon Learning that a Bird Exists
Called the Turnstone

A turnstone turned rover
And went through ten turnstiles,
Admiring the clover
And turnsole and fern styles.

The Turneresque landscape
She scanned for a lover;
She'd heard one good turnstone
Deserves another.

She took to the turnpike
And travelled to Dover,
Where turnips enjoy
A rapid turnover.

In vain did she hover
And earnestly burn
With Yearning; above her
The terns cried, 'Return!'

JERZY HARASYMOWICZ

1933–

A Green Lowland of Pianos

in the evening
as far as the·eye can see
herds
of black pianos

up to their knees
in the mire
they listen to the frogs

they gurgle in water
with chords of rapture

they are entranced
by froggish, moonish spontaneity

after the vacation
they cause scandals
in a concert hall
during the artistic milking
suddenly they lie down
like cows

looking with indifference
at the white flowers
of the audience

at the gesticulating
of the ushers

translated from the Polish by Czeslaw Milosz

ANDREI VOZNESENSKY

1933–

Somewhere a man puts on his shorts,
his blue-striped T-shirt,
his blue jeans;
a man puts on
his jacket on which there is a button
reading COUNTRY FIRST,
and over the jacket, his topcoat.

Over the topcoat,
after dusting it off, he puts on his automobile,
and over that he puts on his garage

(just big enough for his car),
over that his apartment courtyard,
and then he belts himself with the courtyard wall.
Then he puts on his wife
and after her the next one
and then the next one;
and over that he puts on his subdivision
and over that his county
and like a knight he then buckles on
the borders of his country;
and with his head swaying,
puts on the whole globe.

Then he dons the black cosmos
and buttons himself up with the stars.
He slings the Milky Way over one shoulder,
and after that some secret beyond.

He looks around:
Suddenly
in the vicinity of the constellation Libra
he recalls that he has forgotten his watch.

Somewhere it must be ticking
(all by itself).
The man takes off the countries,
the sea,
the oceans,
the automobile, and the topcoat.
He is nothing without Time.

Naked he stands on his balcony
and shouts to the passers-by:
'For God's sake, do not forget your watch!'

translated from the Russian by William Jay Smith and Vera Dunham

MARK STRAND
1934–

The Man in the Tree

I sat in the cold limbs of a tree.
I wore no clothes and the wind was blowing.
You stood below in a heavy coat,
the coat you are wearing.

And when you opened it, baring your chest,
white moths flew out, and whatever you said
at that moment fell quietly onto the ground,
the ground at your feet.

Snow floated down from the clouds into my ears.
The moths from your coat flew into the snow.
And the wind as it moved under my arms, under my chin,
whined like a child.

I shall never know why
our lives took a turn for the worse, nor will you.
Clouds sank into my arms and my arms rose.
They are rising now.

I sway in the white air of winter
and the starling's cry lies down on my skin.
A field of ferns covers my glasses; I wipe them away
in order to see you.

I turn and the tree turns with me.
Things are not only themselves in this light.
You close your eyes and your coat
falls from your shoulders,

the tree withdraws like a hand,
the wind fits into my breath, yet nothing is certain.
The poem that has stolen these words from my mouth
may not be this poem.

JAROSLAW MAREK RYMKIEWICZ

1934–

Spinoza was a Bee

We were not here. Plato was a spider.
We were not here. Spinoza was a bee.

The bee suffices. It is here and there.
It is a July of clouds, a July of July.

The attribute of sting, the argument of sting.
So much for the bee: a central buzzing.

Spinoza the philosopher? Just a nightmare of the bee.
In the dream of a bee. A sovereign being.

A mathematical being. A buzzing cipher.
An analogy of the bee, the pure act of the bee.

Such is the fate of angels. Spinoza was a bee.
He was a predicate of the bee, the bee the subject.

There was no predicate. That was the fear of the spider.
That was the dream of the bee. There was no Spinoza.

So much says Nature. Here the bee suffices.
It is related to the sun, it is here and there.

This bee is only a cipher. A sovereign being.
A dream of Spinoza. Contradictory beings, what of them?

translated from the Polish by Czeslaw Milosz

CARL DENNIS
1936–

In the Middle of the Party

When I saw that the man who stirred the fire
Had teeth and fingers of black wire,
I made an allowance for fangs and claws;
But when he called me by my name
And I heard his voice and mine were the same,
I knew he was the cause.

When I saw that the woman who passed the tray
Had mounds on her back where white wings lay,
I thought of the favors of natural laws.
But when she called me by my name
And I heard that her voice and mine were the same,
I knew she was the cause.

MARIN SORESCU
1936–
Translated from the Romanian

Reading Matter

As usual
this day is pushed into my room
from under the door.

I put on my spectacles
and begin to
read it.

Nothing of any importance,
as far as I can see.
Towards noon, a slight depression
with no reasons given,
and, it says,

I shall take up
my trend towards light
at the point where I broke off yesterday.

The foreign branch
gives information about my transactions
with water, with mountains and with the air,
about their absurd demand
to enter my bloodstream and
my brain.

Then the usual reports
about working conditions,
the way to the bread bin,
the cheerful mood
(but not a word
about conditions
in the liver region).

Where on earth do they print
this stuff,
my life,
when it's full of
inadmissible
errors.

Question

What's today?
A Monday?
But Monday was
last week.

Tuesday?
But it was Tuesday all last year,
nothing but Tuesday.

Wednesday?
The century before this one, as far as I know,
fell on a Wednesday.

Thursday?
On a Thursday
Carthage was sacked,
on a Thursday
the Library in Alexandria burned.
Don't tell me that since then
not one day has passed.

Friday? Saturday?
Yes I've heard
of those days.
No fairy tales, please.

Sunday perhaps?
The time before the Creation
was called Sunday.
I remember that.

You see, all the days of the week *have been*.
For us there's no new one
left.

translated from the Romanian by Michael Hamburger

ANONYMOUS

Titanic, a Toast

*(recorded from Slim, Jefferson City,
June 1964)*

I don't know, but my folks say,
eighth a May was a hell of a day.
News reached the little seaport town
that the old *Titanic* was about to go down.
They tell me on board was a fella called Shine,
he was so dark he changed the world's mind.
Shine came up from the bottom deck below,
he said, 'Captain, there's water runnin' all in the firebox door,
and I believe this big motherfucker's gonna overflow.'

Captain said, 'Shine,' say, 'You go back down,
I got forty horsepower to keep the water pumped down.'
Shine went down and came up with a teacup in his hand,
He said, 'Look here, captain,' says, 'I'm a scared man.
I'd rather be out there on that iceberg goin' around and 'round
than to be on this big raggedy motherfucker when it's goin' down.'
Shine hit the water and he began to swim,
with ninety-nine millionaires lookin' at him.
Captain came out on the second deck, he said, 'Shine, Shine, if you save
    poor me,'
say, 'I'll make you as rich as any black man can be.'
Shine said, 'There's fish in the ocean, there's whales in the sea,
Captain, get your ass overboard and swim like me.'
Now the captain's daughter came out on the second deck,
Captain say, 'Shine, Shine, that can't be a fact,
I got too many pumps to keep that water back.
Go back and get another blow.'
Captain and the major had a few more words,
and the old *Titanic* hit the second iceberg.
Shine come from below the deck
with a lifesaver around his neck.
He say, 'Captain, captain, I can't work no more.
Don't you know there's forty foot a water on the boiler-room floor.'
Captain say, 'Shine, Shine, that can't be a fact,
I got four hundred pumps to keep that water back.
Go back and hit another blow.'
Shine said, 'Captain, captain, can't you see,
this ain't no time to bullshit me!
I'd rather be out on that big ocean going 'round and 'round
than be on this big motherfucker slowly sinkin' down.'
Shine jumped in the water and commenced to swim,
four thousand millionaires watchin' him.
Captain say, 'Shine, Shine, save poor me,
I'll make you richer than old John D.'
Shine turned around and took another notion,
say, 'Captain, your money's counterfeit in this big-assed ocean.'
Then from below the deck came a thousand whores
with their drawers in their hands and their tits around their neck.
They say, 'Shine, Shine, save poor me,
I got the best white pussy you ever did see.'
He says, 'I'm sorry, ladies, but I [gotta] go,
but there's better pussy on yonder shore.'

[475]

Then from below the deck came the Captain's daughter
with her drawers in her hand and her tits around her neck.
She said, 'Shine, Shine, save poor me,
I'll make you the best white wife you ever did see.'
He say, 'I'm sorry, lady, but you 'bout to have a kid,
so jump and split the water like old Shine did.'
Shine took a overhand stroke
that carried him five miles from that sinkin' boat.
Up popped a whale with a slimy ass,
say, 'You a long time coming, but you here at last.'
Shine said, 'You swallowed old Jonah and spit him on dry land,
but you'll never swallow me 'cause I'm a hell of a man.'
but I'm gonna try to save this black ass of mine.'
So Shine jumped overboard and begin to swim,
and all the people standin' on deck watching him.
Captain's daughter ran on deck with her dress above her head and her
    teddies below her knees,
and said, 'Shine, Shine, won't you save poor me?'
Say, 'I'll make you as rich as any shine can be.'
Shine said, 'Miss, I know you is pretty and that is true,
but there's women on the shore can make a ass out a you.'
Captain said, 'Shine, Shine, you save poor me,
I make you as rich as a shine can be.'
Shine say, 'There's fish in the ocean, whales in the sea,
captain, get your ass in the water and swim like me.'
So Shine turned over and began to swim,
people on the deck were still watchin' him.
A whale jumped up in the middle of the sea,
said, 'Put a "special delivery" on his black ass for me.'
Shine said, 'Your eyes may roll and your teeth may grit,
but if you're figurin' on eatin' me you can can that shit.'
Shine continued to swim, he looked back, he ducked his head, he showed
    his ass,
'Look out sharks and fishes and let me pass.'
He swimmed on till he came to a New York town,
and people asked had the *Titanic* gone down.
Shine said, 'Hell, yeah.' They said, 'How do you know?'
He said, 'I left the big motherfucker sinkin' about thirty minutes ago.'

ANONYMOUS

There was an old man named Michael Finnigin

There was an old man named Michael Finnigin
He grew whiskers on his chinnigin
The wind came out and blew them innigin
Poor old Michael Finnigin, beginnigin

There was an old man named Michael Finnigin
He went fishing with a pinnigin
Caught a fish and dropped it innigin
Poor Old Michael Finnigin, begginigin

There was an old man named Michael Finnigin
He climbed a tree and barked his shinnigin
Scraped off several yards of skinnigin
Poor old Michael Finnigin, beginnigin

There was an old man named Michael Finnigin
He got drunk from too much ginnigin
So he wasted all his tinnigin
Poor old Michael Finnigin, beginnigin

There was an old man named Michael Finnigin
He kicked up an awful dinnigin
Because they said he must not sinnigin,
Poor old Michael Finnigin, beginnigin

There was an old man named Michael Finnigin
He grew fat and then grew thinnigin
Then he died and we have to beginnigin
Poor old Michael Finnigin, beginnigin

MICHAEL WULFF

1940–

Der Tragödie erster Teil

Nacht
In einem hochgewölbten, engen gotischen Zimmer
Faust unruhig auf seinem Sessel am Pulte
Faust. Habe nun, ach! Philosophie,
Juristerei und Medizin
Und leider auch Theologie
Durchaus studiert mit eißem emühn.
   a st   ich nun, ic ar er or,
U d in s klug als wie uv r!
H   ße Magi   r, h iße Do t   g r
U dz he sh n an ie z en J hr
H   f, he b u qu u d kr
M n   an er Na   um —
Un   d   ni s   i
             r   d   n n
      e   ,   t   i
   c   l   e   e
                           p

HEIIIIIIIIINNNNNNNNNNRICH!!!!!!!!!!!!!!!

             t
      e   u   p
      b   s   i
             re
   we   z
r   rr   e
  i   op   e
   t   eb   n!
      et   i ht   di   m h rg b!
 e hi oph s.   uF t m! m! i iti im i h.
M rg r te   i ch   re   e mi h!
Ihr E gel,   i en S h en,
Lage t e ch umher, m ch   u be a ren! –

[478]

Heinrich! Mir grauts vor dir!
Mephistopheles. Sie ist gerichtet!
Stimme von oben. Ist gerettet!
Mephistopheles zu Faust. Her zu mir!
Verschwindet mit Faust.
Stimme von innen, verhallend. Heinrich! Heinrich!

From *The Lore and Language of Schoolchildren*
1959

Masculine, Feminine, Neuter,
I went for a ride on my scooter,
I bumped into the Queen
And said, Sorry old bean,
I forgot to toot-toot on my tooter.

Red, white, and blue,
My mother is a Jew,
My father is a Scotsman,
And I'm a kangaroo.

A bug and a flea
Went out to sea
Upon a reel of cotton;
The flea was drowned
But the bug was found
Biting a lady's bottom.

Julius Caesar
The Roman geezer,
Squashed his wife with a lemon squeezer.

The sausage is a cunning bird
With feathers long and wavy;
It swims about the frying pan
And makes its nest in gravy.

The elephant is a pretty bird,
It flits from bough to bough.
It builds its nest in a rhubarb tree
And whistles like a cow.

As I was going to school one day to learn my ABC.
I fell into a washing tub and sailed the ocean sea.
There came by a Chinaman who said I was a spy
And if I did not talk to him he'd poke me in the eye.
He tied me to a cabbage stalk
And cut my head with knife and fork,
I grew so fat that I could not walk
I joined the Chinese army.
The captain's name was Bango,
Bango was his name,
And he played upon his whiskers
Till the clouds rolled by.

'Twas in the month of Liverpool,
In the city of July,
The snow was raining heavily,
The streets were very dry.
The flowers were sweetly singing,
The birds were in full bloom,
As I went down the cellar
To sweep an upstairs room.

I went to the pictures tomorrow
I took a front seat at the back,
I fell from the pit to the gallery
And broke a front bone in my back.
A lady she gave me some chocolate,
I ate it and gave it her back.
I phoned for a taxi and walked it,
And that's why I never came back.

Ladles and Jellyspoons,
I stand upon this speech to make a platform,

The train I arrived in has not yet come,
So I took a bus and walked.
I come before you
To stand behind you
And tell you something
I know nothing about.

One fine day in the middle of the night
Two dead men got up to fight,
Back to back they faced each other,
Drew their swords and shot each other.
A paralysed donkey passing by
Kicked a blind man in the eye,
Knocked him through a nine-inch wall
Into a dry ditch and drowned them all.

Oh ye cannae shove yer grannie aff the bus,
Oh ye cannae shove yer grannie aff the bus,
Ye cannae shove yer grannie
For she's yer mammie's mammie,
Ye cannae shove yer grannie aff the bus.

Long legged Italy
Kicked poor Sicily
Right in the middle of the Mediterranean Sea.
Austria was Hungary
Took a bit of Turkey
Dipped into Greece
Fried it in Japan
And ate it off China.

Salome was a dancer
She danced the hootchie-cootch,
She shook her shimmy shoulder
And she showed a bit too much.
Stop! said King Herod.
You can't do that 'ere.
Salome said, Baloney!
And kicked the chandelier.

The boy stood on the burning deck
Melting with heat;
His big blue eyes were full of tears
And his shoes were full of feet.

Hark, the jelly babies sing,
Beecham's pills are just the thing,
They are gentle, meek and mild,
Two for a man and one for a child.
If you want to get to heaven
You must take a dose of seven;
If you want to go to hell,
Take the blinking box as well.

Good King Wenceslas looked out
In his pink pyjamas.
What do you think he hollered out?
'Lovely ripe bananas'.

BOB DYLAN

1941–

Tiny Montgomery

Well you can tell ev'rybody
Down in ol' Frisco
Tell 'em
Tiny Montgomery says hello

Now ev'ry boy and girl's
Gonna get their bang
'Cause Tiny Montgomery's
Gonna shake that thing
Tell ev'rybody
Down in ol' Frisco
That Tiny Montgomery's comin'
Down to say hello

Skinny Moo and
Half-track Frank
They're gonna both be gettin'
Outa the tank
One bird book
And a buzzard and a crow
Tell 'em all
That Tiny's gonna say hello

Scratch your dad
Do that bird
Suck that pig
And bring it on home
Pick that drip
And bake that dough
Tell 'em all
That Tiny says hello

Now he's king of the drunks
An' he squeezes, too
Watch out, Lester
Take it, Lou
Join the monks
The C.I.O.
Tell 'em all
That Tiny Montgomery says hello

Now grease that pig
And sing praise
Go on out
And gas that dog
Trick on in
Honk that stink
Take it on down
And watch it grow
Play it low
And pick it up
Take it on in
In a plucking cup
Three-legged man
And a hot-lipped hoe
Tell 'em all
Montgomery says hello

[483]

Well you can tell ev'rybody
Down in ol' Frisco
Tell 'em all
Montgomery says hello

Don't Ya Tell Henry

Don't ya tell Henry,
Apple's got your fly.

I went down to the river on a Saturday morn,
A-lookin' around just to see who's born.
I found a little chicken down on his knees,
I went up and yelled to him,
'Please, please, please!'
He said, 'Don't ya tell Henry,
Don't ya tell Henry,
Don't ya tell Henry,
Apple's got your fly.'

I went down to the corner at a-half past ten,
I's lookin' around, I wouldn't say when.
I looked down low, I looked above,
And who did I see but the one I love.
She said, 'Don't ya tell Henry,
Don't ya tell Henry,
Don't ya tell Henry,
Apple's got your fly.'

Now, I went down to the beanery at half past twelve,
A-lookin' around just to see myself.
I spotted a horse and a donkey, too,
I looked for a cow and I saw me a few.
They said, 'Don't ya tell Henry,
Don't ya tell Henry,
Don't ya tell Henry,
Apple's got your fly.'

Now, I went down to the pumphouse the other night,
A-lookin' around, it was outa sight.
I looked high and low for that big ol' tree,
I did go upstairs but I didn't see nobody but me.
I said, 'Don't ya tell Henry,
Don't ya tell Henry,
Don't ya tell Henry,
Apple's got your fly.'

Ballad of a Thin Man

You walk into the room
With your pencil in your hand
You see somebody naked
And you say, 'Who is that man?'
You try so hard
But you don't understand
Just what you'll say
When you get home

Because something is happening here
But you don't know what it is
Do you, Mister Jones?

You raise up your head
And you ask, 'Is this where it is?'
And somebody points to you and says
'It's his'
And you say, 'What's mine?'
And somebody else says, 'Where what is?'
And you say, 'Oh my God
Am I here all alone?'

Because something is happening here
But you don't know what it is
Do you, Mister Jones?

You hand in your ticket
And you go watch the geek
Who immediately walks up to you
When he hears you speak

And says, 'How does it feel
To be such a freak?'
And you say, 'Impossible'
As he hands you a bone

Because something is happening here
But you don't know what it is
Do you, Mister Jones?

You have many contacts
Among the lumberjacks
To get you facts
When someone attacks your imagination
But nobody has any respect
Anyway they already expect you
To just give a check
To tax-deductible charity organizations

You've been with the professors
And they've all liked your looks
With great lawyers you have
Discussed lepers and crooks
You've been through all of
F. Scott Fitzgerald's books
You're very well read
It's well known

Because something is happening here
But you don't know what it is
Do you, Mister Jones?

Well, the sword swallower, he comes up to you
And then he kneels
He crosses himself
And then he clicks his high heels
And without further notice
He asks you how it feels
And he says, 'Here is your throat back
Thanks for the loan'

Because something is happening here
But you don't know what it is
Do you, Mister Jones?

[486]

Now you see this one-eyed midget
Shouting the word 'NOW'
And you say, 'For what reason?'
And he says, 'How?'
And you say, 'What does this mean?'
And he screams back, 'You're a cow
Give me some milk
Or else go home'

Because something is happening here
But you don't know what it is
Do you, Mister Jones?

Well, you walk into the room
Like a camel and then you frown
You put your eyes in your pocket
And your nose on the ground
There ought to be a law
Against you comin' around
You should be made
To wear earphones

Because something is happening here
But you don't know what it is
Do you, Mister Jones?

PETER HANDKE

1942–

The Wrong Way Round

Gone to sleep I wake up:
I do not look at things, and things look at me;
I do not move, and the floor under my feet moves me;
I do not see myself in the mirror, and I in the mirror look at me;
I do not speak words, and words pronounce me;
I go to the window and am opened.

Having got up I lie there:
I do not open my eyes, but my eyes open me;
I do not listen to sounds, but the sounds listen to me;
I do not swallow water, but the water swallows me;
I do not reach out for things, but things attack me;
I do not take off my clothes, but my clothes take off from me;
I do not persuade myself with words, but words dissuade me from me;
I go to the door, and the handle depresses me.
The rolling blind is raised, and night falls, and to snatch air I submerge
    myself in water.
I tread on the stone floor and sink up to my ankles;
I sit on the driving-seat of a coach and place one foot in front of the other;
I see a woman with a parasol and night sweat breaks out of me;

I extend one arm into the air and it catches fire;
I reach out for an apple and am bitten;
I walk barefoot, and feel a stone in my shoe;
I tear the plaster off my wound, and the wound is in the plaster;
I buy a newspaper and am skimmed;
I frighten someone to death and can no longer speak;
I stuff cotton wool into my ears and scream;
I hear the sirens howl, and the Corpus Christi procession passes;
I open my umbrella, and the ground burns under my feet;
I run out into the open and am arrested.

Over the parquet floor I stumble,
with my mouth agape I make conversation,
with the balls of my thumbs I scratch,
with my policeman's whistle I laugh,
from the tips of my hair I bleed,
on the opening of the newspaper I choke.
food with an attractive smell I spew up.
about the future I tell stories.
To things I speak.
me I see through.
dead people I kill.

And I see sparrows shoot at guns;
and I see the despairing man being happy;
and I see the suckling baby harbour desires;
and I see the milkman in the evening.

: and the postman? asks for mail;
and the preacher? is shaken up;
and the execution squad? lines up against the wall;
and the clown? throws a hand grenade into the audience;
and murder? does not happen till there are witnesses.

And the undertaker eggs on his football team;
And the head of state assassinates the baker's boy;
And the general is named after a street;
And nature is painted faithfully after a picture;
And the Pope is counted out on his feet –

and listen: The watch runs outside itself!
And look: The candles burning down grow longer!
And listen: The scream is whispered!
And look: The wind petrifies the grass!
And listen: The folk song is roared out!
And look: The raised arm points down!
And listen: The question mark is commanded!
And look: The starved man is fat!
And smell: The snow is rotting!

And morning sets,
and the table stands on one leg,
and the refugee sits crosslegged like a tailor,
and on the top floor you'll find the bus stop:

Listen: It's deathly quiet! – It's rush hour.

Gone to sleep I wake up
and escape from the unbearable dream into gentle reality
and merrily hum: Stop thief! Murder! –
listen how my mouth waters: I see a corpse!

translated from The German by Michael Hamburger

HUGH HAUGHTON

1948–

The Bollam's Replover: Farewell to Jabberwocky

The wharrupede thrimmered, the glottal stopped,
The millibells lilliped away;
The Bollam of Nadisdrubad morbled his globe
And cajolished the dandrums at play.

'Are nodepells so glibeish, postules so gab,
That boremulls admonate the poles?
Have we crede of modendridons, misoddled the friths,
And gangmolished the bucular noles?

Oh gride on and dremmer! Glem so and durb!
The pollen may climmer and thream!
Mergploisters and pleamen, negmaisters and thrays,
Replover the grundsells of Neme!'

He slighed so. They monished. A mallam.
The groil havered droly madriff.
The Bollam slobe drebwards, the groil at his labe,
And cthonished the grundsellar Gryph.

'Replover the grundsells, remoble the erb!'
Mene slobe raphoristically phleigm,
But the nabobles were faybled, the noles overmairned,
And the Bollam downblendished at Neme.

The wharrupede nemmed. The glottiphars too.
No millibells lilliped away.
The Bollam of Nadisdrubad gried by his globe,
Resturbing the dandrums at play.

Homard à Igor Stravinsky:
Vernacular Variations

The Rite of Spring!
The *right* of Spring!
The 'Write!' of Spring!
The right offspring!

The right-off, Spring?
The wried, 'off' spring?
The writ of Spring?
The write-off's spring.

The wry Toff, Spring;
The wry dove's 'pring';
The 'rye' tough's spring;
The Wright offspring;

The ride of Spring;
The Rye Toff, Spring;
The writer's spring;
The Right; A Spring.

They ride off Spring;
They write-off Spring;
They're eyed of Spring;
Their eyed offspring.

They're right off Spring;
Their write-off's purring;
Their 'right-o' 'f Spring;
Their Ide of Spring.

Their Eye, Dove, Spring;
Their 'I'de have Spring';
Their 'I', Dovespring;
Their eye-dove, Spring.

There! Eyed offspring!
There I'd Hove spring!
There! Ride off, Spring!
There ride, Oaf! Spring!

Thera'd have Spring;
Theoried-of Spring;
The right oaf, Spring;
Theorite of Szpryngh!

The raid of Spring;
The Rye-Dove's spring;
The right 'Ove', 'ffspring;
'*The Rite*' (O'Spring).

Thee! Write off Spring?
Thee, Wright! Dove's purring!
Thee! Ride off! 's Spring!
Thee! Rye! Doff! Spring!

They write of Spring;
The Wright of Spring;
The Right of Spring;
The Rite of Spring.

JAMES FENTON

1949–

This Octopus Exploits Women

Even the barnacle has certain rights
The grim anemones should not ignore,
And the gay bivalves in their fishnet tights
Are linking arms with fins to ask for maw.

The hectic round of rockpools is disrupted
By the addresses of the finny vicars,
With which the limpet choirboys were corrupted.
The knitting-fish produce their eight-leg knickers

[492]

While somewhere in the depths a voice keeps shouting:
'By Jove! that was a narrow bathyscaphe.'
What made the Junior Sea-Slugs give up scouting?
The *Daily Seaweed* tells us nowhere's safe.

Beneath the shimmering surface of the ocean,
The thoroughfare of ketches, sloops and luggers,
With their thick boots and hair smothered in lotion,
Are gathering hordes of ruthless ichthic muggers.

The workers on the derricks live in terror.
You can't stroll out across the sea at night.
Professor Walrus writes (see *Drowned in Error*):
'The lemon sole are taught to shoot on sight.'

The lobsters at the water polo club
Sip their prawn cocktails, chatting over chukkas.
The octopus rests idly in its tub.
The Tunny Girls are lounging on its suckers.

DAVID BYRNE
1950–

Moon rocks, Moon in the Man

Flying saucers, levitation
Yo! I could do that
Get ready, for heavy duty
Go on, give it a change
I saw your hair start to curl
So get up, write it down
You better wait for a while

So take your hands out of your pockets
And get your face adjusted
I heard it, somebody lied
And I'm staring out of the window
Gonna let this thing continue
In its natural time
Roundheads Squareheads

Get settled in
You can hear my belly rumble
There's a voice that starts to mumble
Woo! Its startin' to sing

Protons, neutrons
I ate a rock from the moon
Got shocked once, shocked twice
Let's see what I can do
Man in the moon, moon in the man
I got a rock in my throat
Upside, upside down
My tummy starts to talk . . . (what it say?)

Gonna rock it 'till I shock it
Gonna kick it till I drop it
Woo! Love at first sight
You can kick it, you can poke it
Ooh, I think you broke it
What about that!
Skin from a snake, blood from a stone
You know, that ain't no lie
I got hundreds of expressions
Try to make a good impression
Woo! right between the eyes

I don't mind – let me go
Sounds inside – I don't know
Let me be – why not stay
I feel numb – let me play

I got wild imagination
Talkin' transubstantiation
Any version will do
I got mass communication
I'm the human corporation
I ate a rock from the moon
Moon in the rock, rock in the moon
There's a moon in my throat
You might think I'm wasting time
You might laugh but not for long
Hey! I'm working it out . . . (work it out)

I don't mind – let me go
Sounds inside – I don't know
Let me see – why not say
I feel numb – let me play

ANONYMOUS

An English Alphabet

A   for 'orses
B   for mutton
C   for yourself
D   for dumb
E   for brick
F   for vescence
G   for police
H   for retirement
I   for an eye
J   for oranges
K   for restaurant
L   for leather
M   for size
N   for a penny
O   for there
P   for relief
Q   for a ticket
R   for mo
S   for you
T   for two
U   for mism
V   for l'amour
W   for a shilling
X   for breakfast
Y   for Gawd sake
Z   for effect.

PAUL MULDOON

1951–

Quoof

How often have I carried our family word
for the hot water bottle
to a strange bed,
as my father would juggle a red-hot half-brick
in an old sock
to his childhood settle.
I have taken it into so many lovely heads
or laid it between us like a sword.

An hotel room in New York City
with a girl who spoke hardly any English,
my hand on her breast
like the smouldering one-off spoor of the yeti
or some other shy beast
that has yet to enter the language.

Notes to Introduction

1. *Oxford Dictionary of Nursery Rhymes*, edited by Iona and Peter Opie, Oxford, 1951, p.203.
2. The earliest extant copy of *Mother Goose's Melody* is in fact dated 1791, but it was entered for copyright in 1780 by Thomas Carnan, John Newbery's stepson and successor, and was probably compiled and first printed in 1765 or 1766 for John Newbery, the first man to specialise in publishing children's books in England. Ernest Rhys's Everyman *Book of Nonsense* includes the rhymes with the original notes. (See *Oxford Dictionary of Nursery Rhymes*, 'Introduction', pp.33–5.)
3. See *ODNR* pp.34–5.
4. Lewis Carroll, *Through the Looking-Glass*, Chapter II, *The Annotated Alice* ed. Martin Gardner, Penguin, p.209.
5. *Mack Flecknoe*, written to ridicule Thomas Shadwell, was published in 1682.
6. See Kornei Chukovsky, *From Two to Five*, trans. and ed. Miriam Morton, University of California Press, revised edn, 1968, pp.61–113. Having observed how even before the age of one children tend to spend their time in happy rhythmic babbling, Chukovsky writes: 'In the beginning of our childhood we are all 'versifiers' – it is only later that we begin to learn to speak in prose. The very nature of an infant's jabbering predisposes him to versifying. The word "mama" with its symmetrical syllabic repetition is a kind of model for rhyming' (p.64). In Chukovsky's view nonsense poetry and what he calls 'topsy-turvies' are particularly important to children aged between two and five.
7. Recorded in Anna Kern's recollections of Pushkin and quoted in Roman Jakobson and Linda R. Waugh, *The Sound-Shape of Language*, 1979, p.217.
8. Cited in M. Sanches and B. Kirschenblatt-Gimblett, 'Children's Traditional Speech Play and Child Language', in B. Kirschenblatt-Gimblett, ed., *Speech Play*, Philadelphia, 1976, p.65–110. Also in Jakobson and Waugh, p.219.
9. Claude Roy, ed. *La Poésie Populaire*, Seghers, Paris, 1954, p.28.
10. Klaus Peter Dencker, ed. *Deutsche Unsinnspoesie*, Philipp Reclam, Stuttgart, 1978, p.192.
11. Iona and Peter Opie, *The Language and Lore of Schoolchildren*, Oxford, 1959.
12. My argument about the fascination of nonsense with order owes a lot to Elizabeth Sewell's pioneering little book, *The Field of Nonsense*, Chatto, 1952, which first drew my attention to the nursery-rhyme's predilection for serial order. Though she argues there that 'Nonsense much prefers to be in verse' (p.22), she perversely insists that nonsense is inherently opposed to the mind's 'tendency to oneness, the tendency towards poetry and dream' (p.123), and sees nonsense and poetry as antithetical.
13. Lewis Carroll, *Alice in Wonderland*, Chapter IX, *The Annotated Alice*, p.121.
14. Lewis Carroll, *Through the Looking-Glass*, Chapter VI, *The Annotated Alice*, p.269.

15. *Death's Jest Book*, Act 1, scene 1, *Plays and Poems of Thomas Lovell Beddoes*, ed. H. W. Donner, Routledge, 1950, p.204.

16. Mikhail Bakhtin, *Rabelais and his World*, trans. Helene Iswolsky, Indiana University Press, 1984: 'The greatest writer to complete the cycle of the people's carnival laughter and bring it into world literature was Rabelais', writes Bakhtin (p.12), 'his work is an encyclopaedia of folk culture' (p.58).

17. Text from E. K. Chambers, *The Medieval Stage*, Oxford, 1925 (2nd edn), vol. 2, pp.279–82.

18. E. K. Chambers, *The Medieval Stage*, vol. 1, p.317.

19. The fullest account of the *fatrasie*, with complete texts, is Lambert C. Porter, *La Fatrasie et le Fatras*, Geneva, 1960.

20. Number 50 of the Fatrasies d'Arras in Porter's edition. For my translation see p.50.

21. For an account of 'Bedlamite ballads' and James Carkesse's poems of madness, see Roy Porter, 'Bedlam and Parnassus: Mad People's Writing in Georgian England' in George Levine, ed., *One Culture: Essays in Science and Literature*, University of Wisconsin Press, 1982.

22. There is no modern edition of Taylor's work, but the Scolar Press produced a reprint of *All the Workes of John Taylor the Water Poet*, 1630, with an Introductory Note by V. E. Neuberg, London, 1977.

23. See Christopher Hill, *The World Turned Upside Down*, Penguin, 1975, for the currency of images of the world being inverted and overturned within the radical political debates of the 1640s and 1650s. For the broader iconography of the theme, see David Kunzle's 'World Turned Upside Down: The Iconography of a European Broadsheet Type', in Barbara Babcock (ed.), *The Reversible World*, Cornell University Press, 1978, and Giuseppe Cocchiara, *Il mondo alla rovescia*, Turin, 1963.

24. *The Spectator*, No. 35, Tuesday 10 April, 1711. In *Selections from The Tatler and The Spectator* of Steele and Addison, ed. Angus Ross, Penguin, 1982, pp.334–7.

25. *The Dunciad Variorum*, I.58. *The Poems of Alexander Pope*, ed. John Butt, Methuen, 1963.

26. Henry Fielding, *The Author's Farce* (original version), ed. Charles B. Woods, Edward Arnold, 1967, Act III, line 700.

27. Laurence Sterne, *A Sentimental Journey*, 'The letter': 'Vive l'amour! et vive la bagatelle!'.

28. William Hazlitt, in his lecture 'On the Living Poets' in *Lectures on the English Poets*, 1818, wrote of Wordsworth: 'It may be considered as characteristic of our poet's writings, that they either make no impression on the mind at all, seem mere *nonsense-verses*, or that they leave a mark behind them that never wears out . . . To one class of reader he appears sublime, to another (and we fear the larger) ridiculous'. William Hazlitt, *Selected Writings*, ed. Ronald Blythe, Penguin, 1970, p.225.

29. William Wordsworth, *The Poems*, ed. John O. Hayden, Penguin, 1977, p.295.

30. *Table Talk*, January 20, 1834, in *Table Talk of S. T. Coleridge*, ed. John Morley, London, 1884. In a review of 1816 Hazlitt wrote: '*Kubla Khan* . . . only shews that Mr Coleridge can write better *nonsense verses* than any man in England. It is not a poem, but a musical composition. "A damsel with a dulcimer/In a vision once I saw:/It was an Abyssinian maid,/And on her dulcimer she played,/Singing of

Mount Abora." We could repeat these lines to ourselves not the less often for not knowing the meaning of them'. *Coleridge: The Critical Heritage*, ed. J. R. de J. Jackson, Routledge & Kegan Paul, 1970, pp.208–9.

31. 'Introduction' to *More Nonsense*, 1872.

32. The phrase is Robinson Duckworth's, who asked Dodgson on the trip whether the story was an 'extemporary romance' and was told 'Yes, I'm inventing as we go along'. *The Lewis Carroll Picture-Book*, ed. Stuart Dodgson Collingwood, 1899, pp.359–60.

33. 'Introduction' to *More Nonsense*, 1872.

34. Letter of August 18, 1884. *The Letters of Lewis Carroll*, ed. Morton N. Cohen, Macmillan, London, 1979, vol. 1, p.548.

35. 'Alice on the Stage', 1887, in *The Lewis Carroll Picture-Book*, ed. Stuart Dodgson Collingwood, 1899, p.166.

36. *Through the Looking-Glass*, chapter 1, in *The Annotated Alice*, ed. Martin Gardner, Penguin, p.197.

37. Lear uses the phrase in a letter to Holman Hunt in 1861. Quoted in Vivien Noakes, *Edward Lear, The Life of a Wanderer*, Collins, 1968, p.189.

38. W. H. Auden, 'Edward Lear', *Collected Shorter Poems, 1927–57*, Faber, 1966, p.127.

39. Lear was a friend and admirer of Tennyson and had a long-term ambition to publish a book of illustrations to Tennyson's poems. He also set several of the poet's songs to music, as recollected by Marianne North, who recorded how Lear would sit at the piano 'and sing Tennyson's songs for hours, composing as he went on, and picking out the accompaniments by ear, putting the greatest expression and passion into the most sentimental words. He often set me laughing then he would say I was not worthy of them, and would continue with intense pathos of expression and gravity of face, while he substituted "Hey Diddle Diddle, the Cat and the Fiddle", or some other nonsensical words to the same air': Marianne North, *Recollections of a Happy Life*, ed. Mrs J. A. Symonds, Macmillan, 1892, vol. 1, p.29. In a letter to Chichester Fortescue which also discusses the Tennyson illustrations, Lear includes some of his parodies of the laureate:

> To watch the tipsy cripples on the beach,
> With topsy turvy signs of screamy play.
>
> Tom-Moore Pathos; – all things bare, –
> With such a turkey! such a hen!
> And scrambling forms of distant men,
> O! – ain't you glad you were not there!

12 September, 1873. *Later Letters of Edward Lear*, ed. Lady Strachey, 1911, p.161.

40. In a letter to Holman Hunt Lear wrote of 'this ludicrously whirligig life which one suffers from first & laughs at afterwards'. Quoted in Noakes, *Edward Lear, Life of a Wanderer*, p.246.

41. *Through the Looking-Glass*, Chapter 6, *The Annotated Alice*, p.269.

42. *Ibid.* p.271.

43. G. K. Chesterton, 'A Defence of Nonsense' in *The Defendant*, Dent, London, 1901, p.64, p.68.

44. Sir Edmund Strachey, a close friend of Lear's, wrote an appreciation of his work

after his death with the title 'Nonsense as a Fine Art' (*Quarterly Review*, 1888).

45. *The Waste Land*, Section III, 'The Fire Sermon', in T. S. Eliot, *Collected Poems 1909–62*, Faber, 1963, p.71. Stravinsky records Eliot's estimate of Lear as a great poet alongside Mallarmé and George Herbert in *Themes and Conclusions*. Faber, 1972, p.69.

46. 'J'ai seul la clef de cette parade sauvage', *Illuminations*, in *Oeuvres de Rimbaud*, ed. Suzanne Bernard, Garnier, 1960. The phrase 'le dérèglement de tous les sens', meaning a 'derangement of all the senses', comes in two of Rimbaud's most famous letters of May 1871 about his ambitions as a poet: 'Je veux être poète, et je travaille à me rendre voyant ... Il s'agit d'arriver à l'inconnu par le dérèglement de *tous les sens* ... JE est un autre': 'I want to be a poet and I am working to make myself a seer ... It's a question of reaching the unknown by the derangement of all the senses ... I is an other'. *Ibid.* pp.343–4.

47. See *Jokes and the Unconscious*, trans. James Strachey, Routledge, 1966, and in particular chapter 4, 'The Mechanism of Pleasure and the Psychogenesis of Jokes', pp.117–58.

48. *ibid.* p.131.

49. See *The Interpretation of Dreams*, trans. James Strachey, Allen and Unwin, 1954, pp.295–304, where Freud discusses nonsense words in dreams. Humpty Dumpty's theory of portmanteau words devised to explain *Jabberwocky* can be found in *Through the Looking-Glass*, Chapter 6, *The Annotated Alice*, pp.270 ff.

50. *Interpretation of Dreams*, p.444. The entire section on 'Absurd Dreams' is extremely illuminating about nonsense in general.

51. See Hans Richter, Dada: *Art and Anti-Art*, trans. David Britt, London, 1965.

52. Quoted in Maurice Nadeau, *The History of Surrealism*, trans. Richard Howard, Penguin, 1973, p.60.

53. Quoted in Nadeau, pp.112–13.

54. See C. W. E. Bigsby, *Dada and Surrealism*, Methuen, 1972, p.71.

55. In the declaration of January 27, 1925, quoted in Nadeau, p.113.

56. In *Rrose Sélavy* (1922–3) Desnos specialised in sentences like 'Croyez-vous que Rrose Sélavy connaisse ces jeux de fous qui mettent le feu aux joues?' and 'Rrose Sélavy n'est pas persuadé que la culture du moi puisse amener la moiteur du cul', *Corps et Biens*, Gallimard, 1969, pp.31–46. Edward Lear was adept at the same kind of game: 'What's the difference between the Czar & the Times paper? – One is the type of Despotism the other the despotism of Type'. *Selected Letters*, ed. Vivien Noakes, Oxford, p.132.

57. Reprinted in Vladimir Markov, *Russian Futurism*, Macgibbon & Kee, London, 1969, pp.130–1. My account of Russian Futurism and *zaum* verse is dependent on Markov throughout.

58. In Markov, p.44.

59. Quoted in Markov, p.344.

60. The entire 'Declaration of Transrational Language' is printed in Markov, p.345–6. Terentyev's remark is quoted on p.347 and his '17 Nonsensical Implements' discussed on pp.358–9.

61. Velimir Khlebnikhov, *Snake Train*: Poetry and Prose, ed. Gary Kern, Ardis, 1976.

62. V. Khlebnikov, *The King of Time*, Poems, Fictions, Visions of the Future, trans. Paul Schmidt, Harvard University Press, 1985.

63. *Ibid.* 'Introduction', p.6. It is worth bearing in mind Roman Jakobson's affirmation on the dustjacket of Schmidt's book: 'I have never ceased to consider Khlebnikov one of the greatest Russian poets and perhaps the most important modern poet in the world.'

64. *Ibid.* p.204.

65. George Gibian, *Russia's Lost Literature of the Absurd*, New York, 1971.

66. *Deutsche Unsinnspoesie*, ed. Klaus Peter Dencker, Philipp Reclam, Stuttgart, 1978.

67. *Ueber die Galgenlieder*, Berlin, 1921. Quoted in Christian Morgenstern's *Galgenlieder*, A Selection, trans. and introduced Max Knight, University of California Press, 1966, p.9.

68. *Ibid.* pp.5–6.

69. *Edward Lears Kompletter Nonsens*, ins Deutsche geschmuggelt von Hans Magnus Enzensberger, Frankfurt, 1977. Christian Enzensberger, the poet's brother and an influential literary critic, has translated the Alice books of Lewis Carroll into German.

70. *Notes Towards a Supreme Fiction*, 'It must be Abstract', III, in *Collected Poems*, Faber, London, 1955.

71. *Notes Towards a Supreme Fiction*, 'It Must Change', *Collected Poems*, p. 396.

72. 'Oh! blessed rage for order, pale Ramon,/The maker's rage to order words of the sea', *Collected Poems*, p.130.

73. The critic Morse Peckham, setting himself polemically against Stevens, argues that the urge to disorder is a fundamental impulse of art, and has entitled one of his works on aesthetics *Man's Rage for Chaos*, Chilton Books, New York, 1965.

74. *Finnegans Wake*, Faber, pp.535 and 619. James S. Atherton in *The Books at the Wake*, Faber, 1959, studies Joyce's treatment of Lewis Carroll and his 'loose carolleries', while Mabel P. Worthington has written on 'Nursery Rhymes in *Finnegans Wake*' in *Journal of American Folklore*, vol. 70, 1957, pp.37–48.

75. *Ibid.* p.378.

76. *Ibid.* p.378.

Sources and Notes

Sources for most of the poems in copyright are given in the Acknowledgements.

37 The 'Saxon Fragment' and 'Beoleopard' come from *1066 and All That* by W. C. Sellar and R. J. Yeatman, Methuen, 1930. They have the same scholarly and historical status as the rest of that work.

38–40 'Farai un vers'. From *Troubadour Lyric Poetry*, trans. and ed. by Alan R. Press, Edinburgh University Press, 1971.

41–5 *The Land of Cockayne*. The modernised text is from A. L. Morton, *The English Utopia*, Lawrence & Wishart, 1952. The original text can be found in J. A. W. Bennet and G. V. Smithers, eds. *Early Middle English Verse and Prose*, Oxford University Press, 1966. The MS formed part of a collection of texts of Irish provenance, including a *Missa de Potatoribus* or Boozer's Mass, and the author was probably a goliardic clerk writing in Ireland in the 13th century.

46–7 Cerveri. From Anthony Bonner, *Songs of the Troubadours*, Allen & Unwin, 1973. The original is written in the Provençal equivalent of pig-latin. Its first line – 'taflamart faflama hoflomon maflamal' – can be decoded as 'tart fa hom mal', just as the first line of Bonner's translation can be boiled down to 'It is hard for men to err among good people'.

48 A *fatras* is a 'jumbled medley, hotchpotch of ideas, papers' or 'useless rubbish', and the *fatras* and *fatrasie* were nonsense genres current in France from the 13th to the 15th C. The first poem comes from the *Oeuvres Poétiques* de Philippe de Rémi, Sire de Beaumanoir; the three anonymous *fatrasies* from Arras derive from MS 3114, Bibliothèque de l'Amiral, and date from the late 13th C. The text for all four poems, from Lambert C. Porter, *La Fatrasie et Le Fatras*: essai sur la poésie irrationelle en France du Moyen Age, Geneva, 1960.

52 Skelton. From *The Complete English Poems*, ed. John Scattergood, Penguin, 1983. This is only an extract from the poet's extravagant elegy for a sparrow. *Speke, Parott* and *Magnyfycence* show comparable kinds of absurd linguistic playfulness.

59 'Hay, hey ... I will have the whetstone if I may'. MS. 354., Balliol College, Oxford. From *Early English Carols*, ed. R. L. Grene, Oxford, 1962. The topsy-turvy or lying ballad is a popular oral genre.

60 'Les Mensonges'. From *La Poésie Populaire*, ed. Claude Roy, Editions Seghers, Paris, 1954.

61–2 'My heart of gold' and 'Gebit' from *Christmas carolles newely Imprinted*, Richard Kele, c. 1550, reprinted in *Early English Carols*. ed. R. L. Grene, Oxford, 1962.

63–7 'Il était un petit homme' and 'Monsieur de la Palisse' from *La Poésie*

Populaire, ed. Claude Roy, Seghers, 1954. 'Monsieur de la Palisse' is an example of *lapalissade* or nonsensical statement of the obvious, and is reputed to have been inspired by the death of a 16th C. Marshal of France, Jacques de Chabannes, Seigneur de la Patrie.

68 'The Lily and the Rose'. From MS Harley 7578, British Museum. This text is based on that in *Early English Lyrics*, ed. E. K. Chambers and F. Sidgwick, 1907.

68–9 'Little John Nobody'. An extract from a 16th C. ballad published by Bishop Percy in his *Reliques of Ancient English Poetry*, 3. vols, 1765, and reprinted in *The Oxford Book of Light Verse*, ed. W. H. Auden, 1938.

70–6 'The Antidoted Fanfreluches' and 'The Games of Gargantua', from *The Works of Mr. Francis Rabelais*. Doctor in Physick, containing five books of the Lives, Heroic Deeds and Sayings of Gargantua and his sonne Pantagruel, trans. by Sir Thomas Urquhart, 1653. 'Les Fanfreluches antidotées, trouvées en un monument antique' comes from Ch. 2 of the first book of *La Vie très Horrifique du Grand Gargantua*, c. 1534. The list of Games comes from chapter 22. Urquhart's list is a transmutation rather than a simple translation of Rabelais's sporting inventory, but Peter and Iona Opie note that 'all the games that Urquhart lists were ones known in seventeenth-century England (*Oxford Dictionary of Nursery Rhymes*). The bizarrely Rabelaisian 'Fanfreluches' poem seems to have been the model for many English 17th C. poetic travesties, such as John Taylor's *Odcomb's Complaint*.

77 Peele. Both songs from *The Old Wives' Tale*, 1595.

78–85 'Holofernes's Letter'. From *Love's Labour's Lost*, Act iv, Scene ii., ed. Richard David, Methuen, Arden edn, 1975.
   'Feste's Song'. From *Twelfth Night*, or What You Will, Act v, Scene i. J. M. Lothian and T. W. Craik, Arden edn, 1975.
   'Bottom's Dream'. From *A Midsummer's Night Dream*, Act iv, Scene i, ed. John Dover Wilson, Cambridge Univ. Press.
   'The Fool's Prophecy' and 'Lear's Madness' from *King Lear*, Act iii, Scenes ii and iv., ed. Russell Fraser, Signet Classics.

85 'Will you buy a fine dog'. From Thomas Morley, *First Book of Airs*, 1600. MS 439, Christ Church, Oxford. Reprinted in *Love and Drollery*, ed. John Wardroper, Routledge & Kegan Paul, 1969.

86 'Of One that Died of the Wind-Colic'. MS Harl. 6917, reprinted in *Love and Drollery*, ed. John Wardroper, 1969.

86 'The first beginning'. From *Sportive Wit, The Muses Merriment*, 1656, and reprinted in *Love and Drollery*, ed. John Wardroper, 1969.

87 'Fara Diddle Dyno'. Set by Thomas Weelkes, the text from *Madrigal Verse*, ed. E. H. Fellowes, 3rd ed., 1967.

87–90 'Martin and his Man' and 'The Fly's Wedding'. From Thomas Ravenscroft, *Deuteromelia*, or the Second Part of Musicks Melodie, 1609.

90–1 John Davies, 'The Author loving these homely meats . . .' From *The Scourge of Folly*, 1610.

91–2 John Donne. 'Song' and 'The Computation' from *Poems*, ed. H. J. C. Grierson, 1912.

92–4 Ben Jonson. 'A Catch' from *Oberon, the Fairy Prince*, a Masque, 1616; 'Cocklorrel' from *The Gypsies Metamorphosed*.

95–104 John Taylor. 'Odcomb's Complaint', published in 1613, is a mock elegy for Thomas Coryate (?1577–1617), a legendary traveller and famous travel-writer of the time; son of the rector of Odcombe, he published an account of his travels called *Coryats Crudities* in 1611, and *The Odcombian Banquet*, a collection of verses from The Crudities, soon after. 'Sir Gregory Nonsense his News from No Place' was published in 1622 and reprinted in *All the Workes of John Taylor the Water Poet* in 1630, a collection reprinted by the Scolar Press, with an introductory note by V. E. Neuburg, in 1977. Both texts are printed here in slightly modified and abbreviated form.

105–6 'Non-sense'. From *Wit and Drollery*, 1661, without attribution, but the first eight lines derive from *The Essence, Quintessence, Incense, Innocence, Lye-cense and Magnificence of Nonsense upon Sence, or Sence upon Nonsense*, by John Taylor, dated 1653, and the whole poem is written in his nonsense style. 'If all the world were paper'. From *Witt's Recreations*, 1641, incorporating verse 5 from Ashmole MS 36, a manuscript anthology of the same time.

107–8 Corbett. 'Nonsence' was first published in *Witt's Recreations Augmented*, 1641, with the title 'A messe of no-sense'. Though also published as 'Dr. Corbett's Nonsence', it is classified among his 'Dubia' by Bishop Corbett's modern editors, J. A. W. Bennett and H. R. Trevor-Roper, *The Poems of Richard Corbett*, Oxford, 1955, as is 'A Non Sequitur', first published in *Wit Restored*, 1658.

108–9 Lawes. This is a spoof Italian song composed by Henry Lawes, made up from the contents list of Antonio Cifra's songbook, *Scherzi et Arie*, and jumbling first lines and vocal instructions (songs for 1, 2, or 3 voices); it satirises the contemporary fashion for Italian music, however unintelligible to singer and audience. The song comes from an autograph collection of Lawes' songs in the British Library, add. 53723. Text from Henry Lawes, *Sitting by the Streams, Psalms, Ayres and Dialogues*, The Consort of Musicke, Hyperion Records Ltd: the translation is by Peggy Forsyth.

109 Von Logau. From Von Logau, *Sämmtliche Sinngedichte*, ed. Gustav Eitner, Stuttgart, 1872. In *Deutsche Unsinnspoesie*, ed. Klaus Peter Dencker, Philipp Reclam, Stuttgart, 1978.

110–1 Marvell. From *The Complete Poems*, ed. Elizabeth Story Donno, Penguin, 1972. I have extracted two pairs of stanzas, numbers 59, 60 and 96, 97, from Marvell's long country-house poem about his residence in General Fairfax's Yorkshire estate in the early 1650s, to illustrate the poet's ear for the nonsensical within a far from nonsensical context, and to show the resonance of the 'world turned upside down' idea during a period of social crisis. Fairfax's estate of Denton was by the Wharfe River.

111–2 'Tom Tell-Truth'. From The *Roxburghe Collection*, Volume IV.

112–3 'Ad Johannuelem . . .' From *Wit Restor'd*, 1658.

113–21 Bedlamite Ballads. In 'Bedlam and Parnassus' Roy Porter alludes to the number of beggars who posed as Bedlamites or madmen in the 17th C. 'They commonly sang for their supper' he records, and copies of their songs were presented as 'Bedlamite Ballads', so that 'in the public ear and literary wishes, the gift of tongues established a certain kinship between poetry and lunacy' (in *One Culture*, ed. George Levine, University of Wisconsin Press, 1987). Shakespeare's Edgar in King Lear, who poses as a 'Tom O' Bedlam' is the literary predecessor of this tradition. The texts for this sequence are drawn from 17th C. drolleries, as reprinted in *Loving Mad Tom*: Bedlamite Verse from the sixteenth and seventeenth centuries, ed. Jack Lindsay, with a foreword by Robert Graves, Fanfrolico Press, London, 1927. 'From the Hag and Hungry Goblin' is to be found in *Giles Earle his booke*, 1615 (BM Addl. MS. 24665) and *Westminster Drollery*, 1672; 'Loving Mad Tom' in *Wit and Drollery*, 1682; 'Mad Maudlin is Come' in *Wit and Drollery*, 1661 and 1682; 'From the Top of High Caucasus' in *Le Prince D'Amour*, 1660; and 'To Find my Tom of Bedlam' in *Wit and Mirth*, 1699. I have occasionally lightly modified the texts for the sake of clarity.

122 Francis Ben. From *Wit's Interpreter*, 1671; first edition, 1653.

123 James Carkesse. From *Lucida Intervalla*, containing divers Miscellaneous poems, written at Finsbury and Bethlem, by the Doctor's Patient Extraordinary, London, 1679, reprinted with an introduction by M. V. De Porte, Augustan Reprint Society, Los Angeles, 1979. James Carkesse was a clerk at the Navy Office under Samuel Pepys and later hospitalised in a private madhouse in Finsbury and then Bedlam; his poems were published the year of his release from Bedlam, and many of them, like 'His Petition', are concerned with vindicating his dignity as a 'man of Sense' – though others make strange use of his antithetical status as a 'mad poet'.

123–7 Dryden. *MacFlecknoe*, or a Satyr upon the True-Blew Protestant Poet, T. S., first published in 1682, and in a definitive edition in 1684. From *The Fables and Poems of John Dryden*, ed. James Kinsley, Oxford, 1958. Richard Flecknoe was a minor writer satirised by Marvell; the main target of Dryden's satire is Thomas Shadwell (?1642–92), a successful dramatist and probable author of *The Medal of John Bayes*, one of the attacks on Dryden which sparked off this mock-heroic poem.

128 'Ignotum per Ignotius'. From *The Diverting Post*, 1705. In *The New Oxford Book of Eighteenth-Century Verse*, ed. Roger Lonsdale, Oxford, 1984. 'The Rum Mort's Praise . . .' and 'The Maunder's Praise'. From J. Shirley, *The Triumph of Wit*, 1707. The first of these is described as 'the King of the Gypsies's Song made upon his beloved Doxy or Mistress' and both are exercises in slang or 'canting' songs, a genre going back at least as far as Thomas Dekker's 'Beggar's Curse' in *Lanthorne and Candlelight*, 1608. In J. S. Farmer (ed.), *Musa Pedestris*, 1896.

129–30 *Rum-Mort*, beggar or gypsy queen; *maunder*, beggar; *kinching-cove*, young lad; *rum-pad*, highway; *maundeth*, begs; *quarrons*, body; *clapperdogeon*, beggar from birth; *dimber damber*, head of a gang; *palliards*, beggars by birth; *jockum*, penis; *glimmer*, clap; *crampings*, fetters; *scowre*, wear; *harmans*, stocks; *harman-becks*, constables; *toure*, look; *drawers*, pockets; *loure*, money; *duds and cheats*, clothes and loot; *cuffin*, magistrate; *deuseaville*, country; *chates*, gallows; *crank and dommerar*, fake epileptic and fake deaf-and-dumb beggars; *rum-maunder*, to feign madness; *Abram-cove*, thief disguised as madman; *gybes well jerk'd*, well-forged licenses; *darkmans*, night; *crackmans*, hedge; *glimmer*, fire; *cheat*, duck; *tib o'th' buttry*, goose; *red shanks*, turkey; *ruff peck*, bacon; *grannam*, corn; *lap*, liquor; *poplars*, porridge; *bugher*, dog; *skew*, wooden dish; *filch*, hook; *gybes*, fake pass; *togeman*, cloak.

130 *Doxy*, mistress; *glaziers*, eyes; *glimmar*, fire; *Salomon*, mass; *gentry mort*, lady;

prats, thighs; *wap'd*, fucked; *togeman*, cloak; *mish or slate*, shirt or sheet; *strammel*, straw; *skipper*, barn; *lib*, lie; *ruffin cly the mort*, devil take the woman; *stampers*, feet; *drawers*, stockings; *prig*, steal or importune; *lightman*, day; *Margery*, hen; *boozing ken*, ale-house; *lour*, money; *mill*, steal; *gage*, pot; *nip . . . a bung*, steal a purse; *crash*, eat; *cheat*, pig.

131 Prior. From *Literary Works*, ed. H. Burden Wright & Muriel K. Spear, Oxford, 1959.

131–2 Ward. From *The Poetical Entertainer*, 1713. The attribution is uncertain. In the *New Oxford Book of Eighteenth-Century Verse*, ed. Roger Lonsdale, Oxford, 1984.

132–6 Swift. From Jonathan Swift, *The Complete Poems*, ed. Pat Rogers, Penguin, 1983. 'I walk before no man' was first published in Swift's *Correspondence*, ed. F. E. Ball, 1913. The Anglo-Latin Verses are in fact in an English disguised as Latin, e.g. 'Mollis abuti' means 'Moll is a beauty'. The title and first line of 'A Riddling Letter' come from a second riddling letter, this one being originally entitled 'Probatur Aliter'; the answer to each riddle begins with 'ass', as, in line 1, 'a long-eared beast, and a field-house for cattle' is 'a shovel' (ass, hovel). 'Behold! a proof of Irish Sense' is taken from an anecdote about Swift's madness recorded in the *Annual Register* of 1759, but regarded as 'romantic invention' by Pat Rogers, his modern editor. 'A Cantata' was first published in 1746 with music by the Rev. John Echlin, and intended to poke fun at crudely mimetic attempts to marry words and music.

136–8 John Gay. From the Pope-Swift *Miscellanies*, 1728, identified as Gay's in Bell's edition of the *Miscellaneous Works*, 1773 and never ascribed to anyone else. Text from *Poems of John Gay*, ed. John Underhill, The Muses Library, 1905.

139–41 Carey. From *Poems on Several Occasions*, 1729, first published under the pseudonym of Benjamin Bounce, *Namby Pamby* is one of the numerous satires on Ambrose Philip's poems about children. 'Roger and Dolly' was first published in *The Musical Century*, 1737. Texts from *The New Oxford Book of Eighteenth-Century Verse*.

141–3 Pope. The opening of *The Dunciad, in Three Books*, 1728. Text from *The Poems of Alexander Pope*, ed. John Butt, Methuen, London, 1963.

143–4 Johnson. 'I put my hat upon my head' and 'The tender infant, meek and mild' are extempore parodies of Bishop Percy's 'Hermit of Warkworth', the first recorded in Boswell's journal of 7 April, 1773, the second in Mrs Thrale's journal, Thraliana, printed in the *Works*, 1787. 'I am Cassander' is a translation from a pantomime version of Benserade's *Bal Cassandre*, probably written during a visit to Paris in 1775. 'If the man who Turneps cries' is a burlesque translation of lines from Lope de Vega's *Arcadia*. 'A Song' is recorded in Fanny Burney's diary of November 1778. Texts from Samuel Johnson, *The Complete English Poems*, ed. J. D. Fleeman, Penguin, 1971.

144–51 Rhymes from *Tommy Thumb's Pretty Song Book*. Only Vol. 2 of this little collection of nursery songs survives; it was published by the London publisher, Mary Cooper, and is generally agreed to be the earliest known book of nursery rhymes – though most of the 38 it records probably go back to a much earlier period. John Aubrey records an earlier version of 'Sing a Song of Sixpence' which he describes as 'an old and filthy Rhyme used by base people':

'When I was a young Maid, and washed my Mother's dishes, / I putt a finger in my --- and pluck't out little fishes'. Only the first 4 verses of 'Who did kill Cock Robin' occur in the collection itself, the others are added from 'Cock Robin, a pretty gilded toy for girl or boy', printed by R. Marshall, c. 1770. Only the first two verses of 'There was a Mad Man' occur in the *Pretty Song Book*, the others in *Top Book*, c. 1760.

151 'A Man in the Wilderness' first appears as an MS addition, dated 1744, to the Bath Municipal Library copy of *The Whole Duty of Man*, a devotional work of the 17th C., according to the *Oxford Dictionary of Nursery Rhymes*.

151–2 'The Oath of the Canting Crew'. *From An Apology for the Life of Bampfylde Moore Carew* by Robert Goadby, 1749; in *Musa Pedestris*, ed. J. S. Farmer, 1896. Carew was the King of the Gypsies and may have dictated this canting oath to Goadby or his wife. *Crank Cuffin*, queer cove or rogue; *Stop Hole Abbey*, a nick-name for a favourite rendez-vous; *Abram*, a beggar feigning to be a Bedlamite; *ruffler crack*, expert rogue; *Hooker*, thief disguised as a beggar; *frater*, someone begging with a false patent; *Irish toyle*, a thief acting as pedlar; *dimber damber*, gang leader or exper thief; *angler*, thief operating with a hook; *prig of cackler*, poultry-thief; *prig of prancer*, horse thief; *swigman*, beggar peddling haberdashery to cover theft; *clapper-dudgeon*, born beggar; *curtal*, grey-cloaked beggar of some status; *curmudgeon*, miser; *whip-jack*, beggar with false licence; *palliard*, born beggar; *patrico*, Irish hedge-priest; *jarkman*, counterfeiter; *dummerar*, a beggar feigning to be deaf and dumb; *the family*, the fraternity of vagabonds and thieves.

152–6 Vadé. From the *Oeuvres de Vadé*, ed. Julien Lesner, Paris, 1875. The editor notes: 'Ce genre de plaisanterie fut fort à la mode vers le milieu du dix-huitième siècle. Il n'y a guère de poète de cette époque qui n'ait commis quelques-unes de ces débauches d'esprit, sous lesquelles se dissimulait parfois quelque mordante épigramme'.

156 'This is the House that Jack built'. From *Nurse Truelove's New Year's Gift*, printed by John Newbery, c. 1755. It was used as the basis of William Hone's satire on the political corruption of the age of George IV, *The Political House that Jack Built*, 1819.

156–9 *Mother Goose's Melody, or Sonnets for the Cradle*, probably printed by John Newbery, c. 1765. See Introduction, pp. 1 ff.

159 Foote. Printed, without attribution to Foote, in Maria Edgeworth's *Harry and Lucy Concluded*, 1825, 'The Grand Panjandrum' was said to have been made up in order to challenge the actor Charles Macklin, who claimed to be able to repeat anything he had heard once. It was quoted in an article on Foote in the *Quarterly Review*, XCV, 1854, so it may well have been known to Edward Lear.

160–2 Smart. 'Verses written in a London Churchyard'. From *The Nonpareil, or the Quintessence of Wit and Humour*, being a choice selection from *The Midwife* or *Old Woman's Magazine*, London, 1757, and attributed to 'Mrs Midnight'. Smart edited *The Midwife*, a monthly magazine, from 1750 to 1753, and was its principal writer, and was also involved in producing material for *Old Woman's Oratory*, a vaudeville-style entertainment that took place on the London stage occasionally between 1751 and 1760; though the 'Verses' are not included in Smart's *Poetical Works*, they may possibly be his. In 'The Prologue to Mrs Mary

Midnight's Oratory', he appeals to 'that honest exile SENSE' in defence against 'the manly miss and female beau' who 'think our satire nonsense stuff and low'.

I have given the title 'Reflections on Sounds and Language' to this extract from Smart's *Jubilate Agno*, which was written during his confinement in a private madhouse in Bethnal Green, after his release from St. Luke's Hospital. The text comes from the edition of the poem edited by W. H. Bond, 1954; the sequences are ordered differently in Karina Williamson's recent Oxford edition (1980).

The Greek κατλ ευχηω means 'according to prayer', περι means 'round', αγλαιηφι means 'splendour, beauty', τρνζει 'murmur', *ovai* 'woe!, ah!'. *Mus* is Latin for 'mouse' and occurs as the first person plural ending of the verbs Smart quotes, which mean 'We eat, we drink, we live – let us pray'. αλογος means 'without the Word'. 'Baumgarden' was the name of a theatrical bassoon player who played at the Mother Midnight concerts.

163–7 *Gammer Gurton's Garland, or the Nursery Parnassus*, A Choice selection of Pretty Songs and Verses for the Amusement of all little good children who can neither read nor run, was first published by Joseph Ritson in 1784. Ritson had bought a copy of Newbery's *Mother Goose's Melody* in 1781. 'Quoth he, Miss Mouse' probably derives from the ballad 'A moste strange weddinge of the frogge and the mowse', licensed in 1580, which has the refrain 'humble-dum, humble-dum,/ tweedle, tweedle twine' suggesting it was a spinning song; today it is better known as 'A frog he would a-wooing go'. 'My father died' was originally entitled 'The Search for Fortune' and is the forerunner of the popular ballad 'The Swapping Song'.

167–8 Holcroft. From *Songs . . . in the Noble Peasant*, 1784. Text from *The New Oxford Book of Eighteenth-Century Verse*, ed. Roger Lonsdale, Oxford, 1984.

168 Mozart. The 'Kanonentext' dates from 1788. From *Deutsche Unsinnspoesie*, ed. Klaus Peter Dencker, Stuttgart, 1978.

169–74 Blake. From *Blake, Complete Writings*, ed. Geoffrey Keynes, Oxford, 1966. Blake's burlesque comic fiction was written about 1784 but not published until 1907 in E. J. Ellis's *The Real Blake*. The original MS text is in the Fitzwilliam Museum, Cambridge.

175–85 'The World Turned Upside Down, or No News, and Strange News'. Printed and sold by J. Kendrew, Colliergate, York. James Kendrew was a York printer for 40 years, until his death in 1841. He specialised in little chap-books for children. This idea has a long pictorial and poetic history in popular art, and there is another version in John Ashton, *Chap-Books of the Eighteenth Century*, London, 1882. See also David Kunzle, 'The World Turned Upside Down: the Iconography of a European Broadsheet type' in *The Reversible World*, ed. Barbara Babcock, Cornell University Press, 1978.

186–7 'Old Mother Hubbard'. From *The Comic Adventures of Old Mother Hubbard and Her Dog*, published by John Harris, 1805.

188 'As I walked by myself'. From A Garland of Songs, printed by J. Marshall, The Old Fish Market, Newcastle, *c.* 1810.

188–92 Coleridge. From *Poems of Samuel Taylor Coleridge*, ed. E. H. Coleridge, Oxford, 1912. 'The Devil's Thoughts' was first published in a version with only 14 stanzas in *The Morning Post*, September 1799. 'The House that Jack

Built'. Originally entitled 'On a Ruined House in a Romantic Country'. One of three *Sonnets in the manner of Contemporary Writers*, signed Nehemiah Higginbottom, published in *The Monthly Magazine* in November 1797, and later included in *Biographia Literaria*, 1817. In a letter to Joseph Cottle in the month of the first publication of the sonnets Coleridge describes them as 'three mock-sonnets in ridicule of my own poems, and Charles Lloyd's, and Lamb's, etc. etc.'. 'The Madman and the Lethargist' comes from one of Coleridge's notebooks, and 'The angel's like a flea' (first published in *The Literary Remains*, 1839) is a comment on Luther's observations on devils, as translated by Henry Bell in 1652: 'The devils are in woods, in waters, in wildernesses and dark pooly places, ready to hurt and prejudice people'.

192–3 Lamb. From *The Works of Charles Lamb*, ed. E. V. Lucas, vol. v, 1903. W. Carew Hazlitt in his *Charles and Mary Lamb* records: 'I found these lines – a parody on the popular nursery ditty "Ladybird, ladybird, fly away home" – officiating as a wrapper to some of Mr Hazlitt's hair. There is no signature but the handwriting is unmistakably Lamb's.

193–201 Peacock. *Sir Proteus, A Satirical Ballad* was first published in 1814. I have extracted Cantos ii, iii, and iv from the poem as printed in *The Works of Thomas Love Peacock*, ed. H. F. B. Brett-Smith and C. E. Jones, 1924–34. It is a satirical burlesque upon his poetic contemporaries, and in particular the Lake Poets, written in the artificial ballad-style popular in the period. 'The Wise Men of Gotham'. From *Paper Money Lyrics*, 1837. Written in 1825, it was originally attributed to S. T. C. Esq. Professor of Mysticism. The epigraph from Pindar is from the *Pythian Odes* viii. 95. Peacock uses the traditional nursery story to mock contemporary economists.

201–2 Knight. From *The Broken Harp*, 1815. Reprinted in Carolyn Wells, *A Nonsense Anthology*, 1902.

202–7 Keats. From *John Keats: The Complete Poems*, ed. John Barnard, Penguin, 2nd edn., 1976. 'There was a naughty boy' was included in one of Keats's letters to his sister Fanny, written between 2 and 5 of July, 1818, during the poet's walking tour of Scotland. Introducing it, he wrote: 'we have walked through a beautiful country to Kirkudbright – at which place I will write you a song about myself' (*Letters of John Keats*, A New Selection, ed. Robert Gittings, Oxford, 1970). 'Pensive, they sit' was written on 17 September 1819, two days before the 'Ode to Autumn', as part of Keats's letter to George and Georgiana Keats, composed between the 17th and 27th. He prefaced it with the following comments: 'Nothing strikes me so forcibly with a sense of the ridiculous as love – a Man in love I do think cuts the sorryest figure in the world – Even when I know the poor fool to be really in pain about it, I could burst out laughing in his face . . . Somewhere in the Spectator is related an account of a Man inviting a party of stutterers and squinters to his table, 'twould please me more to scrape together a party of Lovers, not to dinner – no to tea – There would be no fighting as among Knights of Old –' (*Letters*, p. 307). 'Two or three Posies' occurs in Keats's letter to his sister Fanny of 1 May, 1819, where he says there is 'nothing like fine weather, and health, and Books . . . and two or three sensible people to chat with; two or three spiteful people to spar with; two or three odd fishes to laugh at and two or three numskuls to argue with – instead of using dumb bells on a rainy day' (*Letters*, pp. 209–10).

208 'Songs of Lies'. From *Songs of the Irish*, 1960. Trans. and ed. Donal O'Sullivan, Browne and Nolan, Dublin.

208 'There was an old man of Tobago'. From *Anecdotes and Adventures of Fifteen Gentlemen*, published by John Marshall, *c.* 1822. In his introduction to the *Book of Nonsense* Edward Lear described this as his original inspiration for his own 'nonsenses' (the word 'limerick' was not used by Lear): 'Long ago, in the days when much of my time was passed in a country house where children and mirth abounded, the lines beginning "There was an old man of Tobago" were suggested to me by a valued friend as a form of verse lending itself to limitless variety for Rhymes and Pictures; and thenceforth the greater part of the original drawings and verses for the first Book of Nonsense were struck off'.

209 'In the Dumps'. From *Blackwood's Magazine*, July 1824. In *Oxford Dictionary of Nursery Rhymes*.

209–222 Hood. From *The Complete Works of Thomas Hood*, 1906. 'Sally Simplin's Lament', 'Epicurean Reminiscences' and 'The Lament of Toby the Learned Pig' from *Hood's Own*, 1839. 'A Flying Visit', from *Comic Annual*, 1839. The epigraph is from *A Midsummer Night's Dream*, iii.i.

223–6 Beddoes. From *Plays and Poems of Thomas Lovell Beddoes*, ed. H. W. Donner, London, 1950. The poems are taken from *Death's Jest Book*. The titles are my own.

227 'The Lover's Arithmetic'. From *The New Comic Songster*, early 19th C. *Oxford Book of Light Verse*, ed. W. H. Auden, 1938.

228 'Rumble, rumble in the pot'. From *The Counting-Out Rhymes of Children*, ed. H. C. Bolton, 1888.

228–9 Mörike. From *Friederich Hölderlin, Eduard Mörike: Selected Poems*, trans. Christopher Middleton, University of Chicago Press, 1972. Mörike's *Wispeliaden* are what he called *Sommersprossen* (Freckles) associated with a fantastical character named Liebmund Maria Wipfel, and were written out for Ludwig Bauer in 1837.

229–30 Swinburne. From Carolyn Wells, *A Nonsense Anthology*, 1902.

230–1 Thackeray. From *The National Standard*, 1833.

231–5 *The Nursery Rhymes of England*, Collected chiefly from Oral Tradition by James Orchard Halliwell, first published in 1842 for the Percy Society, and then in numerous expanded editions up to 1870. This is the first scholarly, folkloristic edition of the traditional rhymes and divides them up into such categories as Riddles, Jingles, Games and Lullabies. It had an enormous influence on Victorian children's literature and became the basis for all subsequent collections.

236–70 Lear. The first of the two nonsense letters, dated 17 January 1826, was written when Lear was only 14 years old at about the time he began to earn a living as an artist; the second, from San Remo, is dated nearly 50 years later, 16 April 1875. The text for both is from *Edward Lear, Selected Letters*, ed. Vivien Noakes, Oxford, 1988. *A Book of Nonsense*, Lear's first collection of 'nonsenses' – 'limerick' is not a word he used – was published in 1846 under the pseudonym 'Derry Down Derry', with the following epigraph: 'There was an old Derry Down Derry, who loved to see little folks merry; So he made them a Book, and with laughter they shook / At the fun of that Derry Down Derry'. Lear did not put his own name to the book until the third edition in 1861. His account of its origin in the Introduction to *More Nonsense*, 1872, is quoted in the note to 'There was an old man of Tobago', p. 208.

Nonsense Songs, Stories, Botany and Alphabets, published in 1879, was Lear's first book to explore other forms than the limerick – as announced in its title, it opened up a much wider range of genres and possibilities for nonsense.

More Nonsense, published in 1871, contained a second batch of limericks – 'a 4th Alphabet . . . & 110 old nonsense persons' (*Selected Letters*, p. 228). It was prefaced by an introduction, explaining the history of Lear's engagement with nonsense, and his manifesto: '"Nonsense", pure and absolute' had been his 'aim throughout'. He expanded in a letter of the same year: 'The critics are silly to see politics in such bosh; not but that bosh requires a good deal of care, for it is a sine qua non in writing for children to keep what they have to read perfectly clear & bright, & incapable of any meaning but one of sheer nonsense' (*Selected Letters*, p. 228).

Laughable Lyrics, 1876, introduced the Dong, Pobble, Quangle-Wangle, and Akond of Swat, among other mysterious personages. It was Lear's last Nonsense book.

'Incidents in the Life of my Uncle Arly' and 'How Pleasant to know Mr. Lear' were published in the posthumous *Nonsense Songs and Stories* in 1894. In a letter of 4 June, 1884, Lear introduced Uncle Arly by saying – 'a few lines just to let you know how your aged friend goes on' (*Later Letters of EL*, ed. Lady Strachey, 1911, p. 309). It is his last nonsense poem and suggests that it too is as autobiographical as his self-portrait.

'Cold are the crabs', 'Teapots and Quails' and 'The Scroobious Pip' From *Teapots and Quails*, ed. Angus Davidson and Philip Hofer, John Murray, 1953. The phrases in square brackets in 'The Scroobious Pip' are mine; they are simply makeshift fill-ins to repair holes in the original text in the Harvard Library collection.

270–1 Baudelaire. From *Oeuvres Complètes,* Pléiade, Gallimard, 1966. 'Le Pauvre Diable' was ascribed to Baudelaire in *Le Figaro* of 11 July 1878. They are said to have been his improvised response to a challenge to make an epic poem out of lines of one syllable.

271–3 Mummers' Play. From *The English Mummers' Play*, ed. R. J. Tiddy, Oxford, 1923. The play was recorded by a local schoolmistress at Weston-sub-Edge, Gloucestershire, in about 1864.

273 Dickinson. From *The Complete Poems of Emily Dickinson*, ed. Thomas H. Johnson, Faber, 1970.

274–5 'Chequered Poem'. From A. Canel, *Recherches sur les jeux d'esprit, les singularités et les bizarreries littéraires, principalement en France*, 2 vols, Evreux, 1867.

276–321 Carroll. The text of the early verse from *The Collected Verse of Lewis Carroll*, the Rev. Charles Ludwidge Dodgson, Macmillan, 1932. 'My Fairy' and 'Melodies' from *Useful and Instructive Poetry*, Carroll's earliest work, composed when he was 13, for the amusement of his younger brother and sister. 'The Palace of Humbug', written in 1855, was first published in the *Oxford Critic*, No. 1, 29 May 1857; also in *Mischmasch* (1855–62), the last of the 'magazines' he wrote for his family.

From *Alice's Adventures in Wonderland*, 1866. 'How doth the little crocodile' is a parody of the poem 'Against Idleness and Mischief' from *Divine Songs for*

Children by Isaac Watts (1674–1748), beginning 'How doth the little busy bee / Improve each shining hour'. 'You are old, father William' is a parody of 'The Old Man's Comforts and How He Gained Them' by Robert Southey (1774–1843), which begins '"You are old, Father William"' and ends 'I am cheerful young man', Father William replied, 'Let the cause thy attention engage / In the days of my youth I remembered my God!/ And he has not forgotten my age'. 'Speak roughly to your little boy' is a parody of 'Speak Gently' by David Bates, published in 1849, and beginning 'Speak gently! It is better far / To rule by love than fear'. The 'Mad Hatter's Song' is a parody of the first verse of Jane Taylor's famous poem *The Star*, beginning 'Twinkle, twinkle, little star'. The 'Mock Turtle's Song' is sung 'very slowly and sadly' while the Mock-Turtle and the Gryphon are dancing for Alice: it is a parody of the opening of Mary Howitt's *The Spider and the Fly* which begins '"Will you walk into my parlour?" said the spider to the fly'. ''Tis the Voice of the Lobster' is a parody of *The Sluggard* by Isaac Watts, which opens ''Tis the voice of the sluggard; I heard him compalin'. The Knave of Hearts's poem 'They told me you had been to her' derives from 'She's all my fancy painted him', an earlier poem Carroll had published in *The Comic Times of London* in 1855.

From *Through the Looking-Glass and What Alice Found There*, 1872. 'Jabberwocky' begins with a quatrain which was originally written for *Misch-Masch*, the hand-lettered 'periodical' the young Carroll produced to amuse his family, for an issue dated 1855. There it was entitled 'Stanza of Anglo-Saxon Poetry', with spoof linguistic commentary. Humpty Dumpty's explanation of the poem is to be found in Chapter VI of *Through the Looking-Glass*. 'The Walrus and the Carpenter' is written in the metre of Thomas Hood's *Dream of Eugene Arram*. 'The White Knight's Song' is an expanded version of the earlier 'Upon the Lonely Moor' which Carroll contributed to a magazine called *The Train*; it is a parody of Wordsworth's 'Resolution and Independence' from *Poems*, 1807.

The Hunting of the Snark, 1876. Illustrated by Henry Holiday. For Carroll's account of the genesis of the poem, see 'Alice on the Stage' in *The Lewis Carroll Picture Book*, 1899, and Introduction p. 17.

Sylvie and Bruno. 'The Mad Gardener's Song' and 'The Three Badgers' are from *Sylvie and Bruno*, 1889; 'The Kingfisher's Song' and 'The little man who had a little gun' are from *Sylvie and Bruno Concluded*, 1893.

322 Du Maurier. 'Cassez-vous' first appeared in *Punch* in 1887 and then in Du Maurier's *A Legend of Camelot*, Pictures and Poems, 1898.

323–5 Hood, The Younger. 'The Ballad of the Basking Shark' and 'Song' are from *Nowhere to the North Pole*, 1875. ('Confounded Nonsense' from *Fun*, 1866).

325–9 Gilbert. Poems from *The Bab Ballads*, 1869.

330 'J'ai faim'. From *Rimes et jeux d'enfance*, ed. Eugene Rolland, 1883.

330–1 Cros. From *Le Coffret du Santal*, 1873: Gallimard edn, 1972. 'Le Hareng Saur' was composed in an apartment on the Boulevard Saint-Germain, according to Mme Verlaine; Villiers de l'Isle-Adam came to dinner carrying a herring, fell asleep in the *salon*; Cros then suspended the herring over his head and is reputed to have written the poem impromptu.

331–3 Henley. From *Musa Pedestris*, ed. J. S. Farmer, 1896. 'Villon's Good-night'. *bible-sharps*, false clericos; *lurkers on the Abram-sham*, beggars feigning sickness;

flymy titters, saucy girls; *flam*, nonsense; *judes*, women; clobber for *the stram*, dress for the game; *fawneys*, rings; *dexter famm*, right hand; *mot*, harlot; *molls*, prostitutes; *bubs*, boobs; *stand you sam*, pay for; *swatchel-coves*, etc, Punch-and-Judy men; *magsmen*, pattering tradesmen; *jam*, wife; *narks*, informers; *dibs*, warders; *upon the snam*, stealing; *mumps* etc., 'the blues'; *skilly and swill*, food; *gam*, leg; *drink your health* etc, urinate.

'Villon's Straight Tip'. *screeve*, fake begging letters; *fake the broads*, pack the cards; *fig and nag*, play the coper with an old horse; *duff*, sell sham goods; *nose and lag*, act the informer; *get the straight* etc, back a winner; *multy*, bloody; *blowens*, lasses; *mace or mack*, welsh or pimp; *moskeneer*, pawn; *flash the drag*, wear drag; *dead-lurk* etc, house-break during church, or burgle; *pad with a slang*, tramp with a show; *mump and gag*, beg and talk; *tats*, dice; *stag*, shilling; *flash your flag*, sport your apron; *mug and gag*, make faces; *nix*, nothing; *graft*, trade; *stravag*, go astray; *wipes and tickers*, handkerchiefs and watches; *squeezer nips your scrag*, halter pinches your neck.

Like the Canting-Songs in Shirley's *Triumph of Wit* these are written in underworld slang code, but have much of the bizarre effect of *Jabberwocky*-style nonsense. Henley collaborated with Farmer on his *Slang and its Analogues*.

333–4 Rimbaud. From *Oeuvres*, Garnier, 1960. Rimbaud's most avowedly absurd and playful verse is to be found in the 'Album dit "zutique"', but both 'Fêtes de la Faim' and 'O saisons, O chateaux' have a strange incantatory idiom which touches upon the border of nonsense lyricism to my ear. 'Fêtes de la Faim' was written in 1872 and appears in modified form in the 'alchimie du verbe' section of *Une Saison en Enfer*, as does 'O saisons'.

335–7 Housman. From *Selected Poetry and Prose*, ed. Christopher Ricks, Penguin, 1988.

338 Scheerbart. From *Immer mutig*, Munich, 1902.

339 Herford. From *The Bashful Earthquake*, 1898. In *A Nonsense Anthology*, 1902.

340 'Christian'. From *Deutsches Kinderlied und Kinderspiel*, ed. J. Lewalter, 1911.

340–1 Yeats. From *Collected Poems*, Macmillan, 1950.

341–2 'A Chronicle'. From *A Nonsense Anthology*, ed. Carolyn Wells, 1902.

343 Burgess. From *The Burgess Nonsense Book*, 1901.

343–4 Belloc. From *Cautionary Tales*, 1907.

345 Synge. This is the ending of a long folklore told by Old Mourteen to John Synge on the Aran Islands. Synge noted 'the glow of childish transport that came over him when he reached the nonsense ending – so common in these tales'. *The Aran Islands*, 1907.

345–50 Morgenstern. Translations from *Galgenlieder*, which was first published in 1905. 'The Police Enquiry' and 'Korf's Clock' are from *Christian Morgenstern's Galgenlieder, A Selection*, trans. Max Knight, University of California Press and Cambridge University Press, 1963. 'The Midnightmouse' and 'The Knee' are translated by W. D. Snodgrass and Lore Segal, and taken from *The Rattle-Bag*, ed. Seamus Heaney and Ted Hughes, Faber, 1982. The other translations are my own.

350–2 Jarry. 'La Chanson du Décervelage' or 'Song of a Debraining' comes from *Ubu Cocu*, published by Editions des Trois Collines, Geneva/Paris, 1944, though published separately as a song with music in 1898. The translation by Cyril Connolly and Simon Watson Taylor is adapted from their version of the

Ubu plays, Methuen, 1965. 'Le Homard et la Boîte' is from *Gestes et Opinions de Docteur Faustroll*, 1911.

355–6 Chesterton. From *Greybeards at Play*, 1900.

356–7 Graham. From *Ruthless Rhymes* and *More Ruthless Rhymes*, Edward Arnold.

362 *Nursery Rhymes of the Appalachian Mountains*, ed. Cecil Sharpe, Novello, 1923. 'The Derby Ram' is a very old song, but this is one of the fullest and most vivid versions of the ballad. 'Brian O Linn' and 'Finnegans Wake'. From *Irish Street Ballads*, ed. Col. O'Lochlainn, At the Sign of the Three Candles, Dublin, 1939.

367–70 Joyce. 'Humpty Dump Dublin'. This was designed as an advert for Joyce's *Work in Progress*, i.e. *Finnegans Wake*, as recorded in J. S. Atherton, *The Books at the Wake*, 1959.

376 Ball. From Hugo Ball, *Gesammelte Gedichte*, Die Arche, Zurich, 1963. The poem appeared in Ball's novel *Tenderenda der Phantast* with the title 'jolifanto', and is described as follows: 'Sketch of a caravan of elephants from the world-notorious cycle *gadji beri bimba*. The author performed this cycle for the first time at the Café Voltaire in May 1916.

388 'The Billboard Song'. From Florence Maryott, 'Nebraska Counting-Out Rhymes', *Southern Folklore Quarterly*, 1936.

389 'Do you carrot all for me?'. From Carl Withers, *A Rocket in My Pocket*, New York, 1948.

389 'Why are Fire Engines red?'. Quoted in Susan Stewart, *Nonsense*, Johns Hopkins University Press, Baltimore, 1978.

389 'Down in the meadow'. From Lucy Nolton, 'Jump Rope Rhymes as Folk Literature', *Journal of American Folklore* 61, 1948.

400–3 Desnos. 'P'Oasis'. To follow this poem, the reader should pronounce the letters of the alphabet, the numbers, and the musical notes in French. So 'crânes KC' is 'crânes cassés (broken skulls), 'prenez vos 16' is 'prenez vos chaises' (*seize*), and the second musical inscription is 'doré' (from the notes 'do, re'). From *Corps et Biens*, 1930. 'Le Brochet' and 'Les Hiboux' from *Chantefables et Chantefleurs*, 1944.

431 'Doundou Tchil' and 'Syllabes' from HARAWI: Chant d'Amour et de Mort, 1945, for Soprano and Piano, by Olivier Messaien.

479–82 From *The Language and Lore of Schoolchildren*, ed. Iona and Peter Opie, Oxford, 1959. The material is collected from schoolchildren all over Britain, a monument to the nonsense-loving culture of the playground.

495 'An English Surrealist Alphabet'. Based on the alphabet published in the *Daily Express* on 20 June 1936, probably derived from the surrealistic alphabet performed by the cross-talk comedians Clapham and Dyer, with interpolations from other alphabets recorded in Eric Partridge, *Comic Alphabets, Their Origin, Development, Nature*, Routledge & Kegan Paul, 1961.

Further Reading

ANTHOLOGIES

W. H. Auden, ed. *The Oxford Book of Light Verse*. Oxford University Press, 1938.

William S. and Cecil Baring-Gould, eds. *The Annotated Mother Goose*. New American Library, 1967.

Robert Benayoun, ed. *Les Dingues du Nonsense*, Paris, 1984.

Michael Benedikt, ed. *The Poetry of Surrealism*, an anthology. Boston, Toronto: Little, Brown & Co., 1974.

J. M. Cohen, ed. *Comic and Curious Verse*, Harmondsworth: Penguin, 1952.

John Davies, ed. *Everyman's Book of Nonsense*. London: Dent, 1981.

Klaus Peter Dencker, ed. *Deutsche Unsinnspoesie*. Stuttgart: Phillip Reclam, 1978.

Gavin Ewart, ed. *The Penguin Book of Light Verse*. Penguin, 1980.

Edward G. Germain, ed. *Surrealist Poetry in English*. Penguin, 1978.

Geoffrey Grigson, ed. *The Faber Book of Nonsense Verse*. London, 1979.

J. O. Halliwell, ed. *The Nursery Rhymes of England*. London, 1842.

Seamus Heaney and Ted Hughes, eds. *The Rattle Bag*. London: Faber, 1982.

J. H. Matthews, ed. *An Anthology of French Surrealist Poetry*. University of London Press, 1966.

Iona and Peter Opie, eds. *The Oxford Dictionary of Nursery Rhymes*. Oxford University Press, 1952.

Ernest Rhys, ed. *A Book of Nonsense*. Everyman, 1927.

Denys Kilham Roberts, ed. *Straw in your Hair: Nonsensical and surrealist verses*. London, 1938.

Claude Roy, ed. *La Poésie Populaire*. Paris: Séghers, 1954.

Carolyn Wells, ed. *A Nonsense Anthology*. New York, 1906; Dover, 1958.

ON NONSENSE

Mikhail Bakhtin, *Rabelais and his World*. trans. Helene Iswolsky, Bloomington: Indiana University Press, 1984.

Henry Bett, *Nursery Rhymes and Tales*. London: Methuen, 1924.

C. W. E. Bigsby, *Dada and Surrealism: The critical idiom*. Methuen, 1972.

H. C. Bolton, *The Counting Out Rhymes of Children*. London, 1888.

André Breton, *Manifestoes of Surrealism*, trans. R. Seaver, Helen Lane. Ann Arbor: University of Michigan, 1972.

Emile Cammaerts, *The Poetry of Nonsense*. London: Routledge, 1925.

E. K. Chambers, *The Medieval Stage*, 2 vols. Oxford University Press, 1903.

G. K. Chesterton, 'A Defense of Nonsense', *The Defendant*. Dent, 1901.

Kornei Chukovsy, *From Two to Five*, trans. and ed. Miriam Morton. Berkeley: University of California Press, 1968.

Giuseppe Cocchiara, *Il Mondo alla Rovescia*. Turin: Boringhieri, 1963.

Harvey Cox, *The Feast of Fools*: A theological essay on fertility and fantasy. Cambridge, Mass.: Harvard University Press.

W. T. Dobson, *Literary Frivolities, Fancies, Follies and Frolics*. London: Chatto & Windus, 1888.

William Empson, *Some Versions of Pastoral*. Chatto & Windus, 1935.

Desiderius Erasmus, *The Praise of Folly*, trans. Hoyt Hopewell Hudson. New Jersey: Princeton University Press, 1941.

Leonard Forster, *Poetry of Significant Nonsense*, an inaugural lecture. Cambridge University Press, 1962.

Michel Foucault, *Madness and Civilisation*, trans. Richard Howard. London: Tavistock Publications, 1967.

Sigmund Freud, *The Interpretation of Dreams*, trans. James Strachey. London: Allen & Unwin, 1954.

George Gibian, *Russia's Lost Literature of the Absurd*, Selected Works of Daniil Kharms and Alexander Vvedensky. New York: Norton, 1971.

Roman Jakobson and Linda R. Waugh, *The Sound-Shape of Language*. Harvester Press, 1979.

Barbara Kirshenblatt-Gimblatt, ed. *Speech Play: Research and resource for the study of linguistic creativity*. Philadelphia, 1976.

David Kunzle, 'World Turned Upside Down: The Iconography of a Broadsheet Type' in *The Reversible World*, ed. Barbara Babcock. Ithaca, N.Y.: Cornell University Press, 1978.

Ludovic Lalanne, *Curiosités Littéraires*. Paris, 1845.

Jean-Jacques Lecercle, *Philosophy through the Looking-Glass: Language, nonsense, desire*. London: Hutchinson, 1985.

Alfred Liede, *Dichtung als Spiel: Studien zur Unsinnspoesie an den Grenzen der Sprache*, 2 vols. Berlin, 1963.

Christian Morgenstern, *Galgenlieder, A Selection*, trans. and introduced by Max Knight. University of California, 1966.

Maurice Nadeau, *The History of Surrealism*, trans. Richard Howard. Penguin, 1973.

Vivien Noakes, *Edward Lear, the Life of a Wanderer*. London: Collins, 1968.

Iona and Peter Opie, *The Lore and Language of Schoolchildren*. Oxford University Press, 1959.

George Orwell, 'Nonsense Poetry', *Collected Essays, Journalism and Letters*, vol. 4. Penguin, 1968.

Eric Partridge, 'The Nonsense Words of Edward Lear and Lewis Carroll', *Here, There, and Everywhere*. London: Routledge, 1953.

Lambert C. Porter, *La Fatrasie et le Fatras*: essai sur la poésie irrationelle en France au Moyen Age. Geneva, 1960.

Elizabeth Sewell, *The Field of Nonsense*. Chatto & Windus, 1950.

Susan Stewart, *Nonsense: Aspects of intertextuality in folklore and literature*. Baltimore: Johns Hopkins University Press, 1978–9.

Edmund Strachey, 'Nonsense as a Fine Art', *The Quarterly Review*, 1888.

Enid Welsford, *The Fool: His social and literary history*. Faber, 1935.

William Willesford, *The Fool and his Sceptre: A study in clowns, jesters and their audience*. London: Edward Arnold, 1969.

Paul Zumthor, *Langue, Texte, Enigme*. Paris: Editions du Seuil, 1975.

[516]

Acknowledgements

An anthology such as this is both a record of the idiosyncrasy of an editor's eye and the operation of serendipity. In compiling material for the book I have always been conscious of the extent of my natural ignorance, especially of literatures outside English, and of my heavy dependence on sheer good luck in stumbling on isolated nonsensical *trouvailles*, here, there and everywhere. If you go beyond the obvious places and the existing anthologies, it is perhaps an easier thing to find than to look for, and when found it may be that one person's nonsense is another person's sense. I have been particularly lucky with friends, colleagues and editors, and would like to thank them for nonsensical suggestions and advice, in particular: Kyri Argyropoulos, Jacques Berthoud, John Birtwhistle, Jack Donovan, Eva Fox-Gal, Tim Gates, Bernard Harris, Rolf Hughes, John Jones, Paul Keegan, Hermione Lee, Peter Levi, Stephen Minta, Michael Neve, Mark Rutter, Geoffrey Summerfield, and Tim Webb. I am grateful to Andrew Motion for encouraging me to undertake the anthology in the first place, to Gillian Beer and Patrick Parrinder for guiding my early steps across the field of nonsense in Cambridge, to Adam Phillips for conversations over more than a decade, keeping faith with nonsense and desire, and to Jane Turner of Chatto for her sympathetic editorial flair. I owe a special debt to my parents, for bearing with my interest in verbal deformation from a very early age to the present, and to my friends who have had to listen to a lot of and on nonsense over the years. Above all, I am grateful for the personal inspiration of Fiona Shaw.

The editor and publishers gratefully acknowledge permission to reprint copyright material as follows:
For 'Charlie's Sad Date' from *The Owl's Insomnia* by Rafael Alberti, translated by Mark Strand: Copyright © 1973 Mark Strand: Atheneum Publishers, an imprint of Macmillan Publishing Company; for translations of poems by Louis Aragon, originally published in *Le Mouvement Perpétuel*, 1925: Editions Gallimard; for 'Opus Nil' from *Ich bin in der Natur geboren* by Hans Arp, in *German Poetry 1910–75*, translated by Michael Hamburger, Carcanet Press, Manchester, 1977: in German, *Ausgewählte Gedichte* (Neue Arche Bücherei 18) © 1986 by Verlags-AG Die Arche, Zürich; for 'The Domestic Stones' translated from Hans Arp by David Gascoyne from *Collected Verse Translations of David Gascoyne*, ed. by Robin Skelton and Alan Clodd: Oxford University Press; for 'He' and 'Farm Implements' from *Selected Poems*, 1986, by John Ashbery: Georges Borchardt, Inc., New York and Carcanet Press; for 'As I walked out one evening' and 'Alice is gone' from *Collected Poems*, 1976, by W. H. Auden: Faber & Faber Ltd; for 'Karawane' from *Gesammelte Gedichte* by Hugo Ball: © 1963 by Verlags-AG Die Arche, Zürich; for 'franz war' from *Sämtliche Werke*, vol. 1 by Konrad Bayer: OBV-Klett-Cotta, Vienna, 1985; for 'Vladimir's Song' from *Waiting for Godot* by Samuel Beckett, 1955: Faber and Faber Ltd; for 'Sarah Byng' from *Cautionary Tales*, 1907, by Hilaire Belloc: Gerald

Duckworth & Co Ltd; for clerihews from *The Complete Clerihews of E. Clerihew Bentley*, 1981: Oxford University Press; for 'Dream Song I' from *77 Dream Songs* by John Berryman: Faber and Faber, and Farrar, Straus & Giroux, Inc. Copyright © by John Berryman; for 'The Man-Moth', 'Twelfth Morning' and 'Visits to St. Elizabeths' from *The Complete Poems 1927–1979* by Elizabeth Bishop. Copyright © 1936, 1957, 1964 by Elizabeth Bishop. Copyright renewed © 1984, 1985 by Alice Methfessel: Farrar, Straus & Giroux, Inc.; for 'Diddie Wa Diddie' by Blind Blake from *The Blues Line*; a collection of Blues Lyrics compiled by Eric Sackheim: Schirmer, New York, Macmillan, London; for 'Psycholophon' and 'The Purple Cow' from *The Burgess Nonsense Book*, 1901; for 'Moonrocks Moon in the Man' by David Byrne: Warner Bros. Music Ltd, London; for an excerpt from *Three Trapped Tigers* by G. Cabrera Infante. Copyright © 1965 by Guillermo Cabrera Infante. English translation copyright © 1971 by Harper & Row Publishers Inc.; for 'Großes Geburtstagblaublau' by Paul Celan from *Gesammelte Werke*, vol. 3: © Suhrkamp Verlag, Frankfurt am Main, 1983; for 'Un petit d'un petit', 'Pousse y gate', 'Papa, blague chipe' from *Mots d'Heures: Gousses, Rames* edited by Luis d'Antin Van Rooten: Angus & Robertson (UK) and Viking Penguin Inc. Copyright © 1967 by Courtlandt H. K. Van Rooten. All rights reserved; for 'Kiph' and 'Jim Jay' from *The Complete Poems of Walter de la Mare*, 1969: The Literary Trustees of Walter de la Mare and The Society of Authors as their representative; for 'In the Middle of the Party' from *A House of My Own* by Carl Dennis: George Braziller, Inc., New York; for 'Rrose Selavy', and 'P Oasis' from *Corps et Biens*, 1930 by Robert Desnos: © Editions Gallimard 1930, Paris; for 'Les Hiboux' and 'Le Brochet' from *Chantefables et Chantefleurs* by Robert Desnos: Librairie Grund, Paris; for 'Turning into' from *Derivations* by Robert Duncan: State University of New York at Buffalo, for the Estate of Robert Duncan; for 'Tiny Montgomery' and 'Don't Ya Tell Henry' by Bob Dylan: Dwarf Music, New York; for 'Ballad of a Thin Man' by Bob Dylan: Warner Brothers Music Ltd, London; for 'Timetable' from *Anlässe und Steingärten* by Gunter Eich, translated by Michael Hamburger: © Suhrkamp Verlag, Frankfurt am Main, 1966; for 'Mr. Mistoffelees' from *Old Possum's Book of Practical Cats* and 'The Hippopotamus' from *Collected Poems 1909–1962* by T. S. Eliot: Faber and Faber Ltd; for 'Mother, saying Anne good night' and 'Two centos' from *The Royal Beasts and Other Works* by William Empson, and for 'Poem about a Ball in the Nineteenth Century' from *Collected Poems* by William Empson: the Estate of Sir William Empson and Chatto & Windus Ltd; for 'A Child's Guide to Welfare' from *Collected Poems*, 1981, by D. J. Enright: Oxford University Press and Watson, Little Ltd, literary agents; for 'This Octopus Exploits Women' from *Memory of War: Poems 1968–82* by James Fenton: Salamander Press and A. D. Peters & Co. Ltd, literary agents; for 'Don't Let That Horse' from *A Coney Island of the Mind* by Lawrence Ferlinghetti. Copyright © 1958 by Lawrence Ferlinghetti: New Directions Publishing Corporation; for an extract from 'The Listing Attic', and 'The Utter Zoo Alphabet' from *Amphigorey*, 1972 and *Amphigorey Also*, 1983, by Edward Gorey, published by G. P. Putnam's Sons, and by Congdon & Weed: Candida Donadio & Associates; for 'Juego de Picasso' from *Bilderreiches Haupt & (G)liederbuch* by Fritz Grasshof, published by Kiepenheuer & Witsch Verlag, 1970: by kind permission of Fritz Grasshof; for 'Warning to Children' and 'Welsh Incident' from *Collected Poems*, 1964: The Executors of the Estate of Robert Graves and A. P. Watt Ltd; for 'The Wrong Way Round' by Peter Handke from *German Poetry 1910–1975* translated by

Poems of Wallace Stevens: Faber and Faber Ltd and Alfred A. Knopf, Inc.; for 'The Man in the Tree' from *Reasons for Moving*, 1980, by Mark Strand: Copyright © 1963, 1964, 1965, 1966, 1967, 1968 by Mark Strand. Atheneum Publishers Inc.; for 'I, the First Named' from *The Poems* by Dylan Thomas: J. M. Dent and David Higham Associates; for 'Upon Learning that a Bird Exists called the Turnstone' from *Telephone Poles and Other Poems* by John Updike: André Deutsch Ltd; for 'Do Not Forget' from *Nostalgia for the Present* by Andrei Voznesensky, translated by William Jay Smith and Vera Dunham, 1980: Oxford University Press; for 'From Notes Written in Obory' by Aleksander Wat from *Post-War Polish Poetry*, translated by Czeslaw Milosz: Doubleday, New York; for 'Der Tragödie erster Teil' by Michael Wulff from *Deutsche Unsinnpoesie*: Dr. Michael Wulff; for 'The Collarbone of a Hare' and 'High Talk' from *The Collected Poems of W. B. Yeats*: A. P. Watt Ltd on behalf of Michael B. Yeats and Macmillan London Ltd.

ILLUSTRATION ACKNOWLEDGEMENTS

Title page from Edward Lear's *Nonsense Songs and Stories* (Frederick Warne & Co. Ltd, 1894); p. xiv: a reproduction of one of the original woodcuts from the 15th-C. book, *Ship of Fools*, by Sebastian Brandt (the edition used is a translation by Columbia University Press, 1944); p. 32: from Edward Lear's drawing for 'Hey Diddle Diddle'; pp. 40 and 47: miniatures from the 'Romance of Alexander', 14th C., Bodleian Library (from *The Fool: His Social and Literary History* by Enid Welford, Faber 1935); p. 174: from *The Works of William Blake* edited by E. J. Ellis and W. B. Yeats, vol. III (Bernard Quaritch, 1893); pp. 175 ff.: from 'The World Turned Upside Down', courtesy of the University of York Library; pp. 240–59: from Edward Lear's *Nonsense Songs and Stories* and *The Book of Nonsense and More Nonsense* (Warne, n.d.); pp. 279–318: from 1. Lewis Carroll's *Alice's Adventures in Wonderland and Through The Looking Glass*, edited with an Introduction by Roger Lancelyn Green, with illustrations by John Tenniel (OUP, 1971). 2. *Sylvie and Bruno* and 3. *Sylvie and Bruno Concluded*, illustrated by Harry Furniss (Macmillan, 1898). 4. *The Hunting of the Snark*, with illustrations by Henry Holiday (Macmillan, 1896); p. 312: from *The Hunting of the Snark*, illustrated by Mervyn Peake (Chatto, 1953); p. 325: from W. S. Gilbert's *The Bab Ballads*, with illustrations by the author (4th edn, Routledge, 1899); p. 403: 'The Water Wonder, or Fishes Lords of Creation' from *Chap-Books of the Eighteenth Century*; p. 414: a drawing by Stevie Smith from *The Collected Poems of Stevie Smith*, edited with a Preface by James MacGibbon (Penguin Books, 1985), by courtesy of James MacGibbon; p. 496: from Edward Lear's *Nonsense Songs and Stories*.

Index of Titles and First Lines

[525]

[527]

Index of Authors